Powers only !

LP
690.837   Kidder, Tracy
KIDDER   House

DATE DUE			
JE 3 '96			
JE 3 '96			
FE 02 '98			

HOUSE

Tracy Kidder

G.K. HALL & CO.
Boston, Massachusetts
1987

Published in Large Print by arrangement with
Houghton Mifflin Company.

*Part-title drawings and the one on page 114 are by William
Rawn Associates. The drawing on page 86 is adapted from one
by William Rawn Associates. Drawings on pages 257, 310,
311, and 335 are by Jim Locke.*

G.K. Hall Large Print Book Series.

Set in 16 pt Plantin.

Library of Congress Cataloging in Publication Data

Kidder, Tracy.
  House.

  (G.K. Hall large print book series)
  1. House construction.   2. Large type books.
I. Title.
[TH4811.K48   1987]   690'.837   86-33641
ISBN 0-8161-4210-6 (lg. print)

FOR
FRANCES TOLAND KIDDER

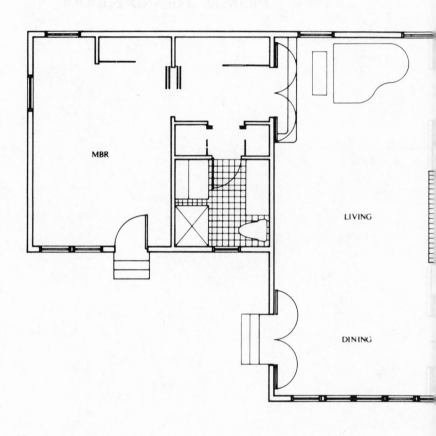

MBR

LIVING

DINING

First Floor

SOUWEINE HOUSE
Amherst, MA.

WILLIAM RAWN ASSO
Boston, MA.

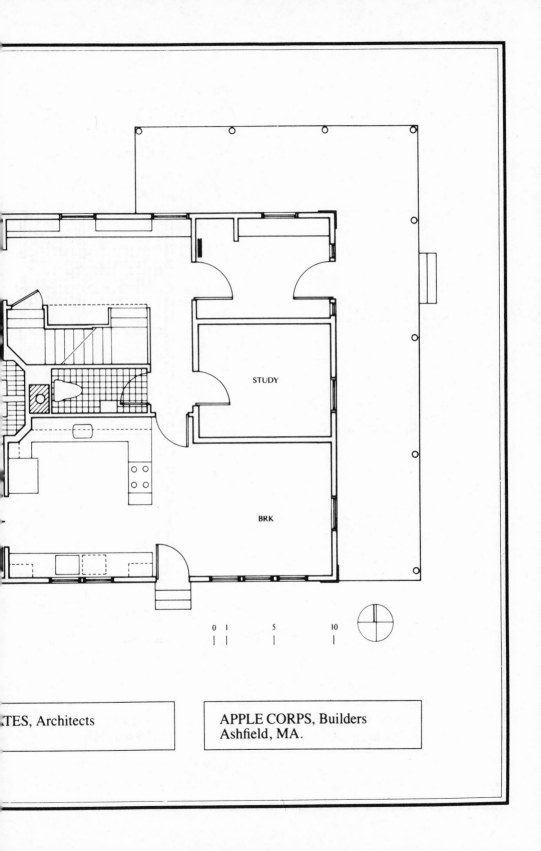

STUDY

BRK

0   1   5   10

TES, Architects

APPLE CORPS, Builders
Ashfield, MA.

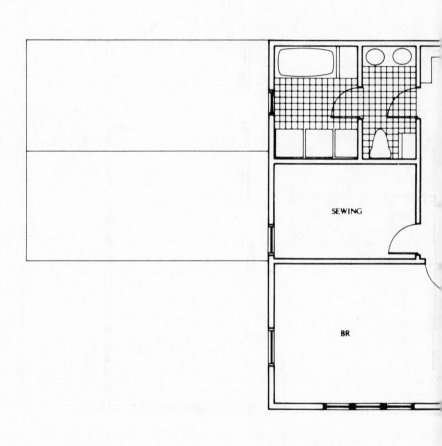

SEWING

BR

Second Floor

SOUWEINE HOUSE
Amherst, MA.

WILLIAM RAWN ASSOC
Boston, MA.

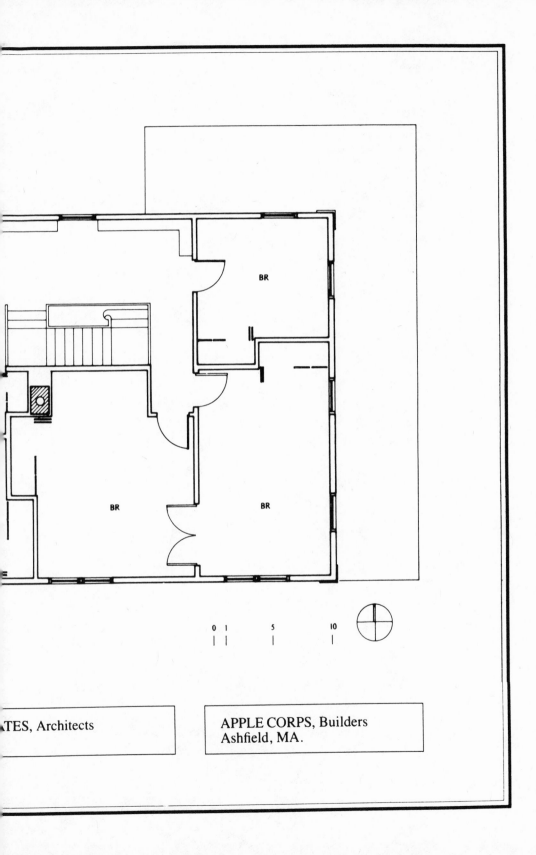

BR

BR

BR

0 1   5   10

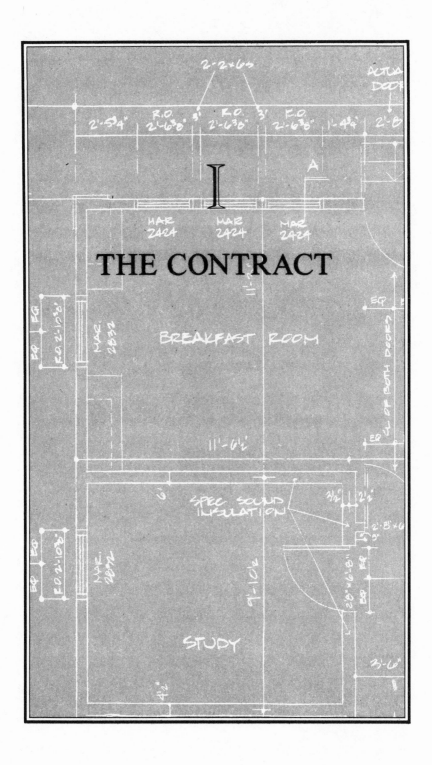

I

THE CONTRACT

Jim Locke sets gently on the undisturbed earth a mahogany box, opens it, and takes out his transit, which looks like a spyglass. It is a tool for imposing levelness on an irregular world.

Locke's transit is made of steel with small brass adjusting wheels and is as old as the century, more than twice as old as Locke, who is thirty-six. He uses it near the beginnings of jobs and first of all for guiding bulldozers. Locke erects the transit on a tripod. He turns the brass wheels until the bubble, encased in glass beneath the eyepiece, floats to the center of its chamber. Then, bending over, putting one eye to the lens of the transit and squinting the other, he transforms his view of this patch of open ground into a narrow, well-lighted tunnel divided by cross hairs. Oliver Wendell Holmes once said, in another context, "The art of civilization is the act of drawing lines." And of course it has also been the act of drawing level ones.

This piece of ground was once part of a New England hayfield. It lies on the southern outskirts of Amherst, Massachusetts, a college and university town, the kind of place that has a fine public school system and a foreign policy. The site has been studied all winter. It commands pretty views. There's a deep-looking woods on one edge. On another, there's a pasture, which turns into the precipitous, forested, publicly owned hills known as the Holyoke Range. And to the north and east there's a panorama. Look north and you see a hillside orchard topped with two giant maples locally known as Castor and Pollux. Look a little east and your view extends out over a broad valley, all the way to the Pelham Hills, which have turned blue at this morning hour.

The air has some winter in it. On this morning in mid-April 1983 a New England spring snow is predicted. The sky looks prepared. It has a whitening look. Several weeks must pass before dandelions, but the urge to build has turned New England's April into May. While Locke prepares for the transformation of this ground, four others pace around, killing time. They have their collars turned up and their hands thrust deep into coat pockets. They wait with reddening noses. None of the onlookers needs to be here, but none would have willingly stayed away. Among them is a very tall man, named Bill Rawn. He is the architect. He has driven all the way from Boston to witness the birth of the first house he has ever designed, and he grins while he waits. There are Judith and Jonathan Souweine, the woman and the man of the house to be. (Their surname is French and is pronounced "Suh-wayne," or if one is in a hurry, "Swayne.") They have spent months planning for

4

this moment, and they have imagined it for many more. Judith and Jonathan smile at each other. Judith takes a few snapshots while Jim Locke works with the transit.

Turning her camera on Locke, Judith sees a refined-looking young man. When she met him about two months ago, she thought, "Obviously, his upbringing was very upper middle class. Even if I hadn't known who his father was, I could have told. Everything about him was—well, you know. He's made a conscious decision not to be a white-collar professional." Locke is wearing jeans and work boots and an old brown jacket, a workingman's uniform. His clothes are clean and he is clean-shaven. He has straight brown hair, neatly trimmed and combed, and a long, narrow jaw. There is a delicacy in his features. You can imagine his mother in him. He has a thoughtful air. He studies his transit a moment, laying two fingers against his lips. Then as he bends again to the eyepiece, he wipes his hair off his forehead and for a moment he looks boyish and defiant.

The building site slopes gently. Locke calculates by how much it does so. He turns the scope of the transit until he sees the cross hairs rest upon a numeral inscribed on a long, numbered staff. Judith's father has volunteered to carry the staff. Locke directs him to and fro. For a benchmark, Locke has chosen an electrical box planted in the ground nearby. He sends his staff-bearer to that spot first. The numbers Locke reads through his scope tell him how far below his transit's scope

5

the benchmark rests. He sends the staff-bearer to a stake that represents the southeastern corner of the house to come, and through the scope he determines how far below the benchmark that corner lies. Locke checks these numbers against ones inscribed on a blueprint opened on the ground beside him. Soon he knows the relative elevations of the land at each corner of the house. He will be able to tell through his spyglass when the cellar hole has been dug to the proper depth. The ceremony can begin, as soon as the bulldozer arrives.

When Locke has begun to wonder whether it is coming at all, it appears—a small, yellow machine on a large trailer. Locke gives the driver his instructions, while the others hang back. The bulldozer puffs smoke, and clanks down off the trailer.

The first pass the machine makes over the ground, ripping the hair off the earth, looks like an act of great violence. The bulldozer does resemble a beast, but the creature is both unruly and extremely methodical. Gradually, the sense of disruption goes out of the scene. The machine makes its first cuts. It goes back over the same suddenly dark ground. Piles of earth mount up. The hole deepens and, as sand appears, turns orange. Watching the bulldozer work is restful and mesmerizing. Its noise discourages speech, leaving each of the party alone and thoughtful for moments.

Ground breaking: On every continent and many islands, people used to undertake elaborate rituals when they undertook to build. Augury assisted choices and planning of sites. In northern Ireland, for example, lamps were placed on stones that marked two corners of an incipient house, and the site was deemed safe to build on if the lamps stayed lit for a few nights. Elsewhere, to ensure the strength and safety of a building, human and surrogate victims—animals and various objects— were entombed under foundation stones. In the Balkans, as recently as the late 1800s, builders digging a foundation hole would entice a passer-by near so that the innocent victim's shadow would fall into the excavation. The builders would cover the shadow with a stone, or mark out the shadow's length and breadth and bury the measurement of it. The ritual ensured the foundation's durability. The victim, it was thought, would die within the year.

No bodies are being buried in this deepening cellar hole. No one has watched for omens. There is only desire. This group does have a few worries. They have not settled all the details of the plan. They have not arrived at a final price for the house. They have not yet signed a contract. Jim Locke wanted all of that done before this day. Locke felt he had to go ahead, knowing that if he delayed he might not get the excavator for weeks. But Locke can imagine events that would leave him holding the bill for this work. Both he and the Souweines have begun to build on faith, without much knowledge of each other.

The party lingers awhile. The bulldozer's cab begins to sink beneath the level of the field.

2

For eight years, Judith and Jonathan shared a duplex with another young couple, but both families grew too large for the place, and reluctantly they all agreed that the time for moving on had come. Judith's parents had settled in a new house on about twenty sloping acres. Jonathan and Judith looked around. They decided that they'd like to buy a piece of her parents' property. Jonathan and Judith liked the idea of locating three generations of their family on adjoining land. It was a traditional arrangement that had grown uncommon. They imagined many advantages. They also thought it was a slightly risky undertaking, but they like to see themselves as people who are not afraid of taking chances. Actually, the only obvious problem was that Judith sometimes bickers with her father, Jules Wiener. She remembers Jules closing out disputes, when she was still a child, by saying to her, "My house, my rules." Now when he visits her house and takes out a cigar, she says, "My house, my rules. No cigars." She smiles when she says her lines, but the joke sometimes leads to sharper words. "I'm pretty direct with my father, and he's pretty direct with me," she explains. "As they say, I come by it honest." As for Jonathan, he is hardly a typical son-in-law. He adores Judith's mother, Florence, and he and Jules have been friends ever since Jonathan was seventeen and came courting Judith. Like Jonathan, Jules is a lawyer, and it's a family joke that if Jonathan and Judith ever sued each other for divorce, Jules would opt to represent his son-in-law.

So Judith and Jonathan made their offer to her parents, who concealed momentarily their great delight, lest they seem too eager and stir up second thoughts. Jules made some vows to himself. "I can see a steady stream of grandchildren coming our way. The door's open. But it's not going the other way. If twenty cars are here for a party, I'm not walking over to say, 'What's going on?' " Jules and Florence deeded to Jonathan and Judith about four acres of land. The Souweines would have a house built on it by the time their twins entered kindergarten in the fall of 1983.

Jonathan is polite and very direct. In conversation he tends to curtness, but let him get on a subject that truly engages him, such as a coming election, and he becomes positively garrulous, tapping his listener's arm for emphasis, talking so swiftly that his words slur. He looks his best at such moments, or running a meeting, or speaking in front of a political gathering, or striding down a street. He clearly likes command. He is an inch below six feet. He has broad shoulders. He comes at you a little sleepy-eyed, wearing a small crooked grin, and carrying his arms out from his body in a way that makes you think of impending showdowns in Westerns.

Jonathan started college on a basketball scholarship, and even now, in a business suit, his hair in middle-aged retreat, he looks like a busy play-making guard—what sportswriters call the spark plug type. He was a good athlete and a better student. He gave up his scholarship, went to Columbia, participated in protests against the Vietnam War and campaigned for a liberal, antiwar congressman, and went on to Harvard Law School. He imagined himself becoming a lawyer who would work for the public good. He spent a year clerking for a federal judge and another in the department of consumer protection of the Massachusetts attorney general's office; in between he took command of the Massachusetts Public Interest Research Group (MassPIRG) and in that capacity led a number of lobbying campaigns, for solar energy and a bottle bill and against white-collar crime. Then Jonathan ran for district attorney of Hampshire and Franklin counties. It was now or probably never, he told Judith. Against all predictions—he was a newcomer, outspoken, and even a little left-wing—Jonathan won the Democratic primary. He lost the general election, and soon afterward he became a country lawyer. For the sake of his family, he gave up running for office, but he has kept his hand in as an epistolary politician. He writes letters to editors assessing political candidates. He writes about burning issues of the day and also about local fund-raising events. He has written so many letters and so many have been published locally that a Jonathan Souweine letter to the editor has become a virtual institution in Amherst and the towns nearby. Some people think he is still running for office, but clearly he is writing letters instead.

A former lieutenant in Jonathan's campaign remembers a quiet day in their office, when a stranger, a middle-aged man, walked in off the street and asked what sort of name was Souweine.

"French," said Jonathan.

The man looked greatly relieved. "Thank God. I thought you were Jewish."

"I am," said Jonathan pleasantly.

"He looked right at the guy," his former lieutenant remembers. "Jonathan told him he hoped that religion wouldn't be an issue in the election. He talked to the guy for about ten minutes, and I remember as I watched, thinking, 'This is Jonathan in one of his best moments.' "

A squash partner of Jonathan's had believed that winning mattered more than most things to Jonathan, and then one day Jonathan made him wonder if he had ever had the slightest idea who Jonathan was. They had played to a dead heat. They were in their fifth and deciding game. The score was tied. It was Jonathan's serve. But Jonathan held the ball. He turned to his opponent and declared that this had been such a fine and even match it seemed a shame to spoil it by going on. Wearing his cockeyed grin, Jonathan offered his hand.

Jonathan says, "If I'm confronted, I'll instantly fight." He has observed in others—in a law partner, in Bill the architect—a quieter way of contending. "What I call Protestant good manners."

He has seen that approach succeed where his own had failed. "I haven't been able to integrate it into my life," he says. "But I can *see* it now." Sometimes—after he's spoken his mind at a school committee meeting, for instance—Jonathan leaves a roiled-up wake. Some people dislike him—that proves he's alive. And maybe he ought to occupy a wider sphere than the one he has chosen. But Jonathan has fun.

He does not deny himself the pleasure of a gaudy necktie now and then. He has a way with children. He emerges from a movie about Robin Hood—his favorite hero—teaching his boys how to swashbuckle down the street. He says, "I love trials. I love the intensity, the action." Losing the race for D.A., he insists, was a fine, enlightening experience, nearly as rewarding as winning, he guesses. After he had lost, he wrote a letter to the local paper, and in it he quoted Teddy Roosevelt, that Achilles of American politicians, as follows:

> Far better it is to dare mighty things, to win glorious triumphs, even though checkered by failure, than to take rank with those poor spirits who neither enjoy much nor suffer much, because they live in the gray twilight that knows not victory nor defeat.

Jonathan seems to believe in coming home with his shield or else on it. Judith likes to mix it up now and then, too. She is small, with black curly hair. She hopes to become a representative to the

Amherst Town Meeting, a yearly congress on town affairs that usually lasts for days. It's some people's idea of torture, and her idea of fun. Of the fights between her teachers' union and the local school board, battles in which she will participate all during the building of her new house, she says, "There's one guy on our team who's not confrontational. But me? My idea is you yell, you scream, you pack the room and have emotional floor fights. What could be better? So we lose. At least we'll go down kicking and screaming." She explains, "If you grow up with a lot of yelling and screaming, yelling and screaming doesn't scare ya. In fact, you kind of like it."

At a party, while standing among old friends discussing current movies, Jonathan reminds Judith that Barbra Streisand in *Funny Girl* on Broadway presided over their first date.

"Remember what I wore?" says Judith, looking up at Jonathan.

"A sort of green thing."

"No, pink. With a Chinese design across the front."

"I don't remember that." Jonathan stares off, as if toward memories.

"It was very pretty," says Judith to a female friend beside her.

"Actually," says Jonathan, "I invited my friend Bruce. But he said, 'You don't invite boys to a show, dummy. You invite girls.' So I invited Judith."

Judith turns to her friend and tells her that just

before that first date, Jonathan broke up with another girl and her most recent boyfriend dropped her. "The reason he dropped me was because Jonathan and his friends came over and gave him such a *bad* time. *Bad*." She turns to Jonathan. "Thanks a lot, guys. That was great. I just lost a boyfriend."

"He wasn't good enough for you."

"You were just jealous because he got eight-hundreds on his college boards."

"He cheated." Jonathan gazes across the room. "You know," he says, "if it'd been the eighties, Jude, things being what they are, I might have ended up with Bruce."

Judith smiles fully at last, and to the woman beside her she says, "Seventeen years old, and I never had another boyfriend after that."

Judith is exaggerating, but Jonathan himself likes to say, "Judith and I have always been married." Jonathan has friends but he does not cultivate many close ones. When Judith points this out to him, he says, "I already have a best friend."

She's the bosomy, softhearted, affectionate, challenging mother, who minds everyone's business and who says, when Jonathan scolds her for offering unsolicited advice to friends, "They want my advice. They just don't know it." She is also a woman in a suit. She has a master's and doctorate in education and has done a great deal of postdoctoral work, particularly in the study of ailments that cut children off from learning. She has worked as a guidance counselor and a special education teacher. She developed and runs Amherst's preschool program for children with special needs. She has written books and papers and delivered many lectures, and has served as a consultant to a number of schools besides Amherst's—they asked for her advice. She has contributed to her field. She is "Judith" or "Judith Souweine," and she sometimes corrects people who forget or don't know and call her "Judy" or "Mrs. Souweine." She also laughs a great deal and often at herself. Her smile has light. It tempers the occasional sharpness of her tongue. She's self-assured, sarcastic, and merry as birdsong in the morning. Most strangers find it hard not to warm to her. She cries easily. Her nose turns red beforehand. She calls Jonathan "Souweine," and "Pook," and sometimes "Pookeroo."

Jonathan has always shared the household chores and Judith insists that he has never put his career before hers. "When our women's group first started, friends in the group had to fight with their husbands over all those things. I'd always go and say, 'I shouldn't say this, but it's not a problem for me.' They'd say 'Oh you must not be telling the truth.' " Jonathan stood for women's liberation before even the term was current. Judith says he felt "a little miffed" when told that he could not join her group.

Of the friendships they share, Judith says, "In most cases I'm closer to the friend than Jonathan,

15

because Jonathan doesn't talk to people. He just talks to me."

"Judith's a very good friend. She likes to chat. I don't," says Jonathan. "If you've got a good marriage and you like your kids, you just don't have much time to make new friendships. I find I get a lot more back from my wife and kids than from any friendship."

"In our family," Judith says, "I take care of the big emotional decisions."

"I like the ceremonial occasions," says Jonathan. "You can feel emotion, but not too much emotion."

She attends to their social life and to matters of aesthetics. Jonathan, she says, has little aesthetic sense, and he agrees. He is their organizational genius, however. His principal tool is the list. If he has a great deal to do tomorrow, as he almost always does, he cannot sleep until he records his obligations in a list. He pulls lists out of pockets, drawers, briefcase. He has some ready-made lists. There's one for a camping trip with children and one for a trip without them. He's devised a kind of list that ameliorates procrastination: If he has a difficult chore of high priority and just can't bring himself to face it right away, he makes a list of his thirteen other chores of secondary significance, in the order of their relative importance. So while he puts off the big job, he still manages to attend to his second and third most important ones.

Judith and Jonathan call themselves "B-plus people," a condition they define this way: "Life's

16

not perfect. Get it done." They keep appointments and don't like to be kept waiting themselves. They revel in being busy and worry sometimes that they carry busyness too far. They astonished their housemates in the duplex at first, Jonathan remembers. "Come Friday, they'd be tired out and want to regroup and sit around and read, and there we'd be with every piece of sports equipment you could have and thirty-two community meetings to go to."

They have a fine, sturdy marriage, which is more than a marriage. It is an enterprise. They make a formidable combination. They are decisive. They know their own minds. And they knew what they wanted in a house. They wanted a study so that Jonathan could work at home more often than he had. They wanted a separate, remote master bedroom and a special domain for children. To ease traffic jams during the morning rush to schools and office, they wanted a bigger kitchen and more than the one bathroom they had in their duplex. "And a place where we can all sit down and play a game," said Judith. "And a place for the kids' markers." They had given huge parties in their duplex, but a larger house would make a better site for parties. "It's nice to have a house where you can do weddings and bar mitzvahs. When I was growing up, there was an unwritten rule that you did those things at home," said Judith. The location of their imagined house would improve their opportunities for hiking and bike riding and cross-country skiing. Because their yard would not be enclosed in woods, as their present one was, they would be able to do a lot of gardening. When Judith and Jonathan thought of a new house, they thought mainly of their family's busy social, civic, working, sporting life, and maybe even of packing a few more activities into it. "When you get more space, you can do more stuff," said Judith, smiling.

Jonathan and Judith had imagined in some detail a house that would suit them functionally. Jonathan had already begun making lists. But they were stuck on the question, among others, of what style of house theirs should be. How should it look to their new neighbors, to their friends, and to people passing by on Bay Road, the old road to Boston, down at the bottom of the hill?

Judith and Jonathan had not rearranged their political philosophy to suit fashion or their growing affluence, and they did not want to display their bank account in the façade of their new house. "I won't be a brilliant lawyer," Jonathan once remarked. "I work hard and I'm a good lawyer, and that's good enough for almost any situation, and it's good enough for me." A plain-styled, sturdy house would have suited him best. And Judith's first impulse was utilitarian. "It's the structural details that can change the quality of your life." They had made up their minds, though, to buy a house of 3000 square feet, in a region where custom-made houses cost about $50 per foot. "By any standard," Jonathan would say, "it's a lot of house and a lot of money." Neither he nor Judith wanted to spend what looked to them like an enormous sum and end up with what Judith called 'just a big box."

Judith grew up in a large and stylish house. It had a foyer and a graceful stair and a full butler's pantry. When the time came to sell it, her mother could scarcely bring herself to sign the papers. Judith did not imagine a reproduction of that house. It would have cost too much, and anyway, she did not want to imprison herself in the past. But she had been happy in that lovely house, and she did think back to it sometimes when she thought ahead to her new one. So did Jonathan. "I grew up in a Long Island subdivision, in a split-level house. All the houses were the same. I didn't mind. I didn't think about it. Then I met Judith, and Judith lived in this beautiful Colonial house. It was just gorgeous. It made me aware that there was something other than split-levels. It made me aware."

Between Amherst and the Connecticut River lies a little bit of Iowa—some of New England's most favored farmland. The summer and fall of 1982 Judith bicycled, alone and with Jonathan, down narrow roads between fields of asparagus and corn, and she saw the constructed landscape with new eyes, not just looking at houses but searching for ones that might serve as models for her own. She liked the old farmhouses best, their porches and white, clapboarded walls. "This New England farmhousey thing," she called that style.

She found one house she liked especially, but did not get much further than that.

Although she and Jonathan considered many options, they began to feel that they didn't have all the right skills to invent their new house by themselves. And time was running out. Finally, late in January 1983, they decided to call in an architect. "We basically hired an architect because we felt the problems of building a house were too complex for us, and we're great believers in professionalism," said Judith afterward. "It looked like a difficult piece of land. We wanted to get someone with a lot of aesthetic ideas, too. Aesthetics are not as important to us as the function. They're important, but they're not where we start."

3

The top of a standard door frame is six feet eight inches from the floor. Bill Rawn's head just misses tops of doorways, like a trailer truck going under highway bridges. Bill is just short enough to live in a standardized world. He is slender. He has thick, dark, shiny hair, hair of good health, and a handsome face. In his office, in Boston, Bill usually wears dress shirts and penny loafers and casual pants—jeans or corduroys. The pants are usually too short. They leave a lot of ankle exposed. When the time nears for Bill to leave his office, to meet a prospective client or go to lunch, all changes. He ducks into his closet. He reappears soon afterward, knotting a tie, dressed in a gray flannel suit, tailored, transformed. He worries that his metamorphosis in the closet may seem "a little false," but there's nothing unnatural-looking about Bill in a suit. He has become a man of affairs. On the street, he catches people's eyes. Passing him, you might wonder if you had seen him in the paper or on TV last night.

Months after he moves into a new apartment, in Boston, many of Bill's possessions sit in corners, still packed. His rooms really aren't messier than many bachelor's pads. He says he has been too busy to organize the place, but then he amends that explanation. "There's a part of me—I realize it's well concealed now—that is exceedingly organized and careful and precise. When I was younger I identified with that precision, that Germanic spirit." He goes on, "Looking beneath all the crap on the floor, I see a real organized, somewhat compulsive person. I like to hide it, because I don't think compulsiveness is a particularly attractive trait."

Bill speaks fluently on other subjects, but it can be nerve-racking to hear him talk about designs of houses and buildings. When he begins a sentence, you worry that he may not find his way to the end of it. He has a very deep voice, prone to cracking in moments of excitement. Words fail him. He stammers. "Bill's appealing awkwardness," says one female acquaintance. When Bill begins to draw, however, he is all authority and purpose. His long fingers move with assurance and grace. Bill's right hand is clearly his proper grammar book and dictionary.

Bill describes the glorious life as "a beach chair, a radio, and a very good book," but there have been years when he worked at two professions and was able to muster passion for both. Bill's résumé is six and a half well-stocked pages long. Its high points suggest the history of a Renaissance man in delirium:

Majored in political science at Yale, graduated 1965, high honors, ranking scholar four semesters. Graduated Harvard Law School, 1969. Spent a summer as an urban renewal specialist, U.S. Bureau of the Budget. Practiced law for two years, in a firm of eighty lawyers, in D.C. Assistant to the President, University of Massachusetts, for another two years. Assistant Chancellor for Physical Planning, University of Massachusetts, Boston campus, for yet another two. In between, 1971 until recently, artist doing serigraphs in limited editions, his work on display at galleries in SoHo, uptown New York, and Amsterdam. In the late '70s, architecture school, Massachusetts Institute of Technology, received Chamberlain Prize (design prize for graduating class) in 1979. Architect for four years, Davis, Brody & Associates, New York.

Some people who have had Bill's vita come across their desks have seen in it the progress of a dilettante. Would he try medical school next? Race car driving, perhaps? Of course, some facts don't show in résumés. Bill was never fired from any of his jobs. In fact, he never left an employer in anger but always parted on the friendliest of terms. After law school, moreover, he earned the money for his adventures. He did not ask for help from his parents, though they were well-to-do. There are other gaps in his official history. Filled in, they lend form to his careers. Bill seems to have spent most of his life trying to become an architect.

He was a very good student and a mediocre basketball player. When he was a child, sick and home from school, he used to draw small cities on old bedsheets. He drew buildings in his room after school—houses, office buildings, gas stations. "I came from a family which frowned on that," he says. He was not encouraged to pursue the fine arts, and he stopped drawing at about the age of thirteen.

On outings, Bill used to coax his family into making side trips to towns he knew only by name. "I had an uncle who loved to do that, too." Maybe a keen sense of place is a recessive genetic trait, a funny ear lobe that appears only once per generation. "I think that's one thing that makes someone want to be an architect," says Bill. "Every little place connotes something. It has a *feel* to it. It's fascinating. A sense of place, and then how to fit a building into it." Some of the happiest moments of his childhood he spent on a wooden boardwalk that runs between a line of houses and the sea in a California town called Alamitos Bay. Other sites he encountered later—part of the Ramblas in Barcelona, and in New York the section of upper Fifth Avenue that runs along Central Park—gave him pleasure that felt similar. For a long time he kept it secret even from himself, but his predisposition shows in the fact that he wasn't content to like those places. He wanted to know why he did. In "The Asymmetrical Spine: A Generator of Design," the thesis he wrote his last year of architecture school, he tried to put his finger on the reasons. The quality of a walkway, a street or boardwalk or arcade, has a lot to do with symmetry or lack of it, with what's on either side of the pathway, he decided. You feel a coldness here, he says, one summer evening, while walking down a stretch of Boylston Street in Boston. You have never felt entirely comfortable here, he suggests, and he is right. Here, he explains, many restaurants and a few stores open on one side of the street, but the other side consists of remote or blank façades, which provide no sense of balance or enclosure. There is no there over there. No one seems to pause on this part of the street, to window-shop or chat or watch other passers-by. It's a place to hurry through. A little farther on, however, there is a lingering crowd. There might be other explanations, but the only visible change appears on the edges of the street. There are stores on both sides now. It's hard to put a name to the difference. Bill talks about "balance" and "a sense of edges." He calls the barren stretch an example of a failed "asymmetrical spine."

Bill thinks that most asymmetrical spines discourage people. The exceptions interest him most. If buildings stand on one side of the street and something else stands on the other, then that something else must make a captivating and enclosing edge: the Central Park wall and the foliage that appears above it, on upper Fifth Avenue; the seaward railing, the beach, and the Pacific along the "weak" side of his beloved boardwalk, where many people stroll even on foggy days. In architecture school, Bill applied these notions to the design of a big hotel on the Boston waterfront. His design was never built, but he won an academic prize for it, and an architectural journal published the design and part of the accompanying essay. Bill offered thanks to many living people who had helped him, and also to "the caliphs of Córdoba, who for 200 years, beginning in 785, pursued an architectural vision for the Mosque of Córdoba, a vision that is as powerful a statement about design and design potential today as it was 1194 years ago."

When Bill arrived at Yale, he went on a tour of New Haven by bus. It was organized for new students, but to most students bus tours were for old folks and most chose not to attend. Bill jumped at the chance. When he made his first trip to Europe, one undergraduate summer, he took architectural guidebooks and made a point of visiting every important building he could. In college he subscribed to an architectural journal. When he got applications for law schools he also got some for architectural ones, but didn't fill those out. His old enthusiasm kept awaking, though. The summer he spent in Washington, he worked on issues of urban renewal, and he also discovered the National Gallery. During law school he worked in a poverty law office, and concentrated there on issues of zoning and housing law. "I was sublimating my interest in architecture in urban housing issues." His third year in law school, he took some studio courses in the fine arts, making silk screens. "It was quite a rebellious thing to do." Later on, he found himself in charge of overseeing the construction of the Boston campus of the University of Massachusetts. He had to deal with contractors, architects, politicians, and twenty-four different, angry groups from adjacent communities. He took some abuse, had some fun, and saw the campus built without bloodshed. "I saw architecture maybe at its most mundane, but it put me in deeper touch with it, and my art was going well."

In 1969, after Bill graduated from law school and passed the bar exam, he went to Greece and roamed around its islands. He had a wonderful time doing nothing. It is mainly the absence of guilt he remembers. That period of wandering proved to him that he was "still a nonconformist," even though he was about to join a large law firm. That short idyll, he believes, gave him the nerve to quit the law, after just two years of practice. To his family's dismay, he went, a renegade lawyer, to Aspen, Colorado, waited on tables, did some skiing, and worked assiduously on his print-making. "Oh, no!" says Bill, wide-eyed, when asked if his family sent him money in Colorado.

After Aspen, Bill went back to wearing business suits. He made himself into a cabinet officer of the University of Massachusetts in the daytime, and remained a printmaker every evening and all weekend long, for about four years. In 1973, Bill went to New York, prints in hand, looking for a gallery. Most unknown artists make such a pilgrimage. It begins with shy, high hopes and usually ends in disappointment. Bill went to SoHo. He walked right up to a little gallery. A sign out front said, "PLEASE SHUT THE DOOR BEHIND YOU. DON'T LET THE BABY OUT. IT IS PART OF THE EXHIBIT."

"They wouldn't like my stuff," thought Bill, and he walked on.

When he finally opened up his portfolio, in front of a woman who seemed pleasant and happy to help, his prints were hung at once. Two years later, a larger, major SoHo gallery took him in, and a year after that the very grand uptown Pace Gallery started hanging Bill Rawn originals on its walls. He had made it. Another artist might have abandoned all else for Bill's success. Bill had enrolled in architecture school by then, however. The time left to him for solitary art dwindled. Eventually, he stopped making prints altogether. He gave up another career when it was just in blossom, but he had come home at last.

27

The prints Bill has kept from the various stages of that career—they sit on the floor of his apartment for most of the summer of the Souweine house—look like pieces of colorful tweed, viewed under a magnifying glass. They are visions of geometry, all lines and color. They are simple and exact. Seen in the order of their creation, they become increasingly refined, the lines thinner, the colors subtler. "Anal compulsive as hell," Bill says. They have some power to soothe. Even people who do not care for abstractions on their walls would spot the desire for symmetry and order that Bill put in them. Knowing that these drawings of an interior geometry are followed in Bill's life by geometrical drawings intended for construction, you can imagine his prints as expressions of architectural values, of tidiness, security, and comfort.

As Bill reads his own history, the summer in Greece made him think he could be happy as a gentle nonconformist and his silk-screening persuaded him that he could be a successful one. It was "a break with the verbal world." The galleries made him feel he had talent. Not long after he started making prints in earnest, Bill started saving the money to go to architecture school. Bill remembers thinking, "If I don't do it now, I never will."

At Davis, Brody, under titles of ascending importance—member of design team, project designer, project architect—Bill participated in a widely lauded plan for the restoration of the New

York Public Library, as well as in the design of several huge apartment complexes, a $14 million building at Brown University, several imposing office buildings, and a convention center. Bill had fun and success, as usual, at the firm. But the title of architect sounds more glorious than the practice actually is. Most architects do not make a great deal of money—$30,000 a year for a seasoned one is about average—and most do not acquire ultimate control over designs unless they become partners in firms, and architectural firms do not as a rule make partnerships accessible. Usually, if you want the chance to make a lot of money and you want to be in charge of the creation of buildings, you have to start your own company. Bill knew what having money was like, but mostly he wanted to be the designer in control and not just an important helper. And so, with the usual good feelings all around—Davis, Brody would throw some work his way later on—he gave his notice. Around that time he went to visit the Souweines.

If Bill had misunderstood himself before, he knew what he wanted to become then. "A very good architect."

Bill and the Souweines had met years before, during a political campaign, and for many years since, they had spent a summer week together on Cape Cod. Bill always took it very easy that week on the Cape, according to Judith. He spent hours alone on the beach, didn't insist that the others join him, always washed the dishes, didn't care if he got a bed but actually seemed to prefer a mattress on the floor. It was Bill, though, who always made sure that the reunions happened. He made the winter telephone calls to the Souweines to ask what they were going to do about the Cape next summer. Without Bill's efforts, Judith thinks, they might have let that vacation lapse. "Bill is a *very good* friend and a *very good* conversationalist," says Judith. "Jonathan and I don't have that many men friends that I consider my friends as well as our friends, because I think men make lousy friends, at least to women. But Bill is really interested in me and in my kids. When Bill calls, he will spend two or three minutes on the phone with whatever child answers." Judith allots a great deal of time to the cultivation and maintenance of friends, but the easygoing, charming Bill is to Judith a truly extraordinary administrator of friendships. "He writes rough drafts of letters! To friends!" she exclaims. "I remember saying, 'Bill, you are *very* strange.' "

She goes on, "Bill is sort of compartmentalized. I think he puts us in: 'Souweines, friends, the Cape.' It's not exactly that he puts everyone in a box, but he covers his bases. He is *the* best in the West, Mr. Contacts. He knows everyone and he keeps up with them. One has the sense that going to Yale, Harvard, and MIT was designed for that. I don't think that he does it totally with an eye to his future or his pocket. Certainly with us it isn't, 'I gotta keep up with the Souweines, because they're good contacts.' And I think that people *love* Bill. My parents just love Bill. Even my father." Judith does a gruff voice. "Ahhh, Bill's all right."

So when the Souweines decided to consult an architect, they thought of Bill. Bill was brilliant. If they were B-plus people, Bill was A-plus—a perfectionist. Jonathan does not expect harmoniousness to prevail in life. If it did, he would be out of business as a lawyer. But hiring Bill might be a way around familiar trouble. Unlike most architects they'd known or heard about, Bill had wide experience in practical affairs. "He knows how to move paper," Jonathan figured. Besides, Bill was a friend, just setting off on another adventure. It seemed fitting to the Souweines that they should help him on his way. Jonathan had never started up a new business himself, but he could imagine how frightening it must be. "You sit there and wonder, 'Will anyone come today? And if they do, why?'"

Jonathan makes a short list of his thoughts: "Wouldn't it be great for this good friend of mine to hit the deck running? And, secondly, wouldn't it be great to have someone who cares about us, do this for us?"

When Bill got the phone call in January, inviting him to Amherst—to explore the possibilities, no commitments either way—he felt grateful. He felt flattered. Even though he was essentially a rookie, they trusted him as a friend. Making and keeping friends did indeed lie at the center of

31

Bill's life outside work. Judith had kept track of the sequence of women in Bill's life, but she wasn't wasting time thinking about what dress she would wear to Bill's wedding. For now at least, Bill was all bachelor. Friends had come to his aid now, to help him through the worry and the loneliness of starting out on his own. The mainstays of his life, friends and architecture, were coming together in his first commission, his first command.

Bill had the feeling he had used up all the time allotted him for trying out new careers. "You start at age forty having done a lot of other things . . . I come from a social world that expects success, whatever that means. It's fine to fiddle around for a while. Your friends are amused, and then you throw all that up to become an architect. You don't do that very many times." There was edginess in Bill about this brand-new start. And there was also confidence, and although he tends to express it softly and diffidently, there was ambition. Bill reveres Thomas Jefferson, the artisan of the Enlightenment. "Jefferson is really thought of as a major architectural figure. It's just nice that he was also a politician," says Bill. "He was also an inventor, and I'm not that," he adds. Thinking of the Souweines' house, Bill says, "Single-family houses are mainly not architected. But they have been a means for architects to acquire reputations."

Bill was bound to attend the ground breaking for this house. He drove out from Boston the night before the ceremony, in his battered Datsun. The car's reliability was so questionable that Bill brought extra clothes, so that he could keep warm if the car stranded him beside the Massachusetts Turnpike. The next morning, he stood watching the bulldozer, and he said, "My dreams are stronger than others' here, perhaps. And they're harder, because someone else has to pay for them. Somehow an architect, if he wants to be more than a paper architect, has to figure out how to build his ideas." Bill gazed at the widening, deepening cellar hole.

4

Compared to towns down near the Connecticut River, settlements in the hills just a dozen miles or so to the west and north seem like outposts. On the night of March 1, a month and a half before the ground breaking, as a dank mist fell on Amherst, it had rained ice up in the hills. In a little community called Apple Valley, limbs were snapping, a sound just like gunfire, and the power had gone out. Inside a house on a hillside, Jim Locke and his partners sat at a kitchen table. They were three of the members of a small building company of equal partners, called Apple Corps. One of the four members, Alex Ghiselin, was out of town. The rest were at the table. There was Jim. There was a broad-shouldered fellow in wire-rimmed glasses, named Ned Krutsky. And there was Richard Gougeon, a bearded man, who owned the house where they had gathered. In the eerie light of a Coleman lantern, the three carpenters' forearms looked enormous, like clubs.

"This is the best-looking house I've seen in a long time," said Jim.

The forearms withdrew as Jim unfurled on the table Bill Rawn's first drawings of the Souweines' imagined house—several depictions of a stately-looking, old-fashioned Greek Revival building. "It's big," said Jim as Richard and Ned leaned in and peered at the plans.

The past year and a half, a time of very high interest rates, no one had ordered a new house from Apple Corps. They had been luckier than many builders, and had kept busy doing renovation work. On one job, though, Ned Krutsky had rebuilt a couple of bathrooms and the costs had run to twice his estimate. Apple Corps had, as they put it, eaten some of the difference. Some customers were taking their time paying up. The year before last, Apple Corps had built three small new houses and had dispensed to themselves Christmas bonuses of $4000 apiece. This past Christmas, there was no money for bonuses. Now, suddenly, all over the country, couples were again emerging from banks, embarked on the pleasures and disappointments of property. "The last year or two it seemed like we were working against the tide," said Jim. "Now a lot of work is falling on us, and I feel real good about it."

"Good!" declared Richard Gougeon, putting on

a parody of a madman's grin. "Maybe this year I can get my truck painted."

Jim and his partners now had before them invitations to bid on three new houses. The Souweine job was the biggest. They could all see from a glance at the plans that the framing would be tricky and the trim challenging. "It's neat," said Jim. In the drawings on the table, in the flickering light, the three partners could foresee a full and interesting summer of building from scratch. They were eager for the smell of clean, new wood.

Even more than Richard and Ned, Jim wanted to build the Souweine house. In their ten years together, Apple Corps had followed a policy that is unusual among builders. The partner who ran a given job—usually the one a customer called first—got paid less for planning the work and dealing with money than he and the others received for driving nails and sawing wood. The arrangement was a statement about the group's early social philosophy. It had the practical effect of keeping any one partner from becoming too fond of bossing the others around. Jim had once favored the practice. Now he thought they should abandon it. Jim was the partner whom Jonathan had called. If the Souweines accepted Apple Corps's bid, Jim would run the job. He wanted to run it. For many years, Jim had viewed as a chore the part of building that is business. He was ready to let himself get interested in business now.

At a lumberyard once, needing to measure the width of a board and having no ruler, Jim spread his right hand on the surface of the wood and declared, "It's twelve inches." He had long ago measured the breadth of his opened hands, to enhance their utility. Only on a very large man would Jim's hands look normal. Just one of them can cover his long face, from ear to ear and forehead to chin. He could keep one hand behind his back and still play peekaboo with a baby. Although a knuckle is likely to carry a wound now and then, Jim keeps his hands very clean and the nails neatly trimmed. His hands look serene, in the manner of small, graceful animals.

Jim was born to work with his hands, but he doesn't feel he was raised to do so. Both of his parents excelled in college. Both were Phi Beta Kappas. His father is an eminent lawyer. "Education was pushed at me as a way of being successful," Jim says. He attended two different elementary schools. He went to a public high school and for a year to a prep school. Some were good schools, some poor, he thinks. Wherever he went, he did badly. He went to two different colleges in the 1960s. "I couldn't really flunk out of college," he explains, "because there weren't really any grades at the ones I went to."

He drifted away from them without a diploma. "It's funny," he says, "because I love learning things and I got some real highs in there, and even now I get purely intellectual joy out of things." Jim speaks softly and always grammatically. He often analyzes his own thoughts, and sometimes analyzes his analysis. He seems to have drawn a distinction between education and schools, the sort that some God-fearing people draw between religion and its churches. Jim reads a great deal. Before he picks up his toolbox in the mornings this coming spring and summer, he will read, among other things, *Understanding Wood, Vanity Fair,* issues of the magazine *Fine Woodworking, Pride and Prejudice.*

Jim had a passion for automobiles as a boy. Drifting around between colleges and afterward, he earned his way as a mechanic. He got married. He was raised near Boston but born in the Connecticut River Valley. In 1972 Jim came back to his birthplace. He bought acreage in the hilltown of Ashfield, in an area of dirt roads and orchards. That summer he set up a tent on his land and built a house. He had no experience working in wood. He and his first wife labored alone, one long summer, just they and a book. "Rex Roberts. *Your Engineered House.* Post and beam, shed roofs, flimsy walls built out of this stuff," he says, gesturing at some thin, bedraggled-looking lumber. Was it a good text? Jim puts laughter in his voice, especially when he's being mordant. "It was okay."

The first carpenters who settled in the Connecticut River Valley came from England, and they built in the ways they knew, both out of expediency and to make America feel like home. They built framed houses, with skeletons made out of

37

large and widely spaced timbers, posts and beams, fastened together with pegs. Jim chose that style because his book made it look substantial and simple. Like the English carpenters in the New World, he relied when he could on skills that his hands had already acquired. He used nuts and bolts, sacks full of them, for fasteners, instead of the tricky pegged joints. "A mechanic's post and beam," he says.

In 1973, after serving that solitary apprenticeship, Jim turned pro. He went to work for a building contractor, and learned the trade mostly by watching carpenters more experienced than he. He did not ask many questions. "The earn-while-you-learn plan," he says. "I'm a good observer, I'm not a good asker. I was worse then. I didn't want to open my mouth for fear of spilling the goods."

Jim and another young settler in Apple Valley worked for the same contractor that year. Their boss's business looked doomed. Jim and the other young man took a job on their own, helping Alex Ghiselin renovate a house. Alex joined them. They persuaded a local architect to let them bid on a new house, and then Richard Gougeon came onto the team.

Richard had a different sort of pedigree from Jim's. "Jim and I," says Richard, "we come from completely different ends of the rope." But Richard, more than the other members of the partnership, has been Jim's alter ego, his improbable secret sharer.

Jim lacked interest in school. Richard was dyslexic. Richard worked hard at his books, but he could not read well enough to keep up. He flunked every grade through the tenth, but was simply passed on to the next, until he was given a chance at acquiring some self-esteem and sent to a trade school. In twelfth grade there, his classmates named him "carpenter of the year." He chose carpentry for the sake of independence, he says. "I figured whatever I knew no one could take away. It wouldn't be like losing your job at the mill. I felt if I got laid off or something, whatever I knew I could take somewhere else and sell it to someone." Jim had moved to the hills west of the Connecticut River. Richard was raised there. He spent most of his childhood in a house trailer. His father's family came from Canada in the late 1800s. His father worked as a farmer, as a lumberjack, and as a repairer of equipment—trucks, tractors, balers. He worked for a boss during the days and he worked in moonlight, quite literally sometimes, for his own one-man enterprise, named Gougeon's Nite Owl Service. Richard's father is well known to the farmers left in the hills. He's a man to be relied upon. He can fix almost anything cheaply and well.

Looking back, Richard says of Jim and his other partners, "When we started, I had more responsibilities than the others, and they had something to fall back on. I didn't. There was no other money I could get from anybody, if I needed it. If I didn't work, we didn't eat." He goes on,

"In this country you busted your ass if you wanted anything. Or you got left behind. It's still that way. The rich get richer. I guess that's true, but there is a way out. Yup. Hard work. I was lucky. I was taught to work. People in the ghettos, a lot of people there never got to work. How can you teach somebody else to work, if you never worked yourself? It must be a horrible life. I come from a different kind of poor."

Richard is short, with a physique that would serve for socialist posters. His beard is full and black. He has a booming voice and usually keeps the volume turned up. His repertoire of laughter ranges from silent mugging, eyes wide and mouth shut as if on something inedible, to bellowing, head back on his shoulders—it could bring down rain. He was raised as a Catholic. He says, "My father never talked much about things besides Ford trucks, you know, but one day I was workin' with him and he said to me, 'You can pray to God as well in a Protestant church as you can in a Catholic one, son.' Then he went back to work. I never forgot that. I don't like churches myself. I guess I'll go to hell, huh? I guess I'm *not* a good Christian. But I don't want to be! I do want to be a good person, though. I care a whole lot about that. Bein' kind to others, and . . . and minding your own business." He grins.

Like Jim, Richard built a house for his family in Apple Valley. He did so in his spare time, on nights and weekends, and mostly by himself. By the spring of 1974, he had reached the roof. On a

Sunday morning, his father came over to lend a hand. They were putting up the rafters when a car pulled in. A moment later, there appeared over the top of the ladder a lithe, thin stranger with a nailbag and hammer hung from his waist. That was how Richard first met Jim, when Jim came unasked to help with the roof. "I think it was more him finding out who I was than anything," Richard says.

"Jim used to intimidate the hell out of me. I told him once I'd put some commercial fertilizer on my garden. He made *terrible* fun of me. Made me think, God, I'm doin' *terrible* things here."

Jim's mechanic's post-and-beam house was large and sturdy and also austere. For two years, until his first daughter was born, Jim's house had no electricity or running hot water. Jim built that house the hard way, almost entirely by himself. "I was dedicated to those propositions," he says. "I don't remember feeling all that solid about them. I guess there was some philosophy behind all of that, but it was philosophy aided by my income. One of my partners says I was trying to make a statement with my place. That sort of makes me feel good, but it was pretty much straight economics. I must have preached about doing things that way, but I think that came afterwards. It usually does, doesn't it?"

Jim's house astonished Richard. "Jim got this hippy-dippy how-to-do-it book. Said, 'Oh-*Kay!* I'm ready to build a house.' The person who wrote that book had a lot of concepts. But he didn't have a *complete* concept. Oh, it came out all right. After we all got in there and fixed it up." Richard laughs. Then his face falls. "Jim's chicken coop. I called it that once. I said that by accident, I think. It hurt his feelings, he told me later. I felt funny soon as I said it. It was one of those things you say and, Oh shit."

Richard also remembers a day when he bragged to Jim about buying an automatic dishwasher. "Jim accused me of bein' bourgeois. Christ! I never had a dishwasher in my whole life, growing up. I was just trying out all this stuff for the first time. I told him, 'I'm trying like hell to be middle class.' It hurt a little. No, it did. Thing of it is, though, here I am trying as hard as I can to be bourgeois, and Jim's trying as hard as he can to go the other way, and he was screwin' it all up." Richard laughs and laughs. "I'm trying to go one way and he's trying to go the other." They seem to have met somewhere in the middle. "When we met each other, we were just twenty-five, twenty-six," says Richard. "Jim was having a hard time dealing with society. He still didn't want to go to prep school. He was still fighting that yet. He was trying to get rid of that past, trying to go without showers, and I was building showers as fast as I could. Jim's changed. *Jim has changed.* Yup. He grew up. I like Jim a whole lot. I have a real good time working with Jim. He works the same kind of pace that I do. We go right along, very at ease, we're relaxed when we're working together." Jim, too, uses commercial fertilizer in his garden now. Richard uses more manure than he did before.

The partnership survived many squabbles. When they named themselves Apple Corps, after Apple Valley, the community where most of them lived, some hilltown tradesmen smiled. This group sounded like another bunch of hippie carpenters. In fact, though all had built or renovated their own houses and Richard had practiced carpentry since tenth grade, none knew much about the business of contracting. Richard remembers their first job: "I was laid off that winter and I was trying to figure out how I was gonna pay my mortgage, when they asked me to work with them. For some incredible rate, like six dollars an hour. 'Hey-eh, great! Let's go to work.' So we estimated that job and came out low bidder. By a lot. Scared ourselves, too. It was a seventy-five-thousand-dollar house, an incredible house back then. We never made any money on it, but we got paid every day. We had a good time. It gave everybody a lot of confidence, that job."

Richard remembers that when they had laid the last of the floor, one of the concluding acts of every housebuilding, they said to each other, "We can do about anything now, in housing." They felt like professionals. The architects won an award for that house. "They were happy as hell," says Richard. "They gave us another job right off."

Apple Corps grew up together, as Richard says. Their skills evolved. Their business practices lagged behind. Contractors get wealthy in part by subcontracting out large pieces of a job, hiring unskilled labor for one aspect of it and semiskilled labor for another, and bringing in the crack carpenters at the end, for the things that show in a house. Even the best contractors cut corners, for the sake of reduced labor costs. Apple Corps always hired subcontractors for the plumbing and wiring, often for the heating and masonry, sometimes for the painting, but almost always they did all the rest of the work themselves. Their reluctance to hire helpers meant that they could keep their overhead low and underbid many other contractors. It also meant that they could build only one large or two small houses in a summer, which reduced their opportunities for profit. Although the practice made Richard shake his head—to him, it was a form of not minding your own business—they had turned down jobs once in a while, because they did not care to execute certain sorts of designs with certain kinds of materials. "I've never put on aluminum siding yet," Jim remarks, with evident satisfaction. They did no advertising to speak of, and you could not find the company's name even in the phone book. In the last good year of forty-hour weeks, each had earned about $20,000, enough to live comfortably, since each had built or renovated his own house, but hardly enough to get rich. They had often talked about making more money, but collectively, they had felt reluctant to change their ways.

"Any of us aren't super craftsmen," says Richard. "There are a lot better craftsmen around.

You know, super cabinetmakers. I'm a carpenter. Nothing special. We'll get good about the time we get in our seventies. It takes a long time to get *really* good at something. You can't do it in just ten years or something. But we do the very best that we can."

In their ten years, Apple Corps had laid hands on more than two hundred houses. They had left their mark on the countryside. They had gotten steady work solely through the recommendations of former customers and the good notices of tradesmen. Jim always hated the company name, but he felt proud of Apple Corps's accomplishments. He had become a carpenter after spending a winter working on cars, in an unheated garage. "I knew I liked to work with my hands," he says. "But I didn't like being dirty and cold all winter, and I knew that if I had my own garage, I wouldn't get anywhere." Carpentry had offered a life of comparatively clean and good-smelling jobs. Jim had known from the start that he could perform well at the trade. He had great, justifiable confidence in his hands. "And being a carpenter is kind of honorable, too," he says.

Jim has said, in his musing, self-reflective way, without a trace of irony, "I can get pretty arrogant about what I do and why I do it."

Richard laughs, thinking of Jim's diplomacy. "He's a lawyer's son. He likes talking to well-educated people and he wants to be accepted by them, too. I don't think Jim's real at ease sometimes. He gets on the defensive. He gets out his dictionary. He overkills what he has to say. It makes him look, I don't know, a little snobbish, which isn't a good thing to do with people you're trying to work for. I don't have that kind of trouble. When I'm trying to talk to a customer, I just kind of clean up my ain'ts." Richard grins and gets serious. "No, Jim has a hard time sometimes dealing with customers. When they're getting a new house built, people go through a real special time of their life. They're putting themselves in debt for twenty, thirty years. It puts kind of a stress on a person. That makes it a little more difficult to get along with people sometimes."

5

With Ned's and Richard's help, Jim came up with an estimate. The Souweines accepted his bid. But Bill had been given scarcely a month to invent a new house and the plans Jim bid on, though nice-looking, were sketchy. The imagined house began to change. Jim, Bill, and the Souweines held many long meetings. During these, Judith made a study of Jim.

"Jim's of, you know, the same genre we are. But he's gone a different way. He made a conscious decision not to do what Jonathan's done. So all that makes it a little more complicated than if we'd hired another builder." Jim's apparent concern for the quality of her new house amazed

Judith. She liked that side of Jim, but other traits she found slightly exasperating. Jim seemed reluctant to bargain, unwilling to enter the fray of normal commerce. "It's sort of naive, sort of purist Yankee." In fact, rural Yankees once made a name for themselves as clever horse traders, but at some point, in the western hills at least, Yankee tradesmen gave up bargaining for the take-it-or-leave-it approach. If you attempt to negotiate with a hilltown Yankee craftsman, or an assimilated one like Jim, you run the risk of suggesting to him that you think he's dishonest or stingy. Judith makes her voice deep and gruff, the way parents will when doing the voices in fairy tales: "My work costs two hundred dollars. If you don't want to pay, that's your business." She goes on, speaking of Jim, "It's cultural practice. The way our life works and his life works. I know who he hangs out with, who he's involved with, who his friends are. Somewhere in his life he made a conscious decision to go up into the hills."

Judith considered the possibility that the slight discomfort she felt with Jim might stem from "an ethnic difference." She had known anti-Semitism, though, and she had not felt that from Jim. It would be odd if she had, because Jim's father is Jewish. Jim had no reason to mention that fact to Judith. Jim's friends describe his looks, accurately enough, as "WASPy." But Judith guessed right anyway. "It doesn't have to do with being Jewish or non-Jewish," she concluded. "It's a cultural-political difference."

Meeting followed meeting, and Jim's original estimate soon disappeared under piles of yellow
notepaper. Jim revised his figures many times.
Finally, he began to approach a summing up. The
bulldozer came and dug the cellar hole. Jim told
Judith and Jonathan that he would deliver a final
price to them the following week, on a Monday in
late April. The preceding Saturday, two days before that promise fell due, Jim drove his pickup
into Northampton, the big town on the other side
of the Connecticut River from Amherst. Northampton has a wide Main Street, flanked by stone
and brick buildings—most of them date to the
late nineteenth century and early twentieth, and
many have been refurbished, like old blanket
chests. Northampton keeps court for a county.
Clusters of surnames appear on many discreet
signs and doorways. These let you know that
deals and trouble are routinely discussed in rooms
all over town. Jim gets to Jonathan's office through
a door between storefronts and up a staircase with
a brass handrail and worn marble steps, scalloped
in their centers by a century of traffic. Jonathan
works under high ceilings, over wooden floors,
and behind doorways cased with thick, wide, elaborate hardwood moldings, the kind of woodwork
that makes some people nostalgic for yesteryear's
carpenters.

Calvin Coolidge lawyered in Northampton in an
office like Jonathan's. It's what a country lawyer's
office ought to look like, reassuring somehow in

its lack of plate glass and gleaming surfaces. Jonathan's desk faces tall windows over Main Street. He's dressed like Jim, in Saturday's casual clothes, but he moves fast. He exchanges quick pleasantries and gets right down to business. For a few minutes, he and Jim discuss the language of the still unwritten contract.

Then Jim says, "I had a little argument with Bill."

"I heard, I heard," says Jonathan, and swiftly he brushes the subject aside, along with a handful of papers. "Now. My feeling is that the date of completion was a strong part of your original proposal. That date was September first."

"Put that date in the wish category," says Jim. "The way we're going to do this, four of us will be working all the time, until we start tripping over each other, and that's as many as can work on a house. And that's not helpers, that's four ace carpenters. Our time is four and a half months and that's with no delays, no bad weather."

"Actually, I wanted it August first," says Jonathan. "But I guess that's impossible. Why four months?"

"Our labor is four and a half months of solid time," Jim repeats. "And there are a couple of vacations in there."

"Why a couple of vacations in there?" says Jonathan, tilting his head. "The farmers I know, the builders I know, take their vacations in the winter."

"Okay," says Jim. He's raised his chin. He

purses his lips now and stares at the wall to Jonathan's right.

"Hey, it's none of my business. But it affects *me*."

"If you've got money," says Jim, turning back to Jonathan, whose face still bears the tan he got on his late-winter vacation in Florida, "you take time off in the winter. If you don't have money, you take time off in the summer."

Jonathan seems to decide that he has not heard Jim's explanation. "Judith wants to be in September first," he goes on. "When I told her you said the end of October, she said, 'No, September first.' "

"It's not a subject of negotiation," says Jim. "That's what I'm getting at."

"It is a subject of negotiation," says Jonathan in an even voice. "I'm going to tell Judith it's October thirty-first or nothing and she may say, 'If it's not by September first, we can't build it this year.' "

Jim stiffens. His large gray eyes widen.

Jonathan notices. "Frankly, I don't give a shit. I agree with you. If you can't do it, you can't do it."

"If the decision is not to build the house until next year, I'm going to be really pissed," says Jim to the wall.

"I don't think she'll decide that," says Jonathan. "I probably shouldn't have said that. You're very worried."

"We just gave up another house to do this one. I don't want to feel screwed."

"Now wait a minute. The first time I heard it wouldn't be September first was a week ago."

They discuss who said what when. After a while Jim has his arm draped over the back of his chair. They seem at ease with each other once more. "I shouldn't have said that," says Jonathan. "I don't feel you proceeded in bad faith on the date, in any way. Now, the only other things I have . . ."

Jonathan says he knows a contractor who allots $3000 worth of time for planning a house, and Jonathan assumes that Jim has made a similar allotment in his bid. Jonathan believes that Bill Rawn's contributions have reduced Jim's expenses, and he'd like Jim to reduce the final price accordingly. Jim protests. Jonathan, who is Bill's old friend, calls him "Rawn," while Jim, who scarcely knows the architect, calls him "Bill." A peaceable discussion, until Jonathan brings up the windows.

When Jim had made his bid on the incomplete plans, he had known that he and Bill and the Souweines would make many revisions, but over the following weeks they had made so many that Jim began to feel insecure about the house's total price. He told Jonathan at one moment that he would like to build the house on the basis of time and materials, a cost-plus arrangement, the safest one for Jim. But Jonathan did not want to spend the coming summer fretting about cost overruns, and he insisted on a fixed contract price. There was no contract yet, however, and there was no single price either. Instead there was a running tally, which Jim kept, as he and Bill and the Souweines tried to find the house they wanted for a price the Souweines could afford. Among the items that changed in the weeks after the original bid were the house's many windows. Jonathan and Judith had reason to hope that they might actually save a bit with the new ones. But the price Jim got from the supplier was about $4000 more than the old one. Jonathan was shocked. He asked Jim to shop around for a better price.

On a contract job for which the plans are settled at the start, the owner is assured of getting a house for the bid price. The builder is under no obligation to reveal how he arrived at that total price, and if the builder finds a bargain on a certain material afterward, he keeps the savings for himself. But Jim and Jonathan were working under a different and, in many ways, more complicated procedure. Since Jim figured 10 percent profit on materials into his ever-changing total estimate, the more the new material cost, the more Jim stood to make. So he had a positive incentive not to shop around for bargains. But Jonathan could hardly be expected to accept blindly whatever new price Jim brought him. Jim agreed that the new window price seemed high. Jonathan had already made one generous compromise—he had agreed to pay $850 for a change in the framing of the roof, though strictly speaking he did not have to do so. And it really was in

Jim's interest, as well as in Jonathan's, that this house not become unbuildably expensive. So Jim agreed to search for a better window price and to pass any savings on to the Souweines. As it turned out, the savings amounted to almost $2000.

Jim felt he had done a good deed. Jonathan was happy, but also concerned. If you were Jonathan and were looking everywhere for ways to make your new house affordable, sacrificing things you wanted, such as a garage, you'd have had to wonder whether Jim's supplier's price for two-by-fours wasn't high by a few thousand dollars, too. And if you were Jim and Jonathan asked you about finding a better price on the two-by-fours, you'd get a knot in your stomach. You'd feel that you were assuming all the risks of a contract job while giving up the important advantage of being able to shop around for your own benefit.

Now, in his office, Jonathan says, "I'm somewhat concerned about your lumber bills. In light of your window bids. You went to five places. It saved a lot of money for you and me."

"No," says Jim. "I make less."

Jonathan understands. He rephrases. "I want you to make a fair profit, but not by enriching the lumber company. And I feel where we have a thirty-thousand-dollar lumber bill you ought to investigate aggressively."

"I haven't been," says Jim.

"That doesn't make me feel comfortable," says Jonathan.

Suddenly, Jim raises his voice. "I know. But

why should it? If our original bid had been out-landish, I assume you wouldn't have accepted it."

Jonathan blinks, and keeps looking straight at Jim. "I imagine some protection was built into your original bid because you had a very vague idea of the house and now you know a lot more and you don't need that protection."

"All of these changes muddy the water," Jim complains.

"Life is full of muddy water, Jim," says Jonathan softly.

"I know, but you want me to take the fat out of the bid for your benefit. You want me to try to figure out where it's padded."

"Exactly," says Jonathan. "Unless you're reluctant."

Jim lowers his voice and looks away, and as if speaking to himself, replies, "I think I'll show my reluctance by not trying very hard to do that."

"Why?" says Jonathan pleasantly.

"That's what a bid is!" yells Jim. He brings his voice down. "If it's fat in some places, it may be thin in others."

Jonathan has his hands clasped in front of him on the desk. He leans toward Jim. "My concern is that the lumber bill may be two to three thousand dollars high."

"But you accepted the price on the fucking bid! Don't you see that's what we're talking about?"

"The reason I think you should bring it in for a little less," says Jonathan, in the same even tone he'd had when he began, "I assume you felt you had to have healthy margins when you made your bid. Healthier than they need to be, now that you know the house. I think what you did on the windows shows that. You shopped around, you got a better price."

"So why did I do that?"

"Because you want to build my house," says Jonathan.

Again, Jim looks away. "It's been nothing but trouble for me. When you take the contract price, you take the price. I'll think about it. I don't know if I'll think about it."

Jim raises his voice, he mutters, he glares at Jonathan, he looks away. Jim has never raised his voice or cursed at any of their meetings, and from time to time Jonathan looks surprised. But then he only blinks and goes calmly on to the next point in his argument. It isn't that he does not respond to Jim, just that he does not respond in kind.

Finally, Jonathan, in the gentlest of voices, says, "I assume that primarily we're on the same team."

Jim replies, speaking softly, too, looking at his lap, then at Jonathan. "I guess there's a lot of money at stake, and we both feel it. We feel it in different ways."

"I said everything I had to say," says Jonathan. "I feel bad that it seems to have upset you. I would feel worse if I hadn't said what was on my mind."

"I'll recover," says Jim. "I understand your position."

"You think I'm crazy?"

"No."

"As long as you don't think I'm crazy." Jonathan smiles. "I don't like to have people think I'm crazy."

Driving away in his pickup, Jim remarks, "He's done everything he can to reduce the price mechanically, so he can afford this house. Now he's asking for mercy."

Jim had gotten divorced, and this past winter he had moved away from Apple Valley. He and Sandy Warren, Jim's second-wife-to-be, had bought an old house in Northampton. Now for the first time in his life, he owed money. It was a mortgage, that most respectable form of indebtedness, but it bothered him. "I'm locked in. I have to make money," Jim said, around the time when he was bidding on the Souweine job. But more than his material circumstances had changed. He went on, "I don't know. It has something to do with success. I want to be successful. Maybe it doesn't have that much to do with money. It's like wondering when you're going to become an adult, wondering when you're going to become successful."

Sandy has long cherished a photograph of Jim as a boy. In the foreground sits an old Victrola. Jim's brother and sister look toward the camera, but Jim stares wide-eyed at the ancient record player. Forever in the picture, Jim wants to get his hands on that machine, Sandy believes. And

56

the notion makes her happy. She feels sure that Jim found a profession that is right for him. Jim agrees, but he does not congratulate himself. All his life he had equated education with success. "And it's *still* there! Even though I see how screwed up it makes some people, all that education, it's still there!"

Jim has not finished looking for his right place in the world. He wants to be more than a carpenter. Like Bill Rawn, Jim hopes the Souweine house is a new beginning.

Two nights later, on a Monday in late April, Jim walks into Jonathan's office carrying a zippered leather case, wedged tightly under his arm. Any purse snatcher would know that something inside is worth caring about. The case contains Jim's final price for the house and, on many sheets of yellow legal paper, the history of that price. It started at $162,000. The Souweines subtracted the garage and half a dozen other expensive items. The price fell to about $139,000. It started back up again, as the Souweines and Bill made new substitutions and additions. Jim's case contains the estimated cost of materials from Apple Corps's usual supplier; firm estimates on foundation work, plumbing, heating, wiring, painting, insulating, from Apple Corps's usual subcontractors; and Apple Corps's estimate of its members' own labor. Jim has put all those figures together and to the total he has added 10 percent, to cover overhead and profit and fear of miscalculation. Jim has come up with a hilltown Yankee's price. It is an exact-looking figure, rounded to the nearest ten dollars.

From his last meeting with Jonathan, Jim knows that the Souweines hope for concessions on the price, and he's not sure that even as it stands, his final price is high enough to cover the cost of this house and a modest profit for Apple Corps. The builders have turned down all other jobs for this one, though. In planning this house, Jim has invested at least two weeks' time, for which he hasn't yet been paid. Losing this job would rank among the large setbacks in Apple Corps's history. Jim feels nervous. He says so, rather nervously, to Judith and Jonathan.

Judith sits knitting in a chair in front of Jonathan's desk. She smiles at Jim and trades some small talk.

Just to build the house they want—and never mind the purchase of the land—Judith and Jonathan must borrow, at 13 percent interest, $100,000, the maximum that the local savings and loans will lend for house construction. To raise the remaining tens of thousands, whatever they come to exactly, the Souweines hope for a good and timely sale of their old house, and, of course, houses aren't always easy to sell. Jonathan hasn't lost much sleep over the money, but the sheer amount makes Judith nervous. She confesses later to a slightly embattled feeling—"It's us against the world, you know." The world is a troupe of unknown lumber dealers and workers, with a building contractor at their head. You turn everything over to a gang of people who don't really know you or have any reason to care about you. You turn over dreams, pride, and money. It's a frightening gamble. Judith and Jonathan don't intend to undertake it without some reassurances and some measure of control.

They once read a book called *It Takes "Jack" to Build a House*. It's a story of woe, with chapters that bear such titles as "The House Is Framed— So Are You." The woman who wrote it chose her builder carefully. He came highly recommended. He talked a good game. He cheated her. Jonathan and Judith feel certain of Jim's competence and honesty, as certain as anyone could be of those qualities in a virtual stranger. They're ready to be guided by him, but not bossed around. Jim should be their partner in this undertaking. Jonathan hopes Jim's final price will be around $142,000. He fears it will be more, and if it is, he'll ask Jim to lower it, if only to get proof that Jim will compromise with them—as indeed Jim already has, on the matter of the windows.

Judith is a trained psychologist, among other things. She can foresee an argument. The prospect doesn't frighten her. She smiles and knits. A button on the lapel of her blazer reads, "GOOD CONTRACT GOOD EDUCATION," a token of the role she plays in negotiations elsewhere. If she feels at all nervous, it's well concealed in the thrust and parry of her needles.

It may not be deliberate, but Jonathan, who's

dressed in a cable-knit sweater and corduroys, is still busy about his office. He says hello to Jim, hands Jim a set of specs, and goes back to examining papers on his desk, occasionally crumpling a sheet and chucking it into the wastebasket.

Jim reads the specs, still standing by the desk. He looks very nervous. He sucks at his lips. He is, unmistakably, not at home.

They begin. "Okay, Judith, tell him," says Jonathan.

"I will really go crazy if I have to live with my father for a month. My sense was it was absolutely clear we'd be in by September first," says Judith to Jim. She smiles.

There's intimacy in this plea. Jim turns to her and leans in her direction. "What can I say? I can't build it any faster. I would like to do it sooner."

Evidently, Judith has resigned herself to October 31.

"Okay," says Jonathan, smiling at Jim. "How much are you going to build this house for?"

"I still don't have the prices on the window casings," says Jim. "My supplier let me down. He went to a banquet tonight. But in theory, with narrow casings, it's one hundred forty-six thousand six hundred and sixty. The reason I'm so nervous, I've been over and over this so many times I don't really understand the numbers anymore. My partner Richard looked at the plans today, and he said, 'It's okay, we can build it for that.' So I guess it's all right."

"What are the high points?" asks Judith. "What have we changed?" She knits. Jim extracts his yellow pad from his case and reads numbers, all the deletions they've made, all the additions.

"Does that make sense?" asks Jim.

No one speaks.

"Something bothers you?" Jim says to Jonathan.

Jonathan has been studying his own sheaf of yellow paper. He looks up abruptly, like a man awakening. "No," he says pleasantly.

Again, there is silence. Again, Jim breaks into it. "I have no idea how to value Bill's time," he says, referring to the architect. "I know I'd have had to do more drawings without him. I know I've been to more meetings than I ever have before, and I don't know if that's because of him. And on the other concerns you had, Jonathan, we just didn't add very much as a fudge factor in our original bid. Frankly, there are a couple of things we left out and we haven't put them back in. So I've allowed two hundred dollars for Bill's work and that two hundred dollars is the only one of the things we talked about that I'm willing to remove."

Judith knits. Jonathan leans a contemplative elbow on his desk. Finally, Judith speaks up. "You and I," she says to Jonathan, "I think we should talk about it."

Judith might just have fired a starter's gun. Jonathan jumps up. Judith arises. They vanish into another room.

Jim's price exceeds the one that Jonathan hoped

for by several thousand dollars. Jonathan knows that an estimate on something as large and complex as a house can't be as precise as Jim's figure suggests. To Jonathan, Jim's price begs for some negotiation. To Jim, the price represents hours and hours of honest addition and subtraction. For his part, Jonathan believes that Jim has been honest, and though disappointed, he's prepared to find the several thousand more than he hoped he'd have to pay, if Jim in turn will round the number down to the nearest thousand. "I think he's gonna go nuts," Judith says. Jonathan stands firm. He just wants Jim to come down a little on the price, and she agrees Jim should.

They're gone only a few minutes. They reseat themselves as briskly as they left. Jim laughs out loud, at nothing in particular. "Okay," says Jonathan. "Some of the things I brought up Saturday I still believe. But what can I say? I came here hoping the price would be somewhere between one-forty and one-forty-five." He studies his papers. He looks up, the trace of a smile on his face. "I don't want to bargain or anything. You take off six hundred and sixty dollars and we have a deal."

Jim is sitting very stiffly. He opens his hands. "Why do you want to dicker?" he says.

"You call that dickering?" says Jonathan. "I call that a round number." It'll cost him $4000 for appliances, he explains, and removing the $660, then adding in the appliances, will bring the grand total to $150,000. "So when my friends ask, I can say it's a hundred-and-fifty-thousand-dollar house."

"Why don't you leave the six hundred and sixty in, and *tell* them it cost a hundred and fifty thousand?" says Jim.

Silence takes over again. Someone's stomach growls. Jonathan has picked up his calculator. Jim has pulled his out. It is hard to imagine what is left to compute. Judith smiles. "Look at this. The war of the calculators."

"That's my proposal," says Jonathan, that brief electronic skirmish over. "We make the deal, I won't bug you or complain."

"It makes me uncomfortable," says Jim. "I'm bargaining with three other guys' money." He adds quickly, "I know that's not your problem."

"I just talked to *my* partner," says Judith, still smiling.

Jim shifts in his chair. "It's stupid, you know. Here I am worried about six hundred dollars on a one-hundred-forty-six-thousand-dollar job." He adds, "But so are you."

"Actually, I'm worried about a lot more," says Jonathan.

Jim laughs. "I feel foolish."

"Don't feel foolish," says Jonathan. "Talk to your partners."

"I've got to," says Jim, who is no longer laughing, all of a sudden. "If it were just me, I'd say, 'No way.' "

The tone of the discussion changes now. "One thing I worry about, Jim. You're building my

house, you have to make decisions. I have partners. If I want to move the office, I'll call a
general meeting, but not if I'm just going to buy
paper clips." Jim stares at a point on the wall. "I
don't want you to feel bad or pressured," Jonathan
adds.

"You gotta make a deal, Jim!" says Judith, not
unkindly. "You gotta make a deal."

"I'm not used to bargaining," Jim says to her.

"Hey, I bargain," says Jonathan. "Judith bargains, and this—I'm kind of annoyed because I
thought I was being magnanimous."

"My job's not bargaining. You accepted the
bid!" says Jim.

"Do you think they just built the Empire State
Building? They didn't bargain over the price?"
says Jonathan.

"It feels to me like if you don't make a little
deal out of it, you won't feel good about it," says
Jim.

"I want to loosen you up, Jim," says Jonathan.

"Loosen me up how?" says Jim, raising his
voice. "By the purse strings?"

"I want the six hundred dollars," says Jonathan,
softly. "But you don't go up on a mountain and
return with the truth. You can't tell me your
estimate is the only possible number. I think
there's got to be a little more give and take, a little
more bending, a little more suppleness."

Jim looks at no one, and no one speaks. Then
Jonathan sighs. "I really did think I was being
magnanimous. I have a short office meeting. I'm

available if there's anything else to talk about. I don't think there's anything else to talk about."

Jonathan leaves. Jim gets up, but leans against a chair a moment, to speak to Judith.

"How does he want to loosen me up?" he asks her. "I think I have a pretty good sense of humor."

"I didn't say you had no sense of humor," she says. "Rigid, yes."

Jim purses his lips.

"I don't believe you, Jim," she says gently. "Everybody has to make deals."

"Our usual procedure doesn't include bargaining," Jim answers. "We don't do that many contract jobs."

"I think you make bargains every day," she says. "Say you want some kitchen cabinets. There's no magic number. There's nothing sacred about those numbers you get on an estimate."

"Then why do estimates?" asks Jim.

"Those may be close estimates, but then the person comes in and says, 'I'll give you a little less.'"

"I just don't understand what the deal is, for that amount of money." Jim seems truly puzzled, but calm.

"It strikes me as a bit holy to think that you don't bargain, Jim," says Judith. "High Moral Tone. HMT," she says. "And I think that's the thing that really gets to Jonathan and me, High Moral Tone."

Jim departs on the instant. He walks out like a

person who has found himself in the wrong neighborhood, wishing but not daring to run.

"There's nothing like a political campaign. But this comes close to it, in terms of intensity," says Judith. She sits in the reception room, waiting for Jonathan to finish his office meeting. "Do you know who his father is?" she says, speaking of Jim. "Number one in workmen's comp. He wrote the book." She gestures across the room toward a bookcase of legal texts. And there it is, in fact. *Massachusetts Practice: Volume 29*, by Laurence S. Locke. Judith adds, with a sad-looking face and a shrug, "Now he's involved with more lawyers, and he doesn't like it."

She calls Jim "very rigid, very rigid." She says, "Jonathan and I are controlling, but we're not rigid. We want things our way. We push people around. But we're not rigid."

Judith sighs. "I thought I was making things better, until I realized I was making them worse. He's mad."

"I wasn't mad," Jim tells Sandy Warren, sitting at their kitchen table. "I was embarrassed. I felt like I was being handled. It was a real familiar feeling. It felt like something that happened to me when I was little. I was put off balance by somebody I expected was going to be allied with me and turned out not to be."

In the bar downstairs from his office, Jonathan

tells Judith that he has given up bargaining. He intends to make no more concessions.

A few days before, the other contractor who had bid on this job called Jonathan, offering his services at a reduced price if for some reason the deal with Apple Corps went awry. Jonathan insisted that he had a moral commitment to Apple Corps, but the other builder's call made him realize he felt that he was going to pay for it—the other builder had good credentials, too. By his own standards, Jonathan has negotiated very gently with Jim and has asked for only a small, token concession. He assumed Jim would accept, and he imagined a handshake and in the next day or two another ceremonial gathering of the Souweines and the carpenters at the site. It was just a small daydream, which Jim has destroyed. Jonathan is openly angry, at last.

He says to Judith, "If you go in to buy a truck, you don't care about the person you buy it from. But if somebody builds a house for you, he becomes a very important person in your life for six months. I'll tell you the truth. He makes me uptight. I feel as if I say the wrong thing, he'll get offended. Tell you the truth, I'm not worried about the money. I'm worried about the deal. If he can't pull it together on one night, how's he going to pull it together on the house?"

Judith worries about the money. "I'm flabbergasted that we're going to spend a hundred and fifty thousand dollars and not have a garage." Of the $660, she remarks, "It's somewhat symbolic, obviously. But it's not totally symbolic. It's six hundred and sixty dollars we've gotta earn, you know."

Now in the bar, Jonathan takes her arm. "Let's go home."

Jim and Sandy sit up till past midnight. "I don't mind the money so much as the way I'm being treated," he says. "I'm being handled and I don't like somebody saying the reason I'm feeling that way is because I have High Moral Tone. It's like going to buy a used car. Well, maybe not. He wants me to be less rigid. It's like he's trying to reform me. The bit about my loosening up. What do they mean? What do they care about what I do? Is that how you welcome someone into your family?"

"Weren't they saying, 'Come on, you're not as pure as that'?" Sandy asks. " 'You're cheating us by at least this much money.' What they said to you over and over is that everybody bargains. They've got to shake that out of you."

"If I keep feeling the way I do," Jim tells her, "the job won't come out as well as it would have this morning. It'll come out less than six hundred and sixty dollars good, and that's what bothers me. I hate that, because that's not the way I want to work."

Sandy looks sad. She says, "I just don't want to face another summer of your getting up and going to a job just because you have to."

Just before they turn in, Sandy remembers their

mortgage. Have they paid it? "It's not the end of the month yet," says Jim, touching her shoulder. "Don't worry about it. You don't have to pay mortgages until the end of the month."

Six hundred sixty dollars represents a very small fraction of what the Souweines will pay for their new house. Divided among Apple Corps, it comes to a little more than a day's pay for each carpenter, against a whole summer of wages, and perhaps, if the estimate holds, a profit of some fifteen thousand dollars. Money is merely the form of the argument. They have asked each other for gestures. They have really just wanted to be friends. They have let each other down.

Jim calls Jonathan and accepts Jonathan's terms. A few days later, they sign the contract. Jim goes over each detail with care. He offers his hand to Jonathan, and Jonathan, glad the hard bargaining is over, takes it with an enthusiasm that surprises Jim. Jonathan gets the better grip, consequently. Afterward, Jonathan feels pleased at Jim's approach to the contract. "My last builder would always say 'Yes,' and he didn't always live up to it. But a man who says he's worried about putting his name on a piece of paper is a man who cares about his word. Jim is a person of integrity. I feel very comfortable having him build my house."

Jim leaves contemplating the handshake. Even in that transaction, he thinks, Jonathan insisted on getting the better of him.

Some weeks later, Judith remarks, "I have a

feeling—I don't know what intervened, between the end of that meeting and when Jim called and told Jonathan he accepted—but I have a fantasy Jim called his partners and they said to him, 'What? Are you joking? Lose this job over six hundred dollars? Call him back, schmuck.' "

In fact, on that Monday night Jim called two of his partners. Alex Ghiselin said, "You shouldn't have gotten angry. Call them back." Richard had said, a few days before, "Well, I guess it's the same situation as a lot of customers. He knows he's gonna spend some money that's going into our pockets, and it's not going to buy anything for him. But *we* take the risk." On the phone Richard told Jim he guessed they'd have to absorb the $660; Jim had better call back and accept the deal. Jim did not call Ned Krutsky, though. He waited until the whole crew gathered, the following morning, at the site of a brand-new barn, which they'd recently erected. They stood together with coffee, their leather tool belts and hammers slung around their waists, looking like a bunch of gunslingers, as carpenters do on the job. Then Jim told his version of the story to Ned.

Ned's voice rose in the morning air. "Fuck them! *Fuck them! Fuuuuuuuck Them!*" he cried.

They sat around on sawhorses. "What a stupid way to begin a job," said Ned through his teeth. "It's goddamn manipulative, and I don't like it. They're taking the spirit away from us. They're not going to get as good a job."

70

"They'll lose a lot more than six hundred and sixty dollars."

"Oh, come on! A house is a house."

"No, the thing of it is," said Richard, "they'll get a good job. We just won't give 'em anything."

For the next two months, not a week passes without Jim or one of his partners remarking on the affair of the $660. Usually, Jim speaks of that sum as money that was taken from them. Generally, he says so while they are performing some little task not specifically required by the contract.

II

ARCHITECTURE

Bill Rawn's heart raced when he first saw the old buildings of Venice. In Barcelona, he once climbed over a rooftop, recklessly breaking the law in Franco's Spain, horrifying his Catalonian friends, just to get a close look at some of Gaudi's work. He made an arduous trek in Alsace to see a church by Le Corbusier, and he knocked on strangers' doors in Berlin and suburban Paris to ask for glimpses of Corbu interiors. Bill, who revels in the works of such markedly different architects as the long-deceased caliphs of Córdoba and the more recently departed Louis Kahn, loves architecture of all ages, and he embraces what is called the contextualist branch of the postmodern movement.

Postmodernism is a slippery term, of course. It says only what it isn't. Paul Goldberger, the architecture critic of the *New York Times*, writes, "The comfort one feels for the modernist ideology today is not much increased by the fact that this style, which evolved with such socialist certainties in the 1920s, became, after World War II, the very embodiment of capitalism, the architectural expression of the corporate state." Postmodern architects reject "the sleek and austere buildings of International Style modernism," the sort of buildings also known as glass boxes. And some postmodernists also disdain the open floor plan, the house without walls.

Bill shares many of the new school's enthusiasms without sharing its scorn for the previous one. He likes certain traditions. "The sense of a building turning a corner, and mullioned windows." He believes that a building should fit its surroundings, both the land around it and other buildings nearby. The contextualist does not believe in form for form's sake, as many modern architects did, but in appropriate form. The principle is perhaps a variation of the environmentalist's creed. To Bill, contextualism partakes of a community's character and history. The contextualist wants to capture some of the spirit of old buildings in new designs. Bill is given to subtlety—sometimes excessively so, he's afraid—and like Judith and Jonathan, he espouses liberal, egalitarian political views. Contextualism suits Bill. He does not like to think of himself arrogantly imposing some wild vision of his own on a client or a neighborhood. On the other hand, what he admires most in buildings is distinctiveness. "Of whatever sort," he says.

As Judith might say, she and Jonathan didn't know from postmodernism, and Bill did not know the Souweines' taste in houses. As Bill traveled up from New York on a Friday night back in late January, he realized that he and his old friends would have to get to know each other in a new way. They began to do so the next morning. Judith and Jonathan packed Bill into a car and drove him all around Amherst, looking at houses. They didn't show Bill any that he considered suitable models. Judith's favorite old New England farmhouse did not inspire Bill. But as the day wore on, Bill realized that his friends wanted a traditional sort of house, and from Judith especially, Bill got the strong feeling that they wanted a little more besides. They drove him to one new house that had what Bill called "historic feeling," and to another that had a couple of arched windows, which Judith said she liked. Bill pointed out that those windows did not suit that house, but it seemed to him that in showing him arched windows, Judith was trying to tell him that she would like a house that was not ordinary—"something a little special," as Bill expressed it to himself, "something with historic feeling."

Bill could not have hoped for better news. Although the day's tour wore him out, it also left him excited. They had dinner in the Souweines' duplex—it was situated in Pelham, a country town adjacent to Amherst. Then they cleared the dishes, and Bill went to work.

They sat at a round dining table with a lazy Susan in the middle, an heirloom from Judith's childhood. The table looked old, its finish gone a little milky. It rested near a sliding glass door in a corner of the living room. The walls of the duplex

77

needed paint. The ceilings looked low, especially when Bill was standing up. The room seemed too small for all the purposes it served. It was filled up with desks, chairs, sofa, end tables, coffee table, wood stove, bookcases, a large corner cupboard, and the dining table, at which Jonathan and Judith sat, in lamplight, facing in on Bill and describing to him the rooms they had imagined in the place of this one. Bill set down on the table a sheaf of yellow tracing paper, and with long, thin fingers, he sketched as they talked. As he sketched, Judith felt excitement rising.

A decade after the first Arab oil embargo, every housebuilding pattern book had something to say about the patriotic or civic or even moral virtues of site planning and architecture that paid proper respect to sunshine. Bill believed in planning for sunlight. Jonathan had proselytized for solar energy at MassPIRG. Judith had read widely on the subject. But the Souweines did not favor exotic approaches. "A million glass bottles stacked up in the living room is not my cup of tea," said Judith. She wanted a house that looked like one and not like an engineering laboratory or a recycling center. She and Jonathan wanted some traditional form with a long wall that faced south and had a lot of windows in it. And that is, of course, one way to solar virtue.

On the phone to Bill in New York, the Souweines had worried that they would have to trade their best views for sunlight, because the dominant vista from their land lay to the north. When they had visited the site today, however, Bill found the broadest view lying to the east and northeast, out over Bay Road toward the Pelham Hills. His friends could have that view and sun as well. The southern view of pastures and woods would be less imposing but charming. "A house wants a place," Bill likes to say, and he had felt pleased to find that his friends' land had meadow on one side and woods on another. They had bought an edge of a woods, and the edge of a woods is a definite place in the sense that an open field or the middle of a woods is not. Creatures congregate and flourish in edge habitats. Le Corbusier called the geometrical guidelines that ancient builders employed "protection against the arbitrary." You could say the same about the edge of a woods.

Jonathan spoke about the front door. The one to his side of this duplex stood out of the way and had invited little use. Jonathan said he wanted an unmistakable front door. If they were going to pay for a front door, he wanted people to use it. Bill had a compatible desire. He believed a house should "respond" to the nearest public thoroughfare. It should not turn its back on public and community, and certainly not if it was the house of Jonathan and Judith Souweine. Bill thought he would also like to keep the new house's windows from opening directly on Judith's parents' dormered Cape, to the east, and on the split-levels down the hill across Bay Road, to the north. Bay Road, he had noticed today, ran past the Souweines' land in a line almost exactly east to west. How to honor the road and the bucolic, while avoiding mundane views of other houses?

As Judith and Jonathan talked, Bill sketched the site and within it a rectangle. One long side of the house that Bill was now building faced roughly south. One of the narrow ends faced west into trees. The other narrow end looked out on the big, open view. On the long south side, he installed a lot of windows. Into the narrower east side he put a front door. He turned the house a little off the east-west axis—15 degrees eventually—so that the front door, while not directly facing Bay Road, would open up in view of it. No one driving up from Bay Road would miss that front door.

The Souweines described their wish to set aside a domain for their children, one large and nice enough to keep them there awhile. Bill drew an upstairs to the house and assigned the whole thing to the children—three bedrooms, two playrooms. The Souweines wanted to recapture some of the privacy they enjoyed before they had children. To the back of the large rectangle Bill appended a smaller, narrower one, a one-story extension with bedroom and bath, nestled into the woods. The windows of this master bedroom would look out upon the woodline, down upon a little brook, away from Judith's parents' house, a little bit away from it all. Judith and Jonathan wanted a big living room. It should serve for formal dining now and then and for parties. It should contain their baby grand piano. It should also invite informal family gatherings. That old home of Judith's childhood had a grand living room and also a de facto one, a den with an unaccountable coziness about it, where the family always congregated, leaving the living room for company. She and Jonathan could not afford two living rooms, so this one room had to be versatile. Bill drew a living room running the width of the house—a well-lighted room with windows on both north and south walls and many fine views through them. Bill made the room rectangular, because in his experience squares attenuate the possibilities for coziness. He installed a chimney at the center of the house behind the living room's east wall and sketched a hearth for the Souweines to gather around. Judith and Jonathan told him they wanted a spacious, sunny kitchen and an ample breakfast nook beside it. Bill gave over the southeastern half of the main floor to those rooms. Jonathan said he had to have a study. Jonathan would like a pantry, but he would trade it for a study. Bill fit the study into the northeastern side of the plan, next to the front door. There the little study's window would command both the grand view and the sunrise. Bill rarely feels awake before noon, but Jonathan rises early, and Bill wanted him to have the morning sun.

"It's a process you just don't go through when you talk to a lawyer or teacher or a therapist," said Judith afterward. She had been watching long-discussed desires get fulfilled on Bill's filmy yellow paper. She had known Bill would be good at this, but she felt bowled over anyway by his talent. "You talk to other professionals and they answer you back with words. Bill answered back with words and drawings. The exciting part was our words seemed to go through his ears, into his pen. He was drawing the whole time. Sort of my lips to God's ears."

At a single sitting, out of the void of virtually unlimited possibilities, Bill had summoned a floor plan that fulfilled Judith's and Jonathan's most important wishes for a house. Bill felt warmed up himself. This basic form could answer his wishes, too. This layout—the rectangular box with a front door in the gable end, more or less facing the road—had a historic precedent. Elaborated in his mind, its roof, its paint, its moldings on, it was a kind of American house that he had long admired casually. They had not stopped at one today, but he seemed to remember passing by some.

"What this house wants to be is Greek Revival," said Bill.

"It does?" said Judith. "How does it know?" She smiled. Her smile is a bit of jewelry that she wears when she teases. It notifies her victims that she feels mischievous and merry because of them and not at their expense. Her smile had always worked that way on Bill. Again and again, and especially when speaking architect's lingo, Bill uses

82

terms that sound obscure and pompous to Judith; she retorts and grins, and often he just goes on, stammering and insisting that he really is "exceedingly serious."

Occasionally, Bill invites her jibes on purpose. This time he had not meant to amuse. He really thought he'd had a brainstorm and he had expressed it in the manner of one of his favorite architects, Louis Kahn, who liked to say that bricks and other building materials *wanted* to become certain kinds of structures.

Judith stopped smiling. "Gee," she said, "what's Greek Revival?"

On Sunday, having seen residential Amherst through the Souweines' eyes, Bill showed them the town through his.

For most of two centuries Amherst was a village. Elderly natives remember its dirt streets. In the 1960s, in a hurry, it turned into a big, busy town. The palpable reason, on the north side of Amherst's borders, is a skyscraper farm, the campus of the University of Massachusetts. It has a library twenty-seven stories high. Seen from a bucolic angle, rising against the sky above the tobacco barns of neighboring Hadley, the university's drab-colored towers look completely incongruous, like a city just landed in a big field. The sight has never amused Bill, the contextualist. The campus disgraces his profession, he has said. With the university's towers have come many modern subdivisions, tidy and pleasant. Bill and the Souweines visited some yesterday. Today, Bill led his friends on a search for something older—Greek Revival buildings. He found them all over Amherst.

Bill has an explorer's enthusiasm and a map-maker's eye for places. Jonathan vividly remembers Bill taking him on a walking tour of lower Manhattan and transforming the place for him. When in the mood, Bill can read a landscape as though it were a novel. Today, though, he kept the focus narrow. In downtown Amherst, among remnants of the old village, Bill found a row of Greek Revival buildings. He and the Souweines ended up there.

They stood a few blocks away from the house where Emily Dickinson lived, their backs to the old village green. It was a fine, sunny, thawing winter day. Bill and Jonathan and Judith ambled down the sidewalk on Greek Revival row. "1838," "1842," "1837," said signs fastened on the corners and near the doorways of the buildings they stopped to examine. Bill, who had never studied the form closely, began picking out its salient features, making the old style his own even as he explained it to Judith and Jonathan.

First in the row stood Amherst's College Hall—an example of what Bill decided to call "civic Greek Revival." It was an imposing public edifice, with a portico for an entrance. The building's roof extended out over this grand porch and was supported by several ample Doric columns. The rest of the row consisted of houses. Some were large

84

and fine, some small and comparatively plain. None had a portico or true columns. Instead, the houses had pilasters at their corners, some of which were molded to suggest the bases and the capitals and the fluting of real columns. Clearly, Bill pointed out, pilasters don't support a thing except the idea of a temple. Front doorways mattered. The moldings around them should suggest columns. Although some of these did not, Bill thought that Greek Revival entry doors ought to open onto the street, through one of the narrower ends of the rectangular structure. A proper Greek Revival roof should not be very steeply pitched. When you look head on at the narrower, gabled end of a Greek Revival house, you should see a pediment, a completed triangle, with the roof forming the two sloping sides and a ledge of wood or brick making up the triangle's base. In most plain, traditional American houses, the base of that triangle is not completed. Bill decided that the completed triangle was crucial. A sketch by Bill of the salient features of a Greek Revival house's "temple end" looked like this:

(see following page)

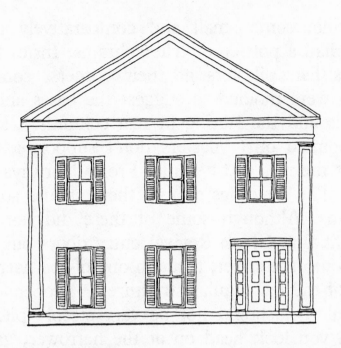

Bill also valued the frieze—the wide surface, sometimes decorated with moldings, sometimes plain, that separates the tops of second-story windows from the line of the roof. The frieze sits on top of the pilasters. The frieze, Bill noted, provides an ample separation between pilasters and roof line. "The frieze raises the house. It's like pushing up your shoulders and standing very frontal."

Looking at those houses, Bill felt blessed with more than his usual luck. Last night the Greek Revival form had seemed to pop out onto his tracing paper, as if he himself were just an intermediary. And today, he had found that form all around town—a contextualist's dream made manifest. "Suddenly, it's not just a house on a landscape. It's a house that's part of the town, that wasn't imposed from outside, that fits in, you know, in a symbolic way."

Bill felt sure he had found the right beginning for a contextualist, postmodern house that would suit him and the site and his old friends. It remained for Bill to help his old friends agree.

2

Many architects have attempted to impose their will upon clients, right down to the furnishings. "Frank Lloyd Wright imposed the furniture, *and* he made it immovable," says Bill. He disapproves in principle. Bill finds built-in furniture "fascistic." He also sympathizes: When architects design rooms, they usually have certain furniture in mind. "I do happen to think that spaces should be occupied by the people in them. The architect shouldn't impose on that," he says. Smiling, he adds, "But I'm a youngster. Give me a few more years, and *I* might be building furniture in."

If he is not disposed to be a martinet, an architect needs to be a salesman. Bill is a good one. He makes his entrances smiling. He leans forward and listens attentively. About his own views, he often seems diffident. He gropes for them. He stammers. His deep, deep voice cracks slightly. What he's driving at is sort of this and kind of that, and he must ask if you see what he means. But then, in the midst of such qualified talk, Bill calls a halt and says, "No. Not sort of. It is."

The first time he met Bill, Jim Locke called him "kind of wimpy, kind of wishy-washy." A month later, Jim would revise his opinion, and say, "He's real mild, and *real* obstinate."

"He beats away at me in his low-key California way," says Jonathan of Bill. "He's stubborn, but so good-mannered."

"I don't think of myself as exceedingly hard-nosed," says Bill. "But I often do get my way."

Bill had given notice but was still working at his old firm. Back in New York the following week, he went to the public library and looked up all its volumes on Greek Revival. There were only a few. He decided not to read them, and merely looked at the pictures in the classic work on the subject, *Greek Revival Architecture in America*, by Talbot Hamlin. Some weeks later, a friend gave Bill a Greek Revival pattern book, a fat nineteenth-century volume depicting all the correct features of the style. The pattern book is an old and enduring institution, and has been one of the vehicles through which styles in architecture have become national, as Greek Revival once did. Bill merely glanced through the pattern book, too. "I'm not an historicist." He wanted to define the style for himself, and he continued to do so, on weekend visits to Amherst.

Back in New York after one of those visits, Bill also did some worrying. He decided that he had placed the imagined house improperly on the site.

He spent some of his evenings repositioning it, and then, a week later, standing on the site again, he put the house back where he'd had it in the first place. Perhaps he felt mistrustful of a plan that had come to him with so little conscious thought and study. It is hard, after all, to feel you own an idea that seems to have appeared of its own accord. Bill never had any doubts about the basic house form, though.

On one of his winter weekend visits, Judith and Jonathan formally hired Bill. Under the standard formula, the customer pays the architect 15 percent of the total construction cost. Bill agreed to work for somewhat less. The pay seemed fair to him. If all went well, within months of starting out in his own practice, Bill would have an interesting building to his credit—a real building, a subtly modern house laid out upon his own synthesis of a historic form, a Bill Rawn original.

On weekends in Amherst, Bill continued to lead his friends on tours. He gathered that Judith and Jonathan admired the Greek Revival houses he showed them and also that she and especially Jonathan worried about the stylishness of those houses. Judith, he observed, was the more immediately receptive. Jonathan's thoughts, as Bill read them, were: "Oh, yeah, because I sort of like these old farmhouses." Bill told them that what he had in mind departed only modestly from the basic form of the farmhouse. Many of the Greek Revival buildings he showed them were, in fact, quite simple. "Not a lot of pretension, but a little decoration. Those are just boxes with a little decoration."

The New England farmstead most comely to Bill was a structure that had evolved, a main house with many ells attached to it. Reproducing the rambling New England farmstead and all its intersecting roof lines would surely cost a great deal more than building just a box and one ell and attaching the appropriate ornaments. Besides, from the start they had all agreed that this house would have a porch, and there is nothing like a porch for adding informality. Greek Revival meant simplicity and economy, Bill told Jonathan and Judith.

They drove in circles, cruised slowly down streets, stopped and looked, got out and gazed. "There's one," Jonathan would say of a farmhouse with a touch of the Greek. And Bill would answer, "No. Not quite." He offered counterexamples. In Sunderland, just north of the university, they found another Greek Revival row. South of Amherst, about midway between the village green and the Souweines' new land, Bill spotted a Greek Revival church. It delighted him first of all because of its location. "It's just such a marvelous symbolic connection between the town and the Souweines' land." He also liked the building for itself. (Later, on a warm spring day, Judith finds Bill lying on the ground beside that church, in deep contemplation of it. Bills wears only sneakers and jogging shorts and for a moment Judith has the impression that he is lying naked before the building. She is greatly amused, and calls Bill an architectural voyeur.) Bill showed them all those buildings and more, partly on the theory that educating his clients in the essence of the form would strengthen his position later on, when the inevitable budget crunches occurred and the Souweines started talking about eliminating pieces of the design. At least they would know what they were losing, he figured.

To his various arguments for Greek Revival—practical, contextualist, and aesthetic—Bill added a political one. "We're not celebrating something from France or Rome or Greece, but something American and populist, and something so simple. A box with some ornament." Bill explained later, "We all come out of this sixties thing that we haven't totally rejected, and that's wrapped up in some sense of social conscience." Greek Revival was in fact a simple style compared to many others, but Bill knew that the house he had in mind would look elegant beside most other new ones in the area. "You're convincing them to do a fancy kind of house. But we're all attached to this kind of liberalism that they feel so strongly." Greek Revival flourished in America during the age of Andrew Jackson, Bill recalled. "New populism. What nicer political heritage could there be for the Souweines than that? A time when this country opened itself to new people, when the proletariat got its first view of power in this country."

This is an interesting hypothesis. Throughout most of the history of the Republic, Americans have held to a notion of a golden, democratic age in housing. Thomas Jefferson was perhaps the most generous and eloquent spokesman for that dream. He foresaw a nation of virtuous farmers living in simple but dignified houses of their own. In reality, though, ever since the first European settlers arrived, American domestic architecture has expressed social distinctions.

In 1630, bound for the New World aboard the *Arbella,* John Winthrop spoke glowingly of the society the Pilgrims would build: " . . . wee shall be as a Citty upon a hill, the eies of the people are uppon us . . ." Some of the other sentiments in his shipboard sermon are less well known: " . . . in all times, some must be rich, some poore, some highe and eminent in power and dignitie; others meane and in subjeccion." In Colonial America, many of the rich and powerful built mansions, with elaborately decorated interiors. In general plan and from the outside, these tended to resemble most smaller houses nearby. "We're all the same, but I'm a little better," those big, early houses seem to say.

In seventeenth-century New England and Virginia, it was an unwritten rule that one could build a house different from the neighbors', but not too different—an injunction that still has some currency. Around 1720, however, some wealthy Americans began to order up large, elegant houses quite different-looking from their poorer neighbors' traditional ones. These new buildings were laid out according to the Georgian plan, a design that creates semipublic and private space within a house. In the opinion of several historians of vernacular architecture, the emergence of the Georgian house symbolizes the withdrawal of the wealthy from their communities. Some of those scholars call the "Georgian moment" a manifestation of the rise of new attitudes, embracing ideals of upward mobility, individual salvation, self-sufficiency. Some think that the rise of the Georgian house implied a weakening in the power of the wealthy and maybe also a decline in fellow feeling within communities.

Americans built according to many other kinds of plans besides the Georgian, and the Georgian was modified and extended, but it became the basic plan for many houses great and small, and its basic characteristics, the essence of its floor plan, survived throughout the main architectural periods of the nineteenth century, including the Greek Revival, the Gothic, and the Italianate. For that reason, some historians of vernacular building think of the period of Greek Revival, which began around 1820, as just one of the many stylistic variations on a theme—the temple look, they argue, was just a new set of clothes for what was basically a Georgian house.

But Greek Revival was a curious and remarkably pervasive style. Women's clothing showed the influence of Grecian tunics, new communities took their names from such distant cities as Troy and Syracuse, and America, as one travel writer expressed it, was becoming a land of "templed hills." Carpenters put up porticoes, pediments, pilasters, friezes, to embellish public buildings and houses and even some outbuildings, in Michigan, Missouri, Indiana, Kentucky, the Carolinas, Maine. Homes that looked like wooden Parthenons, nearly all of them painted white, appeared in Philadelphia, Boston, New York, and many towns along the Connecticut River, including Amherst and its neighbor Hadley.

Where did this romance with antiquity come from? Talbot Hamlin, the pre-eminent historian of Greek Revival, suggests it had these sources: the classical education that the relative handful of educated Americans received in those days, widespread fascination with new archeological discoveries in Rome and Greece, national sympathy for the Greeks, who were just then struggling for their own independence, and a desire to liken American democracy to the ancient Grecian model. Some of America's prominent hated England and English taste, and some felt strongly, as Jefferson had, the need to develop a national architecture that would rival the European. Maybe it is natural that a successful new country would want to make itself look like an old one with deep traditions. Maybe some Americans were trying to borrow the sanctification of the past, like the entrepreneur who strikes it rich and buys a castle. But it's hard to believe that most Americans who embraced Greek Revival did so for philosophical or nationalistic or political reasons.

Fashions had passed through America before.

Greek Revival is notable for its scale. In the 1700s, not many citizens with small and middling incomes seem to have felt they had access to the styles of the rich. By the time of Greek Revival's heyday, in the 1840s, some standard moldings were being manufactured. By the end of the era, one could send away for prefabricated pieces of temples, and anyway a lot of the ornaments were fairly easy and cheap to make. Many people could participate in this latest of styles, the varying features of which traveled around the country in pattern books, newspapers, magazines, and the heads of carpenters. Many new buildings weren't full-fledged Greek Revival ones, but many had classical touches—front doorways got the treatment most often. Greek elements appeared on millowners' mansions and on millworkers' housing, on farmhouses and banks, and even on a few barns and privies.

Greek Revival traveled across lines of social and economic class, during a time when the Jackson administration was broadening the meaning of democracy in America. In this sense, Bill was right in calling the style populist. Of course, he knew that not everyone who built a temple was a Jacksonian democrat. Jackson himself liked porticoes, but so did his arch-rival, the conservative banker Nicholas Biddle. Ralph Waldo Emerson and Nathaniel Hawthorne revered things Grecian, but so did Southern slaveowners—the lavish Southern plantation version of Greek Revival made Bill nervous. As for Amherst, though a liberal college town in 1983, in the period of Greek Revival it took some conservative positions: Its local college was founded partly in opposition to radical religious thinking elsewhere, and its citizens, as well as those of Hadley, voted against the ruffian duelist Andrew Jackson every time he ran.

Bill did not know of Amherst's nineteenth-century voting record, but he suspected that an architectural historian might be able to poke a dozen holes in his theory. The thought didn't trouble him. Bill's deepest aims weren't scholarly. They were aesthetic. He liked the idea of playing a modern tune on this historic form. He liked the form, and it was a part of Amherst and its past.

Afterward, Judith remembered Bill's several arguments for Greek Revival, but only vaguely recalled his political one. It didn't mean much to her. For Jonathan, it carried only a little weight. "It's sort of like an ad, you know. You won't drink a beer you don't like, but if you like an ad for one, it might help you decide. If he had told me this particular design was a favorite of Adolf Hitler's, it would have pushed me the other way."

Shortly after Bill's second visit, Jonathan and Judith took a brief vacation to celebrate their anniversary. A lovely inn in Stockbridge, out at the western edge of the state, was offering reduced, midweek prices. They planned to do some skiing, but when they got there they found the snow mostly gone, so they spent part of their holiday looking at old houses and the rest of it in the town's small public library. Jonathan stacked up on the table in front of him every one of the library's volumes on architecture, and he skimmed through them all. He read about Greek Revival and Judith studied interiors, mainly kitchens.

The only course in fine arts that Jonathan had taken in college was a mandatory one, but it entailed long examination of pictures of the Acropolis. He thinks he may have acquired a liking for Greek architecture then and that without realizing it, or knowing what to call it, he and Judith had grown fond of Greek Revival in the years they had spent around Amherst. "We were already interested in the farmhouse and Bill said, in essence, that if that's what you like in general, what you're seeing is a bastardized version of a great historical form," said Jonathan. Reading up on Greek Revival that day in the library, Jonathan became increasingly interested in the idea.

When it comes to dealing with professionals, many people vacillate between abject servitude and resentment, but Judith and Jonathan believe in choosing carefully, in conveying their wishes clearly, in obtaining second opinions sometimes, and then in surrendering some of their authority. "We really believed we were dealing with someone very talented who could put some form into our ideas," said Judith. " 'You're the design man. You can't tell me how I want to use my kitchen, but you can tell me how it's going to look.' Jonathan and I are pretty good at trusting the professionals we hire."

Judith remembered afterward, "It was pretty clear that there was a big range of what's called Greek Revival. From taking a little farmhouse and adding some things, to those big houses on Main Street. I went along with it right from the start from the passive-solar point of view. I signed off all along the way, but this house is much grander than what we started with."

Somewhere during the progress toward the choice of a style, details of the design began to elude Jonathan, and some months later, he says, "If I'd fully known how grand all this was going to be, and how expensive for the grandness, then I would have said it should be less grand. There came a point when Judith and I realized it, and we felt it was too late to do anything about it." Jonathan is unfailingly forthright. He adds, "But maybe we're just going through the motions of complaining, and we're secretly glad."

3

Bill began to invent the Souweines' house under a schedule that would have seemed unreasonably tight even if this had not been his first time in sole command of a design. When Bill began, he had only about a month to imagine a house and make enough drawings of it for contractors to bid upon, and meanwhile, he had many other chores to do.

After hours and on the weekends that he didn't

spend in Amherst, while still working full-time for Davis, Brody in New York, Bill drew elevations, site plans, revisions of site plans, and revised revisions. He conjured up the names and numbers of friends and acquaintances in Boston. He called them up to say that he would be there soon, on his own and looking for commissions. He had to find a new place to live for himself, as well as design one for Judith and Jonathan. Strong though it was for a beginning, that first floor plan he had drawn at the Souweines' dining room table lacked what Bill calls "architectural distinctiveness." The front door, for instance, led into a hall that headed straight for the chimney, a layout that made for sharp turns. On trains to and from Boston, he moved the entrance and most other passageways to the sides of the house. Stairs and chimney, the mainly functional parts of the house, he placed at the center of the floor plan, channeling imagined movement alongside windows and light, as though, perhaps, the whole house were a boardwalk—a friendly Georgian plan.

When he arrived in Boston once and for all, good luck assailed him. He moved his household on a Thursday in March and on that Friday he was summoned to lunch, there to discuss the possibility of another commission—the renovation of an apartment building in Boston. He had no time to find an office of his own at first, so from an architect friend he borrowed a drafting table in an office in Cambridge, where he sat and drew for the rest of March. Four pairs of glass-paned French doors would enclose the Souweines' living room. He crumpled up many sheets of yellow tracing paper before making sure that the pairs of doors on one wall lined up with those on the other and that one of those pairs of doors would not swing into the space reserved for the baby grand piano. He traveled to Amherst. He talked on the phone to Jonathan and Judith, and a portion of most of those meetings went to reassuring them that they would not be in danger of getting hit with that French door while playing the piano.

By the end of his allotted month, Bill had produced a set of plans, neatly drafted if sketchy in details. He paused long enough to find an office, to negotiate a lease on it, to get phones installed, to assemble a couple of his own drafting tables, to get some work done on the apartment house renovation. However, he still had most of the Souweines' house left to draw.

At Davis, Brody, Bill worked on several examples of what are known as "fast-track" jobs, in which agreements are signed and construction begun with only part of the building planned. On multimillion-dollar projects in an era of expensive money and inflation, accountants choose the fast track because it can save large sums. The temporal value of money has less effect on the construction of a single house, but almost everyone building a new house is in a hurry. Judith and Jonathan wanted a house by fall. Bill was not about to refuse them. He did have reservations about the fast track. He had seen it work quite well and he had seen it make for bad blood, sometimes the spilling of a little real blood, between architects and builders. But there wasn't time for this job to be anything but fast track. Bill figured that they had to find a builder he could talk to and rely on.

In March, Bill visited Jim Locke at Jim's house, in Northampton. Right away, Jim let Bill know that he didn't like this way of building, this design-as-you-go approach. Jim talked about how a fast-track job should be done on the basis of time and materials and not for a fixed contract price, but Jim and Jonathan would have to settle that one, Bill figured, and Bill knew that Jonathan would insist on a fixed price. Anyway, Jim understood the terms and vagaries of this job and Jim wouldn't be making a contract bid if he weren't willing to accept the procedure, Bill figured. So Jim's complaint didn't worry him much.

When Judith had described Jim to Bill, she said, "He looks like you, Bill." Finding instead a man nearly a foot shorter than he, Bill had reported back to Judith, "You just think all WASPs look alike." When they sat together now, other differences showed. Jim's thickly muscled hands defined Bill's as artistic. They used their voices differently. Bill had a lot to say and a lot of it carried excitement. Jim's partners often find him voluble and his talk hard to follow, but next to Bill he seemed the reticent Yankee.

Jim touched the tip of his pencil on a blueprint. He pointed out that Bill had the living room stepping down from the front rooms of the house and then had the master bedroom stepping down again from the living room. It would make the foundation a little less complex, maybe a little less expensive, if the master bedroom stepped back up, Jim said.

Bill leaned forward to look. To himself, he said, "Ah, I like that. I like that. The way he made that suggestion, the clarity and intelligence of the thing, that's the kind of contractor we should have."

Jim made other suggestions. "I agree absolutely," said Bill. "Those kinds of statements I love," Bill declared.

Bill came to this houseraising completely inexperienced in wood-frame domestic construction. He made a clean breast of that fact to Jim, and he observed that Jim did not appear to flinch at the news. Here, it seemed, was a builder who would warn Bill away from extravagant routes toward Bill's goal of architectural distinctiveness. They talked about interior moldings. The preliminary specs, which for the sake of speed were based on the ones for Judith's parents' house, prescribed a stock, manufactured molding known as Colonial casing. Jim called that molding "Colonial clam," denigrating it as just a variation of the moldings used in quickly built development houses. "It's unduly elaborated," Jim said. He and Bill got up from the table to examine the old-fashioned moldings on the doorways inside Jim's house.

Bill gave Jim his pitch for Greek Revival. "I just see Greek Revival as a reasonably clean-cut

form. American. It came out of the agrarian re-
formist Andrew Jackson and Thomas Jefferson
stuff. There's a simplicity about it that's not terri-
bly flamboyant, and these moldings would fit.
They have a sense of pediment and column and
entablature."

"Well," said Jim, "just adding any custom
molding elaborates the job. It just takes a lot more
time than stock molding, and if they're willing to
do it . . . I think they should. I think they should
do something more in keeping with the feel of the
house as you drive up to it."

Bill nodded. He agreed absolutely.

Jim said, "My feeling about trim is, you don't
want to have to look at it more than once. It
should be securely there, it should define the
openings, but it shouldn't be gimmicky."

Bill listened and did not comment. He would
not hold to such a thoroughly self-effacing aesthetic as Jim's. To Bill, it is a legitimate ambition
in an architect to want his designs to attract attention. But he agreed with Jim in some ways. Trim
should be distinctive but appropriate; it should
promote calmness inside the house. In any case,
what mattered to Bill was not the substance of
Jim's statement on trim but the fact that Jim
made it. Bill felt hopeful when he left Jim's house.
At Davis, Brody, Bill had absorbed the injunction
that the only architectural vision that matters is
the one that gets built. No lost masterpieces, thank
you. You want to do something real as an architect, you get along with builders. Bill had man-

aged that trick with many different types of contractors, not to mention those dozens of angry citizens he got to know back in his days as a bureaucrat. Getting along with Jim should be easier. This was an intellectual builder with quality at heart.

Most of Jonathan and Judith's new house was still ideas that wandered freely through Bill's mind. He had not trapped his vision of the front door on paper yet, let alone recorded the door's make and model number. He had not drawn the hearth. Other matters beckoned. Jim needed a foundation plan and also an exact and final floor plan, which Bill couldn't draw until he had imagined the staircase and the width of every tread and the height of every riser between treads. Before anything else, however, Bill had to figure out the number and sizes and styles of the windows, and to do that, he had to settle the question of the house's long south side.

To the rest of the house Bill had already given his vision of the essence of Greek Revival. He had imagined the south wall differently. He thought of it as the modern solar side, the wall that would mark this house as a work of postmodern architecture. He had told Jonathan and Judith that he wanted to make the south wall peculiarly his own and they had agreed in principle. Bill had a theory about walls. One kind of wall emphasizes the enclosing nature of walls and its windows are "punched in." Three walls of the house should have that feeling about them. But a wall can also emphasize its openings. A wall can become the occasion for windows, and Bill was bound to make the south wall seem more window than wall.

In February, Bill had drawn a south wall filled with double-hung and many-paned windows, a rather plain and too simple solution, he decided. Next, he had given it ranks of deeply recessed windows. Then he had made the windows protrude out from the surface of the wall. "Like barnacles or something," he had thought, rejecting that idea, too. He had worried about the porch. Should he have it wrap around the south side as he planned to wrap it around the north? If he did that, the porch roof would keep the winter sunlight from the breakfast nook. Some architect friends had suggested he bring just *the idea* of a porch around, so he had drawn a very narrow, totally unusable piece of porch on part of the south wall, and then he had imagined what Jonathan would say about that. Bill had not liked that drawing anyway, but it had made him stop worrying about the issue of the porch. He would not bring it around the south side. Now, in March, Bill revived his first approach to specialness in a wall. He filled the south wall with standard sorts of windows lying flush with the wall's surface, and he added some small boxlike windows beneath the larger ones. Above some of these larger windows he drew small, half-moon-shaped windows. He wasn't entirely pleased with the composition—he thought of it as a composition in part, as if it were an abstract drawing. But it did look like a fairly subtle departure from the other, traditional walls, and it was also a wall that no one could mistake for a product of the 1830s.

While he was at it, Bill altered the front wall, the house's temple end. He added two pilasters to the front, so that the temple end had four pilasters in all, one at each corner and two between. As a tradeoff, expecting an argument, he removed the two pilasters from the back wall and put plain, cheaper corner boards there. These drawings he sent to Amherst. He followed them out there, on the next to last day in March. The Souweines had some reservations, practical ones, about the extra pilasters and the design of the south wall. Jim had his objections, too, on aesthetic grounds. But the main issue was speed. Bill had to get that south wall drawn soon, because Jim said he needed to know what windows to order. "The windows I need by April fifteen," Jim said.

"What I hear you saying is April fifteen is a real date," said Jonathan to Jim.

Jim turned to Bill. "And also the foundation plan pretty damn soon."

Bill swallowed hard. He had to move in to his new office. He had to do some work on that other job. He got the foundation plan drawn on schedule, though. He found time to make some new drawings of the south wall, but none of those quite suited him. He had gone past the April 15 deadline. He was running out of time.

On April 18, Bill drove back to Amherst to

celebrate the digging of the cellar hole. He and Jim and the Souweines all gathered in Judith's parents' dining room, while the bulldozer worked outside. Bill received an ultimatum.

At every step up until now, the Souweines had invited alternative proposals from Bill, but on the issue of the windows, they now took Jim's side, emphatically. Jim had priced windows for this house two times already. Jim said he would do so only once more. What's more, window prices were on the brink of rising. There was a lot of money at stake, Jim told the Souweines. It was Monday now, and Jim had to have the final list of windows by Thursday at the latest.

Outside, the bulldozer continued to carve the rough outlines of a house. Inside, Bill asked Jonathan and Judith for a little more time. He wanted to redraw the south wall again.

"We know 'redraw' is just a code word for putting off decisions," said Judith.

"I'm very sensitive to that," replied Bill.

Judith smiled. "The ball's back in your court, Bill. You call us Thursday night and tell us the final thing, and don't make any mistakes."

Bill arranged to call Jim with the window list before five o'clock on Friday instead. That gave Bill an extra day. He had three and a half days to resolve the most creative part of the first design that he could truly call his own.

In some corners of Boston, looking up above
storefronts lets you into worlds of dentistry,
martial-arts instruction, dancing lessons. On Tremont Street, just across from the Granary Burying
Ground and Paul Revere's grave, there's an old
office building that houses several small, second-
floor enterprises. Long after dark, in mid-April
1983, passers-by who look up at its second-story
windows can see Bill in his horn-rimmed glasses,
bent over his drafting table.

The huge windows—old, double-hung ones,
which actually open—have been left uncurtained
on purpose. Sitting beside one of them, Bill pauses
occasionally to look outside. Sometimes he catches
the eyes of some stranger who is looking in. Once
in a while, a passer-by whom he's caught peeking
waves up to Bill. Gregarious Bill, sequestered here,
waves back.

When he had set out in independent practice,
veterans in the finances of architecture had told
Bill to keep his overhead down. Bill is thrifty
anyway; thrift had allowed him to explore his
vagabond side and to find his way back to architecture. He had been saving up for this moment
too long to squander money on frills. He decided
not to hire anyone at first, not even someone to
help draw the plans that he would dream up, and
he did not want to spend much on an office. A
fledgling architect usually meets prospective pa-
trons in their offices, not in his own. So a garret,

a rented room facing some alley, would have served Bill's practical needs. This place hardly looks fancy—it is smaller than the living room he has imagined for the Souweines, and the floor is a worn and cracked linoleum tile. But it cost Bill somewhat more than he thought was safe to spend. He took it because of the big windows and the little relief from loneliness he would find in the busy street outside.

It feels odd to be cast in the role of dreamy procrastinator. Bill knows of architects far less practical than he, and he imagines that many would have long ago thrown up their hands at this impossible schedule. As the assistant chancellor of UMass, he had earned a reputation for decisiveness. And it seems to him that he has been as decisive as anyone who cared about this house could be. Two months to design a house from scratch. Look at all I've done, he could easily have said to Jim and the Souweines, but Bill had held his tongue when they had demanded greater speed. Privately, Bill says, "I want a house that is as close to the house I've designed as possible, and I will do anything to get there. And usually, the way to get there is to speak softly."

Bill feels a little worn down now, after all the trips between Boston and New York, New York and Amherst, Amherst and Boston, and after two months of juggling the complexities of this last and longed-for transition in his life. But he works awhile on Tuesday, after driving back from

Amherst. Wednesday he gets to his office at about nine.

The Puritans in the graveyard on Tremont Street would not have approved of the hour at which Bill passes, but if they had understood him, they would have applauded his fortitude in coming in at all before noon. When he walks to his office, Bill passes near two of America's important architectural monuments, Charles Bulfinch's State House and the Park Street Church, but Bill can take inspiration and instruction from them only on the way home. In the morning he travels in a fog bank of his own. Bill knows himself to be a heavy flywheel, slow to get moving, slow to wind down. He comes fully awake when quick and early starters like Jonathan get sleepy. Bill's is a bachelor's trait. He gets a carton of orange juice from the small lobby store in a building down the street, and inquires after the health and family of his new friend, the proprietor. Thus fortified with citrus and conversation, he goes upstairs to his drafting table.

From time to time, the windows in Bill's office become a liability for him. Sometimes he finds himself gazing out at the archway that admits you to the Burying Ground—it is dark stone and carries the figure of the Angel of Death, and he wonders when it will find a way into a design of his. He finds himself looking at the tourists, too, across the street, and especially when spring comes and the tourists appear in shorts, Bill sees beaches he has combed. "You're forty," he tells himself, however. "It's put-up-or-shut-up time." These next three days it is fear, in part, that keeps him at his desk for nine and a half hours, seven and a half hours, eight hours, stretches that most people, including Bill, could not ordinarily tolerate. This kind of close work makes you rub your eyes, but Bill has what he calls a case of first-time-out nerves, and the thoughts that keep him going run this way (while he pulls from the thick roll mounted at the top of his desk a filmy sheet of yellow tracing paper, down onto the slanted drawing board, and fixes it in place): "Nothing will work . . . I'll never come up with a solution that works . . . What if I don't come up with anything that's very nice? . . . What if it doesn't quite work?"

The Souweines had worried about those small rectangular windows he had placed under large ones on the first story of the south wall. Judith's father, Jules, has a bay window; Jules touts bay windows. So Bill begins to sketch a south wall with some traditional bay windows, but he finishes only enough of that drawing to know that is not his solution. He returns to a flat wall of many windows. To make a wall that seems more window than wall, not through some dramatic flourish but some combination of ordinary windows, that would be a wall by the artist Bill Rawn, as Bill understands that person. The artist Bill Rawn really doesn't do much conscious thinking, though.

When he had first joined Davis, Brody, Bill

111

tried for a while to trade ideas for designs with a colleague, a contemporary more experienced than he. "What do you think of this idea?" Bill would ask.

His friend would reply, in effect, "Gee, I don't know, Bill. Why don't you draw it?"

His friend might have been telling a fat man it was good for him to eat candy. Bill had always loved to draw. Le Corbusier once wrote, "Geometry is the language of man." Certainly, it is Bill's.

In previous drawings, to which he now returns, Bill had placed small windows above and below larger ones, on the first story of the south wall. Somehow, that approach feels right. He could hardly have said why just then, but this approach seems to include the imagined presence of a person, sitting inside next to the windows. This approach lets Bill have the south wall two ways: a wall that emphasizes its openings and celebrates southern light, and also a wall that gives the person inside a comforting feeling of being enclosed. Bill could have made a south wall full of huge sheets of glass, and he could have used sliding glass doors, too. But breaking up the window openings, using many windows, large and small, instead of a handful of huge ones, provides opaque, enclosing surfaces that will make the person who sits behind the windows feel unconsciously at ease. The approach gives the house a southern edge. This solution brings in lots of light and at the same time makes that person behind the windows feel inside the house and not at the unfenced edge of a precipice, which is the agoraphobic feeling Bill has when he sits behind sheets of glass and sliding glass doors.

Bill looks at his last drawings. He likes the looks of the small rectangular windows, but not the half-moon-shaped ones. "They look a little goofy." He gets rid of the half-moons, replacing them with rectangular boxes. On the first story of the south wall, there are now small glass boxes above and below large windows—double-hung windows that really open. The three other walls of the house have double-hung, two-over-two windows, ones, that is, with four panes of glass apiece. Bill has never worried about using a different window type on the south wall, but he had worried steadily about mixing window types within the south wall. Now he puts that worry aside. He makes the principal windows of the south wall six-over-sixes. They add a great deal of geometry to the picture. There are, suddenly, many mullions in his drawing, many new wooden, opaque surfaces between panes of glass. A first-story southern window unit now looks like this:

(see following page)

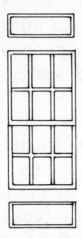

Bill ponders the drawing. "Very dead. There's no dynamic to that." Maybe the second-story windows are to blame. They look unrelated to the ones below. He draws again. On the second story, the children's floor, he draws nine windows, three for each bedroom. This drawing makes him feel he is getting warm. He redraws it neatly and to scale.

One day melts into another. Back when he had lived in Aspen and at Harvard, Bill used to make trial drawings of his silk screens for hours on end, drawing and redrawing far into the night, searching for the counterpart of the images behind his eyes. He had been very happy then, and is nearly as happy now. The drawing he finds on his desk Thursday morning is a complex pattern of lines, a little like one of his silk screens. The whole issue has come down to what he calls "a compositional judgment." He is back in his hometown now, playing with old friends. The drawing still looks dead to him, and now he feels sure those second-story windows are to blame. He has arranged them too symmetrically. That isn't what he thinks as he pulls down another sheet of tracing paper, but symmetry seems to be the subject of his inquiry. He does not want to make the composition asymmetrical. What he wants is for it not to be symmetrical. The distinction has weight for him. It's the difference between wanting to find a cage to get into and wanting to get out of one.

In drawing after drawing, Bill unbalances the second-story windows, trying to make a marriage between the complex first-story window units and the second-story six-over-sixes. What he ends up with, by Thursday evening, is this relationship, the numbers standing for windows ganged together:

$$3 \quad 2 \quad 2$$
$$5 \quad 2 \quad 3$$

For Bill, it works. It looks like a version of something he's had in mind all along. He worries some on Thursday afternoon and Friday morning about the connection between the main south wall and the south wall of the attached master bedroom ell. The wall jogs back several feet there to the ell, and in that space, in the jog, there's a glass French door, opening from the living room to a patio outside. The top of that French door has to be lower than the tops of all the first-story window units, but he wants to bring his composition around the corner. He wants to preserve the vocabulary of the south wall, as he puts it. He places two layers of small rectangular windows over that French door, and then he worries over that piece of the drawing. It might be a particularly difficult version of those puzzles that ask, What's wrong with this picture? Except that this puzzle also asks, *Is* there anything wrong with this picture? He has barely enough time to pore over the window manufacturer's catalogue and pick out the standard sizes of windows that will fit into his last drawing.

Bill finishes around four o'clock that afternoon. He is done only because he has to be, but he feels pleased about the drawing on his desk, during the occasional moments when his eyes manage to focus. At four-fifteen, Bill picks up his phone and dials Jim's home number. Leaning back in his chair, Bill announces that he has made the window list and will read it to Jim.

"That's all right," he hears Jim's voice say. "You have until Monday. I'm only going to do this one more time."

"You can't send me through such a rough time, and then tell me that!" cries Bill.

Jim answers sharply, something about deadlines and how he's still waiting for the location of the staircase.

They shout at each other briefly, long distance.

Later that night, Bill calls Jim back and apologizes for his anger—he was tired, he had been working very hard.

Jim says, "Yeah, I felt bad about it, too."

Bill can't stay angry long. Although a great deal of drawing lies ahead of him, he has done the hardest part, and now something wonderful is about to happen. He is about to see paper get turned into wood.

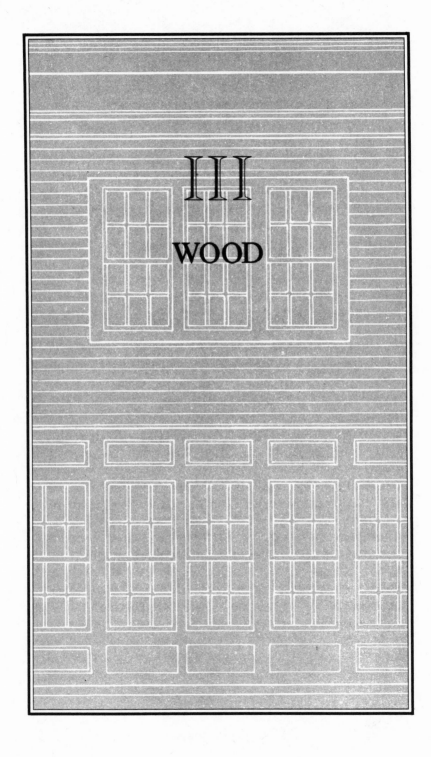

III

WOOD

Jim liked the Souweines' directness and decisiveness. He called them Apple Corps's best customers ever. If you had seen Jim with his clients at the early planning sessions, you would have noticed a slight exaggeration in his manners, a pursing of the lips, for instance, that looked like thoughtfulness itself. It was as though, as Jim listened carefully, he were saying in his mind, "What I'm doing now is listening very carefully." He'd touch his front teeth with a huge index finger, a rabbity look, and then expound on the pros and cons of insulation in the basement walls. "It all seemed so gentlemanly," Jim said later on. "I really liked that part of it."

As it happened, Jonathan had represented Sandy's former husband in divorce proceedings. The first time they met to talk about the house, Jonathan cleared the air. He rehearsed that fact about the divorce, and said to Jim, "It's not an issue as far as I'm concerned. I hope it's not an issue for you." Jim felt grateful for that. From the start, when he sat at the Souweines' table in Pelham, Jim felt like a partner and not a hired hand.

Jim had sparred with Jonathan only once at those meetings, and Jim had given that skirmish an odd twist. If the building permit cost less than expected, Jim said, Apple Corps should get the difference. Jonathan demurred. So Jim agreed to split the savings on the permit, if there were any, but he said he would do so only if the Souweines agreed to apply their share to improvements on the house's interior. The plans for the interior, Jim told them, looked cut-rate compared to the ones for the exterior. Judith was astonished. "He cares that much about *our* house?"

To Richard, Jim confided, "I'm trying to get them to upgrade their house."

"At their expense," said Richard, with half a question in his voice.

"Of course," said Jim.

Jim ran the estimating sessions with his partners. These were a three-day-long rehearsal at Jim's house in Northampton. Jim and Richard and Ned Krutsky—the fourth partner, Alex, was still out of town—first imagined themselves building the house's large sturdy frame, then saw themselves applying the finish. By the time they started doing the vicarious finish work, Ned and Richard were out of their chairs and pacing around the table.

"I'm getting edgy," Ned confessed.

"You want to pound nails," said Jim.

"It's the only way we're gonna make any money," said Ned.

Jim had no trouble staying in his chair.

He called all of the company's usual hilltown subcontractors and took in bids from them. He interviewed a few tradesmen they had never worked with before and got their bids. He arranged for the painting, sheetrocking, plumbing, heating, wiring, brick work, insulation, basement floor, foundation, and earth moving. Jim also visited his favorite lumberyard, to get an estimate on carpenters' materials. Russell Bisbee, one of the proprietors, looked at the plans and said, "The problem with a lot of these specifications is, they're not very specific."

Jim laughed. "We don't want to pad the price. We want the job." Jim was in charge of exterminating vagueness and confusion from this corner of the world and he was having fun. He didn't lose his patience even when attempting to get promises from the power, water, and telephone companies. On an evening in April, Jim sat at the table in his own kitchen, tallying up all the figures on his yellow notepad, and looking up, he said to Sandy, "I really like this." He added, "I'm pretty good at this." Just a few nights later, Jim found himself arguing with Jonathan over $660 and losing the debate, as Jim saw it. "There's a real conflict in my mind, about the difference between hiring someone to do a job for you and hiring a job to be done," he said in the aftermath. He made resolutions: "I feel sort of wounded. I think they screwed up. I don't want retribution. I want them to understand that they changed the tone of the job in my mind."

123

Jim began to profess some doubts about whether being boss was fun. He said he thought he would prefer to work on that house only with his hands. He'd rather not spend time shopping around for bargains on materials, but he thought that he could make more money sometimes by shopping than by nailing. "In half an hour I could make a hundred dollars that way," he said. "Those are Jonathan Souweine rates."

The Jim who planned this housebuilding had reveled in his role. After the fight, he was different, but the tone of the job would have changed anyway, as real events took the place of all the contemplated ones that he had neatly arranged in his yellow pads. He had filled up two. He carried them everywhere in his leather case, hugging them under an arm.

To avoid panic at the end and guilt—"You feel bad for somebody who's got to move out of their old house and you can't let them into their new one, even though they own it"—Jim had named the distant date of October 31 for the house's completion. Jonathan had agreed reluctantly. Jonathan had seen contractors leave jobs unfinished for months, while they worked on other ones. So he applied a penalty clause: It would cost Apple Corps $100 for every day the deadline was exceeded. Jim had shrugged, but it snowed and rained a lot that spring. Jonathan had some trouble getting one of the various permits that precede a house in Amherst. The foundation was delayed.

Jim killed time by building a deck onto his house. He hired his partner Ned Krutsky to help.

"I'm getting anxiety attacks over hundred-dollar-a-day penalties," said Ned.

"Nah," said Jim, but most of Jim's postulated margin for delay had been consumed by the time the foundation work began.

Jim says he won't oversee the making of the foundation. Jim knows the boss's work. Jim trusts him and his crew. "They've never screwed it up before," Jim says on a morning in early May. In the afternoon, he collects his leather case and drives over to the site. Jim learned how to squat on his heels and chat with country tradesmen and farmers during the years he spent in New Hampshire. He squats by the edge of the cellar hole and chats with the old Yankee down in the hole, who is laying out the footings, the concrete slabs on which the tall foundation walls and interior columns will rest. Jim wants to make sure the dimensions are right, but he doesn't let on that there's any question in his mind.

Just before he leaves, Jim says, "You think there'll be any trouble getting cement trucks in here, Ralph?"

Ralph looks up at Jim from the hole, and shrugs.

"I don't have to worry about it?" asks Jim.

"Ya can if ya want to," drawls Ralph.

Jim comes again after Ralph has poured the footings. Jim has daydreamed that the drain pipes laid around the outside of the foundation and the ones laid under the cellar floor got hooked together accidentally. That mistake would someday turn the basement into a swimming pool. It didn't happen. Jim returns again to see the freshly poured foundation walls. He stares at them and says, "It looks good, but I can't tell if it is until I start measuring it. What it *looks* like doesn't matter."

While the cement dries and cures, Jim builds a garden shed for another customer. The job is straightforward. The first day of it goes well. The second day he builds a door. It doesn't fit. He takes it apart, builds it again. Again, it doesn't fit. "I got the pre-job jitters," he confesses, putting down his tools. "It isn't just this job. It isn't just the six hundred and sixty dollars. It happens every job. I guess I think it has a life of its own, the job does. No. I don't think that. It's more the opposite, if anything. It's more a tendency to think I forgot something than that fate was going to come in and screw it up. It's just doubt. If I forgot something, or if I'm going to be able to do it. Performance anxiety, I guess."

The electrician calls that evening, to talk about light fixtures. Jim licks his thumb and turns page after page of his notes on the estimate, looking for the reference to the lighting fixture allotment. The contract allows Jonathan and Judith $1000 for lights, but Jim forgot to put that money in the estimate. Apple Corps will have to eat the lights. He will stay calm, Jim decides. He wonders what other surprises lie in those notepads. Their labor estimate, he thinks, looks a little skinny. But these setbacks are typical. His notes probably hold some pleasant surprises, which haven't revealed themselves yet. Apple Corps has done many jobs that came out almost exactly as estimated, and always for unanticipated reasons. He'll make up for the lights with careful planning. He'll figure out ways to beat their estimate on the framing and pay for the lights that way. He finds it hard to plan ahead, though, because Bill Rawn, working under his own impossible schedule, is still doing his own planning. Bill's drawings don't seem to arrive except at the last possible moments. You can't frame a house, for instance, unless you know exactly where the stairs should be. That information didn't arrive from Bill until the day before yesterday, and tomorrow they start to build the frame. Jim has promised Ned and Richard they can start tomorrow. Ned said, "Hammers are going to be singing over there. They're going to be invisible to the naked eye." Jim talked on the phone with Bill until eleven o'clock last night, making sure about the placement of the stairs. Jim hasn't been able to draw up a final framing plan until today. Their hammers can't sing without a framing plan.

Late in the afternoon on May 16, Jim sits at an old metal desk, positioned under the eaves of his attic, in Northampton. You can hear the rain on the roof. Jim sits beneath uncovered insulation—carpenters often inhabit unfinished space. He rests his chin in one large hand, an ottoman of a hand,

and stares at the drawing he has begun. He's making a bird's-eye view of the underpinnings of the first floor of the incipient house. Jim figures he has used up all of the nineteen days he allotted in the labor estimate for planning and the unpredictable. He says, "I wish I could figure out some way to charge for this."

Jim has said he used to think that anger and unhappiness were twins, but he has decided that they are really more like opposites in him. "I'm trying to stay calm," he says. He yawns. "I can't do this on six hours' sleep." He smiles. "What am I trying to figure out?"

He has to decide where to put a lot of sticks, so that the fewest possible are used and the least amount of cutting is required. Plywood comes in four-foot-by-eight-foot sheets. He has to make sure that the floor joists are spaced in such a way that two edges of every sheet of plywood come to rest on something solid. He also has to determine exactly the boundaries of each room, because some will be floored with oak, some with tile, some with carpeting, and each of those surfaces calls for a different quality and thickness of plywood. The trickiest part, though, is the girders, the beams they'll make to hold up the floor joists. Bill wants a sunken floor in the living room. At one edge of that room a very heavy hearth occurs. In essence there's a place where floors of three different levels will meet. Jim stacks one set of girders onto another, and goes on. One section of floor is a little too wide for two-by-ten pieces of spruce to span. Jim could put a girder under those joists. Or he could use two-by-twelves of spruce. Or he could use Douglas fir two-by-tens. Which is cheaper? Which takes less time to install? Jim has settled on Douglas fir. It comes from the Pacific Northwest. His supplier has to order it specially, and Jim hopes that it will arrive on time.

"Here's a problem, right here," says Jim. He circles a spot where living room and master bedroom meet. He gave the foundation crew the wrong instructions there. Jim isn't in the mood to take the blame himself. "It'll just mean an extra hour in there with a cement drill and a sledge, knocking out cement. It's boring. An unbillable by-product of having this thing wait until the last minute."

Jim consults a drawing of Bill's. He snorts. "He had the house thirty feet, one inch wide. You can't do that. Well, you can, but I don't want to. That floating inch is sure to screw up our measurements somewhere."

Jim peers at his own drawing, which has grown dense with lines. "What am I trying to figure out? Okay. Now I've got to get the stair in here." He turns to peer at Bill's drawing of the first floor. Bill's comes on fine, thick paper, and the words written on it are constructed in the elegant block print that all architects master, like some fraternal handshake. "There's a great slogan here," says Jim, tapping his pencil on a small block of writing next to Bill's drawing of the outlines of the stair. " 'Details by Apple Corps.' As the architect dives

129

over the side of the boat. Home port by Apple Corps."

Jim laughs. He takes his chin off his hand, wets his lips, sucks air in from both corners of his mouth, and leans closer to Bill's depiction of life on the first floor, a division of space into rooms and passageways. Holding his pencil ready above his own much more complicated-looking, much messier drawing of what is behind those walls and underneath those floors, Jim murmurs, "Hmmmm.What's this horsepiss you got here now, Billy boy?"

Jim has never planned a job of framing quite as intricate as this one. He works on it after supper. By the time he finishes, his framing plan looks like an urban street map, and the rest of his household has turned in.

Jim arises near dawn. Just as his favorite weatherman over in Albany promised, the sky out the windows looks perfectly clear. While his house is quiet, just to prove he isn't nervous, Jim sits in his kitchen and reads a chapter of his current novel. Then he slips the framing plan into his leather case and hits the road.

Jim has a long way to go from that complicated-looking drawing to a house built on schedule and for a profit, but today he will have company. Help should already be on the way from Apple Valley.

2

On a horticultural map, a line runs down from New Brunswick through Maine and New Hampshire and divides most of the western half of Massachusetts from the rest of the state. West and north of that line the growing season is a full month shorter than on the other side. Just where this division of climates occurs is hard to tell from the map, but people who live on the cold side of the line, in the hills west of Amherst and the Connecticut River, know that it happens abruptly, halfway up Goshen Mountain on Route 9 out of Northampton, partway up Route 116 out of Deerfield, places where westbound cars in some seasons suddenly acquire mantles of snow. When he ran for D.A., Jonathan went up from the valley into the towns of that colder, hillier section of Franklin and Hampshire counties. Average incomes in those two counties rank as the second and third lowest in the state, and most of the local sources of money—higher education, retailing, agriculture, a little industry—flourish down in the valley beside the big river. On his trip into the hills, particularly in the remotest of the remote hilltowns, Jonathan found more ramshackle dwellings, more yards full of rusting machinery, all in all a stronger feeling of hard times and isolation, than he'd been prepared for. A windswept hilltop, a bunch of houses and a church—that's the pattern of the smallest villages out there. "It was quite an eye opener," Jonathan says. Not enough people live in the hills to make the difference in a two-county election, but Jonathan felt he should go there and is glad he did. He adds, with a smile that recalls those old election returns, that a lot of the people up there didn't like him or his platform much.

During the building of the house in Amherst, Bill Rawn took a trip to the hilltowns. Gazing at old houses, he drew this contrast between the social and economic histories of the valley and the hills: "It's obvious immediately. The old houses are much more modest here." He passed through the villages of Chesterfield, Plainfield, Cummington, Ashfield, and Conway, on little wooded roads and avenues between rows of venerable sugar maples. (Many hilltown roads are known locally by two names—whichever village you're headed for is the name of the road you're on. Many names carry "the" as a prefix—"the Conway Road"—as if to say there's no other road by that name anywhere, or at least none worth acknowledging.) "There's a lot of room between towns," Bill wryly observed. He found some churches to admire. "Very strong and understated Greek Revival." Passing slowly by a main street of white clapboarded houses with peaked roofs, he declared, "Big rambling houses without a lot of decoration. I love it. The houses are modest. They're all set back from the street about equally. None is trying to outdo the other."

Ever since there were industrial cities in the Western world, there have been movements back to the land. In the early 1970s, a wave of young immigrants headed for rural New England, and the hilltown of Ashfield was one favored destination—the town had a long and unusual history of gracefully receiving outsiders. Judith happens to have a friend who lived in Ashfield for a while back then. Amherst, her own chosen town, Judith calls "Granola Valley" and "Cambridge with cows." Looking at the hills from the valley, Judith describes the young hilltown settlers' way of life this way: "Long skirts, baking bread, nursing babies until they're four. Contra dances and potluck suppers. The women in the kitchen and the men out chopping wood. I don't mind any of that. I like doing most of those things. I like baking bread, and I don't want my life ruled by corporate values either. But I don't like being made to feel guilty for having Copco pots. The Ashfield bit, it's the women's role I really didn't like. To me, it seems like they were fleeing one set of stereotypes and falling into others." Judith goes on, " 'You ate some Arnold white bread? You're going to *die.*' Then the kids come. And suddenly the local schools are not good enough for little Summer Morning." Judith says that she once voiced all those opinions to her female friend who had lived in Ashfield, and her friend said to her, "They're no different than you, Judith. They just don't have a hair style." Judith repeats that line, wearing a mischievous grin.

Just after dawn, Ashfield's Boy Scout leader,

Richard Gougeon, stands at the picture window and looks north out of his living room. His house rests on a hillside just down the Hawley Road from the part of Ashfield that someone long ago described as Little Switzerland. Richard says, "Right here, it drops right off. You can see for a *long* ways. A lot of mornings you can see out over the fog in the valleys, and the hills look like little islands out there." The air is clear this morning. There's the ridge up in Heath where blueberries grow by the truckload, and the radio mast, still faintly blinking, that's WRSI in Greenfield, the station he'll probably listen to at work today. Richard's window is a geographer's station. The views are even better from the hill above his house, part of the twenty acres of field and woods he bought five years ago, to add to his houselot. "My father never owned any land when I was growing up. I had to *own* land. *Had* to. I wasn't going to be a whole person till I *owned* land, and two acres just wasn't enough. Lindy felt the same way," Richard has explained. Up on his high meadow the intricate landscape of hills and valleys is laid out as clearly as on a map. Richard has the sort of lofty and expansive views from which the world makes perfect sense. Once, while walking down the meadow toward his house, he suddenly stopped, raised his arms as if to embrace the mountain view, and cried, "I'm king!"

Feeling a little strapped for cash and ready for work, Richard launches himself on the morning. He wears jeans, a checkered woolen shirt, a wide leather belt, brown boots. His clothes have the clean, gently worn, well-oiled look of old, cared-for woodworking machines. He clowns when he walks to the kitchen, dragging his heels, making as much noise as possible, and saying to no one in particular, "I put on three pounds over the weekend. Must be my fat's all turning to muscle. Yup. I'm just a stout little French-Canadian."

This spring, as Richard likes to explain, he made syrup from his own maple trees. At breakfast, he enacts the fantasy of local self-sufficiency. Most things on the table come from Ashfield: the apples in the pancakes from the trees outside his back door, the bacon from a neighbor's pig, the cream from the top of the jug that he and Lindy get filled at the one remaining dairy farm in Apple Valley.

Lindy is about as tall as Richard, and plump, but like him, sturdy rather than stout. She has brown hair and astonished-looking eyes. She talks rapidly, sometimes loudly—maybe from long competition with Richard—and she is given to wry smiles. "I always preferred Edgar Allan Poe to *Cinderella*," she says. She has a fiery side. Richard says, "It's a good thing Lindy wasn't a man. There'd be a lot of beat-up people around. We joke about that a lot. She knows it."

Lindy wasn't always a good cook. "She made pork chops the consistency of my shoe. I didn't even know what it was," says Richard of the first meal she ever made for him. Richard was in the Navy then and they were living on Okinawa.

"When we were there I decided that was what I wanted," says Lindy. "To live on a farm, have kids and animals, and cook a lot. I got good at cooking." She made some meals for Richard's friends. They praised the food. Her cooking thrived on praise. The pastries Richard brings to work in his lunch basket are known in Apple Corps's idiom as "Lindy cakes," and Richard is envied for them.

Lindy planned to go to college when their last child left diapers. When that time arrived, she thought she might not risk college after all. Richard talked her into it. She told him not to expect too much. She went to a local community college and got preposterously good grades. Richard was always telling his partners how Lindy had gotten 104 on her latest exam. She would soon be accepted, with a scholarship, at Smith College, and Richard would say, "This is a dream come true. I always wanted to go out with a Smithie."

Richard reads, but with difficulty. His dyslexia has never been professionally diagnosed, but clearly his long, enduring puzzlement with reading was the cause of his childhood travail in school. When they were first married, Lindy says, they used to fight about her reading. She always loved reading books, and she thinks that Richard envied her then. Many years later, however, it was Richard who urged her to go to college. Lindy knows that encouraging her must have cost Richard something.

"He was very worried last winter," she says. "I

studied with a very bright man in my class. Richard wasn't exactly jealous, but he said to me, 'I thought this would happen.' "

Lindy says, "He worried ever since I started college that I would meet somebody smarter."

Lindy was a proud, shy, rather lonely girl. Of Lindy as he found her, Richard says, "Her idea of a big time, even in high school, was readin' a book." She kept to herself mostly. Richard was a mannerly boy, the sort whom old folks like. "I was a pretty reasonable kid, I guess. All's I ever got was one speeding ticket. We'd swear and cuss, me and my friends, when we got alone. Maybe get some hard cider and drink it at the Mohawk Drive-In. I didn't even know what marijuana was, until I joined the navy." His bedroom in the house trailer in Buckland, where he spent most of his childhood, was very small. You had to back into it, and it was always tidy and his clothes were always decent, but he never had friends over to his house to play, because there really wasn't room. Besides, he always worked, before and after his daily humiliation at school, so he didn't have a great deal of time for friends. He was eighteen, a senior in trade school, and he owned a '56 Chevy and a box of tools. He did odd jobs after school specializing in the repair of bulkheads for cellar stairs and of screen doors. He was fixing one of those at a restaurant outside Shelburne Falls, and Lindy's mother, who worked there, asked him if he would make a rabbit hutch for her little daughter. He agreed and then he put it off. "I was no better then than I am now." Finally, he made the cage, went to deliver it, expecting to find a twelve-year-old waiting, and instead found Lindy, who was sixteen. "I thought she was neat, you know. I *liked her*. I liked her a lot right then." He found her after school a few days later and showed her how to shift the gears in his Chevy. In Shelburne Falls in those days, girls went out on dates with curlers in their hair, all the apparatus done up in scarves. "Probably girls were doing that in the fifties everywhere else. In Shelburne Falls we were doing it in the sixties," Lindy says. Richard liked to pull the pins out of her curlers. He was more like a brother than a boyfriend. Usually they would go on long drives, north into Vermont and New Hampshire, in the '56 Chevy. Gas was cheap. Richard could afford that kind of date. In the car they could talk about themselves without any risk of feeling foolish. "He always said that I helped him a lot just by liking him," says Lindy. "I was somebody outside of his home to talk to. He helped me, too. I didn't think much of myself, either."

When Richard met Lindy, rabbit hutch in his arms, he stuttered. He did not just have trouble reading. He could hardly speak. By the time they were married, after Lindy graduated from high school, Richard's stutter had vanished, never to return in force. They were small-town kids. Innocents, Richard says. He knew little of the birds and bees, as he put it, and they had never traveled far from home. Then Richard got drafted, joined the Navy, and as the old promise went, they saw the world.

Richard took care of airplanes the three years they lived on Okinawa. He flew as a crewman in the planes for which he had responsibility, and he saw a lot of Asia from the air. Then he was assigned to an aircraft carrier bound for the coast of Vietnam. Lindy went home. Richard, meanwhile, was chosen to look after the airplane that transported the admiral of the Seventh Fleet. It was Richard's job to ensure that the admiral's plane was safe for flying. One of Richard's partners says, "What a perfect choice for that job! Richard taking care of the admiral's plane. It almost restores your faith in the military."

Lindy says, "They knew they could count on Richard. Richard would do the job."

As a boy, Richard often accompanied his father on the various missions undertaken by Gougeon's Nite Owl Service. He'd help his father grease trucks. He'd hand him tools and watch him repair machines. It made Richard feel very proud when he overheard a hilltown tradesman describe his father as an artist with the welding rod. Out of all those late nights, Richard remembers one with special clarity. It was perhaps one o'clock in the morning. His father had worked for hours remaking a set of old-fashioned babbitt bearings. A tricky piece of work—you had to pour the bearings molten and everything had to be just the right temperature. This time, it didn't work. Richard's father leaned on one knee, took a cigar from his breast pocket, fired up the cigar with his propane torch, and grinned at Richard. He said to Richard that he guessed they'd have to do that one over again. Richard cannot remember his father losing his temper over a job. He says, "My father has a real good way about him. He has a tremendous amount of patience. A *tremendous* amount." To his father, Richard pays this homage: "He always worked nights. I remember always wanting to go with him."

When Richard's Boy Scout troop pitches its summer camp, on the top of Peter Hill in Ashfield, they run the American flag up a tree. The boys learn woodcraft, mainly, and manners in the woods. Richard does not care for military protocol. They do perform the prescribed flag ceremony, though, and, three fingers raised, promise to be trustworthy, loyal, helpful, friendly, courteous, kind, obedient, cheerful, thrifty, brave, and reverent. The words seem renewed when they're uttered in the woods, without spectators, by a dozen boys and by Richard, who speaks softly for once and stands straight-backed and unusually straight-faced during the ceremony.

Richard began to have misgivings about the Catholic Church while flying repeatedly over remote villages in the Philippines. Grass huts surrounding marble churches—from the air that seemed to be the pattern. "Why?" says Richard. "They should've put the people in marble houses and the church in a hut, because you can pray to God as well in a grass hut as anywhere. That's what I was always told. It started me off it." Richard says he worried for a long time about his inability to believe what he'd been taught in church and about the thought that he would be consigned to hell for his lapse in faith, or as he puts it, become "burnt French fries." Then, he says, he grew tired of worrying. "I figured there was nothing I could do about it, so I decided to forget about it."

Richard left Buckland in 1967. When he returned four years later, he was, like Rip Van Winkle, astonished at the sights. Skirts had risen six inches above the knee. Long hair and drugs were everywhere. He shunned the local antiwar protests, because he disliked some of the protesters. "Some of them were into drugs terrible. I'm not going to go down and march with them. Go down and protest against the war and then go up and sell a trunkload of drugs to the high school kids. I *wanted* to demonstrate, though." He felt lost, but most especially over the changes in himself. For most of four years he had flown every few days to some exotic, distant place, such as Hong Kong or Bangkok or Saigon. Suddenly, as it seemed to him, he was deposited back in Shelburne Falls, in a little town beside the Deerfield River, and he was bored, among other things. "I was owly. I'd fight with Lindy and take off through the woods for half a day."

When Richard came home from Vietnam, he accepted food stamps for a time, but to do so made him sick at heart. So he went to work picking apples. This was a favorite short-term occupation for many youths about his age. Many of them looked like hippies to Richard. He remembers being asked again and again, "Hey, man, what are you working so hard for, man?" He was out to become a fast apple picker, in fact. "I was the fastest apple picker in the valley," he says. "I'd pick seven boxes a day. Some of these guys wouldn't even pick half a box."

Lindy wanted to buy a house. She had found one that they might be able to afford, for $15,000, on the main street of Shelburne Falls. The idea frightened Richard—to buy a real house without a real job. And it frightened Lindy, too, but she reasoned that at the worst they'd simply have to sell the place. She told Richard, "We're going to try." For a short time between trade school and the Navy, Richard had worked for a local building contractor. Richard went to him and got his old job back. Then he went to the bank. He had a job. They lent him the money.

According to Richard, he and his classmates at the trade school were all misfits, "the kids they couldn't do anything else with." They were of two different sorts, however: ones who caused trouble and ones who merely had trouble. He was one of the latter. The troublemakers were kept inside in the shops, where they could be watched. The well-behaved, such as Richard, got to build real houses. He helped to build three while in school. To get a passing grade in English, something he had never before accomplished, Richard found he merely had to keep quiet in class. He actually got an A on one English paper, his only A in an academic subject. He entitled that paper "How to Frame a Roof." The explanation was lucid, the teacher felt.

The first contractor Richard went to work for was a seasoned builder, an able craftsman who was thrifty both with money and with words. "When he picked up your handsaw and it wasn't sharp, there was a lot of snuffing and snorting. Same thing with your block plane." Richard learned the trade mainly by watching. Once in a while, his boss complimented him on a piece of work. "And he wasn't much for compliments either." Gradually, Richard came to feel accomplished. After a couple of years, he went to his boss and asked for a raise. His boss offered him ten cents an hour more. "I didn't understand him. I thought he was saying, 'You're fired.' It hurt." Richard gave that builder two weeks' notice, and went to work for a younger and more congenial contractor. He and this builder worked together, putting up new houses and repairing old ones in a hurry. This second builder worked very quickly, and he taunted Richard when Richard started taking pains and fell behind. Much later on, Richard realized that a game had been played on him. His boss had tricked him into competing for speed. The memory amuses Richard. He still worries, though, about some of the work he did. "Jeez, I did some things I didn't like. Cut the board and nail it on. Still, I didn't do . . . I've

143

seen some terrible things that carpenters do. I do remember that first stairway we did, though. Oh, it was terrible. I still have nightmares of how that came out."

Meanwhile, in the evenings, he fixed up the old house in Shelburne Falls. Then he and Lindy sold it and with that money made the down payment on two acres of land in Apple Valley and on the materials for a new house. They chose Ashfield and Apple Valley first of all because the spot looked beautiful to them and the land was inexpensive. They had ties to Ashfield, too. Richard's mother grew up on a farm within the town's borders, and Lindy is a direct descendant of a Captain John Phillips, a member of the little band of land-hungry Yankees who trekked up through the forest from Deerfield sometime around 1740 and started to build the town.

Not long after Richard had built his house in Apple Valley, he got his invitation to join the brand-new local building company, which until then had been made up exclusively of college-educated carpenters. Apple Corps—funny name, good pay.

In superficial ways, Richard ten years later hardly resembles the short-haired, clean-shaven fellow who looked uncomfortable and very "straight" to Jim on first encounter. In his black beard, Richard manages to look both humorous and diabolical. His hair, now tipped with gray, curls out from under his various caps, and he sometimes lets it grow long enough to cover his

144

ears before he looks up a barber. ("I look quite crisp," says Richard after a haircut. "I look very businesslike.") His politics are unpredictable. He belongs to the National Rifle Association, and he holds opinions such as this: "Communism works great for some countries. It's a lot better than having one fat guy sit up on the hill and eat everything."

Richard's partner Alex Ghiselin, who went to Dartmouth, showed up for work with a wicker lunch basket. "Classy," Richard thought, and he got a wicker lunch basket, too. Lindy says, "I don't think Apple Corps would have survived without Richard. And he's needed them, too. Sharing responsibility and having someone to talk to, working with others as an equal, not always working for somebody else. He's got a lot more confidence now. The other day someone at school asked me what my husband does and I said he's part of a collective. I don't think I should *call* it that, but that's what it is." She laughs. "Richard's never been narrow-minded. No one could mistake Richard for a redneck. And I think Apple Corps has helped to keep him that way. We grew up in small towns. They're mill towns and they're poor towns. I don't think we feel better than the people we grew up with, but we have very little in common with the world we grew up in. I don't want to be part of that world, or the world of the type of people Richard sometimes works for, though in our attitudes and taste, I guess we're a lot more like the people he works for. It sounds like I'm a terrible snob, but I look back and think how terrible it would be if we'd never had a chance to see another world outside of our home-towns. What makes Richard different from a lot of the people we grew up with is more than what he has. It's more that he dreams."

Richard would like to have the time to learn the craft of furniture making and to master fully the art of shooting with a bow. He goes hunting every fall, and afterward Jim always says, "Richard's deer is still intact." Richard would like to get a deer some day. He would like to own a Corvette. Often, in the middle of work, he stops and pictures himself in the wilderness: "What I love is shooting my muzzle loader. When I'm shooting, I fantasize I'm a French-Canadian fur trapper in the 1850s. In the Rocky Mountains. A coonskin cap. A short French-Canadian. I'd fit right in." He goes back to work. A little later, "Next summer I might take a month off and go across the country. I'll have my truck painted, get all new tires, new brakes, be all set. This was supposed to be the year. But Lindy's got to get through college. Same old story. No money." He grins and swaggers: "No. I'm going to work in the summer. June, July, and August. Do a couple of kitchens and bathrooms in the winter. But September to January first I'm going to have to hunt. Take in the turkey season in four states."

Richard's dreams sit lightly on him. They do not have the force of complaints. He counts his blessings with more feeling than he expends in wishing for other ones. On the April morning in his thirty-sixth year when Richard selects the cap with the Jonsered chain saw company's logo and sets out from Apple Valley, fortified with pancakes, to work on the new house down in Amherst, he feels that he has more than he could have reasonably hoped for out of life: a good job that takes him outdoors and is not repetitive, neither a boss nor the difficulties of being the only boss, a house and land of his own in the country, the praise of many former customers, a Lindy cake in his lunch basket. The only thing Richard really has his heart set on in the near, realistic future, is a new paint job for his truck. Richard often says—it is like a favorite grace—"I'm real pleased with where I am in life, compared to how I started out."

To Richard, all the citizens of the world look like candidates for friendly conversation. Jim finds it hard to warm up to people, if he does not admire their opinions and their taste in houses. Richard is much more tolerant than Jim. "Richard gives people a tremendous amount of room," Jim says. But when Richard at last decides he can't abide someone, he dismisses him with a thoroughness that Jim finds a little frightening. What Richard can't resolve he can dismiss. Jim broods, awaiting resolutions. Jim usually assumes that in any exchange among people more is being said than there appears to be, and Richard is usually quite surprised to discover that it's so.

At one time or another every member of Apple Corps has found it hard to work with some other member. From time to time, Richard has felt that way, but none of the others has ever been reluctant to work alongside Richard. "Richard has some way of separating things so that he picks the best one all the time," says Jim. Ned Krutsky says, "I know that when I'm around Richard, he elicits a lot of good stuff from me. Good attitudes, good approaches to things." Jim looked up in the dictionary Richard's surname, and of its literal meaning he once said in front of Richard, "A gudgeon is just a hard, unyielding, unthinking piece of steel." *Gougeon* is the obsolete French form of the term for a metal pin on which a wheel turns or from which a bell swings. Richard's surname lies in the category of things too good to be true. Lindy says that when something breaks around their house, something she could fix, she always waits for Richard to come home and make the repair. Richard makes it very easy to rely on him, she says.

Richard takes care of details. In his world, things run well. His pickup truck is a metallic blue Chevrolet "High Sierra," with four-wheel drive, an eight-cylinder engine, and a black wooden box about the size of a coffin in the bed. The box keeps his tools out of the New England weather. He bought the truck used, a few years ago, has put a hundred thousand miles on it since, hasn't had any major engine repairs, changes the oil every three thousand miles and each time paints the underside with the used oil to keep rust in check.

If you get to know Richard, you get to know his truck. It is a large extension of his competence. Richard is the shortest member of Apple Corps. His truck is the largest. It is a big, high-riding one, and it is just tall enough that Richard, instead of merely climbing in, can swing himself on board, as if he were a long-haul teamster. "You've got to have a big truck, if you're a short person," he says, making his eyebrows bounce.

Answering her phone one day, Lindy says, "No, Richard's not here. He's down the hill on the corner by the mailbox. I can see his truck. He's been there for fifteen minutes, so he must have found someone to talk to. You know Richard." Richard gets so absorbed in conversations that on occasion he drives the wrong way down a one-way street, while chatting. In Northampton once, while Jim Locke sits beside him in the cab, Richard gets to talking and the more Richard talks the more slowly he drives, until, looking back nervously, Jim sees that a traffic jam has formed in Richard's wake. "I wish I was better read. I really miss it now. Everything I know is something I heard," Richard explains. He says, "Life wouldn't be worth it if I couldn't talk."

Here is Richard driving to work, from his dormered Cape, in Apple Valley: "Every house up on the street here, we worked on, or I did. I even worked on that house there, a long time ago. You see that house up there, with the barn? We did a *lot* of work up there. We were gonna do a lot more but he lost his money in the stock market. We built that one two years ago. Came out slicker 'n hell. This house here on the right, lightning hit it back in sixty-six. Burnt a hole in the roof. I fixed that. Last winter I put in book-shelves and some raised panel cabinets in that house, and when I was just out of high school, I put all the windows and siding on that house. Yup. Worked on that house, too, and we put that overhead door in there on that garage. I used to work on a house trailer over there, but it burnt down." He laughs his high laugh.

"Since 1965, I've worked on a *lot* of houses around, an awful lot. It's neat to see the things you did. To be able to go back and talk to the people afterwards is even neater. Sunday, I ran into the people I built the bookcases for. They wanted to show me how they looked with all the books in. They were *real* happy. Then I went over to see the people with the new bathroom. Then I went over to Barbara's, that new house back there, and I got her straightened out. It was a nice way to spend a day. I decided what to do when I retire. I'll go and look at jobs I did." Richard lets out a hoot.

He drives through Ashfield center. He passes farmhouses, ranch houses, pastures, barns, an-other village center, and every view that opens closes again upon surrounding woods. By the mid-1800s these hills were all but denuded. Now they are mostly forests maturing around old stone walls.

For the first time in more than a century, a mountain lion has been spotted in these wooded hills. "Here's a guy," says Richard. "I see him waiting here every morning when I go this way. I'll wave here."

The road drops and twists. Finally it levels out and straightens, like the end of a bobsled run that carries Richard over the Connecticut. "Things change across the river, don't they? It gets at least ten degrees hotter. I was thinking about it. It seems like the real up-to-date, liberated women down in Amherst don't mind shaking a man's hand, but women up in Shelburne or Hawley seem real nervous about it . . ."

It takes Richard about forty minutes to get to South Amherst. It takes longer the first morning of building, because he has to get a new muffler for the company generator at a garage along the way, and he has to spend a while talking shop with the mechanic.

What's left of the big wind that blew all the clouds out of the valley last night still shakes the fruit trees in the orchards along Bay Road, and Jim's path to work is strewn with blossoms. At the site, the foundation's gray walls sit amid wet, rutted, sandy ground and heaps of muddy loam. The foundation looks like a hypothesis drawn in the midst of confusion. Ned Krutsky pulls in just after Jim, and together they pick up various measuring tools to see if the foundation is as good as it looks.

The eight-foot-tall forms that foundation makers use get ragged at the tops. Whenever he can get away with it, Jim specifies foundation walls a little shorter than eight feet. That way the foundation builders have to snap lines below the tops of the forms and pour the concrete up to the lines, and usually, Jim has noticed, the top of a foundation comes out more nearly level than if it's poured right to the tops of the forms. Inducing foundation builders to snap top lines is a small trick of Jim's trade, which he didn't get to use this time, because Bill wanted as much headroom in the basement as possible. Jim hopes this is a good foundation. He does not expect better than what he considers acceptable, because he hired the second most expensive foundation maker in the area. The most expensive is very expensive indeed, and he does not make stronger foundations but ones more nearly of the prescribed dimensions and closer to level and square—issues that matter only to the builders.

Ned is about the same height as Jim and much bigger, thin at the waist and huge in the shoulders and chest, where he looks positively swollen this morning, all bundled up in wool. He wears wire-rimmed glasses. His hair is cut in the shape of an inverted bowl. He looks somber and slightly fierce at the moment. When he takes up a position on top of the foundation, holding the long, numbered staff in place for Jim, Ned looks like a sentinel on a castle wall.

Jim sets up the transit in a patch of poison ivy.

"I always flout things. Always." Then through the transit's scope, Ned assisting with the stick, Jim determines that the tops of the foundation walls aren't level but aren't badly out of level either, just about half an inch here and there. "Just exactly normal. It's a pain. But it's always a pain."

Jim and Ned stretch a long tape measure across the foundation. Jim holds the tape's smart end, as they say, reading the numbers. "Well look at that, whydon'tcha." The foundation measures half an inch smaller than specified, all the way around, which is perfect, or, as Jim says, perfect enough, smaller being the direction in which foundations should err—ones too large require the use of sledgehammers or the addition of an inch or two to the building, a return of the dreaded floating inch that Jim had removed from Bill's plan. Jim and Ned measure across opposite corners. A Euclidean trick. If the diagonal distances match, then the foundation's corners are square. Jim looks at the tape, then looks up astonished. The corners are perfectly square, or as close to that immaculate condition as their tools can determine. Jim measures again, then reels in the long tape, bringing Ned with it. Jim grins. He turns a thumb up as Ned approaches. "That's not classic," he says to Ned. "That never happens!"

"Shhhh," says Ned.

"That's what Sandy says," remarks Jim more softly. "Don't rile the gods."

All the omens are good. The excavator shows

up on time. Then the lumber company truck. Then the electrician. Then Richard, with the generator, which they'll use to run their power tools until they get electricity.

"Hell-oh, Jim. Hell-oh, Ned. God, it's pretty civilized down here, isn't it?"

"Yeah. No snow," says Jim.

Richard climbs into the bed of his truck and stands there a while, taking stock. "It's kind of an odd spot. It's pretty. I live in Ashfield. When you build there, you're supposed to build far away. I can't imagine building a hundred-fifty-thousand-dollar house three hundred feet from another house. It is pretty, though." From his slight elevation, looking east, most of what Richard sees is woods. A bear could travel east from the Pelham Hills for nearly sixty miles, most of the way to the city of Worcester, and rarely leave cover. A bear with a radio collar took that journey not long ago, in fact. Amherst makes an island in a regrown forest, too, but the view from the bed of Richard's pickup is suburban compared to the ones from his own house. He looks all around once more. "I'm in Amherst. It snowed last night in Ashfield," he says to no one in particular. Then he unloads the generator. The motor fires up on the first pull. "God, did that start nice! It liked that new spark plug I gave it. I gave it a treat."

The day is fine. The trees are in new leaf, ones the size of squirrels' ears, the sign by which the Indians knew the shad and salmon runs on the Connecticut were imminent. It is a sparkling blue morning, with a clearing, chilly wind out of the northwest, a day to make horses and carpenters frisky. It's May 17, 1983, the first day of carpentry on the first new house Apple Corps has touched in nearly two years. "This is great," declares Ned. "Building a new house is fun." He grins.

"I haven't built a new house in so long I've forgotten how," says Richard. He grins, too. "New houses are fun. I just get the biggest kick out of it. Always have."

"And we need it," says Jim, who does not grin. "For solidarity. For money. Mostly for money."

The three carpenters stand by a chest-high pile of new lumber. They wear leather boots and jeans and jackets, and Jim and Richard wear baseball caps. Jim's lacks an insignia, though, and it doesn't fit. Baseball caps of whatever size do not suit Jim. They lengthen his long face, as if in a funhouse mirror. The cap sits upon his head like something perching. It looks as improbable as a hard hat on a campaigning politician. Jim seems a little shy and awkward when he pulls out from his leather case his framing plan and lays it on the lumber pile.

Richard peers at the plan. "Fifteen feet, eight and three-quarters inches," he reads from among the many numbers on the drawing. He snorts. "That's quite a number. I like numbers like that."

Ned laughs, too, but more harshly than Richard. "This is a pretty complicated little thing," Ned says over the drawing. "You need a road map to find your way through it."

Jim goes off to his truck for a moment.

Ned and Richard stare at the drawing. "It looks like Jim's got it pretty well figured out, though," says Richard.

"Only *he* understands it," says Ned.

"That's okay," says Richard. "As long as one of us does. Nothing better happen to Jim, though."

Ned shakes his head over the plans and laughs his unhappy-sounding laugh again.

"I don't want to know what every little thing means," says Richard to Ned. "I just want to understand it generally."

Jim returns, and he and Richard hover over the plans awhile, muttering geometry. Ned takes half a step backward and looks around him in a studied way, like a fellow on a street corner who's been stood up. Elbow on the lumber pile, Richard looks Jim right in the eye and declares, "I'm ready to go. We're gonna breeze right through this."

From under his hat, Jim smiles at Richard, and says, "Yeah, this is going to take a while."

Quick and easy as that, Richard has taken charge of the first floor's framing. He has picked up one end of the load. All Jim had to do was set it in front of him. At the moment, Jim feels grateful, not so much to Richard as for Richard's existence.

"Oh-*Kay!*" Richard says and heads off to fetch his framing tools. Ned and Jim fetch theirs.

3

Richard sits on a stack of two-by-tens, the one on which Jim presented his framing plan. The big pile of wood gives off a delicate aroma, like a woods with a pine-needle carpet. The stack makes a clean, fragrant, somewhat expensive picnic table for Richard. Sitting on it, feet dangling over the edge, he shakes his head over that day's Lindy cake, in order to ensure his partners' jealousy, and dislodges the pencil from behind his ear. It vanishes down a crack between the boards.

"Whoops," says Richard, peering after it. "This pile just ate my pencil."

The next day at lunchtime, Richard finds his pencil, on the ground, between two twelve-foot-long two-by-tens, which are all that remain of the pile.

Finish work never seems to end, but the frames of houses go up swiftly. And time passes quickly for Apple Corps when they're framing.

Ned stands on soggy, sandy ground and measures the distances between the bolts that protrude, threads up, out of the top of the foundation's gray walls, and Richard bores the necessary holes in a length of the two-by-six, pressure-treated southern pine. The board slips down right over the bolts. "The first piece of wood. Yaaay!" cries Richard. They install another piece of sill, then another, and then Ned says, "Wait a minute." The sills are sticking out over the edges of the foundation a little too far. Ned and Richard investigate. They measure the two-by-six lengths of pine, which are supposed to be five and a half inches wide. These are five and five-eighths. Maybe they were sawn wrong. More likely, they sat outside and absorbed an eighth of an inch of water. Richard pulls the wood off the bolts. "We can't make this house thirty feet and a quarter inches right at the *start*," he says. They begin again. "It's just work," says Ned.

Observing this scene from the other side of the foundation, Jim nods approval. He says the difference between amateur and professional carpenters lies in the facts that pros make few mistakes and when they err they make corrections at once. Thus they prevent both brooding and remorse. Half an hour later, Jim drives a nail that splits a fresh piece of lumber, one he's spent some time cutting and installing. "This piece of wood just split from end to end," he says. He stares at the ruined board. Then he beats on it with his large framing hammer. But hadn't he said that a pro doesn't brood over an error? "That's right. But I never said you don't let it upset you." He wallops and wallops the board, tearing it along the grain. Jim smiles. He tosses the ruined wood aside. "I never said *that*. Send this back to the factory."

It's clear they do not like to leave mistakes behind. When Ned bends a nail, he withdraws that nail, pounds it straight again, and hammers it back in. Nails are cheap. Time costs the carpenters much more. But Ned seems interested not merely in correcting errors. He wants to erase them.

Each carpenter owns a short-handled crowbar with a rounded claw, known as a cat's paw. There's nothing like a cat's paw for extracting nails from mistakes. "What would a carpenter do without a cat's paw, Ned?"

"Buy one," Ned replies.

None of them carries his cat's paw, but each knows where it is. If he makes a mistake, he has to go and get the tool. They prepare for errors. They don't assume that errors will occur. When one of them does make a mistake, he usually blames it on whichever of the team happens to be absent or out of earshot at the moment.

"Oh, shit."

"Blame it on Jim."

For now, Jim usually gets the blame. Almost hourly it seems, he leaps over the trench near the foundation and trudges off up the hill, briefcase in hand, toward the phone in Jules Wiener's red horse barn, so he can call the lumberyard or a subcontractor or one of the utilities or Jonathan. Jim rarely accepts abuse without retorting, though. He makes a practice of signing his partners' mistakes. "Richard was here," he'll write in pencil on the wood at the site of a withdrawn nail. In Apple Corps parlance, a carpenter gone sloppy is "a beaver," "a jabronie," or "a Hoople," and "thrashing" is the disjointed set of bad procedures that leads to "cobby" work or, worst of all, "a cob job." The last is a very old term. In one of its earliest meanings, *cob* meant a lump of something, and in medieval England to "build in cob" meant to make a house out of lumps of clay, earth, even manure. It was not thought to be a form of high-quality construction. "Cob job" probably came across the ocean with the first New England carpenters and has survived in such sanctuaries of the old-fashioned as the hilltowns. The term is more usual there than in the valley. The carpenters don't remember exactly when they first heard the expression, and they do not know its history, but it has the right pejorative sound for the kind of act that none wishes to be truly guilty of committing. When one of Apple Corps accuses another of thrashing or beavering or cobbing up some piece of work, he usually does so falsely, sometimes even in order to praise, but they also seem to be warning each other and themselves of the nearness of sin.

Usually, if one of them wants praise, he has to administer it himself. When Richard fixes a cobby piece of work, he "tunes it up" or he "fusses with it," and what comes out well is "custom," and for all of them a very good result is "perfect," "perfect enough," or "perfect or equal." And in nearly every case, a satisfactorily completed piece of the job is good enough for whatever town they happen to be working in, in this case, "good enough for Amherst."

"Close enough for Amherst," Ned pauses over his hammer to say. "It's a joke, but it's also a way of keeping perspective. Don't lose the building for the stick. You're always making value judgments, you know, about what's straight or plumb, but sooner or later you gotta nail it. You've got to have confidence it's right enough, or if it's not, that you can fix it."

On the second day of framing, the fourth partner, Alex Ghiselin, joins them. They set up, as they will every morning, a small factory beside the foundation: generator, extension cords, ladders, sawhorses, electric and hand-driven saws. "Tooling up," as they call it, they buckle on belts and make themselves into roving hardware displays, hammers and numerous pouches hanging from their waists, red handkerchiefs in their back pockets, pencils behind their ears. Proper and efficient framing is the art of thinking ahead with clarity, of seeing the end in the beginning, and they have made the exercise of forethought, which is the opposite of thrashing, part of their daily routine in all departments of houseraising.

Alex is their cutter nonpareil. He likes nothing better than to get from Richard an order for thirty two-by-tens, all fifteen feet, five and three-eighths inches long. Alex writes down the numbers. He sets up the company's radial arm saw and the portable bench Jim once built for it. Then Alex measures that prescribed distance down the bench from the saw's blade and nails down a piece of wood at the spot. The end of each successive two-by-ten he'll place against this stop. It takes him a couple of minutes to set up the jig, but once it's done he can cut one board after another

161

and measure only occasionally to make sure that nothing has moved.

Whenever they can, the carpenters assemble a portion of the frame out on the open ground, where they don't have to hang off ladders and there's room to swing their hammers freely. Then, standing on the foundation's walls and on stepladders, they install the construction, a section of floor joists, say, into its place within the frame. Most of the failures of most spare-time carpenters stem from misplaced haste. They haven't got much time. They want to see results at once. Apple Corps spends time now to save time later. It's a form of deferred gratification, which, the psychologists say, is the essence of true adulthood. Apple Corps has acquired the knack for looking calmly on the future. They always pause to remove any nails from boards they cast aside. The practice cuts down on tetanus shots. It was not always this way, but most of them have worked together for ten years now, and they have learned consideration.

Erecting girders, from stepladders set on the basement floor, Richard and Alex struggle to speak geometry. "Move it five-sixteenths that way. No, out that way, toward Pelham. No, up. Whoops. No, down. This sounds like *Sesame Street*," says Richard.

Richard climbs out of the cellar. He studies and restudies Jim's intricate framing plan. He does so out loud: "Oh, I'm being confused right now. That seems rather odd. Unh-hunh. Ohhhh. I see.

162

I see what happened. Oh-*Kay!* Yup, right where it should be. Excellent. Just where it should be. Okay. Good." He adds, addressing Alex, "A *custom*-fit girder." Richard emits a guttural sound, which could imply some twisted pleasure.

"Nicely done," says Alex.

"Custom," says Richard. "I think we're winning."

Not all the two-by-tens they take from that first pile, nor all of the lumber that follows, is of high quality. A few pieces have rotten patches, and a few more than that are twisted. "Goodness gracious, Buffalo Bob, thees somebitch she no good. She crooked, like some beetch," says Jim, with a wild look, sighting down a board. Ned says he thinks the lumber grading standards have declined since he started out. "I don't know, Ned," says Richard. "As long as I can remember, everybody's always bitched about it. 'God, the lumber isn't like it used to be.' We're still sayin' that." They find places for the twisty stuff, where nails will straighten it or it can do no harm, and the worst stuff they cut into pieces for blocking between floor joists.

When he is going well, Alex cuts lumber quickly and to within a thirty-second of an inch of the specified lengths. They attempt to keep their frame within about a sixteenth of an inch of perfection, which is about as accurate as their tape measures are and more precise, in fact, than wood and weather allow. They work in sunshine and a few days into the framing, they even get their shirts

163

off for a while. On the next day, a cold drizzle falls. Jim, who is responsible for worrying, measures the first floor's frame at the end of one sunny day and finds it jibes exactly with the numbers on his plan. Two rainy days later, he measures again and finds that the bottom deck has grown a quarter of an inch along one wall and not at all along the others. They can easily rectify the discrepancy in the next level of the frame. Jim expected this to happen. He is not disappointed. He says again, "Perfection is an insult to the gods." They often speak about the fact of imperfection. The words must have a consoling ring for them.

4

A few towns up the Connecticut River from Amherst there's a village, called Northfield, that belongs in an old lithograph. It has a wide main street, tall trees, and many large, elderly houses that were built to last. The village has a few structures that date back to Colonial times, but most of its old houses were built in the 1800s. Collectively these amount to a text on nineteenth-century architecture. Northfield has houses with hipped roofs and center chimneys, ones with pediments and columned porticoes, ones with the pointy-topped windows of the prototypical American haunted house. The late Georgian, the Federalist, the Greek Revival, and the Gothic, all are represented in the old houses of Northfield's streets. The curious fact about them is that most were designed and built, for about five hundred dollars apiece, by a carpenter named Calvin Stearns and by his sons and brother. You can usually tell a Stearns house. All have classical-looking proportions. In their gable ends, Stearns installed fanlights with shutters that swoop out at the bottoms like bells. Inside, the houses have simple banisters, hand-carved to roundness, and on the trim under most fireplace mantels, Stearns placed two small decorative buttons—his signature. His houses look straighter and squarer than most things one hundred fifty years old. An elderly man who lives in a Stearns Federalist likes to say that someone once put a cable around another Stearns house and tried to pull it over, and the cable broke.

When he was a young man, Stearns worked as an ordinary carpenter on the construction of the India Wharf stores in Boston, which Charles Bulfinch designed, and perhaps Stearns acquired his taste for the classical motif there. For his designs, he borrowed from pattern books, including the one on Greek Revival that Bill Rawn owns but has only glanced through. Stearns farmed. He kept a stable of oxen and horses for hire. Mainly, he was architect and housejoiner, a general practitioner in wood. Carpenters of the American past usually remain anonymous. Often their names disappear long before their buildings do. But Calvin Stearns left a more durable and obvious impression on his town than any of the locally prominent people whose houses he designed and erected. He also left behind a set of daybooks, economic diaries that convey some of the rhythms of a nineteenth-century country builder's life.

Stearns liked to get his children to school whenever he could. He spent generously on their educations. He seems to have had a fairly soft heart. "Boys in Bed after Sunrise," he writes on the Fourth of July, 1839, adding that he gave his eldest the then princely sum of fifty cents. Evidently, Stearns liked the odd glass of liquor. He kept track of his bills for alcohol. He probably passed a bottle among his crew on raising days. His years were round, a cycle of making contracts and plans for new houses in late winter, of building in spring, summer, and fall, with time out for plowing and haying, of making coffins—long a staple business of English village carpenters—and of building furniture, window sashes, moldings in his shop during winter. In the winter, when the sap doesn't run and a sled can travel easily in forest, Stearns also got his wood, for fuel and building.

"Choping wood and tumbling it downhill," he writes in January 1838.

10th   Boys & myself have sledded wood.
17th   We have sledded logs and wood this week
24th   ditto

Stearns, his sons, his brother, his hired men, cut the trees with axes, got them out of the woods on sleighs, and with felling and broad axes squared up the framing timbers, sometimes only flattening one side of a log. They split pine for their shingles. Logs destined to be boards they drove to the local sawmill. As long ago as 1700 every town in Massachusetts had at least one of those. For framing timbers, Stearns often chose American chestnut, that now blighted and greatly mourned hardwood. Also for framing, he took some birch and maple; for banisters, cherry; for plaster lath, any old stuff, maybe hemlock, spruce, or fir; for floors, the hard yellow pine. For frames, shingles, clapboards, doors, moldings, wainscoting, window sashes, he chopped down many tall white pines. It is pleasant to imagine Stearns and his boys making their own selections out of the winter woods, looking at a tree and seeing a floor, a frame, a roof. Stearns's daybooks speak of an era often remembered with nostalgia. Back then the country carpenter worked long hours, for a dollar or a dollar fifty a day, but Stearns's was an age that called for versatility from the country builder. A carpenter was also a woodsman then. Western Massachusetts today has many small sawmills and many trees but not enough large stands of high-quality timber to make lumbering on a modern industrial scale pay. In the hills especially, new houses are sometimes built with pieces of the woods that surround them and with trees that once stood where those houses now sit. Some settlers make a virtue of houses that are grown locally, and for people who build for themselves, the practice can even be economical, but usually not for those who value their time in dollars and cents. Apple Corps has used locally sawn lumber on occasion, and they built a large part of one huge, elegant house with the owner's trees. Like the great majority of professional builders, though, they usually get their wood from lumberyards.

So there's an anonymity to the loads of wood that arrive on the lumberyard's truck and are heaped on the ground beside the foundation. "We better shuffle some of this stuff around," said Ned of the first load that arrived. They made piles. In one went plywood of various thicknesses and grades. Plywood comes in four-foot-by-eight-foot sheets, and is as modern as a jet. Each sheet consists of several thin slices of wood, peeled from trees by veneering machines—which unroll logs like paper toweling—and then bound together with waterproof glue. This is wood rearranged into stuff that by some measurements of strength resembles steel more than it does wood. Of the piles, the one of plywood had come the greatest figurative distance from the forest.

There was a fairly small pile of twelve-foot-long two-by-six lumber, tinted green. This was southern yellow pine, which, the stamp on the pieces revealed, was treated with many toxic chemicals in Culpepper, Virginia, in order to discourage rot and insects. The decline of a house often begins in the bottommost layer of wood. So the sills, the wood that Apple Corps would bolt down onto the foundation, are made of these processed pieces of the southern forests.

"We gotta get these things bolted down in a hurry," said Richard. "They're going to be so goddamn crooked after a day in the sun, they'll look like barrel staves."

The largest pile of lumber stood about as high as Richard's chest and about as wide as his outstretched arms. It contained most of the underpinnings of the first-story floors. This pile consisted of framing lumber, "dimension-stock" softwood lumber, mostly two-by-tens of various lengths, from eight to twenty feet. "Pinkham—S Dry S4S Estrn Spruce Balsam Fir." This code was stamped in ink on every piece. It's a signature. "Sorta dry," said Jim in passing, of the legend "S Dry," but in fact it stands for "surface dry," which means that when this lumber came out of the Pinkham yard, less than 20 percent of its weight was water. The other hieroglyphics say that the lumber was planed smooth on all four sides (S4S), and that it came from trees of either spruce or balsam fir, though all but a few pieces in this stack are spruce.

There are byways within byways of the American lumber industry that make the act of building a house suggestive of the entire economy of the United States. The site of a housebuilding makes a cosmopolitan place. This stack, the one that they're turning into the frame of the first-story floors, comes from as far down east as you can go in the United States. The pile of two-by-tens amounts to 2833 board feet, which represents about six cords of standing trees, or, very approximately, four-fifths of an acre of the spruce and fir forest of northern Maine.

Any child who has studied trees from a bedroom window, and found the faces in them, knows that trees have individuality. When a tree becomes lumber, some of its peculiar characteristics survive. When, for instance, a crooked tree trunk is turned into two-by-tens, some of those homogeneous-looking boards will contain what's called "reaction wood," and they tend to warp. It is as if the lumber could remember the tree. As Calvin Stearns unquestionably knew, out harvesting the winter woods, no two trees are quite alike, but in the woods of northern Maine they are like faces in an urban crowd. From Bangor north, most of Maine is forest, about a third of it in spruce and balsam fir.

An ordinary map of northern Maine promises a wet, green wilderness, without towns or public roads, full of streams, rivers, and lakes. The Big Woods, as it is sometimes called, serves as a sanctuary for moose, bear, brook trout, mosquitoes, black flies. The map shows it to be one of the largest contiguous forests east of the prairies, about 10 million acres in all. A logger's map reveals more, however. It shows that for purposes of ownership the land is divided into squares six miles on a side, each labeled with a set of letters and numbers. The region is called the Unorga-

170

nized Territory, because it contains no human settlements large enough to need government. But it is certainly organized, in the manner of graph paper, for the purposes of industry. When Thoreau visited these Maine woods in the mid-nineteenth century, he found "a damp and intricate wilderness," but he felt vexed at the great amount of logging being done. Nowadays, even vacationing canoeists on the Allagash and hikers in Baxter State Park, the two officially designated wildernesses within this wilderness—islands in a gigantic multicorporate forest—often can't escape the sound of chain saws. A person could easily get lost in this forest but could not walk far in most of it without coming to a logging road.

Lumberjacks used to float logs from the interior down rivers to the mills, until the 1960s. By then the practice was on the wane, and environmentalists finally got a law against river drives enacted. That law has meant new roads, and some environmentalists wonder if they made an even trade. Forest product companies have carved myriad roads through the huge forest, thousands of miles of dirt roads packed with shale—wide, gray main roads and branch roads and branches off the branches, and also many bridges. These roads accommodate skidders, delimbers, whole-tree harvesters, trailer trucks with cranes. You remember most vividly the mandibles and pincers of these machines that all seem to have counterparts in the world of insects. Loggers and truck drivers generally get paid by piece rate. The more they cut and haul, the more they earn. They do not turn off their chain saws for long, and the heavily loaded logging trucks roll through the Big Woods at close to highway speed.

The statistics that apply to the building of housing in America make the business sound like war. Told that more than a million new one- and two-family houses are under way in '83, Richard Gougeon says, "Christ! And we're only building one?" Mainly for building, the United States consumes in the mid-1980s about 30 billion board feet of softwood lumber a year. The national production of softwood lumber accounts for the annual felling of enough trees to cover about 3 million acres of northern Maine, and of course that's only a fraction of all the wood Americans take.

The United States cuts a lot of wood and also has a lot of it, some 482.5 million acres of what is called commercial timberland, a huge figure that leaves out a lot of forests including most of the Alaskan ones. Depending on the system of measurement, Americans and forest product companies remove either a little more or considerably less softwood than is grown each year, and they cut only about half of the growth in hardwoods.

Many stands, cut over once or twice or even three times in the past, have regrown. A great deal of farmland has gone back to woods, particularly in the South and in New England, which is now 70 percent woodlot. Roads have opened up areas once inaccessible to logging. Fires and diseases and pests claim about as much of the forests every year as loggers do, but that is far less than before the era of fire control and of arsenals of chemical sprays.

Meanwhile, the annual timber harvest amounts to only about as much wood as was cut in 1900. That's partly because the mills that turn wood into paper and building materials waste far less of the tree than before and also because America uses less than half as much wood per person as it did in 1900. Americans do not use nearly as much for fuel. A lot more wood is turned into paper than ever before—Americans use about 550 pounds of paper per person each year. On the other hand, the modern house consumes far fewer trees than its ancestors did. Plywood is one reason. To cover 100 square feet of floor with boards, you'd need to use up 10.1 cubic feet of wood, but it takes only 5.2 cubic feet to produce the plywood that will do the same job. Aluminum siding has replaced a lot of clapboards. Such substitutions do not necessarily imply a public good. Substitutes use up resources, too, and in some cases carry nasty social and environmental costs. By most gross calculations, though, America is not courting treelessness just yet.

A forest economist named Lloyd Irland, formerly of the Yale forestry school and now an official in Maine, estimates that the country's woods could supply in perpetuity the needs of 400 million people, provided the citizenry consumed paper at a lesser rate than presently—say the German rate of 300 pounds per capita. Not everyone agrees. The U.S. Forest Service has foreseen shortages, particularly in lumber, by the turn of the century. Such prophecies, both sanguine and dire, rest on many assumptions about many unknown facts. Most scholars of the woods agree that Americans used the forests recklessly for a long time, and left behind large areas of impoverished and genetically degraded woodland. A forest economist named Perry Hagenstein asserts that in general America's woodlands are far better managed now than ever before. Of course, forests have aesthetic and environmental as well as commercial value, and some forms of intensive management serve only commercial interests well.

In the Pacific Northwest, loggers still cut down stands of huge old Douglas fir, felling trees of a size that may soon disappear from America forever. Inevitably, continued heavy use of forests means smaller and smaller trees for lumber. The housing business has relied directly on photosynthesis for centuries. The relationship may become increasingly indirect. A long, straight, clear piece of lumber has already turned into a relatively precious object, in the sense that most of the people who can afford new houses today no longer can afford to use clear pine for trimming their windows and doorways. Composites of scrap wood, such as particle board, will become still more varied and abundant, while structural materials made from metals and from the industrially extruded fibers of stunted trees and slash wood may someday replace most of the forest-grown two-by-fours, sixes, eights, tens, in which much of American domestic life this past century has been enclosed.

Foresters in the Maine woods don't speak of virgin stands. When they talk about notably large trees, large for this region, that is, they use the term "old growth." In the nineteenth and early twentieth centuries, loggers using axes and whip-saws cut their way through most of the region, and the virgin Big Woods was floated down its many rivers. After that, for decades, the forest essentially lay fallow. Since around 1960, paper companies and their subsidiary lumbering operations have been cutting again on a large scale, to feed their saw, pulp, plywood mills. From the air over northern Maine you cannot imagine an end to this forest, and in fact the cut today does not exceed the growth, but over the last decades the industries in wood have installed enough equipment to use all of the growth. Today, the Big Woods by itself provides for about 1 percent of the nation's yearly consumption of softwood lumber, and 4 percent of all pulpwood, and 42 percent of all manufacturing in Maine. The state's many hunters and fishermen, hikers and naturalists don't own the forest but they have made it their playground and refuge. And it is currently under siege from a pest native to the place, called the spruce budworm.

In the natural regime, budworm epidemics besiege the Maine woods every thirty to fifty years.

Left to run its course, an outbreak kills some 40 percent of the fir and the red and white spruce in its path. Then the moths subside. Spraying the woods with insecticides began in the 1950s and has continued intermittently. Chemicals have prevented a lot of damage, but in doing so they have also kept alive enough forage for the budworm population to remain at the verge of an outbreak more widespread and virulent than if there had been no spraying. In this way, spraying has made more spraying inevitable. Insecticides now represent the only barrier against truly catastrophic losses of Maine's spruce and fir, but spraying cannot prevent substantial losses. The budworm has already eaten its way through large sections of spruce and fir. In the worst areas, evergreen canopies now stand all gray and powdery. For a time, industries in the Maine woods will have at their disposal more dead and dying trees than they can use, and then, probably, a time will come when there will be less of the right kinds of wood in the forest than the various mills are designed to handle. For the Maine woods, there seem to be no ways around the budworm that won't have unpleasant consequences, both economic and environmental.

Actually, there's no reason to feel complacent about any of the vast woodlands of the United States. Considering the recent and astonishingly rapid degradation of European forests—almost certainly caused by airborne pollutants—some forests could receive proper management or a proper lack of it, and still be in trouble. One respectable school of scientific thought holds that similar manmade, chemical catastrophes may loom over many of America's big woods.

One day in the winter before Jim and Jonathan signed their contract, when the carpenters were still scouting for new work, Richard sat down with a young couple in a rented house. This couple said they would celebrate the day when they got out of their landlord's house. Richard looked at the couple's sketch of the house they wished they could own. The drawing was rough. It came on a piece of notebook paper. But their rising voices gave it luster: "And here, see, this would be the kitchen . . ." Richard was enthusiastic, too. He helped them improve the plan. Then Richard told them it would cost $50 a square foot. He left in a troubled frame of mind, troubled for Richard, anyway. He thought maybe he and his partners could build something for the couple, perhaps half a house that could be added on to later, but really, he knew those people didn't have the money for a building by Apple Corps. He felt he had rubbed his heel around on their dreams. Maybe Apple Corps charged too much. Other firms, traditionally organized, built for less. Then again, some built for more. Richard didn't make as much an hour as several of Apple Corps's favorite subcontractors. He wasn't getting rich, but these days it seemed as if the only people who could afford him and his scruples about building were much wealthier than he, and it was hard to know where to put the blame.

Seemingly from the start, ideal America was a nation of homeowners. It came close to that condition in seventeenth- and eighteenth-century rural New England, where as many as 90 percent of all families may have lived in houses of their own. By 1645, however, the city of Boston already had landlords and renters, and Colonial Virginia and Maryland always had a much higher percentage of tenants than New England. National statistics on the subject weren't kept until the late nineteenth century, but certainly in some states, Delaware for one, the percentage of homeowners steadily dwindled from Colonial times up until the Civil War. As of the census of 1920, when the country was still largely agrarian, only 46 percent of American families owned homes. After World War II the energies of the federal government and the power of the postwar economy generated a long building boom that greatly altered those statistics. Even then, however, renting remained an inescapable way of life for many. In 1983, about 64 percent of American households owned their homes. That statistic, combined with a few others, meant that Americans were among the best-housed people in the world. It also meant that many millions of citizens of the world's richest nation couldn't afford to buy places to live. For them, the prospects weren't good.

A house in a small town in South Carolina may cost $200,000 less than a comparable one in a suburb of Los Angeles. Average prices both over-state and understate the problem, but they do say something about what many would-be homeowners faced in 1983. Since 1970, the average sales price of a house had risen faster than the prices of almost everything else, including most of what goes into making a house. The construction of the interstate highway system had made vast amounts of new land available and attractive for housing, but by 1970 the government had nearly finished building highways. While the supply of so-called buildable land began to shrink, the very numerous baby boom generation was coming to the age at which, in America, the desire to own a house has the force of biological necessity. Land prices started up. Speculators wait for just such moments of rising prices and demand. Various provisions of the federal tax code, notably the deductions for mortgage interest, deductions that benefit the wealthy most and amount to some $30 billion yearly, heightened speculation. The tax code al-lowed many to buy houses in spite of rising inter-est rates, and swiftly rising prices made investment in houses a means not just of keeping up with inflation but of beating it. Peculiar episodes oc-curred: At the edge of a piece of freshly bulldozed land in a California suburb, a contractor stands surrounded by a gang of excited citizens and auc-tions off to them the houses he has yet to build, houses that the eager bidders do not intend to occupy.

Eventually, towering interest rates sent the

housing industry into one of its declines. As of 1982, the number of new houses under way had dropped by more than a million from the peaks of 1977 and '78. Between 1970 and 1980, the percentage of Americans who own their homes had actually increased, in spite of rising prices and rising interest rates. But in the aftermath, some economists worried that a significant number of buyers had overextended themselves and now stood in danger of defaulting on their mortgages. Partly because the speculative boom included many condominium conversions, the supply of rental housing had tightened. So those who had not managed down payments during the spree now faced rising rents. Average salaries had increased less than prices for houses. By the '80s, people trading up bought two out of every three new houses, while first-time owners bought just one—a reversal of a long-standing trend. As a group, would-be homeowners stood further than ever from becoming real ones.

Taking the long view, an economist named John Pitkin at the Harvard-MIT Joint Center for Urban Studies suggests that if housing prices became abnormally high in the '70s, prices were probably abnormally low in the '50s, at the height of the great expansion of the American suburbs. It seemed certain that Richard would find himself building fewer and fewer houses for people with incomes like his own. Even without high interest rates and speculation and tightening supplies of buildable land, single-family, wood-framed houses would be expensive things. Construction costs run high. They are not likely to decline. One reason is the sheer amount of material that goes into a modern American house. The Souweines' new house will contain 3000 square feet of floor space, about twice the average in 1983. Except for some of its exterior trim—details that will cost a few thousand extra—the plan, as Bill has insisted, is fairly plain. The specs call for basic, standardized materials. These add up, however.

In *Walden,* Thoreau boasts that he has built his 150-square-foot cabin out of this meager materials list:

Boards...............................$	$8.03\frac{1}{2}$	mostly shanty boards
Refuse shingles for roof and sides .	4.00	
Laths	1.25	
Two second-hand windows with glass..	2.43	
One thousand old brick	4.00	
Two casks of lime......................	2.40	That was high.
Hair..	0.31	More than I needed.
Mantle-tree iron	0.15	
Nails.......................................	3.90	
Hinges and screws	0.14	
Latch	0.10	
Chalk	0.01	
Transportation	1.40	I carried a good part on my back.
In all .... $	$28.12\frac{1}{2}$	

Thoreau's framing timbers cost him nothing, because he chopped them down himself.

In South Amherst in 1983, Apple Corps will use 15 gallons of foundation coating and one brush and handle to apply it, 16 ounces of red and blue chalk, 2 rolls of insulation for sills, 4 red lumber crayons, 5 gallons of resin glue, several gallons of roof cement, several hundred feet of aluminum drip edge, 9 rolls of 15-pound felt, $28\frac{2}{3}$ squares of asphalt shingles, 1 folding stair, 1 metal basement doorway, 3 pairs of wooden interior and 1 pair of exterior French doors, 1 single interior French door, 2 single glass-paned wooden exterior doors, 1 insulated steel front door with sidelights, 10 Masonite interior doors, 3 sets of bifold louvered doors, 37 double-hung windows of various sizes, 3 marble thresholds, 2 vanity bases, 2 slabs of Corian, 120 feet of Colorcore Formica, 1 gallon of Formica adhesive, 5 feet of stovepipe, 5 pairs of "cellwood" shutters. Also: doorstops, lock sets, latches, medicine cabinets, towel bars, shelf standards, a robe hook, bolts (toggle, lag, and carriage), screws of various metals and sizes and types, a metal lazy Susan for one kitchen cabinet, 4 dozen sheets of sandpaper, some 30 sanding belts, 1.5 gallons of wood glue, 2 pints of wood patch, and 1 tube of caulk (a very small amount of caulk, an unerring indication of tight-fitting joints).

Altogether, those items and their like cost about $16,000. The rest is wood: 358 sheets of various kinds of plywood, 170 board feet of furring, 612

182

of tongue-and-groove porch flooring made of quarter-sawn fir, 2500 of tongue-and-groove red oak flooring, 1140.76 of pressure-treated lumber, 3 bundles of cedar shim shingles, 244.12 board feet of knotless and 1813.62 feet of number-two and somewhat knotty pine boards, 159.36 feet of staging planks, 165.7 of clear oak boards, 14.62 of bed molding, 4140 of red cedar clapboards, about 250 board feet of sawn but unplaned poplar, 8 wooden columns with caps and bases (each is 8 inches in diameter by 8 feet tall), 1044 lineal feet of Colonial casing, 1422 of baseboard, 396 of crown molding, 402 board feet of tongue-and-V-groove number-two pine, 76 birch balusters, 125 lineal feet of oak nosing, 118 of oak scotia, 11 oak treads, 40 feet of handrail, 6 newel posts and 2 starters, 2 easement sets, 201 feet of drip cap, 45 of yellow pine steps, 32 of particle board countertop, 166 of quarter-round and 8 of half-round moldings. For the pieces of the frame, they'll use about 24,270 board feet of spruce and Douglas fir, including about 1000 two-by-four by eight-foot studs. If you laid all the wood they'll use end to end, you could make a narrow pathway one foot wide and one inch thick and about seven miles long. If you pieced it all together a layer thick, like a jigsaw puzzle, you could cover about an acre of ground. To put all that wood together in the air, they'll use about 950 pounds of nails. The nails seem a relative bargain. The half ton of nails costs about $500. Not including what's in the doors and windows, the price for the wood comes to $30,733.65, or about 20 percent of the total construction cost.

Dozens of industries contribute the pieces of a modern house. Over the past eighty years, the prices of some pieces have risen faster than general inflation, and lumber has been one of those. Far less lumber goes into a house than formerly, but the real price of lumber, adjusted for inflation, has risen by about four times since 1900.

There is a great deal involved in turning four-fifths of an acre of the Maine woods into the stack of two-by-tens lying in Amherst. Probably some of those boards were spruce trees in the grid square T9 R8, taken in snow early in the year by the chain saw–wielding loggers from Mooseleuk camp. Mobile machines—ones that make you think both of Paul Bunyan and of accountants applying the rules of accelerated depreciation—handle the stems (as logs are called there) as if they really were just stems. The trees come out of the woods without their branches and are unloaded among the huge and tidy piles of logs in the concentration yard at the Pinkham mill. The mill looks like an industrial park. It occupies a 300-acre clearing on the edge of the forest, next to the last paved public road between Presque Isle and New Brunswick, and beside the tracks of the Bangor and Aroostook Railroad. The mill itself, the newer of Pinkham's two sawmills, is the sort of factory that dwarfs its operators. Some workers occupy glass booths. Others stand with pickaroons at the intersections of conveyer belts. The noise inside this place seems to occupy every frequency that's painful, and all the workers at their stations keep their ears stuffed up or covered. You pass through in a twilight of sound. The building jiggles gently. The smell of fresh-sawn wood is thick. Resin stiffens your hair.

A giant ant heaves the log up to a slasher saw, which cuts it into rough lengths, the longer the better, up to eighteen feet. Then the log slides into the hot pond, where it thaws and its bark loosens. It enters the mill proper through the debarker, a whirling, sharp-throated esophagus. A system of conveyer belts—taken as a whole they might serve as an improved plan for a small congested city's streets—carries the stem through a gauntlet of huge saws—head rig, twin saw, multiple saw—until all that was round has become rectangular. It's lumber then and headed for the trimmer-optimizer, the sorter, the kiln (one of Pinkham's nine kilns), where it sits for three days in moist tropical heat, which must be administered with care, lest the surface of the lumber dry faster than the innards and the wood crack and check. It goes to another building, through the "tilt hoist breakdown," then board by board down still more conveyer belts, through a planer and past the all-important graders, two Pinkham employees who sit beside the line with crayons, recording on the boards their opinions of them. Then down another belt into another machine, which knocks the lumber into a package, squaring up the ends with sharp jolts as if the big cube of boards were a deck of cards. With the help of one last machine, workers wrap the package in Pinkham waterproof paper and neatly fold the ends.

The new mill turns about 45 percent of each log into lumber. All the rest falls down toward the bottom floor and almost all of it is caught, the bark to be burned at the steam plant for heating the kilns, the buildings, and hot pond, and the scraps of wood and sawdust to be transported to a pulp mill. The saws in the mill, guided partly by lasers and computers, can make every cut to within two-thousandths of an inch of a specified dimension.

As most brand-new Sunday carpenters discover with surprise, a two-by-four is not two inches thick and four wide, but by the standard adopted in 1960, one and a half by three and a half inches. The term "two-by-four" used to describe the approximate size to which a board was sawn before its size was reduced by drying and planing. Mills like Pinkham's newer one make "two-by-four" an artifact. They don't need half an inch of margin. Their two-by-fours never measure two by four, but are rough-cut to one and three-quarters by three and three-quarters. It is a remarkably precise machine, this mill, one of those testaments to the power of thinking ahead. It needs only a handful of people to keep it running, just thirty-six per shift, and on a good day two shifts can guide through about half a million board feet, 1000 cords, the harvest of 100 acres or so. It's a

West Coast sawmill essentially, a piece of western technology brought to the underdeveloped East. When it's tuned just right, this mill can make 1100 board feet out of 1000 crudely measured feet of standing timber. A man who used to work for Pinkham in the summers as a boy remembers that working hard and steadily with old, rudimentary equipment, he and one other lad could do merely one one-thousandth of the work that this mill's sorting machinery, with two attendants, does today. Precision and speed in sawing and handling may make sense at the edge of a huge forest and in a time of strong competition. Clearly, a mill like Pinkham's saves a great deal in labor costs, and it spends a lot of the savings on fuel, highways, interest. The stacks of packaged finished lumber, big as houses, which from time to time accumulate near the railroad tracks, make it clear that risks accompany the creation of so much mechanical advantage, in an industry that depends on the rising-falling sine curve of housing starts. The wholesale price of lumber has fluctuated wildly in the 1980s, from one month to another. Some months Pinkham lacks buyers who will take their lumber off their lot at a price that even pays their costs—this in spite of the fact that Pinkham has the reputation of turning out the best dimension-stock softwood in the East.

Quality in framing lumber rests on the quality of the trees selected and of the mill that saws and dries the wood. Quality also has to do with the instructions that the bosses give to those graders who sit out near the very end of the line. A sawmill that belongs to the Northeastern Lumber Manufacturers Association is allowed in theory to send out packages of lumber that contain no more than 5 percent of subpar pieces, subpar usually meaning improperly grained and therefore weak wood or boards that are excessively waney (lacking in wood at the edges). Some mills shoot for that 5 percent, and as all lumber dealers know, some end up shipping 10 percent or more substandard lumber in their packages. At least several lumber retailers in western Massachusetts, including Apple Corps's supplier, will pay $15 more for a thousand feet of Pinkham's wood than for wood from other eastern manufacturers. A load of bad lumber might cost retailers more than that, if not directly in unsalable wood, then in angry customers to whom they've passed on the subpar stuff.

The white spruce trees that have ended up in Amherst as two-by-tens cost Pinkham $113 when they stood in the forest. Pinkham sold the 2833 board feet to a wholesaler for $880. By the time it reached Amherst, the pile of floor joists and girders cost $1154, less the 5 percent that Apple Corps gets back from their supplier if they pay their bills on time. Between mill and house site, the price of the lumber increased about 77 percent. About 28 percent of that went to transportation, another 4 to 14 percent to the wholesaler, and the rest to the lumberyard, which has had to carry the wood in inventory, store it, and deliver it.

5

Each time Alex slices the end off a two-by-ten, a whiff of the Big Woods comes out. The aroma hangs in the air all day. After a day of carrying the lumber here and there, the carpenters' hands have grown sticky with pitch. It might be the blood you find in the cellophane package of a steak. The pitch reminds you that the wood came from something living. It would be easy otherwise to forget that lumber is a piece of tree, but the *treeness* of lumber is the salient fact about framing. It informs all of the accumulated wisdom and scientific data behind the lumber-grading books and building codes that speak to the issue of sturdiness in houses. A tree can grow tall, withstanding gravity and bending instead of breaking in the wind, because its fibers are very strong in compression and in tension. You can't easily crush those fibers—shorten a piece of wood. And it's even harder to pull a piece of wood apart along its grain. A proper frame for a house reproduces treeness. Studs standing vertically in a wall are trees in compression, withstanding gravity. The underpinnings of a floor—girders and joists laid horizontally on one edge—are trees in the wind as people walk over the floors above. A girder or a joist, properly laid out, will scarcely bend at all if it is as hefty as it ought to be, but it will bend a great deal before it breaks. Jim could have consulted his book of stress tables to learn the proper sizes for the pieces of the frame. This time, an engineer, hired by Bill, has already done most of that job for Jim.

After the sills come the girders and joists, the underpinnings for the plywood, on which the finished floors in turn will rest. Alex and Ned construct the girders on sawhorses, nailing together, sandwich-style, three layers of spruce boards. Ned's face pales slightly with every stroke. He puts down his hammer, and with his combination square, Ned checks to see that the upper surface of each constructed beam is flat and smooth, or as he puts it, "nice." Laminated, the lumber becomes beams, each one too long and heavy for one man to lift. Richard assumes command of the girders' installation.

Richard studies Jim's framing plan, scratches his head under his cap, and says, "I don't think I ever did any framing quite like this before."

The girders span the width of the house, all thirty feet of it, and Jim had the foundation builder make pockets in the concrete wall for the ends of each girder to rest upon. All except for one girder. Complexity arises because of the sunken living room floor. Jim's solution is a short, especially stout girder to hold up both the hearth and two other sections of girder—one end of each of those partial girders to rest in a pocket in the foundation and the other end of each to rest upon the stouter girder, which will rest upon two concrete-filled metal Lally columns, each of *them* resting on cement pads poured onto undisturbed earth underneath what will be the basement floor. To install these girders on top of girders, Apple Corps needs to perform an act of levitation, with Richard as magician and the others the volunteers from the audience. Richard studies the foundation, goes back to study the framing plan, says, "I'll have this under control in a minute," and at last declares, "Oh-*Kay!* I was confused there for a minute. Can everybody dive down in the cellar for a minute? Then I won't get hurt. Otherwise, I might get hurt."

They erect the odd configuration, three pairs of arms held high while Richard scurries around. He tunes up the girder-on-a-girder, centering and leveling the beams. Then Richard on his ladder "temporaries" it, nailing two-by-fours between this construction and the sills to keep the thing from falling over.

"I'll put *two* nails in these temporaries," Richard says.

"You're getting cautious, Richard," says Alex. "You ought to go into banking."

Richard snorts. "Now what?"

"Put the other girders in," says Alex.

"It seems . . ." says Richard.

"Anticlimactic," says Alex.

"Symmetrical to the max," says Ned, staring down at the construction at the center of the frame. It looks simple, now that it exists:

(see following page)

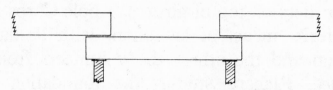

"Moosey," says Jim. "But you won't think it's so much when you see what we're putting on it."

The rest is comparatively easy: Install two other girders, then the floor joists; some of which run over the girders, some of which run flush into their sides. The carpenters crown each joist. That is to say, they sight down the narrow edges of every two-by-ten, to see in which direction each is bent. None is ever perfectly straight, and the eye, what Jim calls "the original laser," can pick up the variations down to about a thirty-second of an inch. They make sure that the crowned edges of all joists face up, so that the joists will bend toward straightness as people walk across the floors in years to come.

Everything else is measuring, cutting, nailing. They move around the sandy ground, carrying the first deck, piece by piece, to the gray rectangle at the center of their outdoor factory of pickup trucks, sawhorses, stacks of lumber, cartons of nails. Soon floor joists begin to cover the space above the cellar hole, like bars above a cage. Jim dances out onto the joists, tightrope walking. Deliberately, he makes the joists wobble from side to side and performs the part of a Charleston that involves the knees. The generator putts. Hammers driving 16-penny nails ring like high-pitched bells, deepening with every stroke. Sometimes the carpenters syncopate their hammers, but that's by accident. The melodious whistling of "Turkey in the Straw"—that comes from Jim.

"Toenails are better than no nails," he shouts.

"Toenails are better than no nails, huh? I don't know about you, Jim. I think Jim's going to need a room with pads on the walls, by the time this job gets done." That's Richard.

The singing in a slightly sour note is Alex's, and the diabolical laughter comes from Richard, as do the occasional startling sounds of planks being dropped, for Richard rarely lets an opportunity to make noise slip by. The quiet and serious one is Ned. Only Richard can bring a laugh from Ned just now. When Ned is asked how his hammer arm feels, he snaps, "I ignore it. You should, too." Clearly, his arm aches, and so do other parts of him as well, but no one talks of pain to Ned again. "We're winning!" and "We're gainin' on it!" Those exclamations come from Richard. The voices you most often hear when you close your eyes and listen to them working belong to Richard and Alex.

After Dartmouth, Alex worked as an advance man in Senator Eugene McCarthy's presidential campaign and as a reporter in New Hampshire, first for a local paper, then for the *Boston Globe*. He was a good journalist. He is a meticulous, hard-working carpenter. What he loves most is farming. Alex has a little farm between the Connecticut and Deerfield rivers. He supports it by carpentry. It was Alex who put up the $2000 that got Apple Corps in business a decade ago. His partners call him chubby, though he isn't really stout, and there's a gentleness about him, a country doctor's air, that would make him suitable for pushing pharmaceuticals on TV. He drives up to the site in his pickup in the morning, with his huge and floppy-eared, dark red Irish Setter, Brewster, sitting shoulder to shoulder beside him. Brewster looks like some cheerful, slightly dimwitted young apprentice in a dog suit. Brewster is a handsome beast. "Brewster," Alex says, "could be the model for statues outside of libraries. I'm going to enter him in the Purina Dog Chow competition." Alex keeps a bed, made for dogs by L. L. Bean, in the back of his truck. This amuses Richard. So does Alex's bumper sticker. Alex is not a vegetarian, but his bumper sticker says:

Love Animals Don't Eat Them
—THE FRUITARIAN NETWORK

Once, years ago, while driving home from work with Richard, Alex put an anti-handgun poster on the front door of the Ashfield Rod and Gun Club, of which Richard is a member in good standing. Alex also took out in Richard's name a subscription to a magazine called *Compassion*. Alex holds a girder steady, while Richard temporaries it and Richard says, "The thing of it is, *Compassion* went bankrupt."

"It shows you where our nation's priorities lie," says Alex.

"And the NRA's getting stronger," says Richard.

"Pain," says Alex. "The pain of animals. It's all going to come back, Richard. It's all accumulating, like the national debt."

Richard heads for the stack of plywood. Sawing plywood for the floors with his skillsaw—the term began as a brand name, Skilsaw, and now seems to be used for every make of hand-held power saw—Richard wonders how many cuts they make to build a house. Maybe, he thinks, they should put little odometers on their skillsaws, and somehow that reminds him of how often, when a tool is lost, the missing item turns up in Alex's box.

"The charge that I gather up my partners' tools is totally unjustified," Alex calls out. "But what can you do about myth?"

Jim stands over at another side of the first-floor deck, laying out a bay of floor joists. He places the blade of his square across the girder, draws a line against the blade with the framing pencil, marks an *X* on the side of the line where the joist should rest, and moves on. As he works, Jim remembers Alex calling out to Richard once, "Hey, Richard, this flatbar here in my box has three little notches in it, just like the one you used to have." And Jim remembers Richard shouting, "That's because it is the one I used to have, Alex."

"This is embarrassing," says Richard now from

over by the sawhorses. "I just lost my whole skillsaw. Alex, where's my skillsaw?"

The bottom deck of the house begins to cover the cellar hole. The house becomes a platform. The days are growing warm. The work runs smoothly. Jim stands at a lumber pile, studying plans. Over on the deck, Alex asks why it is that Richard's trousers always sag, revealing the cleavage of his buttocks. Jim smiles, listens, and studies his plans.

"Levi's don't fit me right. If I get a waist that fits, the legs don't," Richard explains.

"That's because a person with your size waist is supposed to have longer legs."

"That wasn't fair. A short joke on Wednesday morning."

As a rule, Richard turns off the generator and announces, "Lunchtime!" Usually Richard has the most to look forward to at lunch. Alex has often said he wishes that Lindy would agree to serve as the official Apple Corps pastry chef. "Strawberry-rhubarb pie. Chocolate upside-down cake," intones Alex, remembering his sojourns at Lindy's table.

"Gee, Alex, I have three pieces of Lindy cake to eat in front of you. Unless you have something to trade."

According to an article that Jim has read in *Fine Woodworking*, accidents in shops most often occur after lunch. "So if you eat a big lunch, you take your chances afterward," Jim says. Everyone remembers the time, a couple of years back, when the woman next door to the house Richard was working on brought him a piece of cake, because Richard had stopped on his way to work to pull her out of a snowbank. A little later on, Richard was straightening out a piece of molding, thinking about the importance of good deeds and about that piece of cake, and he forgot about his trailing hand. He plunged it in among the spinning blades beneath the jointer's bench. For a couple of weeks he went around with a white club for a hand, and for a few weeks more, Lindy would awaken and find Richard lying at military attention, with his eyes wide open, staring at jointers in the dark.

Food may be risky at construction sites, but lunch is the reward for a good morning's work. At lunch, they take stock. Sometimes they do business. They sit together on the deck, cross-legged in a circle. With mock sneakiness, Richard slowly withdraws from his wicker lunch basket, the one that's just like Alex's, a check at last received from one of the winter's customers. Richard folds the check into a paper airplane and floats it to Alex, who catches it and says, as if he's found a butterfly, "A kited check."

Alex, who serves as company treasurer this year, passes around the new ink-pad stamps he says he plans to apply to customers' bills, but won't, of course. One stamp says, "Pay or Die," and the other, over a picture of a man encumbered with several casts, warns, "Penalty for Late Payment."

Jim wonders whether Alex should send one of

those to Jonathan. Would Jonathan take it wrong? Would Jim feel pleased or sorry, if he did?

They lean back, reclining on fresh lumber, amid smells of wood and fruit, and one of them asks, "Anything horrible in the paper, Alex?"

Alex brings the *New York Times* to work, and often he reads to his partners after lunch, usually from the section called "Metropolitan Reports," which Alex calls "Murders and Mayhem."

"There's a great bank robbery story here. A guy held up a bank. He gave the teller a note on the back of an envelope that had his name and address on it. The quality of crime is going downhill."

"Well," says Jim, "burnin' daylight."

"We better get back to work," says Richard, "before we have to *winch* Alex back on his feet."

The days of framing go quickly by. Richard says it's only four-thirty. He wants to stay and work some more. Alex wants to leave. Alex must be wealthy. "People who are rich want to go home."

Alex straightens haughtily. "Those of us who don't have armories in our living rooms can afford to go home, Richard."

When they put plywood on the joists and studs covering the cellar hole, they fasten the sheets with only a few nails, and then, while the others move on to other tasks, one of them fastens the plywood securely with a pneumatic staple gun. They came across this technology a few years back when repairing a fairly new house. Its builders had used staples to fasten the plywood to the exterior walls and Apple Corps could pull that plywood off with their hands, the staples made such poor fastenings. They assumed they would never use such junk themselves. Staples had improved, though, and now were strong enough. Nailing plywood down had always bored them. Ned already owned a compressor. They needed to buy only the staple gun. They weren't in their midtwenties anymore, either. "When your arm gives out, you turn on the compressor," says Ned, doing just that.

Richard learned the trade in large part from old-timers, as he likes to say, and for many years he carried in his toolbox a ball of string and a piece of soft chalk, for snapping long straight lines. When he went to work for a contractor, Richard found all the other carpenters using modern chalk lines, one-piece devices in which the string winds by crank into a fist-sized housing that you fill with chalk from a bottle. With that tool, the other carpenters could strike a line at least ten times faster than Richard, laboriously chalking up his string. Chalked lines are merely temporary guides. The ones the modern tool made were not of inferior quality to Richard's. A line's a line, he figured. So Richard threw his ball of string and piece of chalk away. Richard was raised in the trade to believe that a good carpenter always kept at least three handsaws in his box: a crosscut saw for cutting across the grain, a ripsaw for cutting with the grain, and a many-toothed finish saw for delicate work. He used the finish saw often, but never the other two. Electric saws did the old saws' work, at high speed and with precision. Richard carried those two handsaws around for years, waiting for a chance to make some sensible use of them. The chance never came. Finally, just last year, he began leaving them at home.

The carpenters of Apple Corps, within the span of their own careers, have abandoned, usually without remorse, many little pieces of the past. A lot of what they have always used is modern, of course. Jim buys a new bit for his router and, examining it, remarks that this new cutting head will doubtless go dull after just a few uses.

"They don't make 'em like they used to," someone says in passing.

"They didn't used to make 'em," Jim replies.

Their routers and the wide variety of cutting heads that tool will accommodate take the place of the many hand-held molding planes that used to be an important part of a housejoiner's kit. Usually, the carpenters don't even use their routers, because most of their moldings come from the lumberyard. For all of that, their modern building site makes an odd, mixed-up place in time.

Terms Apple Corps uses routinely while kneeling on new joists and standing on stepladders seem to identify the sources of many familiar figures of speech. Making things level and straight is essential for giving customers square deals. Going against the grain is always a mistake; the act of partitioning divides up houses as well as nations; sore thumbs make their presence felt. The names of most basic pieces of a house—joists, studs, sashes, collar ties—have not changed for centuries. Richard could sit on the deck of this growing house and talk shop with Calvin Stearns. Richard's portable radio tuned to country and western music ("Go get 'em, Willie," he cries absentmindedly), he pulls from one of the leather pouches at his waist a nail called a 16-penny nail because centuries ago it cost 16 English pennies to buy 100 nails this size, and with several crisp, rhythmic blows of his hammer, he implants that 16-penny common nail into a spruce joist that is called a two-by-ten only because some decades back lumber was sawn roughly to those dimensions. Richard's framing hammer, a large 22-ounce one—"Especially if you're short, you need a big framing hammer"—incorporates significant improvements in the fastening of head to handle. Otherwise, it looks identical to the claw hammers Roman carpenters left behind. The nail is also a venerable device. The ancient Chinese made nails, and so did Thomas Jefferson's slaves. Humanity has probably made nails ever since the dawn of metalworking, and nails have undergone many important transformations, but the most significant of those has been the change in their abundance, an alteration that helped to create the general technique of framing that Richard, pounding in that nail, employs. That technique of framing has led to Richard's easy, practiced stroke—he grips the handle full-fistedly, whereas many part-time carpenters lay a thumb along the shaft for control and reassurance. And that framing technique, more than all the power tools or devices like the modern chalk line Richard carries in a pocket on his belt, makes him a modern carpenter.

According to current research, modern American house construction probably began in the fall of 1832, when a man named George Snow built a warehouse in Chicago. If Snow could have done so, he probably would have built a post-and-beam frame for his warehouse. But that method required large timbers and also carpenters trained in chiseling complex wooden joints and experienced at raising heavy frames. Snow would have had a hard time laying his hands on such wood and workers in 1832 in Chicago. Only 150 people lived there then, and they had already taken the few large trees within easy reach of the town. What Snow could easily obtain were thin lengths of wood. So he put his warehouse together with lumber that, compared to New England's posts and beams, resembled sticks. He assembled the frame with the ancestors of the dimension-stock two-by-four. He placed those sticks close together, making many thin pieces of wood take the place of a few hefty timbers, and fastening the pieces to each other with nails.

Blacksmiths used to make nails one at a time, so nails had been fairly scarce and expensive. In Massachusetts Bay, a trove of one or two thousand nails was once property worth listing in a house-joiner's estate. No one knows how many nails went into the warehouse in Chicago—the building had long since disappeared by the time its importance was understood—but two thousand nails would barely get you started in constructing a typical American house. A modern house of about 2000 square feet takes something like seventy-five thousand nails. Mass production of nails had begun about thirty years before Snow built his warehouse. He had kegs of nails at his disposal. Manufactured nails were a necessary ingredient for his invention, among other reasons because his lumber was too thin to accommodate mortises and tenons. In this sense, the balloon frame, as Snow's invention is called, is one of the products of the Industrial Revolution. It ranks among the important ones.

Architectural historians, the ones who search for social history in buildings, generally agree that balloon framing made possible the rapid settling of the treeless, often carpenter-poor lands west of Chicago. Evidently, Snow did not invent balloon framing out of whole cloth. The technique evolved from others. Within about seventy years, balloon framing had caught on everywhere. With minor modifications, it remains the technique in widest use today. It helped to make housing booms possible, in the face of rising costs for labor and materials. Stick construction allowed for the use of a wide variety of trees, of wood that could be easily found and standardized. It reduced, by roughly half, the total volume of wood needed for a sturdy frame. A balloon frame could be made more quickly and erected with fewer hands than a frame of posts and beams.

Some architectural historians also think that stick construction debased the craft of house carpentry by making framing easy. Balloon framing does require simpler joints than post-and-beam techniques, but it also requires a lot more of them. In balloon framing every joint matters, and laying out a stick-constructed frame is certainly a more complicated operation than laying out one of posts and beams. In an essay called "Carpentry: The Craft and the Trade," a builder named Bob Reckman argues that the occupation has not suffered from the new tools and techniques in the carpenter's box and repertoire. He worries instead about the disappearance of such tasks as door and window making, and the carpenter's loss of control over building sites to architects, engineers, speculators, and general contractors. For their numbers, carpenters make up a disproportionately large percentage of American workers who are described as highly skilled. But carpenters have long since ceded their pre-eminent positions on large-scale building projects. And housebuilding, the last stronghold of American carpenters, is afflicted, Reckman writes, by a well-established and growing tendency toward specialization. Increasingly, the organization of a housebuilding site resembles that of an assembly line. Others organize, design, and finance the work from a distance. Out on the job, young carpenters don't learn how to build houses but how to hang prefabricated doors or lay floors or put up cabinets. Meanwhile, actual factories turn out roofs and walls and floors and also entire houses, in precut and partially assembled packages.

As soon as railroads existed, Americans could buy houses out of mail-order catalogues and have them shipped cross-country. Factory-produced housing has been around a long time. It has flourished and nearly died and lately it has revived. Today, prefabricated wooden structures and mobile homes claim a shifting but substantial share of the market in new housing. Over the past ten years they accounted for about 20 percent of all new houses.

It is worth remembering that production line techniques helped to answer the post-World War II housing shortage and that people who can afford better are usually the ones who despise mobile homes and conspire to make this an outcast kind of housing, through anti-trailer-house zoning. Perhaps the factory should own a larger share of the housing business than it does. At least in theory, the assembly line approach to building can keep down costs. The approach can keep down carpenters, too.

Alone among Apple Corps, Ned Krutsky has worked as a carpenter on versions of the production line. When he moved to Massachusetts, he got a job with a developer who was managing the building of condominium apartments in Amherst.

The foreman put Ned on the baseboard beat. Day after day for about two weeks, Ned was sent forth from the office to places named 8C, 10D, 25G, to work on baseboard after baseboard. Baseboards are for Ned the dullest, least rewarding part of finish work, something he can do cheerfully only if it's a part of his total task. Here, baseboards were his only task. He was lonely, too. After a while, he could not concentrate. One morning he accidentally put a nail through a water pipe behind a wall and the foreman told him, "I don't need you anymore." Ned felt relieved and humiliated all at once. He also needed a job. He ended up at a real factory next. There, he began the day by punching in. Then he proceeded to a wire, pawnshop-like cage. The man at the counter behind the cage issued him a hammer and a nail apron. Ned spent the morning nailing together precut pieces of roof trusses. The way the other workers used power tools amazed and frightened him. Somehow, he felt he had to explain himself to the man behind the cage. "I can't do this" was all he could say, though, when he turned in his hammer and apron that noon. He saw himself as crazy and shiftless, and he remembers how red his ears felt when he hurried out of that place.

The mills of Massachusetts were the destinations of most French-Canadian immigrants to the state, and many of Richard's relatives have spent their working lives in them. Factory work was his heritage, Richard thinks. He only narrowly avoided it, in part because of trade school and also because

206

his parents warned him early—"It isn't healthy for you." "I feel real fortunate," he says, one warm May afternoon while erecting Lally columns in the coolness of the basement. "I'm real glad it's not the same thing every day."

Arguing against the industrialization of the craft, some builders promote a post-and-beam revival. Schools have sprung up to teach versions of that old technique to people who want to build houses for themselves. Some professionals build this way, too. Authenticity varies. Some plane their beams and cut their mortises and tenons by hand, with fine old antique tools from the golden age of woodworking. Some use power tools and a lot of metal fastenings. The results are often comely, sturdy buildings, with chamfered beams exposed in living rooms, real beams that have real functions besides the ornamental one.

Behind this way of building lies a supposition that good old days existed. In *The Framed Houses of Massachusetts Bay, 1625-1725*, the classic work on early building in New England, Abbott Lowell Cummings allows that fine and versatile craftsmen did indeed once inhabit the region. But Cummings says he has grown weary of "the notion that the early craftsman could do no wrong." He writes of one Colonial builder who was constantly being haled into court, to answer charges that he'd made a floor so sloppily a person could put his hands between the boards, that he'd used badly splintered wood, that he'd built a windmill " 'not soficiently undarpined' nor tightly covered." Answering the charges about the windmill, this old-time craftsman's son said that he and his father "did not care 'If the Divell had the windmill' as long as they got their money."

Reverence for builders of the post-and-beam tradition arises from the examples of sturdy work they left behind, but then again it's the sturdy work that survives. The examples of high craftsmanship, ones that have stood for centuries, aren't distinguished by the framing technique so much as by the care with which builders applied it. Those old houses are distinguished, as Jim would say, by the rectitude of their carpenters. And although modern materials, such as concrete and plywood, as well as scientific data about the strengths of woods and structural arrangements, have made it easier to build a durable frame today than formerly, there's still room for rectitude in framing.

Jim and Alex painted the outside of the foundation with tar before the bulldozer returned and pushed the dirt back up against the walls. The tar will help to keep the basement dry. They placed insulation under the sills; the house will be cozier for it. The crowning of every floor joist will tend to keep the floors from sagging over the years. The contract required none of that specifically, but those little pains they've taken, and many others like them, constitute good and reasonable building practice. As for precision in framing, in cutting, measuring, nailing, Jim insists that it will make the finish work go smoothly.

One Saturday, working alone on the house—these days his only escape from anxiety seems to lie in working on the object of his worry—Jim says, "It's a great feeling to realize you know as much as most people about something. I don't feel like we're really a business success yet. But we're doing fine with the carpentry. What we admire, what we emulate, are things done a long time ago. We're not trying to break new ground, but we're trying to get good enough so we can emulate the masters of a hundred years ago. If we're stubborn enough and good enough, we should be able to get there. I often think that's one of the differences between us and a lot of other builders, between a good and a not-so-good job. Often it's just screwing around with something a bit longer." Jim has spoken too openly for comfort. He adds, "That fits nicely with my natural inclination to fuss around with things a little bit longer than necessary. It's good to have your theories support your actions."

When the partners of Apple Corps argue on this job, the dispute often has to do, on the surface anyway, with disagreements on technique and differences in speed. Alex and especially Ned can spend so much time setting up to do a job it makes Jim's teeth itch. Occasionally, Alex gets annoyed with Richard and Ned with Jim, for just the opposite reason. A couple of years ago, Alex scolded Ned fiercely for presuming to question work that Alex was doing. So it seemed to Alex. Ned thought he was only trying to help. Alex and

Ned did not work together alone for nearly a year afterward. Left to himself, each works at a different pace. Richard moves most swiftly through a job, but Richard usually can't work and talk at the same time, so he works fast intermittently. Jim, who rivals Richard for speed, will squander time studying a list of materials, and he'll stop at nearly every chance he gets to discuss literature and politics with a client. In the end, they all accomplish about the same amount in a day. For framing, they have learned a happy medium. Now it usually prevails.

All around them, the hills and fields take on a deepening green. The bulldozed ground dries out and becomes a little desert, and at the center, the gray-walled rectangle and the blond wood that rises from it, in arrays of intersecting lines and planes, look more than ever like an assertion about order. The carpenters, in jeans and T-shirts now, roam the perimeter in ones and twos, bringing lumber and tools and coffee to the shrine. Richard declares he no longer feels the stiffness that his joints acquired the first week of framing. "We're gainin' on it!"

Framing consists of two- and three- and four-man jobs. Each knows what to expect and what's expected from the person on the other end of the board. Jim orders the wood that Alex cuts that Richard and Ned install, in the spots that Jim specifies. Most of the tasks are as familiar as Richard's stories, which he shares with them while they share the framing. Framing is communal labor and rarely lonely, the way finish work can be. Framing is a repetition of tasks, which last long enough for each, except for Jim, to lose himself and put to sleep the parts of his mind that worry about the mortgage and the children. But no task seems endless. Almost always some new kind of job, requiring new forethought, awaits them in the morning or, at the latest, next week. Framing gets results. Work hard for a day, and a huge pile of two-by-tens becomes a floor. While framing, they don't have to wonder if they've earned their pay. They can gaze at all they've accomplished, as they often do when they've taken down their factory at the end of the day, stopping a moment and looking at all they've added to the box full of geometry that has grown out of the sand. A frame is nice to look at. Like a hammer or a bridge, it shows you how it works. Standing in the cool basement, Richard pauses to look up at all the joists and girders, an exercise in geometry class executed in wood. Richard thinks back to that forbidding-looking framing plan and he says, "It doesn't look nearly as complicated now. When you start building, it makes sense."

Builders have loved the framing for a long time. The clearest evidence lies inside old barns, in the huge barns of the Pennsylvania Dutch, in the Shakers' extraordinary round barns, in the chestnut frames of the tobacco barns of the Connecticut River Valley. There's a horse barn in rural Delaware in which some nineteenth-century carpenters left behind a frame of timber braces that look like arrays of pinwheels, a piece of work so stylish and idiosyncratic it could pass for sculpture. It's easy to imagine why a builder might approach the framing of a barn with exuberance and care. In a barn, all the handiwork will be left uncovered, for everyone to see. It is harder to understand why appearance matters in a house's frame, one destined to be covered over by walls, ceilings, and floors.

"In my experience, what looks well works well," Ned says, by way of explaining why he wants the ends of ceiling joists to meet the rim plate just so.

Richard tells Alex, who is cutting a ceiling joist, to stop worrying over a thirty-second of an inch. It will not show or make any other difference here. "It doesn't matter if it doesn't show," retorts Alex. "It ought to be right."

Richard is the most practical one. Richard says to himself, in consternation at Alex, but out of Alex's earshot, "When you work for a contractor you learn not to be too fussy where you cut your wood. If you're only cutting one or two boards, you don't set up horses or the radial arm saw. You find a stack of two-by-fours and use it as a workbench." But Richard also says, "The right way is the hard way," and later, looking down from the field upon the growing building, he muses, "We're fussing with it a little bit. Well, this deserves being fussed on. It's going to sit here a hundred years, at least."

Bernie Herman, an expert on the vernacular architecture of Delaware, who pokes around and catalogues old houses about to be torn down, has a note found in a can sealed in above a porch ceiling. The message reads:

William W. Rose in closed this on November 25th, 1850. On the night of the 23rd of the same month Josiah Ridgeways dwelling house and storehouse and wheelwright shop was burnt down on the corner And this frame suffered from the same fier. With difficulty it was savd. I in close this that when this house is wore out the repairer will know how long it was bilt. James Stevens had this house bilt. He was a Blacksmith by trad the best ax man of that time. William W. Rose was the bilder.

Jim has started leaving messages himself. In lumber crayon, on a scrap of crown molding, Jim writes:

This House Built
for Jonathan and Judith
Souweine
May–Sept. 1983
By
Apple Corps
Builders
Apple Valley
Ashfield, Mass.
For $146,000 By:
Alex Ghiselin
Richard Gougeon

Edward Krutsky
Jim Locke
June 18, 1983

Jim nails the piece of molding in a corner where, once the house is done, no one but another builder doing repair work is likely to find it. It's a note adrift in a bottle, a message sent across time to another carpenter who does not yet exist but who will perhaps understand the gesture and appreciate the work. Jim says nothing of the message. Richard comes upon it by accident. He says he knows that Jim will need a room with padded walls now. Richard does not disturb Jim's letter to the future, though.

Richard has spent a great deal of his professional career repairing old houses. He has found a lot of cobby-looking framing, particularly under the elegant façades of Victorian porches. He has also come upon hidden joinery that could, with some sanding and planing, serve as cabinetwork. "Some did good, some didn't," he says. "The old-timers put a lot of shims in the framing, because their lumber was rough cut and it wasn't closely sized. Nowadays everything's sized so close that you can make your framing *real* close." Often, as Richard pauses on the job to catch hold of a stray thought, he muses out loud about the old-timers and what they would think of Apple Corps's work. Then sometimes he leans on his hammer and tries to imagine how he and his partners will be judged by the carpenters who will follow them into this building. Meditation on the future is an old joke in their community, one they pull out when they are taking leave of one section of completed work—"Good enough. Gotta leave the next bunch of beavers something to do, right?"

Apple Corps has nothing to hide when, the second week of framing, the building inspector visits. Richard, for one, looks forward to that person's visits. "We never had any trouble with building inspectors. They're builders. They know what's goin' on." This inspector comes when the bottom deck is well under way. "I like to see this," the inspector remarks, of the pressure-treated sills. He nods over the girders and joists and initials his approval on the requisite form.

They do not have many other callers. The first morning of framing, Jonathan came by the muddy site at a little before seven, expecting to find the builders there, laying down the first wood for his and Judith's new home. It would have made the sort of small ceremonial occasion Jonathan savors. Jim and the others had not yet arrived, though, and Jonathan had to get to his office. Speaking to Judith a little later on, Jonathan made a joke about the missed connection. Judith passes it on to Jim when she visits, briefly, later that morning. The others have not met her yet, and they hang back, while Jim leaves the foundation and goes to greet her. Smiling, he says, "I know. You changed your mind. You want a thirty-by-thirty-six ranch."

Judith makes her merry laugh. "Jonathan was

215

here this morning. He said, 'They must be Jewish builders. I thought Protestant builders were always at work by seven.' "

Jim smiles faintly, but after she leaves, he says, "Protestant carpenters. Is that what you call being razzed?" He takes up his hammer and star chisel. Squatting on the foundation wall, he gets ready to carve into the cement the girder pocket he forgot about in his plan. "The six hundred and sixty dollars," he says. "It all translates to power anyway, no matter what the ethnic tradition. It's who's on top and who's not . . . I'm not going to tell them I'm half-Jewish. I may need to use that someday." He delivers a few ringing blows to his chisel. Chips of concrete fly. "I don't know," he goes on, a ripple of laughter that doesn't sound real in his voice. "It's a good thing to think about when you're cutting holes in concrete, because it makes you stick with it."

Pausing in his work a few days later, Jim says, "A lot of people would be more comfortable with us if we worked purely for the profit motive. I think Jonathan would be a lot more comfortable if he understood what we're up to that way."

But Jim has little way of knowing now what Jonathan does or does not understand. The frame of the house is rising, and the carpenters and their clients seem to be drifting toward the condition of strangers. In the mornings, Jim finds around the site small neat piles of nails, ones they have bent and discarded, and also evidence that someone has been clearing out the undergrowth in the woods

216

beside the brook, and he guesses that the Souweines have come by in the evenings, their children collecting nails while Jonathan clears brush.

They get used to seeing Judith regularly but for now usually just in passing. Jonathan they see less often. Once, after they have spent most of a day working in the rain, Florence Wiener invites the damp, muddy crew into her kitchen for coffee, and they come away murmuring about Judith's mother's graciousness and wit. The person they see most often for now is Judith's father, Jules. He drops by nearly every day, and stays awhile.

Jules is of middling height, a fit and very active sixty-year-old. He's smoking cigars these days. He's reveling in his retirement. It's an even bet as to whether he's doing more now than he was when he was officially working. He does a little law for Jonathan's firm, serves on a local committee or two, breeds racehorses, studies racing sheets, builds fences, mows and plants with his hired man. Jules's time belongs to him, though, and he likes to spend some of it with the builders.

"Hey, Jules, do you mind if we use the phone in your barn?" calls Jim from his perch on a girder.

"No. Just leave a thousand-dollar deposit," says Jules with a grin.

Jules stands beside the foundation. "Somebody told me you guys whistled and sang like the seven dwarfs."

Alex is laying floor joists with Richard. He

looks at Richard and says, "Only one of us has the physiognomy of a dwarf."

Richard glowers at Alex. Richard grins.

Jules watches the carpenters work. Some joists, those for the sunken living room floor, butt into the girders. That is, the tops of the joists are flush with the tops of the beams. The building code allows flush joists to be fastened to girders with metal hangers or else with strips of wood called ledgers. In the second approach, you spike the ledgers to the beams and notch the joists so that they rest on the ledgers. Apple Corps favors ledgers, the wooden option.

"Hey, Jim," calls Jules. "You're not using any hangers."

"No," says Jim, standing out on one of the thin joists above the cellar hole. "This is better. All wood."

"Oh, hell yes," says Richard. "This is a lot better." Richard climbs down to the basement.

"Hangers are stronger, I think," says Jules.

"We like wood," says Jim.

"I know you do," says Jules. "But hangers are better."

"Hangers look like shit," says Jim.

"Yeah," says Jules, knocking the ash from his cigar. "But who's going to see them?"

Jim goes back to work. Some minutes later, Jules returns to the subject. "This whole living room is hanging on those cleats," he says to Jim.

"Where's the piano going, Jules?" says Jim, a little wearily. "Right here," Jim says, pointing

218

with his hammer to a corner of the floor frame. "It'll have a good home. I'll come and stand under it."

"What's the matter?" asks Richard, poking his head up from the cellar.

"I'm not thrilled with those cleats," says Jules.

"You mean the ledgers?" says Richard.

"Call them what you will," says Jules.

Aside, out of the carpenters' hearing, Jules says, "Jonathan won't be around much. He doesn't know anything about building. I know a little." He smiles, installs his cigar. "Just enough to be dangerous."

Jules is wrong about ledgers, which may not be as strong as hangers but are more than strong enough. But Jules knows more than Jules lets on. He made a prosperous career out of lawyering for builders and developers on Long Island, and he knows a great deal about the business side of building and about standard building practices. He knows more than anyone in Apple Corps about those subjects, and about the general level of care most contractors feel is necessary in the framing of a house. Letting the issue of the ledgers drop, Jules stands silently beside the foundation and watches Jim work. Jim is completing the framing around what will become the hearth. He has to join one piece of wood to another on an angle greater than ninety degrees. He has to make an angled joint—a miter joint—in the frame. Tongue protruding, Jim makes the mitered cuts on the ends of a piece of two-by-ten and puts the board in place, but he doesn't nail it there. Evidently, Jim doesn't like the way it fits.

Jules watches, surprised. Jim tosses that board away and cuts another. He goes through all the motions again. This time Jim seems to like the fit. It looks perfect, in fact, from where Jules stands. It will not show. It will be covered up. Besides, that neater joint is not a stronger one. To himself, Jules says, "These guys aren't builders. They're craftsmen." He has no worries now about the quality of the house his daughter and son-in-law are getting. His observation isn't an unmixed compliment, though. Jules is a businessman, after all. He keeps those thoughts to himself.

By the end of May, they've finished the bottom deck and have begun to raise the walls. Pausing to take stock at their morning powwow over coffee, Jim says, "Whoever thought it would take so long to frame this bottom deck?"

"We're doing okay," says Richard. "It's about what we estimated, isn't it?"

"But this is the time when we usually do better than we expected," says Alex. "This is when we make up for later."

6

Along with many tools you expect a builder to keep by him, Jim carries in his carpenter's box a little tin of aspirin and several small devices—a brad installer, a screwdriver with a variety of magnetic heads that are stored inside the handle, a spokeshave for rounding surfaces, and a kit of small gouges. There's a watchmaker in Jim, also a mechanic. Although he rarely uses it, he carries a file, a metalworking tool. Richard, the welder's son, carries one of those, too. "Richard and I feel comfortable about metal," Jim infers. "Alex and Ned don't."

Each of the carpenters has his own primary toolbox, his doctor's bag, and each box is home-made out of wood. Jim's is largest. He built it out of white pine, a wood usually used for looks and not for strength. Partitions divide the space inside. The central partition, running lengthwise down the long box, curves upward to make a graceful handle. Jim has psychoanalyzed the partnership through its varied toolboxes. His clearly shows a taste for elegance. One day he relates his findings to Sandy:

"Well, mine's the best, of course."

"Of course," she says.

"Alex's is on the style of mine. It has a central partition that comes up and forms a handle. It has a classic line to it, too, but it's smaller, and it always has someone else's tools in it."

Jim goes on, "Richard's is *very* sturdy. It has a plain straight handle, which is made out of a *two-inch-thick* piece of oak. He can stand on the handle and use it for what he calls a ground raiser. And you can never see the bottom of it. It's full of shavings, broken hack-saw blades, and bent nails. Richard dumps it out two or three times a decade."

Last, Jim discusses Ned's wooden toolbox. "Ned has this really complicated box that closes up tight at the corners. It has a cover. It would turn away a mist. And it has a padlock hasp on it."

Ned's brother designed and made that toolbox and then one day presented it to Ned. More than any of his partners, Ned loves his tools and lavishes care on them. Many of his tools come from his father's estate. Some are odd, such as his worm-geared skillsaw. His partners have tried it out and they can't understand how Ned can cut in straight lines with the thing. It must weigh as much as a concrete block. The others don't feel inclined to borrow many of Ned's tools, and that is just as well, because Ned is conscious of having made his hands fit his tools and some of these mechanical appendages now mean as much to Ned as hair did to Samson. It's fitting that Ned should have a box that protects his tools from the weather and thieves, but it's the shyness of the box, the tight-shutting lid, that Jim finds marvelously apt.

As the walls of the house rise, so do Jim's worries about Ned. Both Jim and Richard think high craftsmanship in wood lies in the province of the furniture maker, a land for now beyond them. Of the partners, Ned comes closest to that condition, in temperament and skills, Jim and Richard think. "Ned does beautiful, beautiful work, but

God, is he slow sometimes," says Richard. "He does do beautiful work, though. Sometimes he overkills, too." A few days before they laid the sills, Richard told Jim he felt rusty and counted on Ned to set the example that would bring him back to par. Jim doesn't worry about Ned's work, obviously, or about Ned's stamina. He worries about Ned's state of mind.

Ned's last job, which he did mostly by himself this past winter, was the one that ended up costing twice as much as Ned had estimated. Jim figures it could have happened to any of them. In fact, it has happened to them collectively before, with a lot more money involved. What makes Jim afraid, both for Ned and for Ned's performance on this big job, is that Ned seems to have emerged from that last winter's travail drained of confidence and very angry. Jim didn't call Ned after his argument with Jonathan over the contract price. "Ned would have been ready to throw away the whole job for that six hundred and sixty dollars. So was I, almost." That was what Jim imagined. He knew that at the least Ned would react with anger. Jim wanted Richard and Alex around to help absorb it. So he had waited to tell Ned the story until all of them were gathered. As it turned out, Ned was angry enough to yell, but afterward Ned couldn't say himself which riled him more, the $660 or Jim's not telling him about the squabble right away, as he did the other partners.

When he met Ned five years ago, Richard mistook Ned's shyness for conceit. He thought Ned looked down on him, and he did not like Ned, he admits, but he reserved final judgment. When Richard bought his first grill for outdoor barbecues, he searched his woods for a hickory tree to add flavor to his meat. In twenty acres of woods, he did not have a single hickory, he told Ned one day at work. The next weekend Ned pulled into Richard's driveway with an entire tree in his truck. "Here's your hickory, Richard." That was the Ned beneath the lid, Richard has come to believe. "God, I never had a better friend."

When Sandy Warren lived in Apple Valley, she and her former husband saw a lot of Ned. He was always the best of guests, a gift bearer with "courtly, Quaker manners." Ned is a listener, like Jim. He is not as quick to understand as Jim, but the effort to understand shows in Ned. It can be exasperating. More often it is flattering, he tries so hard to take in all you have to say. When he works up the nerve to speak to them and they to him, most customers, female ones especially, and especially women unused to such attentiveness from workmen, find Ned as charming as Richard has. "If he likes you, he tries to feel *everything* you feel," says Richard. It's obvious that Ned has no capacity for guile. He is also very handsome. He has sandy hair and smooth skin and there is something exotic about his face. His grandfather came from Prague in 1901 and homesteaded in the Dakota Territory. Ned reminds you of the male leads in fairy tales. He might play Hansel. He isn't tall, but he is big, with the muscles and slim waist of a weight lifter, and without the weight lifter's awareness of mirrors. Ned's wife, Tina, who is a midwife and a constantly conscious feminist, a forceful woman, smiles and says, "He's absolutely gorgeous. And he doesn't know it, which is one of his charms, too." Tina can imagine Ned a pioneer. "He would be able to grow the vegetables and build the house and milk the cow. He's able to put his hand to anything—the farming, the wiring, the plumbing, the raising of the children. He might have been better served if he'd lived in the nineteenth century."

Jim and Ned have managed truces but never harmony. This spring Jim seems ready to pretend he doesn't care that they aren't friends. "He's sweet, though," Jim says. "If you can make him smile, you feel you've done a good day's work."

To all who feel they really know him, Ned is kind, competent, and strong. Ned is a birthright Quaker. He has never spoken his mind at a meeting of Friends, but he has taken the injunctions of the faith deeply to heart. He has never struck another human being. His smile can warm a room. His silences can empty one.

As they construct the bottom deck, then the first-story walls, which they build on the ground, sheathe in plywood, then lift into place—all heaving with a loud collective grunt—Ned has bright moments. A wall goes up. Richard puts down his hammer and stares at his own cracked and calloused right hand and wonders why it looks as if it were dying. "You're like a Sherpa, Richard,"

Ned tells him. "Climbing up mountains on his hands." Maybe Ned's bad mood seems longer and steadier than it really is. He does not know how, Tina says, to make himself opaque. In Ned, there is very little mediation between the feelings and the face, very little of the subterfuge that helps to make our companions' sorrow easier to live with than our own. On a warm, sunny day on the brink of summer, while they are making, lifting, and straightening walls, Richard pauses to say, "Alex thinks we shouldn't be paid for working on a day like this."

"Right," says Alex. "This is spa work."

"This is spa work," says Richard.

Ned kneels on plywood nearby, pounding a nail into a doubled two-by-six. When the nail is fully sunk, he delivers a last, violent blow that makes Jim glance up and sidelong at Ned. Ned glares at the nail. Alex and Richard continue their banter. Ned mutters, "No one seems immune from criticism around this place." It is moments such as those that linger with Jim and the others at the end of the day. Richard would like to believe that Ned's angry-looking silences come from Ned's old, bad case of carpenter's elbow. Ned has tried out hammers with wooden handles, fiber glass handles, steel handles, and none prevents the aching in his invulnerable-looking forearm. "Poor Ned," Richard says. "He really likes this work, and he's had such a hard time in his life finding something he likes to do." Jim feels more sympathy and less affection than Richard. "He doesn't need anything like that," Jim says after work one day, of Ned's bad arm. "He needs everything to be perfect, just to stay on an even keel." Jim also says, "Ned's a psychological mess."

Tina knows those silences of Ned's. "They're very powerful, because everybody is terrified of him when he is that way. I used to get angry back. I'd be counting the days when communication was by civilities only. It was restored usually by touch. He can't do that with his male friends."

Tina no longer takes Ned's bad moods personally, because, she says, Ned means to direct them only at himself. She and Ned have talked about his fits of silent, glowering withdrawal, and she thinks that Ned has begun to master them, now that he's found an explanation. "He says it's probably because he was so terrified of his father's rages. It was his technique of shutting himself off. It was safe."

Tina adds, "Isn't it amazing that Ned came out so well?"

Ned built his own house with his brother's help. He sited it like Jim's old place, at the end of a dirt road, in a clearing near the top of a hill in lower Apple Valley. Nearby in the encompassing woods are the ruins of a bridge Ned thinks lay along the old, vanished road from Albany to Boston. The house itself is spacious and unadorned. Wherever possible, Ned left the wood of the frame in sight. He and his brother made the doors by hand. The cabinets on the kitchen's walls have no doors to hide the dishes. Ned's house, unlike his toolbox, doesn't keep a lot of secrets. The house quietly and contemplatively celebrates wood. The most noticeable decorations are a couple of coat hooks by the front door—two stout twigs of apple, the thicker forks of each screwed flat against the wall, the thinner ones projecting out to make pegs. The bark is stripped off these hooks and the white wood has been polished.

Ned has built himself the best woodworking shop in the company, a separate two-story structure. It has a garage and a huge room full of benches and tools, with a high ceiling to make handling long lumber easy, and a loft in which Ned and his partners hoard special wood: the cypress Jim brought back from that job in Alabama, those white oak posts of Richard's, and most notably several huge oval slices from the trunk of a black walnut, which Ned is saving for some special project yet to identify itself. The telephone in the workshop does not ring. Ned removed its bell. He does not mind the telephone, but he dislikes the moment of answering it, and he guesses that's because when he was a boy and his father had taken up residence away from the family, Ned answered a lot of phone calls from female voices asking for his father, and then Ned felt he had to evade the question when his mother asked him who had called.

Ned's living room lacks couch or easy chairs. He sits in a straight-backed chair, his forehead resting on his fingertips. Now and then he looks up and laughs, a barking laugh that makes his shoulders shake.

"Dad left home when I was . . . I think I made a point of leaving that stuff behind. Buried. Dad was a builder in Pennsylvania. I worked with him, under duress actually. Actually, when I was little, I probably really enjoyed it. When you're little, those guys are real romantic. They curse and they chew and they spit, you know, when you're ten.

"I went to the Westtown School, a Friends' school, and boarded there. I was never a real sharp student and I was put almost in the vocational levels of the public school, the sections reserved for slow learners. It concerned my mom, so she got me into Westtown. I was glad. I hated to be home. School work. I wasn't good at it. I was able to fulfill the requirements if I really worked hard. I spent a lot of time as an athlete in school. Soccer was my big game. I got my strokes that way. It was a really old school. It had all these exotic trees. I remember a really big horse chestnut tree.

"I hated my father. I stayed away from him. He beat me once when I was having trouble with my multiplication facts. He beat me because he was so frustrated that I couldn't understand it. He told me to hit him back. All that sick kind of stuff. I was probably ten, eleven, twelve. He would yell a lot and scare me and stuff. I don't remember any other of that stuff. He caught my brother smoking pot and he beat the cylinder heads off my brother's BMW with a sledgehammer.

"He killed himself. He got into the bathtub so he wouldn't make a mess. He was a very tidy kind of guy in a way. He used a Smith and Wesson thirty-eight. He had cancer. It was really painful. He was sick two to three days out of the week and he couldn't work, and the way he relaxed, the way he enjoyed himself, was through his work. Through his work. He was an incredible builder. He spent his own money to do the kind of work he wanted to. He was an incredible, uncompromising builder. A maniac. He was crazy. If something wasn't just the way he wanted it, he would throw away a thousand dollars just to fix it. He was incredibly antagonistic to his labor force. He'd call everybody sons of bitches. He was handy, not a real craftsman, but he was willing to find people who were really good, and later on, he had a head carpenter he got along with. This guy reminded me a lot of Richard. He went through the same intense verbal process as Richard and he'd deal with impossible situations in a completely unruffled manner. My father's foreman taught my brother, who taught me. I didn't have any real fine-tuned skills. I could pile concrete blocks pretty well, but my father never encouraged me to learn carpentry. I never had a tool kit, I never had a hammer, there were never any tools at home. Never. I can think of a dozen hammers I have now and they're spread all over the place—the car, the house, the shop.

"It's funny. I never was going to do that. I looked at Dad, at how stressed out he was all of the time and what a hateful sonofagun. And yet I found myself finished with school and I fell back on the things that I knew and that was one of them. Woodworking is a very, very fascinating thing for me. I enjoy it a lot. It's woodworking that fascinates me more than contracting or house-building. Being with the trees and understanding how the wood accommodates a nail or screw, that's what's sort of magical.

"In high school Dad would come to every one of my soccer matches and stand on the opposite side of the field from the rest of the parents. Here's this island over there on the other side of the field. That sonofagun, calling attention to himself by that kind of isolation, you know. Amazing. After the game I would always go over to him. It was always awkward. It would separate me from the team and its joy or sadness. It was a strange process, to engage in his strangeness. It's the early sixties, right? Everybody's wearing madras shorts and short hair. He's walking around with a beard. He beats me, too. I hate him. And yet . . . Try and figure me out. He had a lot of . . . What a character! What a character! I really love him a lot. I was really mad at him when he blew himself away. I was just getting to know him.

"I went to Earlham College, in Richmond, Indiana. I was never a student. I got in with a lot of effort. If I worked really hard, I could be an average student, if I worked and worked and worked and got tutored. I had a C average in high school but I was captain of all these things—

231

track, soccer, wrestling. I think it was a willingness to really work that they saw. I remember a math teacher told me, 'It's going to be hard for you out there, but if you really work you can make it.' Earlham was a great place, man. Oh, God. I met some great people there. It had a great soccer team. I went there to play soccer. I made the team as a freshman and I was competing with an African for my position, and I broke my leg in the first game. The first game, the first few minutes. I was just completely charged. Me and an opponent were coming to a loose ball; he jammed the ball and I went to kick it. And really kick it. Both shinbones in my leg were fractured. It made a big sound; it made a lot of noise. I don't remember the noise. People remarked on the noise. This is in Wheaton, Ohio. I was in the hospital there two weeks. A week? When I got back to Richmond, the doctor took the cast off and rebroke it and reset it. I was in the cast from the fall to the spring. I had a really great pair of crutches. You could really get around on those suckers. It was a pretty significant time in my life. I was taking a botany course I really liked. The first few weeks of classes I was in the infirmary, I was way behind, and I wasn't a good student anyway, but this botany course. Dad came out. We went to the woods and arboretums. He helped me grab leaves off trees. It was an unexpected visit; he just sort of appeared. He was real nice to me. He went to Penn State, and I don't think he ever graduated either. His major was entomology. He had an incredible insect collection. He grew up on a farm. But the business of just walking around picking leaves, that was pleasure for him."

Tina always liked Ned's father. He was, she says, very handsome, taller than Ned and dark, a man most at ease among women, "a woman's man." Tina says, "He did love Ned. There was a loving, gentle side to his dad, which Ned knew."

Ned says, "When I got married and had kids and gave him room not to be responsible for me anymore, then he relaxed with me more." The moment he came closest to his father, though, the memory that sticks with Ned, was that day among trees, Ned in his hip-to-toe cast maneuvering adroitly on his crutches, his father plucking the leaves, then both of them putting their heads together, studying the greenery in their hands and trying to give it names. Years later, in his spare time, Ned took a course in the management of woodlots at the community college in Greenfield. "He got an A," Tina remembers. "He opened the letter and he stood there and wept. I guess it just brought back all those feelings of inadequacy about his academic experience."

Ned's career as an athlete ended when he broke his leg. The leg healed but he never made the grades he needed to be allowed to play again. Ned sometimes talks on the sorest points in the distant manner of a bureaucrat. "I went way down with the leg issue and my inability to be significant in the area of athletics, because it was the only area I knew how to be significant in."

At Earlham, in the corridors of his dormitory, in long late-night bull sessions, during which he learned to juggle, Ned met a wider world than he had known before. He could come out of the safe rooms of his shyness there. At Earlham, he also met Tina. She was in his class. Her older brother, a soccer player, selected Ned for her, she says, and the choice suited both of them, though at first she had to make most of the effort. "He was such a shy fellow. Would you believe it was six months before he actually kissed me? He asked me out on a hayride, and I gleefully accepted. He had this huge cast on his leg. God knows how he got his jeans on. His buddies had to lift him on the wagon. His pants caught on a nail and they ripped down the back. He was furious, upset, embarrassed, and he went into one of his funks. Everybody in the wagon was passionately making out, and he sat there with his arms crossed."

At the end of his junior year, Ned took a course in the novel, read all of the books, reveled in them, and did not write any of the assigned papers. It had been the same each spring. He'd realize that in the fall he would not be playing soccer. This time he borrowed some money from Tina, bought a big motorcycle, and left college for good. Tina caught up with him in San Francisco. He stayed for a while in a house in Haight-Ashbury occupied by the rock group the Grateful Dead and the rock group's many hangers-on. Ned did not fit in. He did not smoke even a little marijuana. In a dank basement room, Tina helped him write his application for conscientious objector status, and so instead of going to Vietnam, Ned worked at two different schools for young wayward boys outside New York. "It was high stress and horribly deflating to anybody with good feelings about the world. It was a good crusher for a do-gooder. It was hard to go in and see kids angry and abused and how institutionalized they became, and this was just their first stop. Really. In that group of fifteen, I'd be surprised if more than five of them are even collecting their welfare checks."

He and Tina were married then. They traveled around for a time. Eventually, they found their way into the hills west of the Connecticut River. Ned remembers driving up from the valley on a hot day and hitting on the ascending road that spot where, in the winter, rain turns to snow. In the summer, that spot is like a spring hole in a tepid lake. "I was just struck," Ned remembers. "It all seemed a lot cleaner, crisper, higher. The woods seemed like *woods*." The land they ended up buying in Apple Valley was made for Ned. The air enchanted him. There were endless woods for him to roam and study in.

Tina remembers leaving Ned alone for a week once and returning to find an extraordinary spider's web woven on the inside of one of their windows. Ned would not allow it to be cleared away. He called the spider "my buddy." While she was gone, he must have sat and watched the spider spin for hours at a time. She finds that

235

vision oddly moving, as if it held for her all that she finds wonderful and sad in Ned.

Tina became a nurse after college, and later on, she went through Yale's prestigious program in midwifery. A vocation came less readily to Ned, though again and again he ended up in jobs that had to do with trees, in orchard work or forestry or building. He turned to carpentry, once again under duress, after their second child was born. "Typical woman," says Tina. "I went home to my parents and said I wouldn't be back until he got a job." Ned got one right away: his short stint in factory-style building. He painted houses for a time. Then his brother came to town and taught Ned how to build. The Krutskys did renovations. Eventually, they constructed houses. For one client, they concocted a circular staircase. It was a virtual climbing tree. It had a huge oak post at the center, into which they mortised stout oak treads, spiraling upward. This piece of work appears in a book called *Building in Oak*. Ned and his brother had their own way of going about a job. They never took breaks at appointed times. When trouble arose, they would stop and talk about it. Often the discussions were long and metaphysical. More often, they did not need to talk at all. When they finished a large job, Ned's brother insisted on taking a month off. Ned needed a regular paycheck, but he loved those in-between times. They would rehearse their errors, practice new techniques, build furniture and such things as toolboxes and wooden pieces of sculpture for themselves and each other. "It filled a lot of needs I had, in terms of male interaction," Ned says.

Ned and his brother became well-known builders, their reputation growing along with Apple Corps's. The two crews worked together on a large new house in the hills, and Ned's brother, who was leaving for the West after that job, told Ned that he should join Apple Corps. Ned liked their looks. They practiced principled carpentry, too. They were a cooperative, and they reminded him of a Friends' business meeting.

It was Jim, oddly enough, who invited Ned to join them. Jim did so without consulting his partners, and perhaps some of Richard's annoyance with Jim on that score spilled over onto Ned. Jim also stuck up for Ned when Richard complained of Ned's silences and slowness. Once, early on, Richard even suggested that they let Ned go, and Jim pointed out what a fine carpenter Ned was and how many tools Ned brought to their enterprise. Ned didn't hear any of that. He missed his brother, their times of communion over wood, and the freedom they'd given themselves to pause when a job wasn't going well or plans weren't completely understood. He not only missed his brother but he got criticized for it by Jim, who spoke far less kindly about Ned to Ned's face than he did behind Ned's back.

A corner of Jim seems unregenerate, still callow. It's a voice that mocks him after he has spoken earnestly. Occasionally, it also speaks up sarcastically and pokes fun at his partners. When the fit is on him, Jim answers an innocent question with a mordant one—"You can't figure that out for yourself, huh?" Sometimes, in exchange for a compliment, he returns sarcasm: "I like the way you did that, Jim." "Well, that just pleases me no end." Afterward, Jim is full of self-reproach. Sandy says, "Jim thinks I'm the only person who believes he isn't mean, including him. But he's been so nice to me!"

Richard has a knack for making jokes on touchy subjects, and if silence follows, Richard says, "God, I'm sorry. I shouldn't of said that. I don't know how you can stand working with me. I'm a terrible person." When Jim makes a crack that touches an old sore point, he sometimes forces a ripple of laughter into his voice, but it doesn't usually help. Sandy thinks that Jim has wanted to reform Ned. If Jim can't help uttering the sarcastic remark from time to time, it is at least partly because he lacks to an unusual degree the ability to isolate his feelings from the ones in the air nearby. If Ned is angry and morose, Jim invariably shares some of Ned's gloom. To have to do so makes Jim angry in turn. Ned wasn't fitting in. Ned wasn't happy. Jim wanted Ned to trade in his old ways for Apple Corps's. He criticized Ned when Ned wanted to stop and think awhile, when Ned demanded utter clarity before lifting his hammer, when Ned spent half an hour setting up sawhorses and arranging his tools.

"The thing about Jim is, you gotta tell him to

go shit in his hat, when he gets so critical," says Richard. "Ned can't do that, though."

Jim's own brand of shyness, as Richard understands it, drives Jim to use words of impressive length and to talk around a subject. Jim confused Ned. Much later, Ned says, "Jim and I have had some real stormy times. It kind of perpetuates the business of figuring yourself out, almost to the point of injury. I feel real competitive about it. 'Can you do this, too, buddy?' " When Jim criticized Ned's work habits, Ned heard it as an attack on his relationship with his absent brother. Jim meant no criticism of Ned's brother, but Ned took it that way. Richard does a pantomime of Ned enraged. Richard puffs out his chest, stands on tiptoes, and circles his own eyes with his fingers, to show how wide Ned's eyes can get. That was Ned's response to Jim's remarks about Ned hanging on to old ways.

In Apple Corps, everyone keeps track of the hours he works and everyone in effect docks his own pay if he feels he has not done enough. No one has been more scrupulous than Ned. No one has been as critical of his own work or readier to underestimate his hours. In Jim, meanwhile, Ned has noticed a growing desire to make the business pay. Lately, they have had the same argument every six months or so, Jim and Richard insisting that they raise their hourly rates and Ned worrying about the pitfalls of commercialism. Laughing, Richard says, "Ned wants us to keep our rates *way* down, so we can work for people who

239

can't afford us and don't want us anyhow." Between Ned and Richard the subject makes for even-tempered disagreement. Between Jim and Ned, it is an irritant. There are others.

Sandy Warren is small and pretty and bustling. She catches Jim around the waist at unexpected moments and will not let him leave for work without a kiss. She teaches nursery school. She reads incessantly. She went to Swarthmore. She's bright and quick and outspoken. She looks people in the eye. She could stare down even the grumpiest plumber, and she can always make Jim smile. She is very good for Jim, Richard believes. Jim and Sandy left their spouses for each other, and there were injured parties throughout Apple Valley. "I wasn't a bit surprised that it happened," Richard says. "It was just the way Jim went about it. But I don't know how you go about dating your neighbor's wife. I don't know if there's a real clean way of doing that or not." He makes a sad, tympanic laugh.

Sandy was very sick as a young woman, with cancer. Richard was one of the only neighbors who would speak directly to Jim about her. Richard once said to Jim what many felt, that Jim had taken advantage of Sandy in the time after her illness. Jim did not protest. He had his sense of honor. It was as well developed as Ned's. Sandy says, "But *I'm* the one who started having feelings for Jim. In a closely knit community, there's always some very sanitary flirtation. I always thought it was healthy to be attracted to other people, and I thought it was very safe, because I believe in fidelity. I just fell in love with Jim."

This is how Sandy tells the story, over coffee one day, some five years later: "My parents were divorced. It knocked out a keystone and I didn't know it, and then I got sick. I'm sure that had something to do with it. It wasn't that I felt I had to clutch life. It was that it shook some fundamental belief I had about the way the world worked. I had been such a good person all my life, and when I got sick I realized that being a good girl wasn't going to protect me. But it was absolutely devastating to me that I had to do something for reasons that went deeper than my conscience."

Recuperating in Apple Valley, Sandy took up the piano and walking. "I would see Jim often on my walk and the more I saw him, the more I liked him. It was the opposite of what I expected would happen. He's a very quiet, strong silent type, and people project a lot onto that sort of person. Usually, you find out they're sort of rotten.

"I was obsessed. This was really trouble. I decided I would talk to him and he would put it to rest. He was really nice. He said this happens to a lot of people. He came by the next day and said, 'I don't want you to be embarrassed about what you said yesterday.' My idea was to get relief, to stop feeling this way, not to do anything.

We started talking about how I felt. He gave me a hug and I kissed him, and he was startled. He said, 'We can't do this. We can't see each other.' I was walking the next morning and Jim stopped in his truck on the way to work and he said, 'Maybe I made a mistake.' I don't know if I was happy or not. I had decided to get help through my women's group. Tina was in it, and Tina told Ned. So Ned, of all people, had this secret knowledge that kept him from being close to his friends all that summer. Poor Ned. It was horrible. We played volleyball every week and had potluck suppers every Sunday, and poor Ned had to go to all those things and not be able to do or say anything."

In any community, when the news got out, there would have been some late-night talks, about how to go about staying friends with all parties and about all the ways in which the broken marriages differed from one's own. Neighbors would have made conscientious efforts at sympathy and at not looking too deeply. Apple Valley was different, however. This was not a bunch of neighbors thrown together by real estate agents or the coincidences of their children's ages or a mutual interest in lawn mowers. As its founders originally imagined it, Apple Corps was to be not just a group of carpenters but an alliance of all the various craftspeople of the valley, a new arts and crafts movement. The community had men's and women's groups; through them, there was intimacy among neighbors. It had its volleyball games and potluck suppers. When people who helped to create it speak about their hopeful new settlement in the hills, the word they use most often is *safety*. It was to be the sort of place where you'd wish you had grown up, and what made it precious, to Ned for one, was that it bore a strong resemblance to the place he and the others had been looking for.

"A secure, safe place," says Tina Krutsky. "It was a kind of constricted commune, which we all built, to hold on to this image of a safe, happy environment. Jim and Sandy broke that covenant. No wonder there was so much rage. And for Ned, to have his own past replicated . . ." Tina still regrets having told Ned about Jim and Sandy, letting Ned in on the secret that he couldn't divulge. "It was such a dumb thing to do. Because Ned is so transparent. I wish I'd never told him."

Ned was always very fond of Sandy's husband. Ned describes him as "the sort of person you feel privileged to know." Ned would get calls from him, to ask if Ned knew Sandy's whereabouts. Ned could not reply truthfully. He was answering the telephone at home again, and he hated Jim for it.

"I don't think Ned's a man who forgives easily," Tina says. "Jim's one of the few moral disappointments Ned seems to be getting over. Maybe Ned's growing up."

On a morning years later, Jim lays his framing

plan on the pile of Pinkham lumber, and Ned laughs harshly and says, "This is a pretty complicated little thing. You need a road map to find your way through it." Moments afterward, Richard turns away from Ned and facing Jim, declares, "I'm ready to go." Ned takes a small step backward. Ned is conscious of withdrawing. It seems to him that Jim and Richard have made a pact. Ned understands that. He and his brother always shared such alliances over plans. "I thought a third person would've been cumbersome," Ned says afterward. "And yet I couldn't just go at something else. I think that when I'm confused, my tendency is to get anxious. You know, you've got a huge pile of wood and some plans that are a little bit convoluted and I guess in that situation, where I want to be effective, I want to be part of what's going on around me, and if I can't, I get jumpy. In a situation like that, I want a big hammer and a heavy bag of nails."

Later that first day, Jim and Richard and Ned gather at the lumber pile again to plan their working schedules. Richard wants to put in nine-hour days. Ned wants to stick to eight. Ordinarily he and Richard would drive to work together, saving the company some money on gas. Ned offers to pay some of the extra expense out of his own pocket.

"It doesn't seem like you should have to do that," says Jim. "But you can if you want to."

"I want some time to play in my gardens," says Ned.

"I want to do nine hours because I spent the whole winter sitting on my butt," says Richard.

"I'm getting the impression you guys are mad at me," says Ned.

"No, no," says Jim.

"Hell, no," says Richard. "I'm just flat broke."

"I just need to feel okay about putting in eight hours," says Ned.

"I can't *make* you feel okay," says Jim.

Ned looks at him with lowered brows. "You can help by telling me you don't resent my working eight-hour days."

Jim purses his lips and looks away.

"This is a hell of a marriage we got here," says Richard to no one in particular as they disband.

Jim once told Richard that he could not deal with Ned's anger over Sandy. Ned would have to deal with that by himself. That is, in fact, something Ned wants to do. He just has an odd way of showing it. Ned feels confused about the framing plan, he feels excluded, he feels like a hired hand and not a partner. They have not built a new house for over a year and a half. They have worked alone or in teams of two on smaller jobs. Ned feels unaccustomed to this large a crowd. He needs some time to get used to his partners again.

Now, a week and a half later, during coffee break, Jim complains to the others about Bill Rawn. Plans Jim thought he'd have by now aren't here. Jim has not slept well lately. He looks pale in spite of sunshine. Alex and Richard offer sympathy, in traditional Apple Corps fashion, by chastising the absent party, who happens to be the architect. Ned enters the conversation the way policemen enter the premises of armed and dangerous alleged perpetrators. "I just react to your association with me and your kind of antagonistic approach to me," says Ned to Jim. "So. I don't know about the architect, but I know you come at me in a way that puts my hackles right up. Some way, get Jonathan and Judith involved in getting the plans from the architect."

Jim has looked at Ned's eyes as Ned berated him. He sucks at his lips and says, "I agree with that," but he doesn't say whether he means Ned's advice or Ned's criticism, or both.

A few days later, most of that scene is re-enacted. Facing Jim in what will be the foyer, Ned says, "I'm just commenting on your tendency to hang on to things and not call in your friends." Ned says Jim ought to distribute some of the responsibility for this job. They are all partners, after all. The tone of Ned's voice makes what he says sound like an invitation to a duel, but Jim chooses to hear the message, not the voice. Over the past few years, Jim has irritated Ned, hurt his feelings, confused and troubled him, but Jim has also acted honestly, even generously. This past winter, when that job of Ned's had all but fallen apart and Ned was talking about absorbing the loss himself, Jim took the floor at a company meeting and told Ned that they would not let him work for nothing. Then Jim dropped his other work and went to help Ned, so they could get that job finished and behind them, with their reputations still intact. That was the neighborly Jim, the person who showed up unasked to help Ned erect the walls of his house in Apple Valley, years ago. Now Ned intends to repay his debt. He makes his voice pugnacious, maybe because he expects a fight, but this time Jim pauses, touching his front teeth with a finger, and he says that he would very much like to turn over some chores to the others. For starters, would Ned please deal with the phone company? A moment later, Ned strides up the hill toward Jules's barn and telephone. That evening, Jim tells Sandy, "Ned and the others want to take some of the load off me." Sandy observes that Jim, as transparent to her as Ned is to most of the world, feels surprised and also delighted. For the first time in weeks, Jim sleeps well.

A week later, near the end of the afternoon, Jim asks Ned to help him shovel the dirt back into the telephone cable ditch. It's a job that requires no thought. You can see the beginning of the job, at the edge of the house, and the end of it, all the way down the hill at Bay Road. A dreary piece of work for one person, perhaps, but for two, a chance for a long chat. They stand on opposite sides of the ditch, shoveling their way toward Bay Road and evening. Burying the cable, they talk about nothing important, but they have plenty to say to each other, about four years' worth of small talk.

Differences persist. Ned says, "I have the feeling Jim needs to find a more lucrative approach to life. He talks about it often enough. I want to stay real close to the process. Language is a weird thing, man. I don't understand Jim's language a lot of the time, even though it's the same language. Maybe it's frustrating to him. It's kind of jarring. It's not a rhythmic arrangement with Jim."

Ned continues to suspect that trouble with the Souweines and the architect is something Jim encourages, maybe even wants to keep alive. Jim likes a long and argumentative discussion, Ned knows, and he thinks that's part of the reason why Jim spends so much time on the phone in the barn. "But I'm working a lot better with Jim than before. I let go a lot of the anger that I carried, with respect to his arrangements with Sandy."

By the time the second-story walls are raised, Ned's angry-looking silences have grown infrequent. They are gone by the time Ned starts framing the ceiling of the second floor.

Ordinarily, in a modern house, the kind of simply decorated house that Apple Corps usually builds, the joists that make up the top floor's ceiling also serve as collar ties—the horizontally laid beams that connect the bottoms of a pair of rafters, which complete the base of the triangular frame of a roof. But an essential element in Bill Rawn's translation of Greek Revival is the ample frieze board, separating the roof from the second floor's windows. Bill's plan requires one set of joists for the second floor's ceiling and another set, a few feet above those, for the collar ties of the roof. "What there is extra about this," says Richard, "is about seventy-four two-by-sixes, sixteen feet long."

Richard says this while he and Ned haul planks up to the top of the house, in preparation for building the roof. Ned looks up at the completed second-story ceiling and he laughs.

"Too much wood up here," says Richard. "Ridiculous. Talk about something ridiculous. Look at that grid up there. But that's what he wants. It's going to look nice. Shoot, without it, it'd look like a big box, a big shoe box."

"I've never seen anything like it," says Ned. "All that wood to hold up a frieze board. All for a piece of trim." Ned shakes all over with laughter. "Architects!" he howls.

"Pain!" cries Richard, heaving up a plank. "I love pain!"

Now the framing plan makes sense to Ned. He comes to the job and finds before him work that is clear and also clarifying. Looking back later, Ned wonders if some of his problems at the start didn't stem from shyness. Maybe he was still getting used to his partners after five years, and maybe on the frame of this house, he finally felt that they were friends.

When he looks back, Ned thinks mainly of Richard, though. "I get enormously relaxed working with Richard. I understand his language, too. I have learned a lot from Richard Gougeon. About good attitudes and good humor and how necessary they are to a productive approach to anything, particularly housebuilding, with crazy architects, crazy lumber, crazy customers, crazy carpenters. If you can't be good-humored about it, you'll go mad. Richard gets upset sometimes, but then he goes off and walks around his woods and picks blackberries."

Back in February, at one of the company's many meetings, Ned announced, "I'm coming from a place where I need a little rest."

"Rest?" said Richard. "This is spring, when you're s'posed to be getting revved up."

Everywhere Ned has turned this spring looking for a figurative bed, Richard has stood in his way, telling him that he is not only a fine carpenter but also one who isn't tired. There's a kind of gravity in Apple Corps, which takes the place of figuring out who will work with whom. Increasingly, as the house rises, Ned finds Richard at the other end of the board he's working on.

"I got this all figured out now, Ned. But I'm not going to tell you." Richard makes his under-handed laugh.

"Then I'm not going to help you," says Ned.

"You're not as much fun as Alex."

"I know," says Ned. "Alex always has the appropriate witticism."

Instantly serious, Richard explains the task to Ned after all.

Ned and Richard stand on separate ladders, side by side, and Ned says, "Tina's got some great pictures of you, Richard. Of your ass, actually."

"Why was she taking pictures of my ass?" says Richard, leaning back, pushing out his chest and lowering his chin onto it, miming indignation.

"Because it's cute," says Ned. "She thought it was cute."

"I know it's cute and all," says Richard. "But it's a little embarrassing."

Ned explains that Tina plans to blow up the best picture and put it on the refrigerator at a mutual friend's house. That friend had a pinup, a mostly clothed one, on his icebox door the last time Ned and Tina went to dinner there. "Tina was mad at that pinup," says Ned.

"That young lady hanging up there got paid for her picture," replies Richard. "How about me?" He drives a nail and mutters loudly, "Spreading my buns all around town. It must be because I'm losing weight that my pants don't stay up. I know I'm getting better looking, so I must be losing weight. Hey, Ned, why doesn't she take a picture of your buns and hang them there on the refrigerator?"

"Well, she would, Richard. But I keep mine well covered."

"It is embarrassing," says Richard. "I go home and take a shower and I see the tan line way down there." Most of the rest of the day, Ned and Richard discuss pornography, Richard imagining himself a hanging judge sentencing the purveyors of kiddie porn. Ned smiles, listening as he works.

Ned has borrowed from Jim a 22-ounce, steel-handled framing hammer, with a serrated surface on its nailing head, which gives the hammer traction upon a nail. "The checkered demon," they call Ned's hammer. It leaves its checkered pattern on the lumber. That is Ned's mark, and it is prevalent on the frame. Ned's arm still aches from the percussion. Tina knows the malady, an inflammation of the sheath around the nerves of wrist and forearm, called carpal tunnel syndrome. Both carpenters and pregnant women sometimes suffer from it. The only cure for a carpenter is to put his hammer down and get an operation. The pain no longer shows regularly in Ned's face, though.

Ned stands on the deck of the second floor. "What's interesting is when it just goes," he says. "You feel like a Zen master and at the end of the day you feel like you earned your money. What makes it go is anticipating, knowing where the next piece of wood is, where it goes, and where your partner's going to be. It's like playing soccer, you know?" He lifts one foot, turning the toes outward, and makes a perfect pass of an invisible ball to Richard, who is driving nails nearby.

The house looks like a pair of adjacent boxes, one large, one small, a child's outsized building blocks, with many rectangular holes in the plywood walls. To Bill Rawn, though, it is a new reality. Bill has made other inspections while Apple Corps built, but the house lacked shape the last time he saw it. Now Bill can see the refined adult in the gawky child, and he is so moved he can hardly speak at first.

Bill and Judith stand gazing down at the south wall from the field above—the Wiffle Ball field, Judith and Jonathan call it, though in spite of their efforts, it is still as much sand as grass and what grass there is has grown crunchy underfoot.

"Don't you think when you get it all lined up, it starts being a little special?" says Bill to Judith, in a deep voice on the verge of cracking.

"Bill, don't be defensive," says Judith. "It's very nice."

"No," says Bill, staring at the many-holed and otherwise blank wall. "I was just thinking aloud."

"It really is big," says Judith.

"I'm just . . . very happy . . ." Bill's hands attempt to express what his tongue cannot. "This elevation does feel *very* good."

"I know, Bill. It's exciting for you. We've been here more."

"There are two different vocabularies to a wall," says Bill.

"I don't know *what* you're talking about," says Judith, a smile creeping over her face.

"There are windows poked into a solid wall, whereas this south wall becomes almost a window in itself."

Judith looks away to hide her grin. Jim joins them. "Think the house is too big?" he asks.

"I . . ." starts Bill.

"It feels really big to me," says Judith.

"It doesn't to me," says Bill.

Jim shows them around inside. Some of the partitions, the ones that help to bear the weight of the second floor, are in place. There are, as Ned has remarked, lots of places to hide now. In the dappled sunlight that comes down into the roofless house, the uncovered lumber turns golden and light orange. Apple Corps has not yet built the staircase, so the party ascends to the second story on a ladder. "This is totally unbelievable," says Judith when she gets to the top. "Jonathan got up here and said we had to put the principal room up here. Maybe I'll move up here."

"It really is an extraordinary view," says Bill.

The house has risen above some treetops. From the second floor they can see Castor and Pollux again. Those landmark maples have been invisible since the leaves came out. You can see the towers of the university and, off to the east, that gently rolling woodland that stretches out most of the way to Worcester. Judith descends the ladder nervously. Jim stands below and holds it steady for her. He says he understands her feelings about ladders. "I have a dream that I'm getting onto a forty-foot ladder off a slate roof," he tells her. "It's a getting-to-sleep dream."

Sometimes Jim dreams that he is descending a slippery slate roof, trying to get to that very tall ladder. But the ladder does not extend up over the edge of the roof. He must search and search for it with his dangling foot. At that point Jim usually shakes himself awake and makes a fresh start back to sleep. In the daytime, though, Jim loves a height. So does Ned. Ned remembers a hayloft from which he jumped as a boy, and he has an exhilarating daydream of painting the towers of the bridges high above Manhattan's rivers. "We're up here in the treetops," Ned remarks, standing one day on the narrow joists of the second floor's ceiling. The carpenters, Jim especially, pause to look at hawks and turkey vultures and light airplanes, which all seem close, just a long reach away. Planes drone off, a freight rolls down the valley, its horn echoing off the Pelham Hills. In sunshine, they can look into the sides of rainstorms, miles away. When the guests, the paying guests, have gone and the carpenters repossess the place, the house becomes their treehouse, a summertime lookout.

All around the foundation the ground is sand. Off to one side rises a huge mound of darker earth, which is loam they are saving for the final grading, months away. Out of it a textbook's worth of weeds, including a great deal of poison ivy, has sprouted. A black and yellow snake has taken up residence in the mound. The excavator has gotten very busy. For weeks he has left a four-foot-deep trench unfilled. One morning Alex notices a couple of holes bored in the walls of that trench, and with a little patient observation he discovers that those holes belong to a family of birds.

"We've got some cliff swallows in the electrical trench," Alex tells the others at lunch. "They must have eggs."

"What's the morally right thing to do?" says Jim.

"Well, we just won't fill it in until they hatch," says Alex.

Summer arrives and so does the roof, one day in the second week of June. The roof comes in the form of another huge pile of lumber that makes the lumberyard's truck look small. It is, in all, 81 sheets of half-inch exterior-grade plywood, 70 rafters made of eighteen-foot-long two-by-tens of Douglas fir, 70 sixteen-foot-long two-by-eight pieces of spruce that they'll nail together to make the 35 thirty-foot-long collar ties, and 35 ten-foot-long two-by-eights of spruce, to make what they call the drops. "Amazing," Richard says. "All that going up on the roof. The truck was workin' coming up the driveway. We better do this right. If this roof starts coming down, it'll be all the way down here before it stops."

On one of his visits a week or so ago, Jules remarked, "If these guys are any good, they'll cut the rafters with a framing square. Hey, Jim, how do you use the framing square to figure the rafters?"

Jim stopped and delivered a completely incomprehensible explanation, though it seemed clear that he knew the trick. Essentially, he tried to say that you make the square into a miniature cross section of the roof. But Apple Corps tends to show off in product, not in method. They always use the simple but reliable technique that Richard long ago described in that A paper he wrote in trade school, the essay called "How to Frame a Roof." They take out their measuring tapes, chalk lines, and rafter squares and draw a full-scale diagram of one half of the roof on the plywood floor in what will someday be the kitchen. Bill's engineer helped to design this roof. It is to be a very sturdy concoction, with triangular gusset plates of plywood, nailed and glued as fasteners between rafters and collar ties. The carpenters draw a diagram of half a roof; if it were of a whole one, it would look like this:

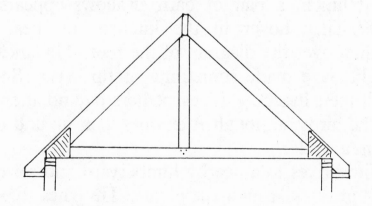

The carpenters spend a long time kneeling on the

floor, worrying about the way in which they'll apply the trim to the eaves.

"There's the rake board. Then comes the seven-foot-four soffit board, which is seven-four but gives us a quarter inch to push in and out," says Richard.

"And we've got three-quarters of an inch for a fascia," says Alex.

"In your fascia," says Jim.

"And actually, we've got the ridge board here," says Richard.

"This is great, though," Richard explains. "Once you got it drawn and you know it's right, you don't have to go and cut seventy rafters hoping they'll fit." Richard stops and recalls a day on his first job. An old-time carpenter said to the boss, "Hey, remember that time we cut forty rafters and none of 'em fit?" Richard's boss said nothing. He just turned away. "It still hurt," says Richard. "But this old guy proceeded to tell us all about it."

At lunch, a pair of barn swallows appears inside. They hover in the kitchen, up near the ceiling, over the diagram of the roof. The ancients might have made something of this visit. Sitting with their lunches, the carpenters pay no attention to the birds, although Alex does look up and offer them a smile.

Jim drives to a nearby lumberyard and selects a load of thick, rough-cut planks. He paws through the pile, rejecting this plank because it's a little twisty, that because it's waney. This is rough-cut staging lumber, not wood for finish work. An imperfection doesn't matter, does it? "Twenty-five feet up in the air it does," says Jim.

Hanging off their ladders, they bolt sidewall brackets made of oak through the plywood walls and into the studs behind. Onto the brackets they heave new planks, making a walkway, an open parapet ringing the top of the house's walls. Each plank spans the distance between two brackets, and at each intersection, the end of one plank rests on the top of the end of another, making for a small, two-inch-deep step. Working on this scaffold, feeling their way along it without looking down, the carpenters encounter these small steps again and again. Always, the step comes unexpectedly. It's a momentary free fall, of two inches. They flinch and grimace and go on.

They set up ladders side by side, between ground and scaffold. Two men ascend in unison, each on a separate ladder, each holding an end of a piece of lumber. Two men up top on the scaffold take each board from them. A chant begins: "Pain!" "Gimme more pain!"

"Ned and I got a system," says Richard to Alex, as Alex reaches the scaffold once again.

"I am glad," says Alex.

"Part of it's hollerin'," says Richard.

They trade roles. Those who play the ladder men request greater diligence in bending down, from the catchers up top. The catchers demand improvements in speed from the ladder men, and every so often one of them asks, "You couldn't get a hoist, eh, Jim?" In this way, piece by piece, the huge lumber pile ascends. They nail the collar ties in place, on the plates that rest on top of the two long walls. They nail and glue the gussets to the collar ties one morning. That afternoon, they make the angled cuts on the upper ends of the rafters, using the drawing on the kitchen floor as a template. On the following day, roof raising commences.

It is a Friday. Jim is supposed to set out for Cape Cod with Sandy and five children. He's supposed to take the day off, but he comes by the site that morning anyway, and helps his partners carry up the rafters.

Alex, on the scaffold, yawns.

"Hey, Alex, stop yawning."

"I'm sorry to offend you, Richard, but this work is not that demanding."

"From each according to his abilities . . ." says Jim, as he and Ned hand over the tops of their ladders the last fat Douglas fir rafter.

"Look at that!" says Richard. "We paced ourselves to the minute for lunchtime."

"Another Apple Corpse operation timed perfectly to end at noon," says Jim.

They are very merry, and merrier after lunch, as they erect the first rafters and section of ridge board. "Look at all those ridge cuts. Perfect," says Jim. Richard and Jim stand on sawhorses, holding up the ridge board with outstretched arms. Ned nails rafters to the ridge on one side, Alex on the other.

260

"You got that rafter nailed good, Alex?" Richard asks.

"Two eight-pennies," says Alex. Eight-pennies would be puny nails for the job. Alex has used much larger ones, in fact.

"The night was calm and the moon was yellow," sings Jim. It is time for Jim to hit the road. Indeed, he is already late. He climbs down. He lingers, though, standing on the ground, looking up at his lofty partners.

"Five kids, huh?" calls Richard. "That sounds like a lot of fun. Why don't you try suicide or something?"

"You send me a postcard," says Alex.

"I always send you one, Alex."

"A nice postcard of a nude reclining on a beach."

"Is that all you think about, Alex?" asks Richard-the-indignant.

"My correspondence with Jim? Certainly."

"So long, Ned."

"Have fun, Jim." Ned waves.

Jim didn't want to leave, Richard observes. "This is glory work, the roof."

"It's the prettiest part of the job," says Ned. "And it's working out pretty well."

The stout rafters of Douglas fir, which are pink like fillets of salmon, make a widening tent above them.

"I feel real good about this detail," says Ned, running a hand over one of the plywood gussets.

"A lot of these old roofs were way underbuilt,"

says Richard, restorer of old houses. "Not this one, though. And this house is framed to the thirty-second of an inch, right to the ridge."

"That should be good enough," says Alex.

In fact, the rafters meet the ridge board nearly perfectly. Richard stops nailing to say, "We should do like they do with a sports car, with a gold plaque that tells how fast it's gone. We should have a little gold plaque in the attic: Framed to a Thirty-second."

A voice calls from below. It's Judith. " 'Lo," says Richard, looking down from the eastern edge of the building.

"Ooo la la," says Judith. "It's wonderful. It looks like a house."

"We'll have you in by Easter," says Richard.

"Oh, great," she calls back. "But we don't celebrate Easter. How 'bout Passover?"

"Okay. Just give me a few Easter eggs," says Richard.

"We don't want to push you," says Judith. "We'll just be in our tent all that time."

When Judith leaves, Richard muses, "If we don't get done until next Easter, it'll cost us a lot of money." He's thinking of those hundred-dollar-a-day penalties for not being done by the end of October.

"Yup," says Alex. "They'll have it for just about free."

"Well, think of it, Alex," says Richard. "Today we're working for free."

"Because it's such a nice day?"

"No," says Richard. "Because we were s'posed to finish the roof yesterday."

Ned laughs. Alex laughs. They are very merry today.

For centuries, perhaps millennia, the raising of the frame of a roof has served as an occasion for ceremony, and often celebration. In what is now Scandinavia and divided Germany, in medieval days, the occasions had great elaboration. All sorts of rituals ensured the luck of the inhabitants. In New England up through the nineteenth century, a large number of relatively unskilled volunteers would gather and, at the direction of a master builder such as Calvin Stearns, push and hoist into place all the heavy precut pieces of a building's frame. Judging from old records of maiming and killing accidents, Abbott Lowell Cummings, the architectural historian, suspects that libations sometimes began before the job was complete. Tradition demanded that afterward strong drink be provided for the raisers of the frame. Often a feast was laid.

It seems obvious why human beings have celebrated after a roof. In the English past at least, the work required the sort of crowd that wants to become a party. In all traditions, the roof represents the essential element of shelter, and once the frame of a roof exists the shape of a building comes clear. It isn't at all obvious, on the other hand, why for centuries builders have fastened small trees or evergreen boughs or flowers (a southern Mediterranean practice) to the ridges of newly framed roofs. Medieval builders who practiced this rite do not seem to have left any clear record of the reasons for it or of its origins.

From James Frazer's *Golden Bough* and the host of other volumes that discuss ancient forms of tree worship, you can infer that nailing a piece of the forest onto the frame of a new roof was meant to soothe the gods in trees, and you can imagine that the ritual has survived as an expression of vestigial wariness about the act of building. A historian named John Stilgoe believes the custom arose from "a pagan notion that the frame is alive." There is, after all, a roundness to the ritual. Having taken wood from the tree, builders bring the tree back to the wood. The tree becomes the house, and in ceremony, the house becomes the tree.

The custom persists here and there. The Dutch use a small white birch for the ritual tree and their grog of choice for the builders is beer. Stilgoe says that in the United States, eastern builders follow the custom far more often than western ones. Oddly, the practice seems to be growing infrequent for wood-framed buildings and flourishing for ones made of steel. Most people who have spent time getting mesmerized by looking through the peephole in a fence around an urban American construction site have probably witnessed this scene: an immense steel girder being swung aloft with a little evergreen bush tied to it. Steelworkers whom Stilgoe interviewed told him that bad luck would afflict a building project if they failed to endow the frame with a roof tree. "They're afraid to stop the custom," says Stilgoe.

Apple Corps has always attached an arboreal flag to the roof of a new house frame. "We do it," Richard says, "because someone else did it before us." Ned can't remember anyone following the custom when he worked for his father in Pennsylvania. He began to observe it when he got to New England, and for the same reason Richard did—other, older builders did it. To Ned, the custom feels right. "My idea is you always try to get a tree that's as close to the material you're using as you can find. I've always interpreted it as homage to the trees."

Richard stands ready to nail the lower end of the last rafter to the gussets. Ned stands at the center of the house, ready to nail the rafter's upper end to the ridge board. Alex stands between them, all the weight of the heavy rafter on his shoulder. At this moment, Richard decides to take a short break, in order to examine his hammer hand. "I don't know what it is. My hand is rotting away."

"It's that French disease, Richard," says Ned, who has been smiling most of the afternoon.

Alex, meanwhile, feels his shoulder going numb. "Come on, Richard," he says.

Richard beats with his hammer on the top of the rafter. Alex's knees wobble but do not buckle. Alex says, "It's his head that's rotting."

Then at last they're done. "What a Friday,

huh?" says Richard, as they put up temporary braces, to keep the roof frame from collapsing should a high wind come. "We got the roof on, on a Friday." Richard leans out from the south wall and sights down the outer edges of the rafters. "Crisp. The cornice oughta go on real slick. We've been hitting everything just right today. Noon was just right. Pickup time is just right."

Back on earth, Richard and Alex carry tools to their trucks. Richard goes off to wash out the pots in which they mixed the glue. Ned vanishes into the woods with his handsaw.

"Got to do it, right?" says Ned. He does not know just what to choose. He counts the Douglas fir among the noblest of trees, but it grows only out West. The house is too cosmopolitan in wood to make this job easy. The white pine, though, is New England's tallest, most elegant and precious softwood. Ned takes a white pine bough from the woods beside the brook, and he carries it up the ladder.

Ned wears a pair of black combat boots and shorts with ragged hems, and nothing else. He has gone bronze in the sun. He stands on tiptoes on the scaffold under the ridge and reaches up toward the top of the house, the greenery in one hand, his checkered demon in the other. Reaching up with difficulty, frozen for a moment against pink rafters and blue sky, Ned is statuary in the heroic tradition. *Ned Triumphant* is the title of the piece.

Alex and Richard have their backs turned at

266

this moment. When they look at the house again, Ned has come back to the ground and the tree is up.

"Hey. A tree," says Alex, with a smile.

"Who put that up? You put that up, Ned?" asks Richard.

"Yeah."

"Great!" says Richard. "I was just thinking about that."

"A good day," says Alex. "Fun times. Much more fun than putting tar on the foundation wall."

They amble, casting backward glances, over to Jules's driveway, which is empty at this moment— the Wieners have gone on vacation.

"This is going to be one stately-looking house. It's going to be wonderful," says Richard. They stare up at the roof. The house, a box this morning, now looks very tall. It begins, as Bill would say, to stand with its shoulders up. "This is *neat*," Richard goes on. "I never thought I'd get a chance to build a house with all the stuff this one's going to have on it. It's like building a thirty-two Ford, you know?"

Ned laughs. "Ah, Richard."

They move back a little farther. "It could be a town meeting hall," says Alex, shading his eyes. "That there is a suitable house for an important person."

"Yeah, if you got the money and you love old houses, build a new one," puts in Richard. "It'll only cost a fraction of the old one to heat."

Richard adds, "I think he's outdone the father-in-law, though."

"Oh, great," says Ned. "Son of a gun. This is a big, big house. I like it."

"It is. I don't think I realized what I was building till now. That thing is *right*. To the very top. Dead on. We fussed with it. That sucker's going to be nice. The cornice'll go on slicker 'n hell. This is going to look like the guest house over here."

Richard ambles over with Ned and Alex to Jules's house. Richard inspects the trim under the eaves, while his partners watch. They circle Jules's house. Richard peers at the finish. "The guy who built this didn't really try too hard. He didn't know what a block plane was. You can tell he just cut the board and nailed it on," says Richard.

"They could have done a lot worse," says Alex, who, like Jim, considers Jules's house a well-wrought example of contractor building. "Okay. Have we all made ourselves feel better?"

They turn back to their house. They stare at it a while longer.

"A *proud* building," says Ned.

"I don't even know of another one being built new, around here," says Richard.

"I guess we're going to shingle it ourselves, huh?" asks Ned.

"Sounds it," says Richard. "It'll go pretty fast, though." Describing how they'll go about the rest of the roofing, Richard walks with his partners to the vehicles. All the way down the driveway, they glance back over their shoulders at what they have built.

About two weeks later, when the builders stand on their high scaffold working on the trim beneath the roof, the excavator returns with a backhoe. As the carpenters work, the excavator fills in the electrical trench. Late that afternoon, in the midst of mopping sweat off his face, Ned suddenly looks up, bug-eyed, and asks, "Did anyone remember the swallows?"

Shoulders are shrugged, pained looks exchanged. Alex hasn't seen those birds for a while. Maybe, he says, they had already flown their nest.

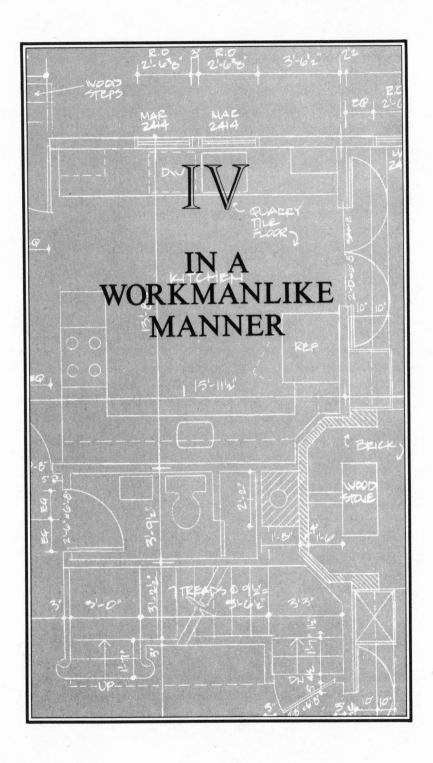

IV

IN A
WORKMANLIKE
MANNER

Even the most prosperous architects have known hard times. Take the case of Richard Morris Hunt, a leader among architects during the second half of the nineteenth century. Most modern architects scorned Hunt's ornate work, and some postmodernists like his buildings. All architects are indebted to him for his diligent efforts to make architecture a profession in America. In his own practice, he designed a number of mansions in Newport, Rhode Island, and once his career really got going, he became the architect to the very deep-pocketed Vanderbilts. He dreamed up a chateau, a villa, and a castle for them. Hunt once said, in his later life, "By the Great Caesar, if this country doesn't take up art, we'll make it, we'll educate it, we'll show it what a great and glorious thing it is." He aimed a little lower on his first commission, the design of a New York City townhouse for an irascible, tight-fisted dentist. Near the beginning of that first project, one of the masons heard Hunt say that he was "going to show New York something" with this building. The project ended up in court, with Hunt suing the dentist for his fee. The carpenter in charge, a man named Thomson, testified against Hunt. According to transcripts of the trial, Thomson told this story to the court:

"Mr. Hunt came there one morning and said, 'Thomson, there is something wrong here; I have made a sad mistake; will you raise those beams? I am a little above the beams with the head of these windows.' Said I, 'You need not trouble yourself; I will raise these beams up so that it will be all right'; and I done so."

This midstream alteration made for something of a cob job, the carpenter-builder thought. "The window trimmings cut into the cornices. I do not consider that desirable architecture, but the reverse."

Hunt had made a mistake in planning some doorways, too. "That was the fault of Mr. Hunt's drawings: the openings were not in the right place to set the trimmings," said the builder, who also remarked that Mr. Hunt had made many drawings: "He figured on paper enough to cover this room nearly; if you would unroll them you would find a good many that were unnecessary . . ." The builder had not bothered to use most of the architect's drawings, he said. Many were quite useless and he had thrown them away. The last is a familiar story, one that still gets told at construction sites.

At one point in his testimony, Thomson seemed to identify the main source of his dislike for Hunt: "There is no use of an architect about a building unless the owner requires it. Nor if he does require it; in many cases there is no use in an owner's requiring it; there are men who do not profess to be architects, but who are just as good as professional ones; a mechanic who understands his business and has served a portion of his time at architecture, but does not pretend to be an architect professionally, may be just as good as a professional architect. . . . It would make a difference if the owner wanted a house different from any other . . ." Thomson adds, and surely there was scorn in his voice, "This house is different from any I ever saw in my life—that is a fact."

From Colonial times until around 1850, clients and builders designed almost all houses in America. Architects had to create their profession against the odds. They had to persuade their countrymen that important distinctions existed between the art of designing and the act of building. Once architects had made some headway with their case, many builders without formal training began describing themselves as architects, too. Doubtless many more declared, as Thomson did, that trained architects were mainly superfluous beings.

Between 1830 and the Civil War, architects published scores of pattern and style books. At one point or another, most of those volumes argue that an architect offers the client protection from the builder. The case is often founded on social class, the architect being the client's ally by virtue of education and breeding. The argument plays upon the suspiciousness of clients about builders, a wariness that seems to have been around for so long that it probably deserves to be called natural.

"There is a glaring want of truthfulness sometimes practiced in this country by ignorant builders, that deserves condemnation at all times," wrote Andrew Jackson Downing in 1850, in one of his very popular style books. In this case, "truthfulness" meant right-minded aesthetic sensibility. Competing with builders for the patronage of people with the money to build, in an age of emerging specialization, architects staked a claim on taste. Pattern and style book writers defined taste in many different ways, but ultimately it seems to have been simply something a trained architect had and a builder didn't. And while clients usually were described as having taste, most needed architects to find their ways to it. An architect could protect clients from themselves as well as from ignorant builders.

The folklorist Bernie Herman tells of a nineteenth-century house that the owner built in imitation of a cautionary picture in a style book. The owner of the book had clearly inverted the architect-author's advice. He had constructed a perfect replica of the house that one was not supposed to build. Most carpenters and owners of the nineteenth century weren't that rebellious or perverse, but most seem not to have given up entirely on tradition and their own powers of invention. In the second half of the nineteenth century, architects greatly affected but did not control building in America, and they don't control it now, not in the way that doctors and lawyers rule their fields.

The competition for hegemony at building sites is hardly at an end. One fairly recent trend puts trained architects inside large firms that both design and build, and the architect isn't likely to wield the power there. At most sites of house construction there is no architect at all. But clients and architects and builders do sometimes gather to create a house, and when they do a century of adjustments has not done much to relieve the tension that's often in the air.

The first time he sat down with Bill to study plans, Jim told him, "When we bid this, we didn't know how much you were going to do. Lacking more input, we felt we'd have more control or input than it appears now." The way Jim said that, it sounded like a mere statement of fact. Jim was just trying to figure out Bill's role, so he could know his own. There was an odd moment, though, that afternoon, at Jim's table. Jim made a joke, a gentle one about Bill's having altered the layout of the kitchen. "I saw that change right away," said Jim, and he grinned.

Bill bowed his head over the plans and didn't smile, and while Jim's eyes lingered on the architect, Jim's smile changed, his eyebrows rising slightly, from amusement to knowingness.

Some days later, Jim sat at the Souweines' round table in Pelham, Bill's plans opened before him, and said, "I have some opinions. These extra columns on the front."

"Pilasters," said Bill.

"I'd rather leave them on the back and not put them on the front," Jim went on, speaking to Jonathan and Judith.

"I appreciate your opinions and want to have them," said Jonathan to Jim. "I encourage and solicit your opinions."

"You'll always get them," said Jim. He added, "I don't want to fight with Bill over this."

"This isn't fighting," said Judith. "You call this fighting?"

Jim put his thumb to his lower lip and studied Bill's drawing. He offered another criticism of Bill's latest drawings. Calmly, Bill defended his concept of the south wall. Jonathan said to Jim, "I definitely want this to be a house you want to build."

"I'll build it anyway," said Jim. He looked shy. He looked as though he had narrowly avoided a smile.

Late that same evening Jim pointed out to Bill a drafting error. If you put Bill's early, hurried plans for the first and second floors together, the chimney would have had to make a right-angle turn to get up through the house. Bill winced. Jim had chosen to show Bill the mistake at a moment when Judith and Jonathan were talking to each other. It was a favor of sorts. Driving home in the dark, Jim said, "Bill hasn't had a lot of experience with houses. Experience is what really helps on things like that. But he won't ever do *that* again, get a chimney out of line." At the next meeting, Jim explained a number of technical details to Bill, such as the usual height of cabinets on kitchen walls. A few hundred years before, in England, this same species of information would have fallen into the category of "secrets and mysteries of the trade." Some historians think that the publishing of books that revealed those secrets partly accounted for the decline of the apprenticeship and guild systems in carpentry and opened the way for the rise of professional architects. Jim seemed glad enough to pass on the information, but on the way home that night, he said, "I'm kind of mad at Bill. I don't know why. His relationship with the Souweines seems fuzzy. I still don't know how much he's supposed to do, and I don't think I should have to tell him how high a kitchen cabinet is."

A few days later, Jim and Bill had their spat over the phone about the deadline for the window list. Afterward Jim felt sorry, but not very. His supplier had told him, inaccurately as it turned out, that window prices would rise that Friday. Of course, Jim didn't have to tell Bill the deadline wasn't real, just when Bill had finished racing to meet it, but Jim wasn't thinking about Bill's problems. Jim felt entitled to get items such as window lists well ahead of time, so that he could shop around and plan the work.

Apple Corps had usually collaborated with customers on designs, and the carpenters liked to build that way. To imagine, then to build—there's a roundness to that kind of work that's pleasing. The carpenters liked the intimacy and the friendliness that sometimes comes from serving people with their ideas about houses as well as with their manual skills. Building had never been quite the same with an architect involved.

Apple Corps had made plenty of mistakes all on their own, of course, but somehow those weren't as memorable as the ones that architects had caused. Richard likes to tell about the time an architect specified that a roof be ventilated only under the eaves. "I wanted a ridge vent, and he's telling me we don't need it, the air's going to do something impossible. I'm telling him that and he's telling me I don't understand." Richard thinks he knows what that architect had in mind: "I only went to trade school."

Chatting in his kitchen with Sandy and a friend one day, Jim said, "You know what? I haven't ever built a house that I *really* like."

"You should be an architect yourself," the friend told Jim. Sandy agreed. She knew Jim had the ability and the temperament.

Jim's cheeks flushed. Turning half away, he said, "I can't do it. I can't conceive the grace of line, starting from nothing."

Another time, Jim said, "When you see a house written up in the *New York Times Magazine*, they usually give the name of just the architect and the owner, and I think the builder has every right to be pissed off." Jim leaned against his kitchen counter. "The thing about the architect is, the architect is sort of the artist, and the practical person who works with his hands always disdains the architect. Why should a guy be able to make a living doing that, just because his head works in a different way? But there are these things that Bill should know, and I have to come up with them."

Jim raised his voice slightly. There was a little new color in his face. What was the cause of his argument with Jonathan? It was money, obviously. When the Souweines want to add something to their house, Jim's the one who has to put a price tag on it. He's the one who has to put a meter on their dreams.

"I've gotta bring reality to the Souweines. *He* brings them the pretty pictures. I bring that." Jim smacked his fist into his open palm. "I've gotta bring them that." He punched his hand once more. "And that," he said, and then he smiled.

The blossoms came and went and the apples set on the trees in the orchards along Bay Road. In between rain showers, the frame of the house went up, and Jonathan lay awake part of one night worrying about his plywood getting wet, even though he knew a little rain wouldn't hurt it. The roof was framed and decked with plywood. Now Jim wants a detailed drawing of the cornice. By "cornice," Jim means all the trim on and under the eaves of the roof—the frieze, the soffits, and so on, a lot of different pieces of wood that meet each other at various angles, a complicated piece of work. Bill comes to Amherst and consults with Jim about it, in the Wieners' dining room, a breakable-looking room, prettily decorated in blue, with a bay window and a round table.

"Needless to say, the last forty-eight hours I've spent a lot of time thinking about this. I imagine the old-time architects spent all their time on this stuff," says Bill. He tells Jim and Judith "I worked hard yesterday walking home from work." He studied the cornices of many old buildings, he remarks earnestly. "I walked by Bulfinch's State House, too. Of course, it predates this."

Evidently, that last statement is vintage Bill, to Judith. She covers her face with her hands. She leans toward Bill, shaking with mirth, and lays her head on his shoulder briefly.

Jim looks at Bill's latest drawing of the temple end. It still shows those two extra pilasters. Jim smiles. "God, he's persistent."

"You've never seen me stubborn, have you?" says Bill, smiling, too.

Bill says he'll return to Boston and draw the cornice again. Jim tells him, "Might as well take out those middle pilasters while you're at it."

Judith says, "He just likes to draw 'em in. That's as far as he's going to get. Maybe he can imagine them there, when the house is built."

Bill shares the general amusement in his usual way, by bowing his head, as if he's being knighted or absorbing blows.

This would rank as one of their most pleasant

meetings, everyone calm and smiling, except that in between the jesting, a fencing match proceeds.

"You would recommend a drip cap?" Bill asks Jim.

"No," says Jim.

"You wouldn't?" asks Bill.

"No," says Jim. He wouldn't *not* recommend one either.

Bill, with assurance now, declares, "You *do* recommend the drip cap."

"No."

Jim explains, "I just want you to have what you want, from a design standpoint."

Judith looks at the ceiling and seems to bite back a grin.

Bill: "So you're recommending . . ."

Jim: "Suggesting."

Judith looks away, leaning back in her chair, and she clicks her tongue, just audibly, the sort of sound fond grandparents make when reproving children.

Jim: "You're in charge."

Bill: "He's teasing me. I love it."

Jim: "No. You *are* in charge."

On the question of the style of molding for the round window in the temple end, Bill says to Jim, "You don't have an opinion, of course."

"You think he's going to answer an aesthetic question?" says Judith.

"I don't want to," says Jim. "I have strong opinions about all of this, but—" He turns to Bill.

"I want you to do your work, and I'll do my work."

The meeting lasts most of the morning. When Jim, briefcase in hand, trudges back to the house, his partners meet him in what will be the foyer. What took so long? they want to know. They're losing time with him gone from the job so often. And where are the drawings for front door, hearth, stairs, cornice? Jim says he's asked for all of those. What can he do? Alex suggests they stop the job and assess penalties for every day those drawings are overdue, $100 a day, just as the contract penalizes them for every day they're late.

They mutter and scowl—and Jim has the feeling some of their consternation is really for him. Then Richard says, "Well, like we say, every job with an architect gets a little screwed up."

"With architects, there's always some kind of a fight," says Ned.

But Ned suspects that Jim draws out those meetings deliberately. Jim likes to get involved where he doesn't belong. He likes a little conflict when things get dull. Ned says so to Jim. Jim merely looks at Ned.

It's true. Jim knows Ned is right, but he does not want to go to any more meetings. He knows he doesn't. He wants to do some work with his hands for a change, some long continuous work. He doesn't feel the way he did a month ago, when Jonathan filed his motion, as it were, encouraging and soliciting Jim's opinions on design. If Jim felt now as he did then, he might have asked Bill how the frieze boards should be attached to the house. Jim didn't ask. He just wanted to bring that meeting to an end.

Afterward, when the affair of the frieze board has run its course, each party will recite a different accounting. Apple Corps will blame Bill, who will mildly blame Jim, and Judith and Jonathan will blame both Bill and Jim. They could as easily conjure up a trickster god, who oversees construction sites, and who arranged the joke this way:

Jim plans to put on the shingles once the roof is framed, so Jim gives Bill "a reprieve" on some of the drawings, including the drawing of the cornice. The Souweines, meanwhile, have begun again to worry that the design of their house has grown excessively distinctive.

If you come upon the building from behind, out of the woods, its height surprises you. The thing seems to pose the question of how it came to stand here. Its surfaces are plain, all reddish-blond plywood, but it no longer looks like an experiment in geometry, an assemblage of parts. It looks like a whole thing. It looks tall from the driveway out front, too. The mind's eye can easily add the Greek Revival trim and give it a limousinelike air. Jonathan stands in the driveway, looking up at the house. "Enough is enough. It has a taste of a Greek temple. Fine. But it's not a Greek temple, and we're not Greeks." He and Judith have resolved to put red shingles on their roof. "That gives it a little color, a little fun, in what could be a pretentious house," says Jonathan. He thinks the red roof will resemble a necktie, he says. He owns a few ties with generous amounts of color in them. He grins.

But New Englanders, Jim learns to his slight surprise, have not taken to red shingles. No one has them in stock. Apple Corps will have to wait for the shingles, and in the meantime, the only thing they can do is build the cornice. So they start on that trim about a week earlier than Jim had intended.

Jim drives to his favorite lumberyard in Amherst to buy the pine boards for the job. He goes to that yard partly because they let him choose his wood himself. The specifications call for number-two pine on the exterior, which generally means white pine with knots in it. There are knots and there are knots, though. Dead knots, roots of branches that died before the tree did, tend to fall out of a board. Knots left by living branches will bleed through paint, but you can treat them and they won't fall out. Knotless, number-one pine for the cornice would cost at least $1000 extra. The Souweines seem strapped for cash now. Jim feels sure that Jonathan wouldn't spring for number-one pine, so he doesn't bother to ask. Jim does spend over an hour, in the lumberyard's fragrant hangar full of wood, searching through piles of pine, rejecting every board with dead knots in it, except for one. He can't find any more boards without dead knots, so he has to take one that has them, and he decides to make that board symbolic. He looks it over and addresses these remarks to it, as he loads it on his pickup: "There, Jonathan, there's your six hundred and sixty dollars."

Back east in Boston, meanwhile, another sizable design job, a generous gift from his old firm, has been delivered to Bill. That makes three jobs. Jonathan has been telling Bill he has to get the remaining drawings out to Amherst much faster than he has. Bill is now searching for an assistant, but he finds the time somehow to draw the cornice in detail. This drawing makes it plain that the two wide frieze boards are supposed to be built out from the wall three and a half inches. The drawing that makes Bill's intentions unmistakable arrives at the bus station in Northampton on the date Jim named when he gave Bill the reprieve. Jim picks up the drawing of the cornice on the morning Apple Corps begins to build it.

At that moment, Jim's thoughts lie mostly with the staircase. Hoping to save some time, he sent Bill's drawing of the stair to a stair-making firm. That firm has reported back that Bill's drawing will cost more than $4000 to execute. Bill hadn't drawn the stairs when Jim signed the contract, but that document includes an "allowance" for stairs. It's only $2500. What's more, the contract doesn't say whether or not that $2500 covers the main staircase and also the three small ones that lead into the sunken living room. Jim thinks the figure covers all. He also thinks they put a figure into writing in the spirit of a guess, one that they would add money to when the real cost of the main staircase revealed itself. Jonathan feels differently. He says the small stairs are covered in the general contract price, and he's told Jim the $2500 covers only the main stair and that he does not want to pay any more than that for stairs.

When he ponders an issue of this sort, Jim usually develops a crippling awareness of the opposing point of view. In his own mind, he tends to argue the other side's case more forcefully than his own. As he puts it, "I don't feel sure enough I'm wrong to say I am." Anyway, the stairs will need redesigning. Stairs are just a way of getting to the second floor, Jonathan has said. A new argument looms, Jim thinks. He's bracing himself for it. The work on the cornice begins.

Jim and Richard feel stumped about how to build one detail of the cornice that every drawing has included. It has to do with the application of some crown molding to the eaves. Jim and Richard spend an hour of that morning, crouched on the kitchen floor, trying to solve that problem. Preoccupied about the crown molding, Jim does not think about the frieze. He thinks he knows Bill's intentions for that detail. Jim does not consult the new drawings, the ones he just picked up at the bus station. They sit inside his leather case, over in a corner.

The carpenters must be making an especially nice job of all the trim for the cornice, because for the next week or so Richard keeps singing out, "Crisp" and "Custom," and there's a lot of talk about beavering and cob jobs. All around the house lie handsaws, and block planes for shaving saw cuts to near perfection, and other finishing tools. The carpenters sit high up on the parapet of staging, among treetops.

"Hey, Alex, you ever hear of a razor-sharp block plane?"

"Oral tradition says there were sharp block planes once, just as there were unicorns," says Alex, as with his razor-sharp block plane he gently smoothes the butt end of a section of frieze board, and, per Jim's instructions, nails it to the house, flat against the wall. You know the cornice went on nicely because on the back of one of the last pieces of molding, before he nails it in place, Jim writes,

APPLE CORPS BUILDERS 1983

They've built the cornice and the red shingles have arrived, when Jim calls Jonathan to talk some more about the stairs. Jim mentions, by the way, that they've improved on a feature of Bill's plan. The improvement has to do with the crown molding on the eaves.

Jonathan doesn't know exactly what Jim's talking about, but he does not like the sound of it. Neither does Judith.

Back when they got stumped over Bill's drawing for that molding, Richard had declared, "That isn't proper." He had decided to apply the crown molding differently, the way the old-timers used to, a modification that costs Apple Corps about $30—a small price for propriety. A few weeks later, passing by an old house, Richard stops in his truck and looking up, he sees that very same molding applied in just the way that Bill had specified. "Whoops."

The crown molding is a false issue, though. Troubled by Jim's call, Jonathan phones Bill and tells him he'd better come to Amherst soon. Bill must visit in any case, to talk to Jim about redesigning the staircase.

A tall wooden ladder leans against the high staging on the temple end. It wobbles as Jim climbs. Bill follows, looking slightly nervous. Bill stares at the crown molding. Bill shrugs. "It's different than what I expected," he tells Jim. "I don't have a lot of problems with it."

Back on the ground, Bill and Jim sit down on separate sawhorses, facing each other. The temple end stands high above them. The blondness of the raw wood in the bright sunshine obscures the trimmings, but if you look twice you can see many new crisp, angular surfaces up near the roof. Bill and Jim discuss the stairs.

"The question I raise is, it's all Brosco stock items. The whole stair was designed straight out of the book. My problem is, they seemed like minimal stairs," says Bill.

"Yeah, but you picked the most expensive parts. I think."

They talk on, another fencing match, Bill saying that an assumption existed from the start that these would be traditional stairs with newel posts, banisters, easements, balusters, and Jim answering that he cannot price assumptions at the lumber-yard nor build a house from them. Bill asks, "You need the front door drawing for when?"

"For Wednesday last week," says Jim. There's sarcasm in Jim's voice. Bill lets it pass.

They talk about the grading and the hearth and half a dozen other issues. Richard and Ned wander by, stand sideways listening in, then go back to work.

When Bill had driven up to the house, he had noticed the knots in the cornice right away. He had decided not to think of them again. Too many other potentially explosive subjects already lay between him and Jim. Every time he has glanced up at the house, though, Bill has seen those little round black spots, like pox on the crisply installed trim beneath the roof. After a while, when Bill looks at the house, he can see hardly anything but knots, and he can't contain his worry.

"I assume there's no problem with knots in the trim wood?"

Jim looks up with widened eyes.

"I wondered why we didn't have clearer pine," Bill adds.

"Because it isn't in the contract," Jim says. He explains the issue as he sees it. Then Judith comes over, and the meeting ends.

It's late. The other carpenters have left. Jim

heads for his truck. "Are we okay, Jim?" Bill calls.

"I don't know what you mean by 'okay,' " replies Jim. He adds, "I'm just in a hurry. I'm not upset."

Then it's just Judith and Bill, in front of the shell of the house in the bright summer evening.

Judith says that she fears they must write a change order for the master bathroom's fixtures.

Bill grasps her arm and lays his head upon her shoulder for a moment, a contortionist's trick for big Bill to perform with little Judith, and he says, "Look, my friend, if that's the only change order that comes out of today's conversation, you'll be lucky."

Bill tells her about the knots. She says, "They did an awfully nice job."

"Oh, yeah!" says Bill, with feeling. But those knots are driving him crazy, he tells her.

"There's some things you can worry about, but I think it's a little late for this one," she says. Bill tells her clear pine would cost $1000 extra. She says, "Forget it, Bill." In a moment, she leaves him standing there, in front of the skeleton of his first house.

Didn't the contract call for clear pine? Bill asks himself. He stares up at the cornice and laughs a short, deep, sorrowful laugh. "Funny how something like that can really get to ya. Boy! I'm really . . ." Bill knows those knots will bleed through the paint. He's always thought of knots that show as a sign of general shoddiness. He suspects that the contract doesn't call for clear pine. He has always specified it on buildings in the past, on occasions when wooden trim was involved. "I'm surprised I didn't catch that."

Bill gazes up at the cornice, and suddenly he looks puzzled. He's taken off his sunglasses and hung them by an earpiece from the *V* at the breast of his short-sleeved shirt, the better to see the knots. He walks backward, away from the house, all the way back to the Wieners' woodpile. He tilts his head, for a slightly sidelong view. He makes his hand a visor for his eyes, and he says softly, "I always thought it came out a couple of inches from the face of the house." He stares. "It's . . ." He laughs. Then he groans, "Ohhhhhh," like someone desperate for a bed.

The frieze, one of the most important elements in Bill's synthesis of Greek Revival, lies flat against the house, a broad band extending out just the thickness of the boards that make up the frieze. Those boards are only slightly thicker than the clapboards that will lie below them. The frieze won't stand out to meet the eye. It won't create the proper look at all. "It just doesn't seem substantial enough."

Bill gazes. He groans. He tries out reassurance. "It'll look a lot better." But he adds, "It better. Because it looks really weak right now." He laughs, and it sounds like an echo from an old well. "You pour so much of your soul into it," he says. "It's very different from most fields. There are so many vagaries that can change things and explain why it

293

didn't come out in exactly the form of your vision." Bill stands beside the Wieners' woodpile, staring up in the evening light at the tall, elegantly proportioned skeleton. Standing in that same spot ten days ago, Ned called the building "proud." Now Bill says, "It's so funny, because every time I look at this house now, all that I can see is the frieze."

The following morning Bill and Judith and Jonathan, who is dressed for the office, hover in a ring around Jim. He sits on the opened tailgate of his truck, a pencil behind his ear, and extracts from his leather case the most recent and detailed drawing of the cornice.

"There was always an assumption that the frieze would extend out from the face of the house," says Bill.

Jim studies the drawings for the first time. He looks up at Bill. "Well, I guess the solution is to get the drawings before we build the house." Jim throws the papers down onto the tailgate. He stares at Bill. Judith and Jonathan glance at each other and don't speak.

"It's been different from the way you did it, all along," says Bill.

"Not all along." Jim picks up the blueprint and shakes it. "These drawings right here are dated six-fourteen. It's makin' me mad, all this stuff." He hurls the plans down, glaring up at Bill. Bill and the Souweines stand around the angry builder, wearing helpless, worried looks.

"Your drawings have all these assumptions and implications in them," says Jim. "Now I feel I'm on the carpet."

"I'm on the carpet, too," says Bill, very softly. "My feeling is we have to try to correct the frieze in some way that makes sense."

Jim looks away. He takes a deep breath. He purses his lips. He gazes up at the frieze. He studies the drawings again.

Jonathan doesn't understand the problem fully. Judith explains it to him, to one side. Smiling, she tells Jonathan that perhaps the solution is to change not the frieze but the name of the house's architectural style. "Maybe we can call it something else."

Jonathan returns her smile. "It'll explain why the Greek Revival didn't sustain itself."

"There are more drawings on this house than on most five-hundred-thousand-dollar houses," Bill says to Jim, very softly.

Jim studies the detailed drawing once again. "It's on here," he says. "I guess I didn't have it in my mind that way."

Bill stares up at the frieze, chin on hand. Jim stares up at the frieze, a forefinger against his lips. "Hey, Bill, what about the idea of having the frieze go down a little lower?"

"Below the vents?" asks Bill. "I think that would look very strange." Jim's solution would not preserve the proper effect, the sense of a roof floating on the frieze.

"It would be neat," says Jim. "There'd be a line there under the soffits."

They stare upward.

"I would like to be able to say that that's good," says Bill. He looks pained. "I just don't think it is."

The architect and builder go back to silent, upward staring. There is, it seems, no other way around the problem but for Apple Corps to take down the frieze and put it up again. The repair looks hard to Jim, because they assembled the cornice so carefully and because to change the frieze they must alter the soffits. The right repair will mean, among other things, that one of the carpenters must spend a day or more inching along the high staging on his back, cutting over his head with a skillsaw while twenty feet up in the air. A neat job won't be easy. Jim says he doesn't want to ask anyone to do that job.

Jonathan has to get to the office. Bill and Jim should try to invent a new design for the staircase and find a way to fix the frieze, he says. Then Jonathan turns to the subject of the knots, and Jim has the feeling all at once that he is in the witness box in court. "I would consider it an acceptable solution if you will warrant that the knots won't come through the paint for five years," says Jonathan to Jim, "since I do have tremendous respect for your integrity and judgment as a builder, and I know you wouldn't put anything there that wasn't satisfactory."

"Jonathan's strategy. It's real familiar. I'm used to it. 'You're a real good, a great, craftsman and I know you wouldn't do anything wrong, so why did you?' It's just what my father would do," says Jim.

Apple Corps has retreated to an Amherst sandwich shop and fruit store, for coffee.

"The frieze?" cries Richard. They will not redo the frieze, Richard declares.

"I was ready to punch that guy," Jim says, referring to Bill. "It feels really funny. I never felt that way about anybody before."

Ned gets up from their table. He lifts a watermelon out of a bin. He laughs. "We could drop this on Bill's head."

Jim explains that Bill won't accept the easy-looking solution.

Ned says to Jim, "He seems kind of soft and mild in his requests."

"That's just his manner," says Jim. "He gets an idea, he sticks to it."

"I knew it was going to be like this," says Alex. "An arm-wrestling match."

They vote. It's unanimous. They will not guarantee the knots. The three others vote no on repairing the frieze. When that ballot reaches Jim, though, he doesn't vote. He says, "I wish these issues were perfectly clear. I'm not quite sure when those plans arrived."

"Aw, shoot," says Richard. "I'll take your skillsaw, get up there and thrash it. I don't mind.

I'll do it on my back with a rope around my neck."

They return to work, on the roof.

"Upbeat!" bellows Richard. "Let's have this upbeat!"

"Turn on the radio," yells Jim.

" '*Kay!*'" answers Richard. To himself, he says, "Upbeat. Whatever we do, we gotta be upbeat."

For the rest of the day, Richard accomplishes little. He drops tools off his ladder. He climbs up to the staging around the master bedroom ell's low roof, remembers he forgot the tool he needed, climbs down, climbs up again with the tool, drops the piece of wood he was working on, climbs down again. None of them gets much done. Several times, they gather in their usual circle, to discuss the issues—the stairs, the knots, the frieze.

Sitting on the floor inside, Ned searches for a general explanation and a remedy. "I sort of feel Jonathan and Judith need to know how much of an imposition this guy's being on us," Ned says. "The guy wants to build a Cadillac, and they only want to buy a Chevrolet."

"They know he's upping the ante all the time," Jim tells Ned. Jim lifts opened palms to his partners, that old gesture of innocence, and he says, "Everybody knows everything. But everybody wants something different."

Mornings have grown warm, afternoons hot. By afternoon the carpenters are dressed for an outing at the beach, in shorts and sneakers and no shirts, all except for Richard, who insists on wearing boots and jeans, because, he says, his legs are very handsome and are worth protecting.

"You can barely get up there by yourself, Alex," Richard says, at the bottom of the ladder. "How are you going to carry up a bundle of shingles?" The first rule of roofing, Richard says, is you never ascend a ladder without bringing a package of shingles. "Sweat a little, Alex."

Halfway up, a package of heavy shingles on his shoulder, Alex stops. "Even allowing for religion and national origin, Richard, you're a terrible person."

One of the crew, following Alex up, confesses, "I lose courage near the top."

"Hemingway must have an appropriate line for that," says Alex as he relieves the worried climber of his load of shingles.

"Know why roofers always carry straight-clawed hammers?" Ned stands on the slanting plywood roof, then suddenly, letting out the shout of an Oriental warrior, he lets himself fall to the plywood, and falling, he smashes the claw of his straight-clawed hammer through the plywood deck. In this vivid way he explains that your hammer is your tool of last resort, the ice axe you implant when you have lost your feet and are slipping toward the edge of the roof.

"It *is* hot."

"It *is really fucking* hot. It's real hot up on the peak of the roof right now."

Standing on the high staging, Richard can't see

Ned, who's up near the peak on the far side of the roof. But Richard hears Ned's voice say, "I gotta put my head in the hose or I'm going to fall off the roof."

"Oh-*Kay!*" says Richard. "I think we'll just pack up our tools now 'n' go home."

When Ned gets down, he sits bare to the waist beside the house in the sand, empty shingle bags all around him. A board clatters inside the house, and Ned flinches. "The thing that scares me, you go past where it's safe, just to get the job done and not be called a weakling." Ned barks a soft laugh. "It's stupid. And I think the thing that's good about it, we care enough about each other to do like Richard and just call a stop to it." They head home long before their usual quitting time.

They start their shingling very early in the mornings, because by midday the heat begins to make them wobble and the red shingles begin to soften and crumble under their feet. Bits of gravel from the shingles' surfaces lodge beneath their wet T-shirts, and the roof feels like a sloped highway radiating smelly heat. So on these roofing mornings, Jim sets out from home in the dark, alone in his truck, and as he turns down Bay Road the weird and lovely jagged hills of the Holyoke Range, the apple trees and fields, emerge slowly from the mist, first the outlines, then the color, like a photograph in a pan of developing fluid. Driving out Bay Road, climbing a little, the oceanic views of the Connecticut River Valley awakening around him, Jim finds some peace. Dawn is lovely in this valley. He's glad he lives here.

In morning light, the carpenters stand at mountain-climbing angles. They move gingerly across the roof, then up, then across again, turning the roof brick-red in swaths. But building the house has begun to seem just an auxiliary function, the builders being the crew who hurry to prepare the set for the next unpleasant scene. The night after the affair of the frieze, Jim sleeps fitfully. He rises feeling all worn out. "I would really like to work on this house and not be in charge of it, because it's a nice house." The windows have arrived at the lumberyard. They must take possession of the windows soon. They can't charge Jonathan for the windows until they install them. They can't install the windows until they finish the roof and fix the frieze. If they can't charge Jonathan, they can't pay for the windows. If they don't pay for the windows on time, they lose their builder's discount. It's another way to forfeit a few hundred dollars. Jim will figure out a way around that problem. What really worries Jim is the meeting with Jonathan tomorrow.

Jim had felt so angry at Bill about the frieze, he had scared himself. For Jim, the residue, now that the tingling is long gone, is a feeling of stupidity. Immediately in those situations, he wonders, What have I done wrong this time? He feels cornered. He won't fight with Bill and Jonathan anymore, he has decided. "They're too powerful for me," he says. But if Jonathan won't yield on the issue and Jim's partners won't, then there's no way around another fight. Jim can feel it coming. He can feel himself getting hot all over again, and the only way out he can think of is to take Ned's advice and get some help. He has always dealt all by himself with the Souweines and Bill, one against what sometimes seems a multitude. He has wanted it that way. He has coveted the role of boss. But Richard is a much clearer, straighter talker than he. In all the years that Jim has known him, Richard has never had trouble talking directly on any subject, including money—Richard has never had enough money to feel embarrassed by that subject, Jim thinks. In bed the night before the meeting with Jonathan, Jim thinks that tomorrow he might ask Richard to join him. The next morning, Jim resolves to do it.

Sandy is surprised. "I would have thought that Jim would be jealous of Richard joining the negotiations." She is very pleased with Jim.

It's a new tableau that morning, three men standing in the dirt by the driveway, two in T-shirts, the other in a pink seersucker suit. The short one with the black beard keeps his arms folded on his chest and smiles when he's listening. When he talks, his voice booms and somehow still sounds friendly: "See, the thing of it is, Jonathan, we don't want to buy your stairs."

Jonathan appears, as ever, both completely calm and in a hurry. When Richard speaks, Jonathan wears a crooked smile. Clearly, Jonathan enjoys Richard's brand of direct talk. "Things seem to go more smoothly when Richard's there," Jonathan has noted.

Jim thinks a traditional staircase, like the Wieners', could be built for about $2900. Insisting that the allowance named in the contract was $2000 for the main staircase, Jim thinks that Jonathan should pay $900 extra. Jonathan disagrees on all counts, but he offers to split the difference: They'd each ante up $450.

Jim and Richard don't feel they can afford to eat $450, because they have decided already to eat the frieze. Politely, they fail to agree on the stairs.

"Ummm, the cornice, the frieze board issue, we decided we would absorb the cost of that," says Jim.

"Thank you," says Jonathan.

"We put the roof together and we had to think it through ourselves, and then he comes in the *day* before with detailed drawings," says Richard. "It's going to cost us three hundred dollars to rip it all apart and start over. But we should've looked. So we want to pay for it."

Jonathan nods.

"On the knots," says Jim. "The specs call for number two. We don't feel we should guarantee them."

"We're gonna seal all the knots," says Richard. "There are going to be some knots come through. I'm not going to tell you they won't. But the next time you paint, they'll be gone."

Are all those boards up there number-two pine? Jonathan wants to know.

"All except for one of those wide boards," says Richard, pointing to that one piece of pine with dead knots, the one that Jim had to take. The symbolic board has become part of the wrongly built frieze.

"But you *bought* number two," says Jonathan. He pauses. "Okay," he says. "It's all right with me."

Nearly every night Jim makes nervous calculations, attempting to compare their estimate to reality. One evening around this time, he discovers that they forgot to include the cost of framing the interior walls of the house, an item worth perhaps $750. True to form, though, it seems that they overestimated some other parts of the job. The sheetrockers bid $2500 less than Jim and his partners allowed for dry wall, and the insulator and the maker of cellar floors Jim hired have promised to do their jobs for hundreds less than Jim expected. So far, he thinks, they're about even, but not for any of the right reasons. And what about the stairs?

To build a set of rough stairs, you think about the finished ones, because you build the finished stairs on the skeleton of the rough ones. Jim doesn't want to make a rough staircase without assurances that Jonathan will pay all the cost of the stairs, but the plumber, electrician, insulator, and sheetrockers are coming soon and they'll probably go away if there aren't stairs.

Jules suggests to Jim one day that Apple Corps build the staircase and settle up with Jonathan later. "Settle it at the end, huh?" Richard says when he hears that advice. "That's not the way Jules got to be driving a Mercedes. They're takin' *real* good care of themselves. We're going to take care of ourselves." The next day, Richard tells Jim he might as well build the rough staircase. What good would it do to stop the job or slow it down for lack of stairs? "We've gotta build the house anyways, sooner or later," says Richard.

Items for Jim to discuss with Bill today include: the staircase, appliances for the master bath, towel bars, casings for the interiors of windows, a granite lintel for the hearth, grilles that Bill wants placed in the ceiling above the wood stove, material for vanity tops, the bases and capitals of the columns that Jim has ordered for the porch, the final grading of the site, the thimble and clean-out for the chimney, the locations of electrical outlets and lights, the size and style of the round window for the gable of the temple end, and bed molding for the frieze. Bill wants to know by how many inches it is customary to overlap one clapboard with another, and what knot sealer Jim's painter will use.

Shortly before the battered Datsun came up the drive, Ned and Richard counseled Jim. Jim should curb his proclivity to argument and palaver. He should say only what needs saying. Keep the meeting short, Jim, they said. They need his hands. Now Jim sits down with Bill, at the table in the Wieners' dining room. Jim is patient at first. He is helpful. As the meeting continues, though, Jim turns testy. He tells Bill that weekdays are not the time for meetings; he has work to do. And Bill replies that he's always been willing to discuss these issues after hours. Jim baits Bill. Once, he actually gets Bill to snap at him: "Don't give me that shit." Jim smiles briefly. He goes back to being helpful, and partly because of Jim's experimental stratagems, the meeting drags on.

Jim begins to say something about vanity tops. Abruptly, he quits. "I don't want to raise any new questions."

"They will be very disappointed if something important is not pointed out to them," says Bill.

"Well, it's not my problem."

"Yeah, but in terms of people being happy . . ."

"But the only one it costs money is me!" says Jim. "I care only because I care how the house comes out. But I'm pretty worn down."

"Yeah, but in terms of your pride as a builder . . ."

"Yeah," answers Jim. "But let's not spend that money. Jonathan's been spending it and there isn't any left."

They return to their discussions. What to do about the stairs? That's between Bill and Jonathan, says Jim. That's between Jim and Jonathan, says Bill.

Passing through his own dining room, hearing talk of money, Jules offers a jibe that seems more sharply pointed than he can know: "Why are we

letting money come between our beautiful friendship?" Jules grins and goes out.

Jim points out to Bill that the drawing of the
porch roof is wrong. The roof should be hipped.
Jim leans across the table and draws the correc-
tion onto the plans.

"You're changing things and I applaud that,"
says Bill. "Isn't that nice? Applause from the
snide architect?"

"You aren't snide," says Jim. "It's me that's
snide."

Jim doesn't want to estimate the cost of new,
possible staircase designs, not off the top of his
head, and he says he doesn't want to take the
trouble to make another estimate of something
that won't get built.

"But you know you have to answer those questions in this world," says Bill.

In all, with time out for lunch, the meeting
lasts about five hours. When Jim gets back to the
house, it's nearly time to pack up for the day.

From time to time, before they stop to "hoe it
out," as Richard says, trash heaps of sawdust,
scraps of wood, and coffee cups accumulate inside. Studs lie helter-skelter in other piles. The
house just now might be not in progress but in
demolition. "I didn't earn any money today," Jim
says. "I have a sort of feeling that I get trapped
into these things. I'm real aware of that because
it's something I do. Blub, blub, blub." He picks
up a two-by-four and throws it onto a pile of
studs in a corner of what will be the foyer. The

noise attracts Ned from the second floor. To him, Jim says, "I just wish we had something else to do. I'd just stop this job. I don't really want to stop."

"I really do need to keep a paycheck coming," says Ned.

The others climb down to the foyer.

"What that fellow needs is a case of lockjaw," says Alex, referring to Bill.

"I wish they'd get all their shit in one bag," says Richard.

"Get your shit in one bag!" Ned yells, toward the still-empty window holes that open toward the driveway, where Bill's small car is parked.

"We're taking the Fourth of July off," says Alex.

"With pay," says Jim.

"With what money?" asks Alex.

When Jim gets home, Sandy is in the kitchen, reading. "I worked for about forty minutes today," Jim tells her. She puts down her book. She can see Jim needs to talk.

"They're pissed at me because I'm not working," Jim tells her, referring to his partners. "Well, I'm gaining. I'm teaching Bill how to build a house. That meeting, I was mad for part of it, nice for part of it, conciliatory for part of it, but it didn't make any difference. He keeps taking his six-foot strides. I made him mad once, but it didn't make any difference."

"People who work with their minds can accelerate the process," Sandy says. "It works for mental labor, but you can't go home and in the bathtub put the shingles on the roof." She doesn't think Bill or the Souweines fully understand that.

"Bill's an able person, clearly. He's a real charming guy," Jim goes on. But he wishes he had not allowed Jonathan that $200 for Bill's contributions. "Bill's tuition," Jim calls the money. "I hope he remembers me in his memoirs."

Someone driving around Amherst with Jim, on a morning in June a week or so after the affair of the frieze, might think that Jim is following an air show. He drives very slowly and he keeps ducking his head and looking skyward, through the driver's window. After a while, it's clear that Jim is examining the brick chimney tops of some of Amherst's old houses. Many of those chimneys don't have plain, flat sides, but fancy designs, called corbeling, in the brickwork. Some people think that corbeling had functional origins. Jim doubts it. "Corbeling says, 'This is where the chimney ends,'" he remarks. Judith would smile if she heard, as she smiles when Bill makes statements like that. "Hmmmm," says Jim, driving along with his eyes on chimney tops.

Bill has envisioned nothing special for the chimney, just a square, well-built one that comes up through the center of the house and is faced with brick where it protrudes above the roof. He's left any other details to Jim. "Bill punted on the chimney," Jim says.

Jim hired Apple Corps's regular hilltown mason, Dick Staelens, months ago, and Staelens gave Jim a price for a chimney with a flat-sided brick-faced top. Jim made that price part of the final contract price for the house. Staelens works fast. He starts laying the chimney down in the basement one morning, and by midmorning the next day he's brought it all the way up into the attic, which has become a steamy spot. You climb up and at once your face turns moist. Jim joins Staelens there, under the rafters.

Jim squats on his heels beside the mason. "It's a fancy house without being extravagant," Jim says to him. "I wonder if we could do something to dress up the chimney."

Burly Dick Staelens hitches up his pants and takes out a fat barn-building pencil. "Over to Westhampton we did somethin' like this." Staelens draws a diagram of a chimney top in profile, on one of the two-by-sixes that makes up part of the roof truss.

"Corbeling," Staelens says. "Or like the one I did in Apple Valley."

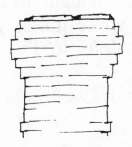

Jim stares at the two drawings, lips pursed. "Damned if I know."

"Everyone has their own preference," says the mason.

"Yeah," says Jim. He points to the second, more elaborate diagram. "Why don't you do it that way?" He adds, "I know it'll cost more, but it's not a lot, is it?"

"Nah."

So the chimney comes out of the house corbeled. It looks just like some of those old ones Jim studied on the way to the lumberyard. Florence tells Jim she loves it. Judith says the same.

Jim says nothing to his partners about the chimney. Standing outside looking up at it, he admits that he has, in effect, designed and bought the corbeling. He smiles. He wipes his hair from his forehead. "Yeah," he says, still gazing up. "But it looks really nice."

Masons sometimes sign their work, as carpenters do. When he was finishing off that chimney cap, Dick Staelens wrote in the wet concrete on the very top. Jim had been leaving messages around the house, describing Staelens as an "old goat," and Staelens thought he'd get even. You can't see what he wrote unless you climb up to the chimney and look for it. The message reads:

GENTLEMAN JIM 83

2

Jim thinks Jonathan must feel strapped. Instead of spending another thousand dollars or so to have his own water pipe laid, Jonathan has decided, against Jim's advice, to tap the line that runs from Jules's house to the town water system.

The water pipe often comes up in the talk at morning coffee break. Richard imagines a day in the future when Jules is singing in his shower, and across the way the Souweines turn on dish and clothes washers, baths and showers, all at once. In Richard's vision, Jules appears outside, clad in a towel, and strides across the driveway. " 'Hey, Judith, get the hell out of the shower,' " says Richard, doing a fine imitation of his new friend, Jules.

The water company has doubts, too. What will happen if some day strangers occupy the two houses? one of the employees over there asks Jim. Relieved, Jim tells Jonathan they'll have to lay a separate pipe, and Jim thinks the case is closed. The next time he goes to the water company's office, however, all the "working-level people" seem to talk out of the sides of their mouths to

312

him. "Who is that guy?" they want to know. "A doctor or a lawyer or something?" Jonathan will be allowed to share Jules's pipe. Jim is amused, also impressed. He couldn't have pulled that off himself.

Another time, Jim mentions to Richard that Jonathan is buying his wood stove at a nearby store.

"He'll pay a lot more for it there," says Richard.

"I bet he won't," sings Jim.

Apple Corps holds a conference on how to become more businesslike than they have been, an annual, sometimes biannual soul-search of an event at which many motions are made and many are tabled. Tonight, they agree that they ought to think about hiring a lawyer.

"We could hire Jonathan," says Ned.

"He'd probably do great things for us," says Richard.

"I wouldn't be surprised if he was *real* good," says Jim.

When Jonathan sent them his first bill, they could knock $660 off it, Jim says. They laugh and turn to other business, but they meant what they said. They believe Jonathan could handle their problems easily—the customers who take months to pay, for instance—if he handled their problems half as adroitly as he has handled them.

A psychiatrist in Northampton remembers testifying against a client of Jonathan's, in a case that Jonathan wasn't likely to win. Jonathan was giving the psychiatrist a cool, brisk, hostile cross-examination. From little signs, meanwhile—a tilt of the head, an imperceptible nod—the psychiatrist got the decided feeling that his responses were making increasingly good sense to the judge, who was also jury in the case. What interested the psychiatrist was that Jonathan clearly read those signs, too, and abruptly ended the cross-examination. Jonathan was probably a very good lawyer, the psychiatrist figured. Jim has little doubt of it. Jim, the lawyer's son, has felt drawn to Jonathan from the start and also increasingly wary of him. Every time they meet to discuss money these days, it seems to Jim that Jonathan begins by praising Apple Corps: "The main thing is that you're doing a great job building my house." Jonathan closes a big meeting on change orders in the same way: "I think this went exactly as I hoped it would. Not everyone's happy about everything, but that's life . . . Again, keep up the good work. The house is looking great. Everyone who sees it says so." He looks to Jim and Richard. "The work looks great." He looks to Bill. "The design looks great." And then he's gone.

At those moments, Jim feels as if he's being played in several keys at once. He is reminded of a phrase from an old song whose name he can't remember: "a handful of gimme and a mouthful of much obliged." But Jonathan's praise also sounds authentic to Jim. It pleases Jim to hear it, and it dismays him to feel the strength ebb from the grudges that he's nurtured, just when he needs them most, to make himself want to hold the line in every disagreement from now on. When Jonathan raised the issue of the knots and said, in effect, "You're a fine builder, so I know you'll guarantee those knots," Jim was so taken aback he didn't think to describe the pains he had taken to do more than the specifications required and find the best number-two pine he could. The upshot of the next day's meeting with Jonathan looked at the moment like a symmetrical exchange. Apple Corps gave in on the frieze without an argument, and Jonathan gave in almost as easily on the knots. But when he thinks about it afterward, the trade seems less than even to Jim. He and Richard yielded on a somewhat debatable issue—one very early drawing had shown the frieze nailed flat against the house—while Jonathan merely acceded to the undeniable fact that the specs call for number-two and therefore knotty pine. Jonathan leaves them feeling fairly contented, though, and impressed that they are.

"He's a pro," says Jim, a while after Jonathan has left.

"Yeah, he is," says Richard, who has just seen Jonathan in action for the first time. "When I was on jury duty, I learned a lot about lawyers. The good ones took a course in theater. 'Here's this poor little old lady got run over by a tractor trailer.' Actually, she jumped right out in front of it. I thought it was nice, though, that he thanked us for the frieze."

"Thank you for giving us another three hundred dollars," says Ned, who's working nearby.

"It's not exactly that, Ned," says Jim. "Or we wouldn't do it."

"I expect, though, we'll get credit for a good deed," says Richard. "A bonus. We never got a bonus from a customer. Just one party once. A bottle of wine."

"The reality is that if these guys weren't quality workmen and quality people, there'd be fewer problems," Jonathan reflects. "They'd say, 'Fine,' and then just go and do what they wanted. You know why I gave in on the knots? Suppose Jim said, 'Okay, I'll guarantee the paint.' Suppose four years later I called. 'The knots bled through.' What could I do if he said no, he wouldn't fix them? But the point is, if Jim said to me he would do it, Jim would do it."

Jonathan seems to say that he would rather not force from Jim a concession on the knots, because to do so would amount to penalizing Jim for having more integrity than most builders do.

"I love trials," Jonathan has said. "I love the intensity, the action." Clearly, he likes some of that in his daily life as well. The fast track suits him and Judith. It also carries some liabilities. Designing as you go undermines the security of the contract price. Every addition to the design seems to cost more than they feared. Every deletion saves less than they hoped.

If you sit in Jonathan's chair and daydream

316

briefly, looking out over Main Street, it's clear he made an even trade on the knots and frieze. Sure, the specs call for number-two pine, but Jim should have explained the difference between numbers one and two. Jim never said there was an option. So Jonathan did have some grounds for argument about the knots. He gave them up. Jim and Richard gave up no more in agreeing to pay for the frieze.

Jonathan remembers telling Bill again and again that one of these days something would get built wrong, if Bill did not deliver drawings well ahead of time. Imagining himself Apple Corps's lawyer, Jonathan tells the builders, "Don't you touch that cornice. Not until you get the detailed drawings and have time to study them." He'd have added, "If you build it wrong, you're screwed, and if you're right, no one thanks you for it." He would have advised them, "Go tell the owner his architect's holding you up and he's got to adjust the completion date." As the lawyer representing himself, he figures that having hired an architect and builder, he has a right to expect them to get the house built correctly, and not to pay for their mistakes.

Jonathan feels sorry for the trouble the frieze caused, but not for the little imperfection it represents. No one else will see it, but Bill has said that even when repaired, the frieze won't quite reproduce his intentions. Orthodox Jews have a tradition that until the Temple in Jerusalem is rebuilt, they will not erect a house or building without

317

giving it one deliberate imperfection. Though not a member of the Orthodox branch of Judaism, Jonathan believes in the inevitability of imperfection. So why not celebrate it? "There's a flaw in the house . . . ," he says, and he flashes a smile, a shooting star of a smile, ". . . which the pernicious part of me sort of likes."

Long ago, early in their marriage, Judith sometimes began to talk of pending worries, right when Jonathan was heading off for sleep. "It just set me off," he remembers. "Write it down," he'd tell her. "I can't do anything about it now." He does not let himself worry very much at bedtime. He takes up issues like the staircase in the morning.

Jonathan has known of building contractors who play a subterfuge nicknamed "the lowball." They underestimate on purpose the costs of unspecified items, in order to underbid competitors. Once they get the job, the contractors squeeze the real costs out of the owners: Pay up or buy yourself a ladder to get to your second floor. Has Jim lowballed the staircase? Jonathan has considered the possibility and rejected it, utterly. The Jim he's seen across the table many times lacks that sort of guile or intention.

Jonathan could swear he remembers Jim saying that the allowance of $2500 should cover a staircase. Now it appears that Jim was thinking of building, not for $2500 but for $2000, the kind of modern, simple stair that Apple Corps has usually constructed. Jim has offered to build one of those for Jonathan, but a stair like that in an old-fashioned house like this would be completely inappropriate. "He might as well offer me a kangaroo." The stairs were not designed when Jim put a price on them, but the specs for the Wieners' house have served as the model for this one, and the Wieners' house has a traditional staircase with an expensive, rounded tread at the bottom— Jonathan likes that rounded tread. He does not want Jim to build the very expensive stair that Bill designed. A stair like the Wieners' will do. Jim says he can build such a stair, minus the rounded bottom tread, for $2900. The problem is Jim wants $900 added to the contract price, $900 to build a staircase for which Jonathan thought he'd already paid.

People who do the work have a certain advantage over those who merely pay. The workers occupy what Alex calls "the moral high ground." But Jonathan works hard for his money, too. "Jonathan would work all the time," says Judith, "if I let him." He does not want Apple Corps to work for nothing on his behalf. He does not want to throw away $900 worth of his own work either. Judith has said they shouldn't pay any of the $900. Jonathan has no doubt that he would win his case before an arbitrator. "But the world is full of people who think they are right and don't get anything done," he says. "It's traditional in this situation to say, 'Let's split the difference.'"

Jonathan has already agreed to pay hundreds of dollars for extras that didn't seem like extras to him: for "kickboards" on the front wall (those seemed to appear in the earliest drawings), for "stops" in the small fixed windows (he thought windows always came with those). And Jonathan has already struck many compromises with Jim, including some that Jonathan did not have to make—the roof, for instance. After he'd made his original bid, Jim had realized that Apple Corps would have to put into the roof's frame a lot more labor and some more wood than they'd imagined. Jim was only partly to blame, but Jonathan could have insisted on the sanctity of the original estimate and forced Apple Corps to shoulder the increase alone. Instead, he looked Jim in the eye and asked for a compromise. Jim said the extra labor would come to $850, the materials to $450. How did Jonathan feel about paying for the extra labor?

"Sounds fair to me," said Jonathan, scribbling a note.

Jonathan had accepted the larger part of the change. Jim had paid him back by shopping around for windows.

Now, on the phone to Jim one evening in June, Jonathan again proposes a compromise for the stairs. He will forgo the rounded bottom tread, and he will surrender, for the sake of amity, his conviction that the $2500 allowance was meant for the main staircase alone. Jim has said the stair will cost $900 more than Apple Corps anticipated. Jonathan offers to pay half of that.

"I'm uncomfortable on this," Jim's voice replies. And then Jim says, "The fact that you already knocked the price down six hundred and sixty dollars makes me reluctant."

Jonathan is astonished. He remembers the evening, of course, but he had forgotten the exact figure they'd argued about. He'd known Jim wasn't pleased at the time, but he'd believed that Jim felt satisfied with the contract in the end. Jonathan shakes his head and makes a puzzled smile. "That's like me saying I don't feel right about paying more for the stairs because I wanted the house for a hundred and forty-five thousand, not a hundred and forty-six."

When you agree to buy a two-story house, you have a right to expect that a staircase is included in the price. Cars come with steering wheels, houses with stairways. It seemed like a generous offer that he made to Jim. It was money he had not planned to spend. It cost him some anxiety.

People he trusts told Jonathan to stretch for this new house, and he has done so. He's had to count on selling the duplex in Pelham for a tidy profit. They put that house on the market a month ago, and almost no one has come to see it. Jonathan does not feel frightened. "We have a back-up plan." Any day now, though, Jim will hand him a stack of change orders, amounting to several thousand dollars that Jonathan will have to raise. Jonathan has already agreed to some changes, without knowing their exact costs. Those he has to accept. There are some other change orders coming, ones Bill wants but Apple Corps hasn't yet built. Jonathan does not have to sign for them.

Adding one nice detail after another can become an addiction. You say, "Oh, it costs a little more and it'll make our lives much nicer." Even sensible people get caught. Jonathan is a vicarious veteran of most kinds of ordinary trouble and mistakes, including that one. The day before the big change order meeting, Jonathan wins a case he thought he'd lose. He takes charge of the meeting, with a grin on his face and caution on his mind.

Bill, Judith, Jim, and Richard have gathered at the table in the Wieners' dining room. The table is round, but Jonathan defines the head of it. He raises the issue of casings.

Bill badly wants to substitute custom-made Apple Corps casings for the manufactured Colonial casings that the specs say should surround the living room's array of south-facing windows.

"I'd love to do it that way," says Richard to Jonathan.

"I understand," says Jonathan. "It's the right way, but you can only go to the hole so long. Hey, there's lots of things I'd rather do. Life is full of compromises."

"I'm not happy with Colonial casings," says Bill.

Jim insists that custom casings, though contemplated, were never in the contract price.

Bill thinks that an assumption of custom casings existed.

"You can't build on assumptions, my friend," snaps Jim.

At meetings like this, Jonathan sometimes brings to mind the steady captains of nineteenth-century seafaring lore. He's brisk, efficient, and calm. Jonathan lets Bill plead the architect's case a little longer, and then Jonathan leans back in his chair and sweeps an arm around the dining room, directing the attention of the fractious crew to the despised Colonial casings on these windows. "This," he tells them, "this is fine for me."

Jonathan knows that with the kindest intentions in the world, Bill and Apple Corps could arrange his bankruptcy. He wants Bill to be happy with the house, but the house has already been endowed with enough elegance and expense for Jonathan.

Jonathan can't easily imagine himself doing Jim's job. Few of the details look difficult, but the whole job does. When Jonathan imagines himself in the trades, he thinks of earthmoving. "The dirt part." He could do that.

Jonathan has long sympathized with people who earn their livings with their hands, and in some of his practice he has made their points of view his own. He has a client this summer who has lost most of a hand to his job. Thinking of him, Jonathan says, "One thing middle-class Americans don't realize is how often working-class Americans get hurt. I wouldn't be aware of it, except for my job."

When he insisted on an overall contract price for this house, Jonathan did so partly because he knew that the alternative, the time and materials arrangement, would mean six months of worrying about the length of the carpenters' coffee breaks. A fair contract, he thought, would allow him to relax and enjoy the process. He hoped to get friendly with the builders, and he has been willing all along to pay something for peace and harmony. Small incidents, such as Jim's mentioning their early and now old dispute over $600—or whatever it was—have disappointed Jonathan. He seems vaguely troubled. "I feel like I'm the enemy, and I don't think I *am* the enemy."

Jonathan, stopping by the house on his way to the office, hands Richard a check for $14,280, to cover work already completed. Richard stashes it in his wicker basket. "I hope I don't eat this for lunch." Garrulous Richard pursues him, but Jonathan really has no time at all to chat.

When Jonathan comes to the house in clothes that could pass for a workman's, it is usually when the workmen have gone. They see him only briefly as a rule and usually in his lawyer's uniform. Often, he bears lists to them, messages from Bill or the latest information on such issues as the water pipe. Some days these lists come on small slips of paper, which he pulls from various pockets and reads aloud, to an attentive-looking, faintly smiling Jim. Jonathan will pull out three, crumple up one, and divulge the contents of two. One day he pulls a slip of paper from his shirt pocket, looks at it, looks again, and finally says to Jim, "Well. Sorry. I can't read this one." Some days he comes when the house is still empty and leaves a list on a yellow sheet of paper for Jim to decipher by himself, or with help from Judith, who is often nearby, once school lets out for the summer.

"Does this say 'rheostat'?" asks Jim.

"Very good," says Judith. "I saw Jonathan's report cards from grade school. He got straight A's in everything, except in penmanship *and* behavior."

Judith exclaims one day, "This friend of mine is seriously talking about building a house. People just have *no* idea. I can't imagine doing this without Jonathan as my husband. Someone who can bargain and deal with the building inspector and yell at the right people and just move it along— and how could you get it done without someone like him?" He handles the money, presides at the meetings, deals with the arguments, incipient and real. He makes the decisions on items such as the water pipe. He pleads for decisions on aesthetic questions, and once, Jim notices, the man without aesthetic sense or opinions, who once said he had no feeling one way or the other about the south wall and if he accepted Bill's creation he did so as a matter of faith, this neutral party to beauty in buildings decides all on his own that he wants six-inch casings on the outsides of the south windows because he wants those casings the same size as the mullions that divide those myriad windows.

Maybe he's just assaulted another unmade decision or maybe he's left a glimpse of slip beneath the hem. In any case, the aesthetic is usually Judith's turf. She attends the long discussions and shopping trips with Bill, worries about the make of the windows, the colors of the tiles, the styles of knobs and coat hooks, the layout of the kitchen, the paint, the lamps, the appliances.

Richard and Ned notice, rather late in the summer, that Jonathan sometimes speaks to Judith reprovingly—even harshly, to their ears.

Jonathan: "Do you want to joke or do this?"

Judith: "I like to joke."

Jonathan: "Fine. Do it on your time."

"He seems kind of rough on her," says Richard.

"Pisses me off," says Ned.

It would amuse Judith to hear these chivalrous remarks, both for the obvious affection for her that they convey and also for their inaccuracy. The builders would have to revise their opinions if they saw Jonathan wistfully saying good-bye to her when she departs for most of a week on a long-contemplated trip and leaves Jonathan alone to manage his busy practice, three children, and an incipient house.

It begins to look like a long summer for Judith and Jonathan. Many times when they're alone, they feel it's necessary to tell each other, "Hey, we're on the same team." Many couples have divorced by the time their new houses are finished, but this house won't break the Souweines' home, or even their pact. Gradually, the carpenters see less and less of Jonathan, more and more of Judith. He's at work while they are, too, and when he meets them at the site or talks to Jim on the phone, he has an air that's not exactly harried but rushed and businesslike. "I always feel like I'm wasting his time," says Jim.

Jonathan rises in the middle of a change order meeting, to call his office.

"This is Jonathan. Are they reading their wills? Tell them to get a cup of coffee. Tell them to do anything. I'll be there in fifteen minutes."

Jonathan's withdrawal begins with busyness, but that's not all there is behind it. When he ran MassPIRG, the school year brought many students into the organization's campaigns. He would make friends with some of the young volunteers, and then when school let out, they would be gone from his life, usually for good. Vanished. He hated the little holes they left behind. When a case is long, he says, there's time for him to acquire opinions about clients and they about him, and once in a while an enduring bond gets formed. He had not planned to stand aloof from his builders. He wanted to be friendly with them. Somehow it just isn't turning out that way. He does not blame them or himself. His role seems to lie in administering disputes and arguing his and Judith's side, and gradually Jonathan realizes that he feels most comfortable at his new house when the builders aren't around. After a while, when he has a message for them, he sends it via Judith.

"No, you go, Jude. You get along with them better."

He assumes the role of outside man, before he quite knows he has done it. Then one day it becomes clear to him that Judith has assumed the role of friendly representative to the builders, while he does not know them well enough to feel, in negotiations with them, the disadvantages of friendship. "Judith, this is good," he says.

Judith plans to save a little money by performing some carpentry on the house herself, alongside the pros, probably in August. Jonathan looks forward to the stories she'll bring home. "It should be interesting."

Sometimes Jonathan could wish for a quicker, more decisive, and less persistent Bill. And then again, he isn't sure. Maybe he needs the slowing down that Bill provides. Anyway, Bill is the sort of person for whom one makes allowances. "Bill's an artist," says Jonathan. "I'm not." As he has for months, Bill is still arguing for those extra pilasters on the temple end, and Jonathan is resisting, because he fears those additional decorations will add to the grandness of the house. Jonathan also feels torn.

"You'll like it better," Bill has told him more than once.

"He may be right," Jonathan says, though not in front of Bill. Bill has been right before, about the south wall, for example. Jonathan had his doubts, but looking down on it from the Wiffle

Ball field in the evenings, Jonathan really likes the looks of that wall, now that it has taken shape.

Jonathan believes that Bill got his easygoing style from growing up in California and his stubbornness and drive from attending Yale. The combination is formidable. The application—Bill beating away at him on issues such as the pilasters—grows tiresome. After a while, especially when Jonathan has spent a long day trying to solve the problems of people with real trouble, some of Bill's arguments sound ridiculous. Sometimes it seems that every tiny detail has become, in Bill's parlance, "exceedingly important."

"To put so much energy into these personal aggrandizement things," says Jonathan one day at lunch, just down the street from the office, "well, it's okay. It's great but . . . I know it sounds incongruous, given this elegant house, but Judith and I are just not people who are that into houses."

Bill will put on his deep stammering voice and say, "Oh, I think it's *exceedingly* important."

After months of hearing that phrase, Jonathan says privately, "When everything becomes exceedingly important, it becomes a joke."

That summer the network news carries many grisly images of Southeast Asian refugees packed into leaking boats. "What about the boat people?" says Jonathan when Judith worries about coat hooks or says that Bill is upset about the style of the front door. "You think they care about coat hooks? You think they worry about front doors? They'd be happy if they had a pot to piss in."

After a while, he can feel himself losing interest in this house. He had always eagerly awaited the summertime reunion with Bill, but as this summer wears on, he sometimes wishes for less communication with his old friend. He doesn't blame Bill, though. Bill *should* be meticulous. That's what he's paying Bill for. Jonathan assumes his weariness will pass.

"Architects and builders, Arabs and Jews. They don't get along," Jonathan observes. Back in April, when he heard that Jim and Bill had words about that deadline on the south wall, Jonathan took the news as an omen. "In general," he'd told Jim, "it may be better for you to tell me to tell Bill, which is fine. Any problems, call me right away." He's had reason to regret that offer. When acquaintances ask about his new house, Jonathan imagines them thinking, "What a lucky guy." But at those moments he finds his own thoughts turn to Bill and Jim. Are they getting along? Does a new problem loom?

It's a little sad, the way things have turned out. Here are two honest, competent men with complementary passions for building. Jonathan imagined Bill and Jim would become collaborators. He wonders why they haven't. Almost all of the complaints he hears about that relationship come from Jim, while Bill tends to say that no important problems exist. Jonathan understands Jim's view. Jim thinks that Bill is costing Apple Corps money and aggravation, but Jim exaggerates, Jonathan believes.

Bill is Jonathan's old friend and, procedurally, his ally. When it comes to personalities, Bill clearly has the more accommodating one. Jim is puzzling. "There's a part of Jim that's a very nice guy and part where I find him . . . a little difficult, and I can't get my hand on it," says Jonathan. "I don't know where it comes from. I don't know if Jim knows where it comes from." When he listens to Jim complaining about Bill, Jonathan hears whispers of emotion.

3

Hands pressed against the air, feet splayed for a probable landing on all fours, Ned looks like a big cat pouncing, as he sails out off the edge of the roof of the master bedroom wing.

On the ground, Richard looks up, with widened mouth and eyes, and can't even manage a shout.

One cost of building in America is about six hundred deaths per year. Falling is the most common cause. Vehicles and heavy equipment, electricity, fire, gas, explosives, and even bullets also claim some lives. General construction ranks among the most dangerous professions in America. Large buildings make the riskiest sites, but one can grow old quickly building houses, too.

Lindy says that Richard has always been a little hard of hearing, in the sense that he hears what he chooses. But none of the carpenters' ears work as well as they did, back when they started out and saw no reason to wear ear protectors while running power tools. That twinge in Jim's knees when he bends down to nail, that wasn't there two years ago. Alex recently started wearing kneepads, which make him look like a hockey player. They have been younger. They are old enough now not to feel embarrassed about wearing some armor. They all wear safety glasses, Richard most diligently, because he never again wants to have a nail sticking out of the white of his eye. Richard figures they should probably wear hard hats, though they do not. He remembers the time when a concrete block fell off a roof that they were building and landed right at the feet of one of their subcontractors, and the time when Alex's framing hammer brained their electrician. ("Yup. Brought him right to his knees," says Alex.) Richard also remembers the days when the joint compound used in sheetrocking contained asbestos. It said so right on the label—but who knew what that meant then? Richard was just learning how to work with that stuff, and he had to sand the dried compound a great deal in order to make it smooth, but he didn't think to wear a mask. Richard sees no point in worrying about what's irretrievable. They have taken the asbestos out of joint compound now but none of Apple Corps goes near the stuff anymore without dressing up their faces with masks.

Protection has its limits anyway. Some accidents seem unavoidable. Cut enough wood with power tools and sooner or later, you're bound to make a mistake. You climb up enough roofs, you have to run afoul of gravity sometime.

Jim is over at the Wieners' conferring with Bill, and Ned must have been thinking about Jim over there and the stern words he'd said to Jim about Jim's tendency to waste time in palaver. Ned has just finished putting the last of the red shingles on the roof of the master bedroom wing. That is the lower of the two roofs by a considerable distance. It's about twelve feet from the eaves to the ground. It does not feel very high, perhaps because the other roof defines what a height means for them this summer. For that reason, the lower roof is perhaps the more dangerous one.

Ned's fall begins slowly, to him. He's facing down the roof and beginning to reach with his foot for the staging that he knows is out there below the edge. His hammer, slung at his side, must have gotten cocked somehow, so that it sticks out at right angles from his hip. It catches on a roof jack and pushes Ned outward. Reaching for the staging with his foot, Ned has the feeling he's suspended over a puddle, and knows that he won't make it to the other side. Then he leaps. Afterward, he's reminded of the familiar dream in which he is falling and perpetually awaits a landing. This flight happens very quickly, and in daytime. Richard watches Ned hit on all fours. Ned ducks his head and rolls, once, twice, and comes to rest under a shower of nails from his pouch.

"Are you all right?"

"Is Ned all right?"

"He's okay!"

"I'm a little sore," says Ned. "But we roofers are made of tough and significant stuff."

"Did you see what the skydiver did?" says Richard, flushed and jubilant. "He didn't yell or nothin'. I like a little noise."

Jim has returned with his briefcase. Out front near the trucks, Jim pours water over Ned's hands, which are covered with tar. "I don't want the beer can to stick to them," Ned says. Then he climbs into the bed of Richard's pickup and sits, with an arm draped over the erect tailgate. "The trouble with these accidents is that you start feeling it late at night," Ned says to Jim.

"That's the value of shock," says Jim.

"Really," says Ned. "It allows you to go off somewhere and die in peace." Ned grins, eyes half-closed. Then he shouts, "Where's the beer? I want to celebrate the end of this day."

A few mornings later, Alex climbs a ladder and begins tossing down the staging planks.

"Hey, Alex, you got Ned hiding inside, right in the middle of the house," cries Richard.

One after the other the planks hit the ground. "Some people are just nervous Nellies," calls Alex.

The roof is done, the frieze repaired. They won't be going up there anymore. For the rest of the summer they'll risk bad falls only in their dreams. Gradually the house is emerging from its skeleton, like some reversal of life's progress. The store-bought windows are in place and paid for on time, Ned is making the small rectangular windows for the elaborately fenestrated south façade, Jim has started to build the frame of the stairs, Richard and Alex have created the floor of the porch.

For the porch floor, Jim bought tongue-and-groove quarter-sawn fir. Where the porch wraps around the north corner of the house, Richard and Alex have made a graceful turn, a sort of fan in wood:

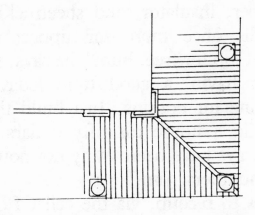

Bill hadn't ordered this touch. It will delight him when he sees it.

They shovel sawdust out the window holes. A couple of big piles form like snowdrifts on the sandy ground, and among those heaps have rained down a lot of small wooden blocks and ruined strips of number-two pine, scraps from the rebuilding of the frieze, beside which Jim stops one day, as if to pay respects. The pile represents, he figures, $320 lost, about $80 per partner. "It's like giving away something you really like that costs eighty dollars," says Jim. "I guess another way of looking at it is that it's real money, but only a quarter of it comes out of each of our pockets, and when the Souweines pay for something like that, *all* of it comes out of theirs."

Jim's notebooks are a depressing place for him to visit now. Question marks surround the stairs. A number of items are missing altogether, including the cost of those frames for the interior walls, as he discovered not long ago. The morning when they start creating those interior walls, carving up the house's space to make ready for the electrician, plumber, insulator, and sheetrocking crew, Richard calls once more for upbeat attitudes. "Pretty good job for free, huh?" he says, toenailing studs. "I'm havin' a good time today, talking about working for nothing. Just build the house. We can build a house for fifty dollars a square foot. We always have been. Why not now? Throw away your numbers, Jim."

Jim hopes to recoup, via the cellar floor, some of the money they have lost on the interior walls. He hired a subcontractor they had never used, to pour the cellar floor. Jim visited an example of the sub's work and found it satisfactory, and the fellow's price is low. The floor comes in a concrete truck and rumbles through a cellar window. The sub is still smoothing out the slab when Jim leaves for the day. He pays the sub. Next morning, Jim looks down in the basement and finds the floor all hardened and all wrong. In some places it is not as smooth as Jim requires. Worst of all, the drain is set into a little hill of concrete, at the highest point in the floor. Water won't run into the drain. Water will run away from it.

"Well, we've got quite a bit of difficulty with your slab there," says Jim on the phone to the sub. "It looks like shit. Even an amateur would be embarrassed. Well, maybe you wouldn't." Jim lugs his collection of sledgehammers and mason's cold chisels down the ladder to the cool basement. He spends half a day destroying concrete around the drain and half a day in patching it. Pausing to catch his breath, Jim says, "This guy gave me this line about having old-time hand trowelers working for him. He made it sound like something to be reverent about somehow."

"The easy part's done," Ned says. The carpenters have brought their woodworking factory indoors, now that such a place exists. You can't buy all the windows that Bill has drawn. Jim has given Ned the job of making the 19 small, fixed rectangular windows that Bill drew for the south wall. Ned has turned the basement into his window-making shop. He stands under bare light bulbs, before his tuned-up table saw—he's waxed its bench and changed its blade. To his left sits his jointer, for straightening edges. To his right, a table full of clear pine lumber, the pieces all stacked as neatly as cards. He'll cut for length, then sand and joint each piece of the window frames. He'll dado channels into side pieces, assemble the four-sided boxes with glue, fit the glass, apply the stops, and emerge with armfuls of windows. Posted to the basement and a roomful of tools, Ned is in his element, but on the brink of all that pleasant work, Ned contemplates the pile of clear pine about to become windows and he swears this house gives him the oddest feeling. It seems like a hole into which lumber, nails, sheetrock, and a hundred other things are pouring. A new house always uses up a surprising amount of material, but this one feels different to Ned. The sheetrockers, for instance, veterans at close estimating, appear to have underestimated this house. They're going to have to use seventy pails of joint compound, weighing a ton and a half when wet, and that's twice what they thought they'd need. The electrician says that at the end of a long day at this house he feels he has accomplished nothing. Ned does not want to say this job feels jinxed, but to him this house seems to have seductive power, over even wary veterans.

"It's not mystical," Jim says.

In the hallway to the kitchen, there's a spot in the framing where two beams do not quite come together. The little gap between the beams makes no difference structurally, and in a few days it will disappear under plasterboard. For weeks that gap has caught Jim's eye in passing, and sensibly, he's passed. Now one morning, before the others arrive, he cuts a small block of wood and makes it fit snugly in the gap. The house had a hole in it, Jim says, and if he had left it behind all covered up, it would have troubled him, like a leaky faucet that couldn't be fixed.

Richard says they're winning. Maybe they are, finally, Jim thinks. The first week of June was fraught with trouble. The first week of July runs smoothly—no arguments, no money lost. That Friday afternoon, Jim takes his list of change orders to Jules's horse barn and calls Jonathan. Dick Staelens built the chimney weeks ago. Tomorrow he's returning to construct the hearth. "On the hearth," Jim says over the phone to Jonathan, "the brick Bill's got figured is the most expensive brick." Staelens bid the hearth imagining it would be made with used brick. The brick Bill has chosen will add $250 to the job, and Jim wants to know if Jonathan will pay for it. Or should the mason buy used brick? "The mason's coming tomorrow," says Jim to Jonathan. "Unless I call him off. I know it's kind of late."

Jonathan decides on used brick. Bill is on the road and can't be reached at once. When Bill gets the news of the change of brick on Saturday, the mason has already begun to build the hearth.

In ancient Greece, the flame in the hearth was the goddess Hestia. First to be invoked in sacrifices, she was the only important deity who did not like to fight. The Greeks' regard for hearths, for reasons that seem obvious, has been widely shared around the world and across the millennia. A hearth still stands for what most people want from home. Like many New Englanders, the Souweines participate in the era of the wood stove. Bill sets out to give them a stove place that feels like a hearth. Bill has never designed one of those.

Jim has waited a long time for Bill to do so, but Bill has not been stalling. He's been thinking. He's been shopping. Every trip Bill has made to Amherst, he has spent some time looking at bricks. In the process, Bill has rejected used bricks. In any given batch, the dimensions of used bricks vary widely. In search of the crisp look, Bill chose "water-struck brick," a kind of brick that comes in a uniform size and has a deep red color. Bill has a nose for quality. It led him to the most expensive of bricks, though he did not know that then.

Bill threw himself into the design of the hearth. He tried to make it a distinctive and inviting thing. What he draws is certainly a novel-looking plan. In the drawing, the hearth has a floor of brick for the stove to sit on and three surrounding walls. A tall wall in back with a slab of granite for a lintel—a lot of discussion with Jim has been spent on that lintel—and two smaller wing walls. In the drawing, the hearth looks a little like a huge armchair with the seat flat on the floor, an armchair for a legless giant. The pattern of bricks and mortar joints counts heavily for Bill. He spent at least two days at his drafting table, drawing every brick and mortar joint, and he sent the picture out to Jim a couple of days ago. Bill is horrified on Saturday when he gets the news about the change in bricks, and he decides at once to come to Amherst Monday, to avert what has the feel of another error like the frieze.

"Hey, Googie," Dick Staelens says to Richard

Gougeon that Saturday morning at the house. "A guy said, 'Rome weren't built in a day,' and the other guy said, 'No. And I weren't foreman neither.'" Staelens can do the second voice with conviction. He puts up a substantial chunk of the hearth's walls that morning, before knocking off. Paul Korpita, a mason who works for Staelens, takes over the job on Monday. Paul looks puzzled. He studies the plans with Jim. "It's awful easy to do this with a pencil. It's a lot harder with brick," says Paul.

The living room exists. It lacks a ceiling, walls, and doors. Its floor is plywood, with sawdust and shavings and red brick dust for a carpet. For furniture, it has stacks of brick and lumber, mortar troughs, Jim's table saw and sawhorses. Jim sits on one of those, conferring with Paul, when Bill arrives, with Judith. Silence gives way to unhappy faces and then to consternation. "The problem is those little pieces of brick in the corners," says Bill. "They kind of look like they were patched in. You see the problem, Jim?"

Jim puts his elbow on his wrist, his chin on his hand. "Yeah." He says he guesses the problem arose mainly because the used bricks are of a different size from the ones Bill planned on.

There are conferences. Bill confers with Judith. "I'm exceedingly unhappy. One would have designed the hearth differently, if one knew one were using used bricks. I'm angry because the change was made at the last minute." Bill explains, "It's not a matter of ego, it's a question of quality."

Judith confers with Jonathan by phone. "It is horrible communication," she says. They'll ask the mason to stop and tear the work down. She's afraid Jim will yell at her, she says over the phone.

Judith confers with Jim, who doesn't yell but says instead, "If you don't like it this way, you shouldn't have it in your house. Masonry is enduring." Jim also tells her, "I didn't think about that size change. I don't feel *responsible* for it."

Bill confers with Paul, the mason. Together they devise a way to rebuild.

Bill confers with Judith: "It's not perfect. It's . . . okay."

Jim and Bill and Judith confer, to assign the blame. "Who's buying the lunch?" asks Jim.

"I think this is your problem," says Judith. "Meanwhile, Jonathan thinks you're both idiots. You *and* Rawn."

"Me?" says Bill. "I didn't even *know* about it." Coloring, Bill says that he'll produce the phone records, to prove he was not notified in time. It's outrageous that this should have happened, and infuriating that he should be blamed for not being consulted on the change.

Judith says: "I think that this whole thing about the hearth was poorly handled by everyone, except for us. We just weren't given enough information."

Back at the house, Paul and Richard, working

near each other in the living room, are trading stories about an old-time mason, named Ernie, who used to light his pipe and, forgetting it was lit, would put it in his trousers pocket. "He used to start his pants on fire with his pipe," says Paul. "Old Ernie's dear to my heart."

"Oh, I like the hell out of old Ernie," says Richard.

Jim trudges into the living room and sits down on a sawhorse. "Googie told me you had stock in Rolaids, Jim," says Paul.

"I'm workin' on it," says Jim. "Oh, pain. Agony."

"Hey," says Richard. "There's a certain amount of pain you gotta have every day."

"Yeah," says Jim. "But who decides how much?" Jim adds, "I guess we're going to get blamed for presenting them with a choice. I don't feel responsible, but I'm afraid we're going to pay for it." He looks out the windows. "I'm not blamin' anybody."

"The brick day," says Richard. "A lot of action. Ned's got this one named. He calls it the brick day."

When the conferences end, Jules comes into the living room, contemplates the hearth, and says, "It's fine the way it is. When you start using a house, these little things you go over with a fine-tooth comb disappear."

When Bill stands in front of the finished hearth a week later, however, he sees what should have been. The brickwork looks better than it would have if he had not stopped the work, but it still looks awkward at the corners to Bill. On the phone to Jim a few days after brick day, Bill airs his grievance. Why didn't Jim warn him about the cost of water-struck brick?

"Well, you gave me the drawing the day before we were supposed to build it," Jim says.

That's true, Bill allows, but nearly a month ago he had told Jim about his plan to use that sort of brick.

True, says Jim, but the decision wasn't final, and he was tired of chasing down prices for items that would never get used.

Every contractor Bill has ever dealt with has been willing to give him comparative prices on various materials, and usually right away. Those were big building contractors. Bill supposes it's harder for small ones to do that. But how much would a phone call to the mason have cost Jim? Bill does not relate those thoughts to Jim. He merely tells Jim that many days went into designing the hearth.

"It's so big!" That's what most friends and acquaintances tell Judith when they visit the site. Sometimes it makes her feel uncomfortable. She calls the house "the Taj" now, when Bill brings up those extra pilasters he wants on the temple end. Bill won't quit. She won't give in. In a town near Amherst, Bill finds a house with pilasters marching across its temple end, but Jonathan and Judith won't even go to look at it.

On the Cape, where he has joined the Souweines and other friends in July, for their annual holiday, Bill discovers a Greek Revival house without extra pilasters on the front. He is bike riding with Judith when he spots the house. He stops. He points out the house to her. Doesn't she think it looks a little squat? She thinks it looks just fine, and still he's not ready to quit.

While Bill lies on the beach, wondering how to convert his friends, back in Amherst Richard and Alex put the decking on the porch roof. They hoist up a piece of plywood. They stand on ladders in the sun. Richard puts his end in place. Alex puts his end in place, taking Richard's out of place. The piece of plywood has been cut to the wrong size. Richard grabs his end and puts it back in place. Then Alex does the same. From their ladders, they glower at each other, until Alex smiles. Then Richard lets out the laugh he was holding in. The next day, they begin to construct the two pilasters at the corners of the temple end. Two days later, they finish those decorative columns—almost finish.

Driving the last nail into a piece of thin molding, Richard misses with a stroke and hits the wood, leaving a dimple, known as a rosebud, on the molding. Working around the corner on the southern wall, Ned hears Richard cry out. Ned comes around to investigate and finds Richard sitting on a sawhorse on the porch. Richard's arms are folded. He looks studiedly unconcerned, like an inexperienced shoplifter with the goods behind his back. Behind Richard's back, nailed by Richard to one of the pilasters, is Richard's cap. Ned eyes Richard, eyes the cap, begins to smile. Ned lifts an edge of the cap and peeks in at Richard's rosebud.

"Here's a guy in Billings, Montana, who stole a tank. He was apprehended on the interstate," says Alex, at lunch on the porch the next day.

"What was he doing with a tank?"

"He said he was going to visit his relatives in Minnesota."

Even Jim is having fun this week. "These hippie carpenters. By God, they're all right."

The temple end is Grecian now. Doric columns support the porch roof. The pilasters look old, fancy, and crisp. Richard thinks the whole concoction handsome. "We got the old-timers grinnin' in their graves now." Richard feels so pleased, he wants to get the porch roof shingled right away and complete the picture. To do that, though, he and Alex must first cut and install clapboards on the wall above the porch, in the space between the two pilasters at the corners of the temple end.

Red cedar clapboard comes from the forests of the Northwest. It contains the loveliest of smells. It is the Château Margaux of woods. It resists rot and is far less prone to warp and check than clapboards made of pine or spruce. Timber thieves favor it. A two-foot-long piece of thin red cedar clapboard costs about a dollar. It will cost about $4000 to buy the red cedar to cover this house. You put it up carefully.

Richard and Alex stand on ladders set on top of the porch roof. "State-of-the-art clapboarding, Alex," says Richard. He adds, "You know, the kids today are *real* serious. They're into high tech and not having a good time." Alex is working too carefully, thinks Richard. "Jesus Christ, Alex, this is Bay Road, Amherst, twenty-four feet up in the air."

"It's the front of a stately Greek Revival home, Richard. Well, we got that piece in. Only took two tries."

"Don't you think it would be nice, though, to be the only person who did good work?" asks Richard.

"No! You want to be part of a fraternity of good workers."

"We don't want craftsmanship to go downhill, though. Do we?"

"No. Not rapidly anyway. All right, Richard, this is a contract job. No more talking."

And so while Bill sunbathes and schemes on Cape Cod, to find a way to talk his friends into two more pilasters for the temple end, Richard and Alex make the issue moot. Cutting and nailing up red cedar that no one would want to have to pay to remove, they cover up the space where Bill has dreamed long and hard of pilasters.

Jonathan and Judith return. "I like that porch," says Jonathan. The Souweines stand looking up at the temple end.

"If we ever sit on it," says Judith. "Do you think those pilasters make it look squatter? I just know Bill's going to say that." Then she notices the clapboarding. She grins. She laughs. That case is closed. "Or as they say in Yiddish, done is done."

One time Judith orders up a change in a part of a Bill Rawn plan, and Richard, at her service, effects it. She's the boss, but Richard worries a little. "Really, some architects would go crazy over something like this. It's like the artist painting his masterpiece. Sells it to someone, then they go home and touch it up."

On the day when Bill had lost his case for custom-made Apple Corps casings on the living room's south wall, Ned saw the lanky architect come into the living room, take up a piece of wood, and hold it next to the windows. He's imagining custom casings there, Ned thought. "Here's Bill with his baby watching it get thrown out with the bath," Ned said afterward. "It seems like with Jonathan you've gotta stop him or be ready to move on. He's a speedy cat."

Jim knows a secret he figures he might as well keep to himself. He never liked the idea of those extra pilasters, and when Bill first proposed them, Jim thought of putting a high price on them. "If you don't want to do something, you oughta get paid a lot to do it." He didn't act on that principle, though. He priced the extra pilasters in his usual way—adding 10 percent to their estimated actual cost. But Jim felt so sure the Souweines wouldn't buy those extra decorations that he had never put any blocking behind the wall of the temple end. If Bill had gotten his way, there would have been nothing for Apple Corps to nail the extra pilasters onto. Jim has secretly won a round with Bill, but Jim doesn't get much pleasure from it.

Months afterward, Jim finds in a copy of *Fine Homebuilding* an article about architects from a builder's point of view. Architects want most of the authority and accept very little responsibility— that's the gist of the article to Jim, and he finds it apt. Bill contributes to mistakes, but only Apple Corps pays. It feels that way to Jim. Sometimes, though, Jim allows himself to realize that Bill's time is, like Apple Corps's, convertible to money. In fact, Bill spent more designing stairs that never got built than the $900 that Jim and Jonathan dispute. Designing the hearth that went awry, Bill didn't just spend the $250 difference between used and water-struck brick, he spent more out of his own pocket than the whole pile of water-struck brick would have cost.

Bill's losses look considerable to Jim. Bill wanted wooden doors inside. Instead, the Souweines have saved a lot of money buying Masonite doors, which look remarkably like wooden, paneled ones. Bill has also lost his fight for wooden shutters, because Judith vividly remembers seeing, one time on the Cape, a couple scraping paint off wooden shutters on a lovely summer's day, and it was a vision of a fate that she would not accept. So she has insisted on vinyl shutters that don't need paint. Bill dreamed of a staircase like ones he has seen in Boston's old Back Bay. He did not even try to draw one of those, and now even the stairs he thought slightly cut-rate won't get off the paper. He has lost out to the economies of scale and labor that make manufactured Colonial casing much cheaper to buy than plain Apple Corps casing. Bill always imagined a front door made out of wood, with an oak threshold, but Jonathan has watched his wooden front door in Pelham come gradually apart, and Jonathan insists on steel, and the best steel door comes with a metal threshold. A wooden one is an expensive extra; they don't make them that way in quantity. As for the frieze, and especially the hearth, they look fine, but they don't quite measure up to Bill's visions of them.

At a bar not long after brick day, over a beer—Jim rarely drinks more than one—Jim tallies up Bill's losses. He says, "I sympathize that he's been rushed, but there's some difficulty between him and the Souweines that's never been worked out. They think he's just refining now, and that isn't true. The inside was sort of prefab, stock parts, when we first started, and we bid it that way. Now Bill's trying to correct that, but he's working for nothing if they can't pay for what he wants."

Jim says, "I feel sorry for Bill, now that he's down."

In Boston, on Tremont Street, at the end of the hall upstairs, there's now a new sign on the door:

The young assistant architect Bill has hired had to rearrange those letters once, at the boss's soft insistence, to get the composition rightly centered on the door. Now the assistant is drafting the façade of an apartment building, apparently unmindful of the slight commotion around him. The phone rings regularly. "Do I have any more calls to make this morning, Katie?" Bill asks the part-time secretary and bookkeeper on the far side of the room. Four months in business on his own and Bill has two employees, and he's looking for at least one other fledgling architect. He has three commissions on the drafting tables, and there are several other prospects. Sitting in his chair, in dress shirt and tie and sockless feet and too-short corduroys, all professional above the waist, all beachcomber below, Bill gazes his way through the stack of photographs he has taken of the house in progress out in Amherst, and self-pity seems to be practically the only enjoyable emotion he doesn't feel just now. "I love going out to the site. It's so *real*." Friends have been asking to see some snapshots of the house. That's why he took the pictures, partly. He says he feels the way a new father must, when friends ask to see a snapshot of the child. He studies the photos with appropriately fond smiles.

"Here my very first commission is producing a house," Bill says. He can hardly believe that within six months of starting out he'll have a house he's proud of and can show. The pilasters were a disappointment, but he thinks he understands. "They are sitting there in the eyes of Amherst with a big house, with a house that looks like it cost a hundred thousand dollars more than it will, I think. They are picking up vibes that people think, 'That's a very big house.'" Judith and Jonathan have given in on every other issue that really mattered to him. Except for the bricks, and if he'd had half an hour to make his case, he knows they would have given him his bricks. "You can't win *every* one," says Bill. He still can't imagine better clients. And what of Jules? Jules's well-known dour view of architects frightened Bill a little once. Some parents would resent a child's building right next door a house that dwarfs their own. But Jules and Florence have housed and fed Bill, and all he's heard from them is praise for the design. Bill counts himself a lucky man, all the way around.

Most people in the building trades know stories about architects. In so many tales the architect sacrifices the client's dreams and comfort for the sake of his own art that you have to suspect arrogance is a hazard of the trade. But here is Bill with Judith in the Wieners' dining room, trying to talk her out of her vision of a kitchen with a lot of unpainted wood: "It *is* a matter of light, no matter what you say. In the winter it gets real dark around here. And if that's what one believes, one has to be perseverant. I just worry. This room's

352

going to have so much wood in it and so much going on."

She has been teasing him. When he described one kitchen plan as "very beautiful and very European," she said, "The wrong people. We're kind of 'Merican, Bill."

Now as he conjures up a picture of her children home from school, and of a daughter entertaining in the breakfast nook, she begins to listen gravely. "And when she's fifteen and the love of her life won't look at her because he hasn't reached puberty, all that's going to go on there," says Bill. "Think about that. Ultimately, on the kitchen, *you* have to be happy. I can talk about the aesthetics of trim on the south wall, but that's stuff you learn to live with. But the kitchen is more than a matter of aesthetic judgment. It's something you really *have* to live with."

Judith studies the samples of colorful Formica that Bill has brought her and she says softly, "We could have gray counters and white cabinets."

"With a gray Formica backsplash," says Bill.

"You like that a lot better," she says.

"I think it could be beautiful, and it keeps the clean lines."

"What else you got in Formica?" She sings, "Formica, Formica." She murmurs, "This is hard."

In the end, Bill travels with her so unobtrusively to the color scheme, and it suits her so perfectly, she will have the feeling she came up with it all on her own. If you watch Bill help Judith make decisions for herself, and then you conjure up the wrathful ghost of Frank Lloyd Wright, advancing in his flowing cape across the driveway, to register his feelings about the frieze, the front door, the interior casings, the pilasters, then it's clear that Bill is not a martinet. He has a reservoir of what the Romantic poets called sympathetic imagination. He's an ideal architect for human beings. Of course, he is capable of mistakes.

On a Monday morning in early August, Richard kneels among the beginnings of the kitchen, scratching his head over a set of plans. "Rawn's redrawing these plans and he sent them, but Judith isn't here and I can't get in her mailbox," he says. "Oh, well."

Building a kitchen, Richard replicates the building of a house. He frames it, then he finishes it, and the framing must be crisp because crispness underneath gives him the proper attitude for making the finish custom. Crispness in this framing also carries its own justification. A degree of crookedness no eye could discern in an outside wall would make the doors of kitchen cabinets so cockeyed that even the sub who poured the basement slab would feel offended. Richard is snapping lines on the plywood floor just now, because he does not believe in the straightness of the newly sheetrocked wall, when Alex enters and surveys Richard's meager-looking morning's accomplishments. "Hey! Lookit that. *Four* red lines," says Alex.

Richard smiles.

"I wish I had a full-fledged plan here, instead of all these vague corners," Richard says to himself. "I sure wish I had those other plans. I'm right into it now. I got it all figured. Oh, well, you can't have everything. I laid this out wrong Friday. It's because the plans weren't here. Another good deal. Another fast track."

Alex comes through again and stomps on the plans Richard has unfolded on the floor. "Childish," says Richard, as Alex leaves. Richard turns to repairing his error of Friday. He takes up his bottle of wood glue, pulls the plug out and pretends to sniff deeply from the spout, rocks back like Frankenstein awakening, sniffs from the bottle again, and then spots Judith's black Chevrolet pulling in and goes right out to get the plans.

She's checked her mailbox. "The plans weren't there. Are you really stymied, Richard?"

"I'm going to be."

He follows her to the Wieners' phone and listens as she gets Bill.

"What did you do with the plans for the kitchen? . . . Oh. You didn't do it."

"Humph," says Richard. He actually says that occasionally.

"Put any more boards up, or are you just resting?" Alex asks when Richard gets back to the kitchen.

"No. I talked to the architect. 'Oh, I was supposed to send the plans, but I forgot.' Betcha he hasn't even got them drawn."

"You're kidding. I think we should just go in there to Boston and give him a thump."

The next few days—Bill's plans arrive on Thursday—Richard loses some of his usual composure. He puts in a shelf upside down. Realizing his mistake, he pounds on a piece of wood, so maniacally the sound brings Ned around the corner from the living room. For Ned, Jim has observed, Richard represents stability itself. Ned depends for his own equanimity on Richard's. Now Ned comes in with a worried face and says softly, "Is everything under control in here?"

"If some six-foot-seven-inch feller walked through the door right now, he might catch a little shit," says Jim, grinning broadly.

The relationship between an architect and builders can explore the limits of sympathy in sympathetic people. It is not in either party's interest to understand the other one's too well. In Amherst, Jim and Richard complain about the time they've spent in meetings with Bill, and in Boston, Bill says he was taught that the good architect confers often with the builder. In Amherst, Jim remarks that getting plans at the last minute slows down construction. "The fast track. Slow track is what it is. There's nothing fast about it." In Boston, Bill says, "I was starting a business, and if the drawings were not needed until next week . . ." In Amherst, Richard mutters over a set of plans, "It's real easy to draw this. Oh, yeah, you can *draw* this real fast," and in Boston, Bill remem-

356

bers how he had to scramble to dream up the pieces of this house and meet the crucial deadlines.

When someone praises his design, now that the house's shape is clear, Bill often smiles at his shoes and praises Apple Corps. Of Jim, Bill says, "He's an intriguing person, and I find myself feeling very fond of him. I suspect that he carries some heavy baggage and out of that came a real dedication to quality, and the strength that comes out of that . . ." Bill has tried to get acquainted with the carpenters. Once, he joined them at lunch. The conversation never blossomed. "I felt . . ."

"A chill?"

"Yes."

Through Jonathan and Judith, Bill has heard most of Apple Corps's complaints. Some make him stiffen. "I don't think they're losing their shirt and if they are, they signed a shitty contract," he says. "Timing is not a major issue once one accepts the fast-track method. If you don't want to accept that, say it in April, not in September." He declares, "The whole point is to get the house built and built well, and it's very clear to me now that these guys are building it well."

For a while, suffering from too many commissions and too little help, Bill had felt compelled to perform an architectural form of battlefield triage. It wouldn't happen now that he has assistants and an office routine. Back then, any time he spent on one project he stole from another. That was the cause of what he calls his "one flagrant mis-promise." "I had other work to do," Bill says. "I felt badly, because poor Richard was put in a bad position."

So was Jonathan. He had to go to the house and apologize for the absence of the revised kitchen plans. He had to ask Richard to halt work there for a day. "A mild Jonathan Souweine this morning," Alex observed.

"I like that a lot," Jim said.

Those several days of the missing kitchen plans, Jim grins a great deal more than usual. "It's good for me," he admits. Indeed, even for Richard, Bill's undeniable lateness seems a tonic in the long run. Apple Corps has always made a joke out of the psychological advantages of assigning blame to distant parties. For the next few days there's excitement in their voices when they discuss the architect, especially in Jim's. Judith notices the general hilarity. For a day or two, she and Jonathan were very angry at Bill. Now when she stands in the house and hears the builders calling imprecations about architects to each other, she feels for Bill. She's also begun to get a firsthand look at building through a carpenter's eyes. "They love it," she says. "They love any chance to get mad at Bill." She shrugs. "This time, they're right."

The house is all but designed now, including the kitchen. Gradually, Bill becomes an infrequent subject at coffee break and lunch time. Late in the week of the missing plans, Richard announces, "I had an interesting call last night. William Rawn called last night, and *apologized!* He said he'd been meaning to do it all week."

"Did you accept his apology?"

It's as if he's been asked whether maple syrup comes from trees. "Oh, yeah," Richard says.

4

On a Sunday in August out in Pelham, Jonathan sits in a deck chair under the tall pines in what will soon become someone else's back yard. Just when he had begun to feel no one wanted the duplex, some people came, saw, and bought. One large worry has vanished, and on this day Jonathan has no others. For the first time in his recent memory, no impending obligations loom. He feels at his leisure in the back yard, to a degree he rarely felt when this ground belonged to him— then, if he had some spare time, he'd be as likely to work on the yard as to loaf in it. He listens to a concert on a portable radio and reads the Sunday *New York Times* from end to end. A long time has passed since he saw either Bill or the builders. For weeks no one has called to complain about plans or to ask for decisions. Tranquility took longer to arrive than he thought it would, but the hard bargaining and trouble seem to have ended. At last, it seems as though he can watch his house get built in peace.

Jim leaves work last and gets there first. Some

mornings, summer fog settles over the valley, so thickly that you can hardly make out Judith's parents' place across the driveway. Then the new building seems as lonely as a lighthouse. Jim sits by himself inside the empty house, in gray light, surrounded by gray walls, his calculator on one knee, a yellow pad on the other.

Jim combs his hair before work, but Sandy says it would part itself if he didn't. "Jim's hair comes that way." At the end of a day, Richard often looks as if he's been rolling in sawdust. Jim seems to perspire rather than sweat. He almost always looks unruffled, but these days he rarely is.

Jim got the sheetrockers to agree to begin hanging the interior walls and ceilings on July 15. He had to make sure that the lumber arrived soon enough for Apple Corps to frame the walls before the plumber's, electrician's, and insulator's promised arrivals. He remembered to call the building inspector, who would insist on seeing the place before the sheetrock went up. You build a job out of a host of promises, and if the insulator's truck breaks down or the electrician gets the flu, the whole procedure can collapse. You might have to tell the sheetrockers to delay a week and then you might lose them for a month. Timing is everything, and in spite of the vicissitudes of the fast track, the job has not halted or even slowed for the lack of the right materials or the next subcontractor. That is thanks to Jim's forethought—both his choices of subs and his scheduling. The house, in this sense, really exists in the meticulously printed notes he carries in his leather case. The plan in there is sound. In the mechanical sense, this job has gone more smoothly than most construction projects. Jim could congratulate himself for that, as Jonathan and Judith have, but Jim doesn't seem to be able to find much comfort there.

He has never known a job that aroused such complicated feelings in him. The electrician's bill arrives. It comes to $780 more than the estimate. No one is to blame, Jim thinks, but the Souweines certainly have some cause to balk at paying this overrun. "Here we go again," Jim says, when he makes up the change order. But Jonathan does not argue. In fact, he says cheerfully that he will pay the extra charges in full. Jim goes deadpan. "Okay," he says. He actually seems slightly annoyed at Jonathan's largess. "They've changed their ways," says Jim afterward, "but it's a little late for that."

Jim has a long, exacting memory, especially for his own miscalculations. Sometimes he looks around the house and nearly every piece of it looks like a reproach to him. Then he speaks as if the job has gone so far off course already that no matter what happens from now on he will not be able to salvage any satisfaction from the work he's done. The act of saying so often cheers him up.

Nearly every day Jim talks about success. His ruminations have a tentative quality. Will he feel successful if they make their hoped-for profit? Will they make any profit? He has resolved to

361

hold the line and charge the Souweines for every change, no matter how mean and small-minded the act will make him feel. Then, in the natural course of the job, an issue such as the windowsills arises.

The specs say nothing about windowsills. The contract would allow Apple Corps to surround all the windows with stock Colonial casings as if the windows were pictures—to "picture-frame" the windows and leave them without sills. It's a fairly common practice that saves a builder time. That's what Jim plans to do. This is a contract job. He assigns the task to Ned, the cabinetmaker. When the time for giving Ned his instructions comes, however, Jim can't bear the thought of their leaving a house without windowsills, and he does not want to ask Ned, of all people, to do a job wrong on purpose. Jim doesn't ask the Souweines' permission, perhaps because he fears permission won't be granted, and anyway, how can you agree to build a house for someone and then not give them windowsills to rest their chins and elbows on? So Jim tells Ned to make sills. He does not even ask for recompense. Evidently, he doesn't get much pleasure from the gesture either.

On his next visit, walking through the rooms, Bill notices the sills right away. He sees what Apple Corps has done. He finds Ned and Jim in the living room. He thanks them. "Gotta please the architect, right?" says Ned. "No, I'm glad you're pleased."

To Jim, Bill says, "It has mostly to do with

362

taking extra care. That's the nature of quality work."

"Or of not being businesslike," says Jim. Jim adds, "This contract's wide open. There are fifty places where we could've stuck it to them."

"Oh, I'm sure," says Bill. "That's the nature of . . . Well, I'm sure."

Ned laughs. His shoulders shake. "We don't know how."

"Maybe we should take a couple of years off," says Jim to Ned. "Go work for some honcho condo builder and get back to where there's some compromise."

Whether or not they are making money, they have to build this house. The financial side of the job had become immensely complex anyway, a labyrinth of bills they hadn't received and ones they hadn't paid and ones they hadn't yet incurred. Late in July, Jim decided to take Richard's advice and give up trying to compare their real progress with their estimate. He would let Alex keep track of the accounts paid and received and stop worrying about the rest. By the second week of August, Jim admits, he feels much better. He still thinks about money. The issue is always there, he says, but for the time being it sits more lightly on him than it did when he still believed he could control it.

"I do have a sense of humor," Jim protests to Judith, as he accepts a Popsicle from the box she's brought for the crew one hot August afternoon. "It's buried under piles of paper."

"Things seem to be gettin' real smooth," Richard says aloud to himself in the kitchen. "Everybody seems real relaxed."

The first mouse is sighted in the basement, by the plumber, late in August. The house has rooms, windows, a hearth, some plumbing, exterior doors, electricity, and heat. It still has plywood floors, which now look old and worn. Odors of mortar and special glues come and go. The house always contains the smell of wood and faint sweetish smells of sweat.

The station to which the carpenters most often tune their radios offers the weekly predictions of an astrologer, who comes on and says one morning, "The moon will sesquiquadrate Venus tomorrow. You might want to watch out for lashing out at someone."

Painters have recently appeared on the job, and one of them tells the radio, "The moon's in Uranus." An old joke. The painter is the only one who was listening to the warning, which seems to coincide with the start of unprecedented tranquility around this building site.

Apple Corps had talked of stopping the job. They had threatened to call in an arbitrator to decide the issue of the stairs. But it is as if merely imagining hostile acts can satisfy their grievances. The project has left the fast track now. "I think the fighting's over," says Ned after work one day in mid-August. "I could be wrong, but we're trying to get done now." Ned laughs. "The stair.

Jim will probably be dealing with Jonathan about the stair well into 1986."

Ned's good mood, to Jim's astonishment, has held for months. The assurance Ned has always had about a job in wood seems to have spread from his hands. At the end of a hot August day, Richard stands in front of the hearth complaining about a detail in a drawing of Bill's, a little piece of metal Bill has ordered them to place between the hearth and the cabinets that flank it, this for the sake of extra—excessive, Richard believes— protection from fire. The day is exhausted. Richard thunders, "Ugly! Horrible! I wouldn't mind doin' it if there was any purpose behind it. You gonna catch something on fire through eight inches of brick that's already two feet away from the stove?"

Jim looks rumpled for once. Wearily, he answers. "All I can say is I'll tell him it's stupid and he'll say, 'I feel very strongly about this.' "

"He's gonna worry about this and not about the floor catching on fire?" shouts Richard.

"Hey," says Jim. "Don't yell at *me*."

"I'm not yelling at you," says Richard, in a voice slightly short of yelling.

Ned lies down on his back on the dirty plywood living room floor. It seems a sacrificial act. At any rate, it draws his partners' attention. "Exhausting, this job," says Ned.

Jim smiles. "I know. We could've done four jobs easier than this one."

"How much energy all of us use up worrying about a stupid piece of metal," Ned goes on.

"God's on our side, not on his," says Richard, who looks recovered.

"I think we're doing wonderfully, though," says Ned, from his resting place. "To get this far and not be crazy. Just amazing."

"I'm relaxed. I just can't eat regular," says Richard. Then he hollers, "Oh-*Kay!* I accept it. Wire mesh." Richard stares at the hearth and puffs up his chest, playing the characters Astonished and Indignant. The spat avoided, they go home.

The role of peacemaker is new for Ned. At the end of another day in early August, Ned calls a meeting. Apple Corps sits down together on a plywood floor in a bedroom upstairs. Branches of trees rustle behind them just outside the windows. Ned says it looks as though he'll be leaving them this winter, and he's not sure for how long. Tina is going to take a job as midwife in a place where midwives are wanted and needed, perhaps in Alaska, more likely in rural South Carolina. Ned calls his departure "a sabbatical from Apple Corps."

Out on the porch two days later, Jim says suddenly to Ned, apropos of nothing they've been talking about, "I'll be sorry to see ya go."

For years they have contemplated alterations in their enterprise, and usually Ned has spoken against change. Now he says, "Sooner or later we have to hire some younger men. Someone to carry the plywood. And when that happens we're going to have to be in the mainstream of taxes and benefits. So maybe incorporation's part of the aging process." Someday, they've often said, Apple Corps would have to hire carpenters, divide itself into crews with a partner in charge of each, and undertake several large jobs at once. A reorganization should increase their incomes, but even Jim, who's argued for change, has felt torn. He suspects reorganizing would mean he wouldn't get to work with Richard anymore. Now the prospect of Ned's departure sets a limit on how long they can go on tabling the issue. Alex plans to go traveling for most of the coming winter. At least for a while, Apple Corps will be a company of two, and they already have more work lined up for next winter and spring than Richard and Jim can do alone.

After Ned's announcement, they seem more careful with each other than before. When Ned criticizes all the work he's done on the south wall—mainly out of weariness, he's been at that job so long—Jim tells him it looks fine. Richard says, "It'll look like a silk purse, Ned." And when Jim describes this job as "all screwed up," Ned tells him, "It's just a hard job. I think you're doing fine. Gotta give yourself some credit, Jim." Apple Corps is a courtlier group of carpenters in August than it was in April. It is as if Ned has lent them some of his manners, on the eve of his departure from them.

Once the carpenters had framed the walls inside the house and the plumber and electrician had woven the miles, literally miles in all, of wire and pipes into the skeleton, like so many nerves and arteries and intestines, the insulator came and Jim said, "The house will change today." By nightfall it was all muffled up in pink and yellow fiberglass and loud sounds no longer echoed. That was the calm before the sheetrockers. The carpenters, the plumber, the electrician, the insulator, had all seemed to work quickly. The sheetrockers showed what quickness meant.

When Jules saw the sheetrockers pile out of their cars and van, and troop across the sandy ground up onto the new porch, he said, "It looks like the Nicaraguan invasion."

"He's an incredible worker," said Richard, stopping to watch, through a downstairs window, one of the bosses, a muscular young man named Dave Pogue.

Cutting and running, as he himself described his technique, Pogue trotted through the house, slapping huge, heavy gray sheets of plasterboard against the studs, cutting holes for outlets, screwing the 'rock in place with an electric drill that— along with the several others constantly running— made the house sound like a giant dentist's office. All the while Pogue instructed the new employee who was trying to assist him: "Pay attention and I guarantee you'll learn . . . You might hate me, but I guarantee you'll learn . . . Don't get hurried. I've got to hurry. Even though you're new, I've got to hurry. Gonna lose my ass on this house . . . Don't stand there. Do something. Don't

368

stand there watching me screw up, way I just did."

Richard grinned, looking through the window. "These guys are good. They're some of the best sheetrockers around."

The novice, as it happened, grew weary by three that first day. Pogue paid him off on the spot and sent the fellow into an early retirement. Through the windows, the sheetrockers really looked like people working at the wrong speed. They came and went like a swarm and left behind a maze of gray walls with many smooth white seams that would vanish altogether under the first coat of paint.

The carpenters went outside to work when the sheetrockers arrived. Around the time when the sheetrockers left, Apple Corps finished the exterior. Ned put in the last of the little southern windows—"Done, by God, Bill Rawn." Alex and Richard finished clapboarding the house. And Jim endowed it with a front door. He built from scratch, following Bill's drawing, a Greek Revival molding for the entryway. He did so without uttering a single complaint about architects. Joining the door's molding to the clapboards, he got to use a number of his small, watchmaker-like tools. The finishing touch was a piece of quarter-round molding only a quarter of an inch long, which he had mitered on one end and coped on the other. He installed it on tiptoes. It fit just so. "Oh-hoh," said Jim, standing back. "So much talent in such a young feller."

Richard admired the front door greatly. "Crisp. That's the way it should be. This is the front door."

Then, more or less at once, they went inside, to finish.

Near the end of August, during a coffee break out on the porch—those intervals at which they satisfy what Jim has called their "unrelenting quest for sugar"—Alex produces a list of figures: They've worked so far 2441 and a half hours. They've billed the Souweines $104,715. "We paid all our bills, paid off our debt, and we're just about even," says Alex. He figures they should make some $13,000 profit, on top of the $14 an hour each has been making. Assuming that it will take only another month of labor. Jim thinks a month sounds reasonable, although he hasn't checked. "By and large, it seems to me our finances are pretty good," says Alex, concluding his report.

"Good," say Jim. "That's the way they should be."

"If we hurry up and finish this house, we'll have a lot of money," Alex says.

Back in March, after they had estimated the framing and turned to imagining the finish work, they had gotten up and paced around Jim's table. In a hurry to get to real saws and hammers, they had estimated the finish work swiftly, but they have never been able to do the actual work any way but slowly. Jobs usually slow down at this point, when carpenters begin to apply the thin surfaces that people live with. Finish work tests the conscience, and they are moralists in wood.

The expense of framing and sheathing and roofing lies mostly in materials. Afterward, little by little, increasing amounts of labor are applied to dwindling amounts of new wood and nails. Now the time of swift, dramatic changes in the house has passed. At the start, they used hundred-foot-long tapes, then ones sixteen and twenty-four feet long. Now they carry six-foot folding rules. These are long enough to measure most of what is left to do. Their fields of vision are narrowed, and their rulers, which they can use more accurately than tapes, are magnifying glasses for them.

One of the hemlock planks that Jim selected with great care for the high staging, back in June, has gone all twisty in the sun. Jim carries the plank inside and turns what was a tool into part of the house. Out of the twisted board he cuts stringers, underpinnings for the wide short sets of steps into the sunken living room. Aligned and nailed into place, each set of stringers looks like a row of sharply angled knees. At least they do to Alex, who says, "That looks like a chorus line just exiting."

Back when they were framing, Richard dropped his metal tape and bent the hook that's on the end, and his tape threw off a calculation or two, until he bent the hook back and recalibrated his with the others'. Equality in tapes mattered then. It would not matter now. That was communal labor. Finish work is mainly solitary. Most of the time now, they work alone in different rooms, conversing with each other around corners.

5

Once in a while, one or another of them pauses to counsel Judith. She has joined them, as a sort of apprentice, for two or three days a week.

"Jim? Can I borrow a screwdriver?" asks Judith.

"What size?" Jim kneels, sharpening his block plane.

"I don't know. For these screws." She holds out a handful.

"I *do* know, and it's a number eight." He takes from his toolbox a screwdriver with a wooden handle that his hands have oiled and polished over the years, an old friend of a tool, and smiling up at Judith, Jim hands it over.

There are a number of Judiths and, it sometimes seems, a new one can hatch at any moment. There's the Judith who teaches shoelace tying. There's Dr. Judith Souweine, who has enough degrees for an office wall and a résumé as long as Bill's but who feels the need to further her primary career that summer and travels to Boston once a week for postdoctoral work in the diagnosis of neurological disorders, at the famous Children's Hospital. (The Doctor sometimes meets the public in a skirt, blazer, and necktie. "I'm female. Want to make something of it?" that outfit seems to say.) There's Judith the labor negotiator, Judith the politician, Judith the athlete. Once Judith was a photographer. Now she has discovered carpentry. She started making things in wood a few years back. She made a platform bed that still pleases her, though she confesses that after she made it, she found out it was too big to haul up the stairs. "None of it looks all that hard to me," she says she told herself. "Let's give it a try. Carpenters can't be *all* that smart. I'm smarter than most people."

A vanity, a cabinet on which two sinks will rest, is the first task she's set herself. It's her first time out building a cabinet. She comes in with an armful of tools, wearing an old pair of red pants, and she gets right to work.

"I like her. She's sarcastic," Richard said after he'd had his first real chat with Judith. Now he stops from time to time to give her tips about her cabinet. But it is Ned, the fussiest craftsman, who seems most interested in making Judith feel welcome and who takes the greatest interest in her woodworking education. He is creating windowsills when she calls from the bathroom.

"Hey, Ned?"

He puts down his tools at once.

She wants to know if her frame needs more support. He studies what she's done so far, hand to chin. The vanity will have a top made of Corian, a synthetic material that looks like marble. "I'm not going to install that," she tells him.

"Oh, I am?" says Ned. He smiles at her. Then

he tells her that her frame is "perfect." It could, however, use a few more struts across the top, for holding up the Corian. She has put in her struts with fat-headed roofing nails instead of finish ones—that isn't proper to Ned—and she's cut the struts a little more raggedly than Ned likes, but this is her work, the struts won't show, and he does not mention those small deficiencies. The important problem is that she's placed the struts on edge, thin sides up. Ned thinks she'll need to supply some wider surfaces onto which to glue the Corian top.

She makes a worried face.

Ned puts a hand on her shoulder. "It's all right."

"It won't fall down, will it?"

"Oh, no," he says. "It won't fall down."

"I may have to ask you for some assistance putting on the doors." She puts a hand on his large shoulder. "Don't tell Jonathan. He says, 'I have to tell you, Judith, I get a little nervous when you tell me how many mistakes you made.' I told him, 'I correct all my mistakes. I just make a lot of them.' "

Ned promises to keep her secret. He tells her how to add struts. The ones she adds, he says, should lie flat and not on edge. She thanks him. He goes back to work. In the evening, when she has left to collect a carload of children, Ned and Jim gaze in at her work, from the bathroom doorway.

"A lot of nailing there," says Jim.

"A lot of roofing nails," says Ned. "I appreciate her efforts, but I know that when it comes time to put on the Corian, we're going to have to do some work. Gutsy of her, though. Shoot, my first projects didn't come out nearly as well. I probably used up twice as much wood, too."

Jim laughs. "She's used a lot."

"Is this an avocation of hers?"

"Ummmhmmm. This and the banjo."

"She plays the banjo, *too?*" says Ned. "Neat."

"It doesn't seem like her instrument to me," says Jim, departing.

Ned lingers, laying his head from side to side in contemplation of the vanity. "I think it's really excellent. I think it's great that Judith built it, and it's going to work out fine. A little caulk and it's going to look fine, and it'll hold up the sinks, and the next one she builds is going to be better, because *I'm* going to draw her a bigger picture." A very large grin comes up slowly into Ned's face. He approaches the vanity. To himself, he says, "I told her twice to lay those new struts flat. Didn't I?"

She has added struts but has put them in on edge, like the first ones. She's supplied sufficient bearing surfaces, but not in the way Ned prescribed. Ned shakes and shakes his head, grinning all the while. "I think it would be hard to have her for a student. Stubborn, by God. It's interesting." He says in her voice, without much verisimilitude: " 'No, by God, I'm going to do it my way.' "

A couple of days later, Jules pays a visit. Jules is on a first-name basis with all of the carpenters and many of the subs now. Several days back, Gene Poissant, the electrician, began putting in the electrical heating. The system is a fairly new sort, located in the first floor's ceilings, between two layers of sheetrock. Gene was stringing the wires when Jules entered and in a very friendly voice remarked to Gene, "As far as I'm concerned, you're doing this all wrong."

Gene, an unflappable sort, just smiled, and he and Jules conversed pleasantly.

Jim often talks back to Jules, and Jules will sometimes say, on entering, "Mr. Locke, sir, may I have a word with you? Front and center, Mr. Locke, sir." Richard loves to talk to Jules. They chat about the service and about hunting. "I get the biggest kick out of Jules," says Richard. Today, Jules comes in with a cigar, and says to Alex, who is laying the oak flooring, "I thought I'd hear bang-bang, bang-bang. I hear, bang . . . bang. Pretty slow, Alex."

Alex smiles.

Jules heads upstairs and stops outside the bathroom door. Judith kneels inside, wrestling with the tricky problem of hanging cabinet doors.

"Hey, this tub's better than ours."

"Hey, you know. First class," she says.

"I'm glad these kids are so rich," says Jules. He adjusts his shoulders, flicks at his cigar—she's too busy to complain about his smoking—and, from behind Judith's back, he smiles. "Flush-mounted doors with cheap hinges."

"Dad. Please."

"They're just not first-class hinges."

"Dad. This looks pretty cool, don't you think?"

"Nice. It takes three degrees to do that."

"Hey, Dad, you only paid for one of them."

"It seems to me I had something to do with your master's." He makes sure those are the last words. He goes downstairs and exits through the study window.

Of course, the builders can't defend her from her father's criticism, but Ned takes her side against other visitors. Stopping by, a friend of Ned's observes that something looks wrong about the doors on Judith's vanity. "Nothing's wrong with these doors," says Ned. "They're perfect. What's wrong with *you?*" He bends down and examines them. "They're just a little hinge-bound. We'll just get her a powerful magnetic catch. And *no problem.*"

Early in the morning, when the house is still empty, Jim spots Judith's block plane lying in front of her cabinet. She has left the tool with its blade exposed, on the dirty plywood floor. Jim takes her plane to his toolbox. He disassembles it, cleans all the pieces with a rag, sharpens the blade on his whetstone, and puts the plane back. He does not tell her what he's done, and if she notices, she never says so. Jim insists he did it only because he couldn't bear to see a perfectly good block plane fallen to such a low estate, but on several mornings over the next weeks he plays secret sharpener to Judith's tools. Once, he even sharpens up her pencil.

Judith turns to closets next. Jim tries to instruct her in the fabrication of an Apple Corps closet. The interior of such a closet should be a little room, with casings on the insides of the doors, with baseboards and finished floors. You have to rummage around and risk a stiff neck to notice the difference between an Apple Corps closet and a more easily constructed, less elaborate one. Instructing Judith on closets, Jim mentions baseboards.

"I don't think we're going to have baseboards in these closets," she says.

"You have to."

"How come?" She puts her hands on her hips. "Who says?"

Jim's face colors. "If it's going to be finished, you just have to."

She does it her own way. No baseboards. She makes the shelf above the closet bar out of plywood. When Apple Corps makes a plywood shelf, they always glue a strip of clear pine along its outer edge to hide the plywood's laminations. Judith simply covers the edge with wood dough. She stands back. "Very good," she says. "Almost just right. I cut a few corners. It's a closet, right?"

Richard stands in the same spot at the end of the day. She's gone. He says, "Paint is not going to help this closet one bit."

"Is she *done* with these closets?" asks Alex.

"Yes, I believe that's right," says Jim. "Garbage to garbage. Oh, well. Different strokes. I don't care, as long as she proudly points out to her friends that she did it."

"The closets are intense," says Ned. "The thing that I find curious is that she didn't ask me for any help on them. Well, she did, but just once."

"Maybe she doesn't know any better," Richard says.

"No, she knows," says Ned. "She's just in such a hurry she doesn't care."

Judith lacks their experience. She has children to care for, a case to argue in her union's negotiations with the Amherst School Committee, work to do in Boston, fixtures and appliances to find. She does her carpentry on stolen time, and getting done is her main goal. Her work isn't bad. It just isn't Apple Corps's. And hers clearly improves. One late set of shelves she makes with facings on the outer edges. She makes a complicated bench and cabinet in the master bathroom—by far her best and toughest piece. Even that is not crisp enough for Apple Corps to praise, although Ned, at least, does find some complimentary things to say about her work when she's nearby. None ever complains, not even privately, about the time they lend her, as they have when Bill has come asking questions. On Judith's carpentry, Richard takes the long view. "Oh, cobby," he says, when asked his opinion on her closets. "She gave the impression she was real serious, but if she was real serious she would've done them the right way. I

379

know she can see the difference between what we do and what she's done. She has the ability, though. She knows how to use the tools. Way she goes about it, with a little practice, she could do good. She's real forceful. 'Oh-*Kay!* Here's what I need, let's do it.' " He imagines a gradual elevation in her standards. Conversions often take time, but it's never too late for one. "Those closets can be ripped out real easy and redid," says Richard.

At first, Judith always asks when she wants to borrow tools from the builders, and they loan them gladly. Then, for a little while, she borrows some without permission, usually when the owner isn't there and she really needs a tool because she really needs to get a certain piece of work done today. The trouble tool borrowing causes is venerable. A turn-of-the-century book called *The Village Carpenter,* by Walter Rose, describes the ways of the carpenter's profession in a rural part of England in the late nineteenth century. Rose writes of the "unity" woodworkers felt with their tools:

> No true craftsman but loves his tools and groans to see them abused. It is not lack of courtesy and good feeling that causes the carpenter to refuse to lend his handsaw to a novice. . . . The saw after many years of service is still as straight as when it left the maker's hands; one careless handling alone may, and often does, result in a bend that can never be put right, and for ever after the saw will be unfit for good work. . . .

Many misunderstandings have arisen from

this simple matter. . . . For this simple reason, the carpenter has often been credited with a churlishness that does not belong to his disposition.

Alone with Judith in the house on a Saturday, Jim hears her start up Ned's jointer, down in the basement. "I have to talk to her about the tools. She's gotten quite wanton about them. Shit, when I borrow something from Ned, I ask. High Moral Tone, right?" Jim goes back to work, instead of talking to her. "It's plain that she likes to be one of the boys. Trouble is"—Jim sets a nail—"even the boys ask each other if they can borrow each other's tools."

Ned will not speak to Judith himself, though he worries, too. "He's damned if he won't be courteous," says Jim, who finally performs the hateful chore himself. She accepts the remonstrance without protest. In fact, she has not harmed any tools. Afterward, she always asks.

"Richard. Are you using this saw at this minute?"

It's the old twelve-point finishing saw that Richard found at a junk shop many years ago. He sharpens that saw himself. Once on this job, he threw it down in anger, because, as he said, it cut him, and five minutes later, he started to worry about it. "God, I hope I didn't hurt it." He lets Judith take it now. "For a minute," he says. "I'm a truly nice person."

She returns with the saw. "Is that a minute or what?"

"Yup, just in time."

Ned stands with Judith in the master bath, explaining to her his techniques for making a cabinet. She should scribe it to the wall, he says. Scribing, he explains, is the technique for cutting the edge of something like a shelf or cabinet so that it will fit snugly against a wall—inevitably, walls are never quite flat, even in a new house.

"The scribe part sounds a little hard," she says.

"Take a little more time on this end and it goes much easier on the other," Ned says. "I use this one-dollar compass." Compass in one hand, a board in the other, he shows her how to catch the mirror image of the wall on the inner edges of a cabinet. He hands his compass to her.

"Where should I put it when I'm done?" she asks.

Ned beams.

Most houses get bought and sold with the insulation of middlemen between makers and buyers. Perhaps the nation's courts and emergency rooms are a little less crowded for that fact. Apple Corps once built a house for some people they never met. Architects played go-betweens in that case, and Apple Corps could speculate about the owners only on the basis of the floor plan and specified decor. Usually, they've had more to go on.

Back from scouting a new job, Jim describes some new prospective customers to his partners at coffee time, in the incipient kitchen. "I know they have some dreams hidden in the work. Clearly, they hadn't discussed much. 'Well, there'll be a bookcase here,' she said. Then he said, 'What do you mean?' "

"Sometimes I think people wait for a disinterested carpenter to come, to have those kinds of conversations," says Ned.

"You get a lot of people," says Richard, "where usually it's the guy who'll walk out and say, 'All right, as long as it makes you happy.' "

"Yeah," says Jim. "It's kind of unfair, laying it all on the wife and the carpenter. So if it comes out wrong, it's all on her."

"It all depends on the marriage," says Richard. "Usually one or the other has the power. It's great when it comes out equal."

"Right here," says Jim. "Jonathan always has an opinion, even if it's that he doesn't have one. I like that."

Once inside for the finish work, the carpenters begin to populate the bare rooms of the house with visions of the life in them to come. They foresee parties in the living room, mornings in the kitchen. "I don't know if these people will sit on this porch or not. They run pretty wide open," says Richard. Looking at the porch, he imagines Jonathan and Judith, gone gray, sitting there in rockers. Jim observes that the staircase is going to be fairly steep. "It'll get Jonathan upstairs fast," he says. "Jonathan's stair comes down into Judith's foyer," he remarks, adding, "A foyer's fancy. Just having one is fancy." As Jim begins to build the staircase, he imagines Judith descending it in a party dress, and he smiles. When the upstairs bathtub is plumbed, Jim fills it partly, opens the drain, and runs down to the living room to listen for gurgles. "Not too bad. They can't object too much. A house *lives*."

Jim stands outside on the sandy ground and looks over Judith's shoulder at a catalogue of bathroom fixtures. He advises. She selects soap dishes, holders for toilet paper, bars for towels, a hook for Jonathan's bathrobe. She turns and looks at Jim. "It's so weird. Discussing these intimate details of my life. Where my husband hangs his bathrobe."

"Yeah," says Jim. "And you already admitted you like to sit in the bathroom and watch Jonathan shave."

She smiles wryly. There's sudden color in Jim's cheeks.

Alone in the evening, Jim stops in front of the closet Judith has built for Jonathan. A blue and gold necktie hangs from a peg. Jim fingers the cloth. He guesses that the reason he has never dared to wear a tie so wild was the training in being staid that he received at boarding school.

Alone again in gray morning in the basement, Jim finds a castle on the floor, built of scraps and sawdust. "Cute." He steps carefully around it, moving on. And later, working on the stairs, Jim thinks of children on them and puts lots of screws into the newel posts. He anchors the posts to the framing stoutly enough for the juvenile traffic he foresees. He slaps a post when done. It does not waver. "Strong like bull."

In the hilltowns of western Massachusetts, friendliness often awaits friendship and does not always come then. Usually, it takes time and a lot of circling to penetrate the reserve of Yankee carpenters, assimilated ones included. But Judith would find a way to make friends with extraterrestrials. She has moved right in with her tools, and in no time at all she fits.

Judith asks Jim why the closet she's finishing isn't perfectly square.

"I remember distinctly my first recognition about closets," answers Jim as he shaves a stair tread with his block plane. "I complained and somebody said, 'Hey, man, that's the way it is.' I wasn't used to wood. I used to be a car mechanic. Steel. It stays put. I realized I had to loosen up."

"Was that the beginning of your loosening up?" calls Judith from her closet.

"I knew I'd catch some shit for that. Judith, you're a bad person."

"But Richard just told me what a nice person I was."

People who share a special passion tend to find each other out. She spends a lot of time chatting with Richard in the kitchen. He leans an elbow against an unfinished counter. She does the same. She's telling him about some people she and

Jonathan once visited. "They were so aggressive and sure of themselves."

"Not like you." Richard aims a sneaky, sidelong grin at her.

"No! I mean *really.*"

"It's my sixteenth anniversary tomorrow," he says.

"That's a long time."

"We started dating when we were sixteen."

"You really did rob the cradle. Jonathan wasn't even twenty-one when we got married."

"I wasn't either. You guys got married really early, too."

"He wasn't even done with college. Well, that's exciting, Richard. Congratulations."

"Yeah, I been thinkin' about it all day. Sixteen years."

She brings them beer on several hot afternoons, also ice cream and doughnuts. At coffee time, they spread themselves around the kitchen or the porch and they hear about her union negotiations. She tells them family legends. She draws from Ned the news about his sabbatical from Apple Corps and the fact that he is taking it for the sake of Tina's work.

"I'm very proud of you," she says.

"Well, I've known Tina a long time, Judith, and I really, you know, I really like her a lot."

She's smitten with that statement, she confesses afterward. Ned's a sweet man, she thinks, although something about him also makes her think of him as "a simmering pot." She also calls him "gorgeous." Alex she hardly knows at all, but she thinks that he must be the gentlest of them, because her children head for him and he seems to like them at his knees. Richard is gruff and blustery, the steady one, and yet she saw that he could get disconcerted, during the affair of the missing kitchen plans. Of all the carpenters, Jim is most like a friend, and the most difficult. She thinks him kind, thoughtful, honest, and adept, but she wonders if he could bear the stresses that routinely fall on businessmen. Richard is accommodating. To get along with Jim, you have to build your house his way. His wariness irritates her sometimes. He's frank and even voluble on some subjects, but he never offers an opinion on the house in general or on the choices that she's made for it.

Judith carries home reports of her days among the carpenters. Her tone makes Jonathan feel that in the future she probably should not try to negotiate with them over money. She does not protest. The builders' work is hard and sometimes boring, like any job, she feels, but she likes especially the "teamliness" of their approach to it. But lately, deep in August, they seem to work with diminished cheerfulness. Maybe Ned's coming departure makes them sad. Maybe, she thinks, they've begun to feel "separation anxiety" in anticipation of the end of this job. Comments she's heard around the house also make her think they're worried that they might lose money. Judith's thoughts pivot there. She has friends who are building new houses without contracts and who are now receiving bills for thousands of dollars of extra costs. She feels very glad, she says, that Jonathan insisted on a contract price. In effect, she says she's glad this worry lies only vicariously on her. She is not one of the builders, after all, but an ambassador to them, sympathetic with the problems of their country and mindful of the interests of her own.

"Judith being there," says Jonathan. "That's why we've all been getting along." He is probably right. When they want to alter slightly a feature of Bill's design for the three small sets of living room steps, Jim doesn't have to call Boston. He goes to her instead. He brings her to the living room. He explains the problem. She knows about problems in carpentry. She soon understands this one. "Fine. Do it that way."

"Thank you, Judith."

Jim has another question, on another day. He finds her in the kitchen. "The second floor is all carpet, right?"

"No way, José," she says. It is carpet in the bedrooms, tile in the bath, and oak everywhere else.

Jim drops his pencil.

"You obviously are surprised."

"Oh," he says. "Ohhhh. That would have made a lot of difference. The underlayment on the second floor is all for carpet."

She understands. He had planned carefully for

carpet. "Oh, dear. I feel bad you didn't know that."

"I do, too."

"Is it in the contract?"

"It oughta be."

The kitchen fills with light and rubble every day. As soon as Richard creates a counter or a shelf, someone drops an old set of drawings on it, someone else deposits an empty doughnut box and coffee cups, and these sit there attracting other droppings until Richard goes into one of his housekeeping frenzies and hoes out the place. Walking through the kitchen, you're always stepping over boards or toolboxes or Richard, who often works on his knees. Judith and Jim sit down in a clear spot, inside the frame of an unfinished cabinet, a sort of booth on the floor. She looks over Jim's shoulder. They groan together. The contract doesn't speak clearly on the issue of carpet versus flooring. Jim takes out his yellow pads, to see if they can help, and gets diverted right away by history—notes on his first squabble with Bill and on his efforts to get the Souweines to "upgrade" the house's interior. "This is where I was going to give a speech to Jonathan," he says.

Judith smiles. "A real speech? With jokes and everything?"

"No jokes. This is when I was very serious."

Judith remembers an angry letter she once wrote and never sent. "But it was therapeutic to write it."

Jim reads on, but the yellow pads speak only

ambiguously about carpeting. "It's not clear," says Jim. "Jesus, a long time ago, there was a big lack of understanding here."

It is about $100 gone, for plywood thicker than was needed. "Well," he says. "It makes no difference."

"I think we should have gotten stock in yellow pads before we started this job," she says. "Got any more questions? Maybe we should get out the assumptions file."

"That would take all day."

They smile at each other.

"I'm working late. I'm working till the end of *Sesame Street,* if you want to know the truth. It'll help them get into Harvard," says Judith from a closet.

Alex sits in the study on his Apple Corps workbench—each carpenter has one essentially the same—sharpening his block plane and answering questions from the children near his feet. Richard is in the kitchen nailing, pausing now and then to wonder what cap he should wear with his new Jack Daniel's T-shirt when he attends the Willie Nelson concert out at Tanglewood this weekend.

A lumber delivery truck driver finds Jim out on the porch and asks, "How's your sense of humor?"

"Better than it's been," says Jim.

Together at the end of the day, like viewers at a museum, Jim and Judith ponder from the living room the casings on the southern windows. Jim fears that Bill won't like them much. Doubled studs in the framing between windows have necessitated wide mullions. "But I think they're going to work out all right."

"No," she says. "He isn't going to like that, but, hey, the world's not perfect. The boat people. If they had a stud, they'd be happy."

The sunlight comes deeply into the house from the south, now that fall is near. Shadows of leaves flutter across the barred shadows of the windows, on the as yet untiled kitchen floor and over the freshly laid oak in the living room.

6

Once, a customer called Apple Corps's team of favorite subcontractors "a hilltown Mafia." That client insisted on hiring some of his own subs. He regretted it. His plumber did not do leakproof work.

Most of Apple Corps's subs are, in fact, like relatives. Norm Nye, the plumber, is somewhat older than they. He has great respect for water, the knack it has for finding its way to holes, and, when superheated, for exploding, and he tends to eschew newfangled materials and techniques for managing the unruly substance. Jim believes a plumber ought to think that way. Norm's truck might be a gypsy caravan, it is so full of tools and fittings, and for this reason Norm tends to park it in spots most convenient to a house. Jim says he often thinks they could use Norm as a sort of dowser. They could wait to decide on the locations of driveways and front doors until Norm arrives and parks.

Gene, the electrician, hunts with Richard and is such a close relation that all of Apple Corps gathered one Saturday not long ago and put a roof on his barn for free. There's the stalwart mason, Staelens, and his assistant Paul, and the sheetrockers, Pogue and Schmidt. The sheetrockers don't have much that's good to say about their job. "The material kills your body," says Dave Pogue. Theirs is heavy, dirty work, but it's the pace of it that really seems inhuman. So much of the expense that the world can allot for making the surfaces of walls has been invested in sheetrock factories that there's hardly any money left to buy the time for putting up the stuff. And sheetrock is a material that can be put up quickly. Therefore, it has to be. "The satisfaction," says Pogue's partner, Jeff Schmidt, "is walking away knowing no one else can do any better."

That is what all of Apple Corps's subs say, whether outright or by doing neat and sturdy jobs. They say they enjoy working for builders who do consistently good jobs themselves. The painter, Bert Willey, who has the freshest eye, because he is a newcomer, says he and his partner, Tom Kennedy, are lucky. "We work on nice jobs like this. It's not always the best profit, but it's fun to turn out a nice-looking piece of goods."

Some of the subcontractors grew up in the

trades, as Richard and Ned did. Some of the younger ones came to their specialties after other adventures, which for some included college and studies in the liberal arts. Paul Korpita, the mason who works for Dick Staelens, started constructing mortar joints part time, while he was still in college. He got a scholarship to graduate school in history. He found out he had made a mistake. "You know how when you go from grade school to high school, people tell you you're going to learn the real truth now? I just got tired of waiting for the real truth, I guess. I had this job. It was a real good job, a lot of fun."

Bert, the painter, took a degree in European history at the University of Massachusetts. He did well. "I loved my philosophy courses." He had a chance to take over his father's business afterward, to work as a procurer of material for large construction projects. He spent a couple of weeks at the job and saw it wasn't for him. "I almost died. It was the toughest work I've ever done. Miss a couple of things and you do the job for nothing. Trying to collect is no fun either. It didn't suit me, being at a desk." Now as a painting contractor, Bert works extraordinary hours—Bert makes Richard feel slothful—often eighty hours a week, and he earns, he says, anywhere from two to twenty-five dollars an hour, depending on a host of variables. Sometimes, when a customer sues a builder or a builder goes bankrupt, Bert, who comes in near the ends of jobs, "goes yummy," as he likes to say. He has no complaints, however. "I was hitchhiking one time in Canada," Bert explains. "I got a ride from a religious guy. Finally, I told him, 'I believe in a warm, sunny day.' You know. In the spring when you feel the sun on your back and you feel wild and nineteen again?"

In England, even after wood had lost its place as the primary building material, carpenters often remained the bosses of construction. Apple Corps preserves that tradition. Each year they have subbed out another task or two that they once performed themselves. Although most of Apple Corps enjoy it, they hang and mud and tape far less sheetrock than formerly, because, Jim says, they are too finicky about it and so they just aren't fast enough. They still reserve for themselves a much wider range of jobs than any one of their subs practices. They also do the paperwork and planning. The subs have their own businesses to run, but their individual jobs are less complicated than the builders', and the subs don't deal directly with architects and customers as often as these carpenters do. The difference between being a sub and a carpenter-builder is often the difference between being in the building trades and being an intermediary between those trades and other worlds, usually ones better endowed with money and formal education. The carpenter-builder has occasion to stand at the windows of the expensive houses that he builds. Sometimes, if his ambitions lead him that way and he has luck, he gets to buy what he can build.

One of the sheetrock crew saved the money he earned at his trade and went to Alaska searching, literally, for gold. He went bust up there. He came back to sheetrocking, to earn some capital for another attempt at the big score. He told the story on the porch, at lunch. It was an unusual tale, unique among the histories of the assembled workers. By contrast, Jim's history reads like a story about contentment. But among all the other workers who have laid hands on the Souweine house this summer, Jim clearly feels most restless, not for an escape from his trade or even for great riches, but for some reconciliation of his visions of what he might have been and what he is and what he could become.

The something about Jim that makes him a little difficult to Judith and Jonathan has not escaped Jules's notice either. Jim interests Jules. After a season of observing Apple Corps, Jules will say, "They seemed very nice, friendly, humorous." He will say, "I like 'em a lot." About Jim in particular he expresses less warmth and a lot more curiosity.

Jules is a pianist, not a dabbler but an accomplished musician. He's a graduate of Cornell. He's a well-read, well-traveled, thoughtfully religious man, and an experienced and successful lawyer. He has managed to keep many of those attainments under cover, at least around the builders. If you saw him with the workmen, poking around, as Jim says, for his adversaries' soft spots, in what is intended to be friendly verbal combat, or building fences with his hired man for hours at a time without a break, or diagramming the rearrangements of earth that he and his favorite bulldozer operator made on his horse farm, you would think that all his life Jules must have harbored a secret ambition to work in the trades. Most likely he'd have driven bulldozers. Unquestionably, Jules loves building, the movement of dirt, the camaraderie of workingmen. But these seem to be recreations for him, which he keeps in perspective as some adults do their favorite sports. With puzzlement and even occasional heat, Jules ponders Jim Locke's choice of profession. Many fathers of Jules's era must have spoken words like these, alone and in front of wayward children: "A guy comes, swings his hammer, gets a day's pay, and goes home. I don't think there's anything very exciting about it to them. I don't know about the other guys, but Locke's father is exceedingly eminent. Where's Locke trying to go?

"That background is interesting. A professional background and the boy turns out to be *in* the background. From riches to rags in one generation.

"If you've got a reasonably middle-class family with an educational background, you expect that the kids'll do something with their heads. Be a builder, not a carpenter; be a real builder, something that's not just swinging a hammer. You can say they get a lot of satisfaction, it's enjoyable. Like the kids you see in communes, weaving straw. That's a lot of crap." Jules grins. "Who says you're supposed to be happy?"

Sandy watches Jim bending studiously over the kitchen table. Night after night he sits there, past his proper bedtime, making lists of people to call and material to order. Once, he looks up and says to her, "I want to make some money."

She knows that Jim has a long history of feeling that he has done, is doing, or is about to do something wrong. "Irresponsibly wrong." It comes, she believes, from his failures in school. He has recalled for her even the times when as a boy he failed to take out the trash. "He's determined not to be irresponsible now," she says. "He was going to do this job right. I think Jim saw this job as his chance, almost, to be a grown-up."

Jim has often spoken to her about that long-contemplated reorganization of the company into something larger or at least more lucrative, and about his fears that in the process he and his partners might lose control of the quality of their work. She worries, too, because the pursuit of quality seems to lie near the center of what makes Jim happiest, what has made him stick with this profession, and what makes him rise willingly from his bed around dawn to work on other people's property and dreams. Sandy isn't at all sure, on the other hand, that Jim and his partners could make the compromises they'd have to make to run a large and thriving construction business.

"They can make mistakes," she says. "They *can't* make them on purpose."

Jim has been bound to the phone in the barn, to his briefcase, and to his calculator. He has had satisfaction being boss, but always with some strain mixed in. Many days he has been unable to use his body strenuously enough for exercise to sedate him, and then he has lain awake worrying about plans already carried out and arguments over money that have not materialized. He has stopped to wonder, wistfully, how he and Bill and the Souweines would get along if he weren't playing the role of boss. Occasionally, he has escaped.

Jim drives his pickup to Vermont, to buy from a small woodworking establishment the round window that Bill has drawn in the gable of the temple end. The woodworking company's building looks slapped together. It sits on a lonely dirt road. Jim eyes it warily as he parks. "Hippie architecture." Once he gets inside and has poked around awhile, though, he finds a lot of finished work to admire. The round window is beautifully made. The owner claims he has the best shop in the East. Driving back to Amherst, Jim says, "I think it's probably true. I like it now when people say they're the best and their work backs it up. I used to feel boastful about saying we do a really good job ourselves, but I realize now we do. Because we care. That's the difference. We don't have any more skill than anybody."

Another day, fetching the granite for the lintel

and front steps, Jim drives deep into the Berkshires, to the shop of a stonemason, a tall and handsome man about Jim's age. "Thirty years ago," the mason tells him, "every little town had a monument shop. Now all that most big towns have is a showroom. Italy's producing marble cheaper than I can make a sawcut. There'll always be someone handling marble, but there won't always be someone cutting vertical, broached granite posts, unless we're careful." The mason gestures toward an object of that description, lying on the ground nearby.

"Notice how he stands with his feet wide apart?" says Jim on the way back. "As if he's about to lift something. That's certainly a material you don't fight with. Granite. You don't win the argument if you do, I imagine. I liked him. He's a smooth guy. Smooth but not shiny."

Those trips to other craftsmen's lairs seem to lend Jim reassurance, which begins to fade when he turns up the driveway to the house, and comes back to the phone, briefcase, and calculator. Working with those businessman's tools, when thinking is his job, Jim rarely thinks out loud. His tongue loosens and his thoughts complete themselves when he works mainly with his hands.

On Saturdays, Jim can be all carpenter again, and he keeps on coming to work Saturdays, even after the others have begun to take the weekends off. On Saturday mornings you find Jim alone in the half-finished house, in a white T-shirt that looks as though it might have been pressed, kneeling by his toolbox, sharpening a chisel or sawing the end off a new pencil so that it will sit easily behind his ear. Then he is the spirit of Saturday mornings, when the world is quiet and easy and handyman fathers initiate sons to the wonders of lumberyards. Jim is putting up stairs to the attic. This prefab staircase is one of those that fold up into the ceiling.

"Everything tacky that you ever dreamed of is incorporated in a folding stair." Jim wrestles the contraption out of its big cardboard box. "And this is the best, absolutely the best. This is 'The Aristocrat of Folding Stairs.' " It says so on the box, also on the directions, which Jim reads silently. He whistles. He reads them aloud:

When installation is completed and whenever the stairway is used, the stairway must necessarily be slanted at an angle from the ceiling to the floor, *but* the stairway must *always* be aligned originally and used thereafter in a completely straight line along that required slant, which straight line will run all the way along that slant from the ceiling to the floor below.

Jim whistles again. "That's almost like an English sentence translated into Japanese and back again."

The stair in place, in no time at all, Jim begins to surround the opening in the ceiling with the disdained Colonial casing. He's making a picture frame, four pieces, each mitered on both ends at forty-five-degree angles. He cuts the first piece on his German miter box, and he nails it up. "We can build for thirty dollars a square foot," he says. "I don't know. Maybe we can't. I suppose that's what we should be doing here. Bid at fifty, build at thirty, and reap the difference."

Jim dislikes mitered joints. As a house heats and cools they tend to open up. Making the joints tight to start with is in itself often less than satisfying. The process often denies him feelings of mastery. "You almost have to trick them into being tight." His usual technique for tricking those joints is to cut all the pieces, tack them in place so they can be removed, and then shave them here and there until they fit just so. Fiddling is necessary unless the opening is perfectly square, the surface perfectly flat, the miters perfectly cut. This morning, though, Jim cuts one piece of molding and nails it solidly in place. Then he cuts the next and nails it securely, too. He does the same with the third piece, saying meanwhile, "It's just the same thing as that six-hundred-and-sixty-dollar deal. You tell yourself, 'Well, the hell with it, I'm not going to take this pain to get it right.'" The way Jim proceeds, if he makes a slight error, he will have to rip all the molding down or else—it seems unlikely—leave loose joints behind in the ceiling. *Hubris* is the condition of pride, *ate* is the act, and *nemesis* is supposed to follow. Jim turns all his attention to the job now. He measures the opening for the last piece of the frame, murmuring, "This side should be just exactly the same as the others. Well, by God, it is the same." He cuts, goes back up his stepladder, and slips in the last piece of molding. You couldn't fit a razor blade between any of the joints. Jim smiles. He conceals nothing at this moment. He does not try to spoil it with bitter thoughts. "These hippie carpenters," he says once again. "By God, they're all right."

Among these four at least, carpentry is not inimical to acts of cultivation. Now Alex has discovered a passion for geology. Weekdays he works with his partners to apply finished surfaces to the house; evenings and weekends he studies what lies underneath the hills and river valley. In a quarry near his farm, he finds the tracks of a dinosaur, and soon a part of lunchtime has become a lecture series on the history of the terrain around them. Richard studies in the woods, alone and with his Boy Scouts. He sharpens his skills with bow and rifle. He celebrates the discovery of a new blackberry patch. Richard, adept in woods and garden and house, has taught himself to fix nearly everything in sight. Ned and Jim are fixers of things, too. Ned also studies trees and the spider, his new spider, that has found its way inside his car. Ned reads but not as much as Alex, who reads about as much as Jim. Jim has set his own curriculum and done what many real students fail to do, which is to read the books. He's stuffed his head with American and English literature. This summer he has taken on the Victorian novelists.

"Vanity Fair got a little long, but I finished it,"

he says as he sharpens his block plane. "Time for its morning tune-up." He always sharpens that crucial tool of finish work in such a way as to leave the blade slightly convex. That way its edges won't bite into the work, gouging wood and ruining surfaces that should feel smooth. Jim and the others always run their fingers over joints and other surfaces they've planed and sanded. These unconscious movements of the fingers have a reassuring quality and also an Epicurean one, like sniffing wine or laying a cheek on velvet.

Jim makes his lips into a trumpet and plays "Sweet Georgia Brown" as he diagrams a piece of work on a scrap of wood. Jim often draws small diagrams of projects he's about to start and almost always he draws on the appropriate material. If it's a Corian top for a vanity that he plans to cut, then he makes his diagram on a scrap of Corian, and if white pine is his material, he finds a scrap of pine to draw on. He slaps his four-foot level against the jamb of a door he's just installed. Finding it quite plumb, he says, "By God, this is a class act." He cradles the level in his arms. He takes from a cloth pouch in his toolbox a gouge and starts removing some superficial knots from a piece of pine that ought to have been knotless, saying, "Yup, sure would be nice if trees grew without branches." He works awhile. Then he observes that this tool is made for outward-thrusting strokes. "All Japanese tools work toward you," he says. "That's the way you commit harakiri, too. Western tools all seem to work away from you. They're less introspective. You have more control pulling a tool toward yourself, because you have *no* inherent tendency to go too far. Whereas, going away, you can be as ebullient as you want."

There are two categories of finish work inside the house. One sort is repetitious and fairly easy to perform. They must install dozens of window casings, nail in hundreds of lineal feet of baseboards ("Baseboards are the low point of the finish work, if you'll pardon the pun," says Jim), plug in a truckload of doors, lay some 1500 square feet of oak flooring. They divide these chores. Jim takes the doors. Doors can be challenging, especially if a builder makes them from scratch and even if he buys them but hangs them himself at the site. Apple Corps can make doors, but not cheaply. They enjoy hanging store-bought ones, too. But they long ago found out that they can't do any of that work better than their favorite door-making establishment, and they can't do the job nearly as cheaply. So they buy doors that are already hinged to jambs and simply install those prefabricated units. The procedure takes some tinkering, but there's nothing very interesting in it for Jim. Or there wouldn't be, but this time the doors have come improperly prepared for their knobs, with mortises—holes—that Jim must patch. These repairs involve small and delicate cuts. He makes patches that will become invisible under paint, and while at this chore Jim seems mildly entertained. "I have to Dutch these suckers in. That means to patch a hole. I think it comes from the old finger in the dike. But can the hippie carpenter run this patch through the bench saw without cutting off his thumb?"

For one day, only one, Jim helps Alex lay oak floor. They use, as always, a nail-driving device, which gets its power from a large rubber mallet. Alex lets Jim handle the machine.

"Very early in my life, I learned to trust machines over living things. The opposite of most people. You, Alex."

"Right. I believe machines are inherently capricious acts of God."

"That's why you don't try to keep the tools you steal."

"I don't know. All these tools look the same to me."

"Just like the devious Orientals. I'm sure it's connected to your deep-seated distrust of machines. Hey, Alex, stop making so much noise."

"That's the only thing wood responds to, James. Noise. I'm getting bored."

"Yeah."

"Even under the best circumstances, it's hard to keep this from being a boring job."

"We're both in the wrong profession," says Jim.

Alex does not always say he minds laying floors. "It makes the time go by quickly. You keep busy. No thinking." Alex takes on willingly the repetitive tasks that make up one part of finish work, but he has also asked Jim to let him build the TV cabinet and the woodlift (a dumbwaiter to transport wood from basement to hearth). The second is an especially demanding job, which combines mechanic's work with cabinetmaking. Those are Alex's share of the second category of finishing.

Only small piles of wood lie in the corners now. They dwindle slowly. Richard has the kitchen, a task of great complexity. He's making all the cabinets from scratch. "If I had to do one thing all the time, I could probably do kitchens," Richard says. He's making a lot of this kitchen from rough-cut boards of poplar that he planes and joints himself at a friend's woodworking shop in Apple Valley. Richard now divides his time between the hills and Amherst, but when he's away the others do not seem to miss him as much as they would if each did not have something special to build.

Ned has three sets of living room steps. He builds the treads himself, gluing together long thick boards of red oak. "Oak. It's really nice working with oak. I love this winy, uriney smell it has. Piss oak." When he has made the oak floor of the foyer turn seamlessly into the first tread of one set of stairs, Ned stops to say, "I love this sea of oak in this living room. An Oriental carpet, some contemporary furniture. Hell, anything would look good in *here*." The stairs won't take more than a week, however, and then, Ned fears, it's the baseboard beat for him. Making steps is a fine job. Ned wishes he could make it last.

"It's like geography," says Jim. "The interesting parts are the edges. Where things come together. The middle parts that are all the same are not so interesting to me." The main staircase will have dozens of edges and joints, all out in plain sight. Once, Jim was ready to give the staircase to a subcontractor. Now he has claimed it for himself, and he feels a little selfish.

Jim rips the rough treads off the frame he built a month ago, exposing the spruce stringers, those many sharply angled knees. The frame of the main staircase has a treacherous look. Jim turns on his radio and tunes it to a country and western station. "Jim's becoming a human being," calls Richard from the kitchen. For Jim, the radio plays "babysitter to the world": "It lets you know the rest of the world is still there and all right, and you can concentrate on what you're doing." Jim stands in front of the frame of the stairs, studying them. From his radio, to a raucous country melody, comes a tale of unrequited love. Jim snaps it off. "I can't build the stairs listening to Dolly Parton."

The front door leads to the mud room, which leads—through a French door—to the foyer. The frame of the stair stands to the left. Just across the foyer from the bottom of the stair, there's a window with a view of sand, then grass, then woods, under all of which Jim sets up his shop. He always stops to sharpen a tool at the first sign of dullness. He won't usually lavish time on arranging his tools, materials, and sawhorses, the way Ned does. On the brink of finishing the stair, though, Jim spends half an hour laying out half the tools from his box and several from his truck: chisels, belt and pad sanders, twelve-point hand-saw, miter box, framing and try squares, wood glue, razor knife, block plane, C-clamps, saber saw, electric drill, finishing hammer, nailsets, workbench, ear protectors. He waxes the base of his skillsaw to make it glide. He puts a handful of sawdust in his nail pouch, to take the oil off the nails he'll use, so that he won't smudge with oil what he's about to do. The stair makes two right-angled turns, and requires six newel posts. When he has anchored the first post to the framing, Jim loops a spare extension cord into a hangman's noose and drapes it over the post. It's the gesture of a monk who keeps a skull beside his bed to remind him why he prays. "This is what happens if you cut the treads wrong."

In stair building, the steeper a stair, the taller the risers between treads and the narrower the treads. All the books, ones such as the handbook Richard pored over in trade school, prescribe that the width of a tread and the height of one riser should add up to seventeen or eighteen inches. The collective, successively refined wisdom of the tribe of carpenters seems to have produced that formula. It is the one that works best for the largest variety of human feet. A more basic rule for stairs says: Every tread must be as wide as every other, and every riser must be as tall as every other one. "Within a thirty-second of an inch," says Jim. "It has to be that fine. It's amazing. You start up a stair and after the first step your legs know what the next rise should be. You can trip on a bump in a flat sidewalk. A quarter-of-an-inch variation will do it. It's amazing. I bet if you took pictures of people climbing stairs, you would find their toes *just* clear each tread. You let your legs and feet take charge, but they're pretty literal-minded." In fact, it is very easy, a common mistake, for a builder of stairs to forget to add to his calculations the three-quarter-inch thickness of a finish floor that's not installed yet. Then he builds the stairs and lays the floor, and suddenly he has a staircase with a bottom riser that is three-quarters of an inch shorter than all the other risers. A stair like that will never stop tripping people, even ones who know its flaw. Stair-making carpenters are like school crossing guards or trainers of seeing-eye dogs. They take on one of society's small sacred trusts.

Jim awakens early, thinking of the staircase and its manageable dilemmas. If he lays the treads and then inserts the newel posts through them, he can't make the posts as sturdy as he wants them. So instead he anchors the newels deep in the framing. Then he cuts precise holes into the several treads that the newel posts will pass through, tight collars to surround the newels. The bottom tread must slip down over two posts. This is the most exacting moment on the stairs. Jim cuts, chisels, whispers precautions, and at last, he lowers the tread over the two bottom posts. Wood squeaks, birch against oak. "You couldn't get a razor blade in beside any of these posts, by God. How much? Five dollars? What's the statute of limitations? Tight for twenty years? Tight fits are what matter. Some people don't feel that way about life at all, but I know what quality feels like to me. What quality means to me is how tightly things fit together. Joints are the essence of it to me. But an old stairway that hasn't got tight joints can still look good to me." Laying another tread, one of the many without a newel running through it, Jim says, "Usually, when you're done and there's a place where it's not quite perfect, you find a way to tighten it up. If you have a guilty conscience, you do that. Sounds right anyway. . . By God, that's close enough. . . Pretty good stair so far. The question is who's going to pay the extra nine hundred dollars. *That's* the question."

Doesn't a thing like a stair need some small imperfections, in order to look real?

"I don't want it to look real. I want it *absolutely tight.*"

Jim has gone to the barn and left his ear protectors on a newel. It looks as if the post has earmuffs. Richard ambles into the foyer and looks the stair up and down. The first time he worked on a job with Apple Corps, Richard found Jim building a staircase. Jim was doing it in a way that wasn't wrong but wasn't best. "I immediately made some suggestions," Richard remembers. He sees one of them re-enacted here. Jim has set the risers in place before cutting the apron—the piece of trim that lies against the stairwell wall like a baseboard over the stair treads and risers. You can simply nail the apron board to the wall and butt the treads and risers against it. Or the stair maker can install the risers first and then fit the apron board around them, a procedure that requires a dozen or more precise, toothlike cuts in the apron. Jim has taken the second and more exacting approach. Now, as the various woods of the stair move, most of the cracks that open will be hard to see. "It does a better job this way," says Richard. "Takes longer, too. That's why we never make any money. It would be fun, though, to make some money on this job. Wouldn't it?"

Richard goes back to his kitchen, where he is constructing the frame of a cabinet. He's making a box out of birch-faced three-quarter-inch plywood. He mates the sides of the plywood box with dado joints, cutting a channel with his router in one piece of wood, then fitting the edge of the other piece into the groove. There is a catch, however. Dado bits cut grooves very nearly three-quarters of an inch wide, but three-quarter-inch finish plywood is never quite that thick. The edge of the plywood lies only loosely in the dadoed channel. Taking up his screw gun, Richard fastens the two pieces together from behind, and as he does so, he drives the screw at a slight angle, forcing the edges of wood tightly together along the side where the joint will show, if anyone ever decides to peek behind the dishes. Richard discovered some years ago that the technologies involved, the one that produces dado bits and the one that's responsible for plywood, did not marry well. He found this way around them then. He does not think about his adaptation now. His trick is a choice he made long ago, and his hands make it now by themselves.

The carpenters kneel on the floors of different rooms. Harpsichord music emanates from Jim's radio. Hammers ring now and then. Fine-toothed finish handsaws rasp away, a sound like the music of the nighttime summer woods. First thing in the mornings, the house usually has a sylvan stillness, while the carpenters settle into their work.

"One of you guys is dead in there," calls Bert the painter through an open upstairs window. "There's a vulture circling around out here."

"How do you know it's one of us?" calls Jim.

"I check the heartbeats of my crew every hour. Actually, we're all dead from the necks up."

In the living room, Ned turns on his radio, right in the middle of a once popular song called "Patches." It's about an orphan. Jim had hoped he'd heard the last of it some years ago.

"Hey, Ned, it's about your radio."

"Yeah, Ned," calls Judith. "Bad, Ned. Bad."

It's a mistake to complain. Judith is one of the boys now, so she gets the usual treatment. Ned turns the volume all the way up. In the kitchen, Richard's saw stops. A moment later, from the kitchen, at full blast, comes a song about a gambler.

Up in Apple Valley last night, Lindy laid a

412

farewell feast for Tina. Tina's going on ahead to South Carolina, and Ned will join her there after this and one more job. On his way to the woodlift, Alex stops to ask Richard, "Did you stuff yourself with quiche last night?"

"Yeah. And a pear tart for dessert."

"It sounds quite fattening," says Alex. "Bad for your health. I'm glad I wasn't there."

"I bet they're glad you weren't, too," calls Jim from around the corner.

The morning wears on. Richard broadcasts some news that easily reaches all the rooms. "I told Alex I was going to give him a piece of my pear tart and he told me how healthy it was and that I wasn't fat. What kind of a patriot would you be, Alex?"

"A fair-weather one," calls Alex.

"When the going gets tough, Alex leaves," says Richard. "When the going gets tough, Alex leaves."

Alex sings that country and western song about the gambler, who twangingly advises a younger man that one must know when to hold one's cards, when to fold them, when to walk away from a table, and when to run.

"Read the book *Little Big Man*, Alex?" asks Jim, after a stanza or two.

"Yes, I did, Jim."

"Way the guy changed sides all the time. Alex, the master of the quick change."

"Hey!" It's Richard's voice. "Where's my goddamn ruler? Alex?"

"It's over here someplace."

"Thanks, Alex. Probably ruin the rest of my day. If anything goes wrong the rest of the day, it's your fault, Alex."

"My God, Richard," says Ned.

"Tell him to stuff it, Alex," calls Jim. "Richard's so excited he got his cabinet up, he can't think straight."

"Alex took my ruler and he hid it," mutters Richard. "Hey Jim, what are you building anyways, a stairway or a fort?"

Silence for a moment. "Hey, Ned," Jim calls. "What are you building, a stairway or a fort?"

"Say what?"

"Richard just asked me that, and I sputtered for a while. I think he's just getting cocky because his cabinet's on the wall."

Immersed in finish work, the carpenters have grown as cheerful as when they were mounting the air with the frame of this house. Then, on a day in September, Judith stops by Jim's half-completed staircase and asks him his opinion of the newels. He guesses they're all right. Afterward, he says to himself, "Keeps you on your toes. Makes you wonder if you're doing the right thing."

A day or two later, delivering a check, Jonathan stops, too, before the stair. He tells Jim he admires the craftsmanship in it. Indeed, he feels aghast at all the work a staircase takes. He's not sure that he likes the style of this one, though.

Jim applies nosings—rounded edgings—to the treads, perfectly mitered nosings, and sands them into silkiness, and while he works he utters misgivings. The posts at the bottom are different from the rest. "It's kind of mongrelized," Jim says of his staircase.

Judith must have overheard, because she comes to Jim again one morning. "I'm sorry that you're spending so much time and energy on something no one seems to like."

Jim thanks her for the thought. Afterward, he says, "She's learning." He admits he feels very warmly toward her then. But every day now, as he adds new pieces to the stair, he finds new faults in it.

After they had thrown out the designs that cost too much, Jim told Bill he didn't want the stairs redrawn. Verbally, they worked out a new, less costly design. Jonathan made one alteration, but Bill and Jim did most of the planning and they had thought they understood each other.

A staircase encompasses baffling geometry. As soon as Bill had drawn a floor plan, back in March, he realized that he would have to make the space for the stair a little cramped or else add nine inches to the length of the whole house. He chose the less expensive-looking option, and let the stairs be cramped. That did not mean that the stairs would look cramped, but Bill had to plan some tricky adjustments in order to make the banister run in a continuous line from newel post to newel post. The continuous banister was important to Bill, and his now-discarded drawings of the stair had one running down over the tops of the newel posts. In the new plan, the banisters run into the posts instead. Bill thought that all the pieces of banister would intersect the newels at the same height, but the last section of banister has a curve in it. The curve makes up for part of those missing nine inches.

To make the curved section meet the newels at the same height as the section of banister above, Jim would have had to make the bottommost newels much taller than all the other posts. Either the lower section of banister or else the bottommost newels had to diverge from the rest of the stair. Jim thought of calling Bill. He did not want to call him. There were many reasons why, and one of them, Jim knew, was that the thought of calling Bill made him feel less than fully competent. Besides, Jim would have had to halt and wait for Bill to come to Amherst. There would have been another conference. Jim had seen the problem solved by making bottom newel posts tall. He thought he would prefer the composition if he altered the height of the banister instead. Jim made the choice, and eagerly he began to build.

The architectural profession's standard argument against those firms that offer both to design and to build holds that only independent architects can protect the customer. Architects must spend some time looking over builders' shoulders and they must feel free to cry out whenever they detect inferior materials and poor workmanship. Bill doesn't worry much about those issues, though it was lucky, he believes, that he caught the hearth and frieze in time. Bill knows that building anything is an adventure into the unknown, and he believes that when the unforeseen problem arises, having an architect on hand can make the difference between a distinctive and an ordinary, even a poor, solution. He has spent three busy weeks in Boston. He drives out to Amherst again on the fourteenth of September. As soon as he gets in the front door, Bill sees that he has come too late.

There's a lot to look at and a lot to praise, but the staircase—all but finished now, except for the balusters, the pickets in the fence, as it were—draws Bill to it and won't let him go. He gazes at the staircase, Judith at his side.

Jim stands on the lower landing. "There's a lot of staring and not much talking here," Jim says. No one speaks. Jim goes away to fetch a tool.

Softly, to Judith, Bill says, "The problem is, I'm thinking of what might have been."

"Oh, Bill," she says. "Keep those thoughts to yourself."

It sounds like a plea, not a command, but when Jim returns, he can't help asking for the news that Bill can't keep from his face.

"He's remembering his tact lessons," says Jim to Judith.

"No," says Bill. "Because I have utterly no criticism of the way it's built."

There's no angry talk. The others leave, by

ones and twos. Jim and Bill stand at the stairs discussing the problem of banisters at different heights. Bill asks, softly, what it would cost to tear out the bottom section of stairs and do them over.

"I won't do it," Jim says. He speaks softly, too. He wets his lips. He says it might cost $450. Abruptly, Jim excuses himself, gathers his tools, and leaves.

"I don't know why Jim was so upset," says Bill. "Maybe it was just the end of the day."

Later, reflecting on that inspection tour, Bill says, "Sometimes I feel forced into the position of being the guy who comes out and sees the problems. And Jonathan's played the bad cop. In a sense, he was forced into that because of Jim's style, which is sort of arm's length, and there's probably a sense in which Jim feels he's forced there, too, to be a contractor and not a time-and-materials builder. It's ironic. In a sense, we're all forced into roles that are not quite suited to our personalities. Yet in a sense we've all made choices." At this moment, though, Bill can't be thinking clearly. He leaves to do some other business, to render some advice to friends who have a new house in progress, too. He looks down a hallway. "Am I getting taller?" he murmurs. Then he laughs. "Every window I see today seems too low to me."

Bill has prodigious powers of concentration. Once fixed on something, his mind sticks. It's dark when he returns to the empty house. He sets up a lamp. He fetches some masking tape and with it attaches several of the balusters to the banisters. He stands back. He rearranges balusters. He stands back. He finds a can of wood dough and places it on top of a newel, to simulate a taller newel, and that, he sees, would fix the problem altogether. He stands back. The balusters alone, when actually installed, won't correct the problem, but, he thinks, they will ease the impression he had the moment he walked in today, that the bottom section of stairs is a vestigial appendage. Bill leaves the balusters tenuously applied, and drives to Pelham, where Judith has an ample supper waiting. Bill renders his report.

Jonathan's objections to the staircase aren't the same as Bill's. Jonathan thinks all the banisters should be higher, for the sake of safe passages, and overall, he thinks the stair a little boxy, "a little clunky." Judith says that Jonathan is thinking of the elegant stair in the house where she grew up, and he does not disagree. Anyway, Bill's solution won't cure Jonathan's objections. A week from now Jules is taking Jonathan on a golfing holiday in Scotland, and Jonathan does not want to disturb the peace on the eve of his departure, and he does not want to spend $450. "But you can buy another stair if you want," he says to Judith.

She does not want that. Bill doesn't either, really. He thinks ripping out the bottom section probably isn't worth the money or a fight with Jim. They turn to the subject of knobs for cabinet doors. Should they be brass or porcelain or a mixture? The discussion lasts late into the night. Afterward, Judith says she feels a little angry at both Bill and Jim—God gave them a common language; her house is not the Tower of Babel—but mostly she seems to feel sad. "When the stair is done, everyone will like it. No one will know, except me and Bill and Jim."

When Richard walks up onto the porch the next morning, he hears laughter inside the house, and when he comes in he finds Jim standing in front of the stairs. Jim is shaking his head and laughing. Jim points to the taped-up balusters, and then Richard laughs, too, but more indignantly than Jim.

"Jim's pretty down. Everybody's dumping on his staircase, and it's only part built. It's going to look beautiful. It is. People come in and look at things part built . . . Humph . . . Thing of it is, way Jim's got that stair built it's almost one piece. I don't think you could rip just part of it out."

Jim stands beside his stair, looking at the taped-up balusters. They remind him of a routine in which the comedian Jonathan Winters declares that he is going to Scotch-tape forty-seven pigeons to his arms and try to fly. Jim leaves the balusters as Bill had left them, until his amusement is expended. Then Jim takes them down.

Jim pulls from his wallet what looks like a business card. An architect once gave it to him at the end of another job, telling Jim he might need to use it on some architect in the future. The card reads:

We Sincerely Appreciate Your Criticism
Fuck You Very Much

"I wish I'd given this to Bill."

Jim has felt much angrier at Bill than he does now. In fact, Jim feels impressed at Bill's bravery. Jim doubts he'd walk into a house full of hostile carpenters and speak his mind. What Bill did, architects have done forever. Bill's not uppermost on Jim's mind anyway. "I want the stair to be good, as much as anyone," he says to the foyer in general. "I did my best. I don't feel guilty. I don't!" He begins to install the balusters, drilling holes and putting dabs of glue on the ends of the thin round posts—"A little dab on each and after this, you can get a job at a Carvel stand." As he works, Jim says again, "I don't feel guilty. Thing is, I think they'll like it when it's done."

Each of his partners stops by that morning to praise Jim's staircase. The distaff side of the owners' family must have conspired. First, Judith comes by. She recites to Jim the adage about builders and architects being necessary adversaries. ("I think she was trying to make me feel better.") Next, Florence brings a visitor, and, passing by Jim, declares, "This is the master builder of the century." (Jim had sent Florence flowers on her birthday. He smiles.) Finally, the

Souweines' daughter enters. "I love the staircase, Jim."

"I'll work for you anytime," Jim says.

That Thursday, Jim recovers. By Friday, Bill has once again become the distant scapegoat of Apple Corps tradition, and spirits lift generally. On Saturday, Jim shows the house to his visiting father. Afterward, Jim says he knows that in showing the house, he meant to say to his father, "Here's something I've accomplished in the world."

Monday morning, and the carpenters sit on the kitchen floor, eating a peach pie by Lindy, collecting their paychecks from Alex, and discussing finances for the first time in a while.

"Alex, this check looks awful skimpy," Richard says. "God, I hate responsibility."

"I figured out how much I spent on those living room stairs," says Ned. "A thousand. Nine hundred labor."

"God, why did you do that?" asks Jim. "To depress yourself?"

"How much do we have in the estimate for them?" asks Ned.

"Depends on who you talk to," says Jim. "I don't even know who's going to pay the extra nine hundred for the staircase." Jim laughs. "But that's okay. Richard's gonna save our ass in the kitchen. Right?"

"Right!" declares Richard.

"We put in twelve-fifty for the woodlift and

five hundred for the TV cabinet. So *Alex* saved you, Ned," says Jim.

"All right, Alex," says Ned.

"Alex did both for a thousand," says Jim.

"You are amazing, Alex," says Richard. "You are an amazing person."

Alex half-shuts his eyes and looks beatific.

They disband and scatter to their various corners of the house, but Jim doesn't go to his staircase. He lingers in the kitchen with Richard. He says, when the others have left, "My father was over here and he didn't like the design at all. He liked the workmanship." Jim looks around the room. "I know what we're doing is good, but I want people to like it."

"It kinda hurts," says Richard.

Richard is holding his skillsaw. He's halfway to work already. Jim leans against a counter, empty-handed, and he looks off through the southern windows toward the Wiffle Ball field and the woods beyond. "Usually when you show a new house to people when it's not finished, they're not sure."

But Richard has gone back to work. To himself, Richard says, thinking of the snack he's just eaten, "I never knew. I never really knew how much peach pie hurts."

Jim returns to his staircase. He has to put a cap, called an easement, onto the top of one of the bottommost newel posts. It's a matter of planting firmly a round peg into a round hole, and Jim has decided to do it without fasteners or even glue.

He makes a cut across the top of the post and inserts a wedge partway into the cut. He forces the easement down onto the post, which drives the wedge deeply into the top of the post, spreading it so that it holds the easement tightly. "Blind wedging" is the name for this trick. Jim performs it with a slice of tongue clasped in a corner of his mouth. He does not speak. When he finishes, he says, "Well, I hope everybody likes it, because it's *good* enough."

Jim has nearly finished the staircase now. While he works on one remaining chore after another, he is silent. When he finishes one, he speaks, and then it's as if he were emerging from a dream he would rather not leave. "We've gotta make this house right," he says.

From the living room comes the sound of Alex singing: "I don't care too much for money. Money can't buy me love . . ."

Jim ducks his head and smiles. He loses himself in another task. He looks up and says, "Whether we're going to make money or not is something I think about all the time. I think it's beyond calculation now. It's easiest to build it and not recalculate until the end. We have to build it anyway. But it bugs me. I feel responsible for it, making money . . ."

Over in the living room, Alex has switched tunes. "Bee bop a lula, she's my bay-bee . . ."

"The house looked good two weeks ago. It probably still does," says Jim. "It *looked* good, but it wasn't all figured out. It seems that at the end of a job there's an endless number of little things to do, which throw your calculations off. It's scary, I just ignore them. I don't count 'em. I'd feel out of control if I did."

"Hey, it fits!" cries Ned from another room. He has been tuning up an exterior door. "It's a little snug, but we gotta leave something for the carpenters to do in years to come."

Alone with his own thoughts, Jim works on. "My father had never seen a house I'd built. I'd rather have done the same work and have had everyone think the house was stunning. I wanted him to *like* it." Jim knows the feeling isn't reasonable, but he says that he is angry at Bill Rawn.

Jim looks at the stairs. "Well, what can I say? In a month we'll be gone, and I won't give a shit."

Summer lingers in September. In the kitchen, Richard's router whines. "Why, that boy is makin' the most piteous wailin' and caterwaulin' you ever did hear," says Jim. On his own radio an old English ballad plays. Jim applies a delicate sliver of wood to the outer wall of the staircase. And now, after weeks of labor, he is done. And really, Jim has to admit, it's a pretty good-looking stair.

These days are hot and humid in the valley. The carpenters and painters eat lunch out on the porch, while Alex's dog, Brewster, sleeps underneath it. Bert tells them stories about falling, of "come downs" and also "high come downs"— "the ones that twist your stomach"—and about the time he dropped a bucket's worth of paint on a customer's Mercedes-Benz. Sometimes Bert catches a bee in the morning, when bees are sluggish. He carries it up his ladder and then hands it to his partner, on the ladder next door. Alex discourses on geology and as always reads from oddities in the *New York Times*. Jim laughs. He loves these family gatherings, but for now he seems troubled and lonely, and what's most on his mind, he speaks about when his partners are elsewhere and he works by himself.

"I wish this job was over," Jim says. "There are a few interesting parts left. It'll be neat to see it all painted."

7

The written agreement separates emotions from transactions. If you put your deal in writing, you can head off misunderstanding and deter malfeasance. Those are the old and enduring promises. Americans have always believed in them, and in every era, significant numbers of people have prepared for the construction of houses as they have prepared for death, by getting their wishes down in writing.

Both old and modern building contracts name dates for completion. Both usually prescribe penalties for lateness. In the old documents, payment to the builders may take the form of grain and corn or land or occasionally a slave, but old and new contracts always specify payment and usually a schedule for it. Often, they also share a common general injunction. Some Colonial contracts require that the house be built "wall and workmanlik." "In a substantial and workmanlike manner," says the contract that Jim signed.

Laid side by side, the contract for this house and ones written in the seventeenth and eighteenth centuries look surprisingly alike. The main difference between them is weight. The specifications and original drawings that Jim found skimpy and the modifications attached thereto make a sheaf nearly as thick as the local telephone book. The old building contracts, however, rarely amount to more than a page. Often, nothing in them resembles even a slender set of modern specifications. In the old, dimensions are set down, the number of chimneys is prescribed. Seventeenth- and eighteenth-century contracts may admonish the builders to make roofs "tite in all wayes," stairs "convenient," a mantelpiece "plained and handsome," a frame of "the best oake." But often not even that much is recorded, and owners and builders seem rarely to have attempted ahead-of-time definitions of terms such as "handsome" and "convenient" and "best."

It wasn't, presumably, that people in the old days were careless or stupid. Bernie Herman, the folklorist, believes that the phrase "in a workmanlike manner," and its variants, covered what was left unwritten. Herman has found records of old lawsuits that appear to have been settled on the basis of those words alone. Back then, apparently, the court could easily find witnesses who would speak with authority on whether or not the builder had performed in a workmanlike manner. The injunction has survived in modern contracts because it can serve as a pretext for introducing expert opinions on matters the parties have neglected to specify. But experts called to the stand today would have a hard time agreeing on what "workmanlike" means.

Starting around the middle of the nineteenth century, contracts grew long and specific, perhaps because the Industrial Revolution introduced a great and new abundance of varied building materials and designs. But while the number of house forms was very small before the nineteenth century, builders constantly varied those several forms. Herman points out that "in a workmanlike manner" was confidently applied to agreements for building all sorts of different structures, from barns to mansions, and he insists confidence was justified. In a given place, at a given time, he feels, people involved in building could apply the phrase to almost every possible case.

The change in building contracts can be gauged by the amount of paper expended to say what "workmanlike" means. Obviously, old and new contracts speak of worlds that differ widely. Jim once said, not long after he had signed the document, "We wouldn't need contracts if we trusted each other." Many old building contracts seem to speak of a time when, as Herman puts it, "customary relationships superseded commercial ones." And it is tempting to think that trust and understanding were easier to come by back in the eighteenth and seventeenth centuries than they are today, and that life, even building houses, was gentler and simpler in the good old days.

In fact, builders and owners have always bickered in America. "Certainly New England was an incredibly litigious society in the eighteenth century," says a lawyer and historian named Jack Michel. "Those people fought a lot, about building houses and everything else. Any quick trip through the court records of the eighteenth century tells us that." No statistics show whether the old-timers fought more often and fiercely over housebuildings than owners and builders and architects clash today, but clearly houses in progress have always been potential battlegrounds. The kinds of arguments that went to court in the seventeenth and eighteenth centuries appear to be timeless. Builders sue to get the money that they think they have earned. Owners demand recompense for uncompleted work that they think they've paid for.

On a Monday morning in September, while the carpenters and painters work, the promise of a revelation comes over Jim's radio. It's a program called "Getting Your Money's Worth from Home Contractors."

"Hey, listen to this," says Jim.

Paint-speckled Bert walks over to listen.

"The reason there are so many problems with contractors is there are so many handshake deals . . ."

Jim snorts. Bert laughs. But the old advice seems nicely timed. Not that it's very much on Jim's mind, but Jonathan came by earlier this morning, and he and Jim discussed a problem about the paint. Afterward, Jim started to explain the issue to Ned, but the explanation promised to take longer than the issue seemed to warrant. Jim said to Ned, "Anyway, I'm not worried about it."

Many of the specs for this house come from the specs for the Wieners' house, and those specs required that one coat of a product called Cuprinol stain be applied to the clapboards. Bert, as it happened, had painted the Wieners' house, and the builder had paid him to apply two coats of solid-colored stain. Bert had asked Jim about that detail, back when Jim was soliciting estimates. The specs said one coat of stain, however, and Jim was bidding the job on the basis of those specs. The competition, Jim figured, would put one coat in their estimates, so Jim told Bert to do likewise. If Apple Corps got the job and the Souweines wanted two coats of something else, Jim could always change the specs and increase the price accordingly. Somehow, though, the subject never came up.

They could cover clapboards with one coat of clear stain. The house would need at least one more coat within a year, but that didn't represent to Jim an outrageous proposition. At some point, though—he can't remember when—it became clear that the outside of this house was going to be all white. Jim never told the Souweines that by choosing to paint it white, they were in effect buying two coats of paint. He can't remember why he didn't. Probably the subject got buried in his mind under all the other changes they were making. It was a fact, anyway: You can't put just one coat of white paint on clapboards. The wood will show through, like the skin of a dog with the mange. Bert said so to Jim about ten days ago, when Bert and his crew started painting the clapboards, and of course, Jim knew Bert was right. A second coat would cost an extra $750, and Jim needed authorization to spend that money soon, because if Bert had to leave and come back to do a second coat, it would cost Bert considerably more to do the work.

So Jim looked back through his yellow pads, and for once he found what he looked for. It was right there in the specs: "Paint: exterior 1 coat Cuprinol stain on clapboard. . . ." Jim gave Jonathan the news. Jonathan clearly didn't like it. Jonathan said they must resolve the issue before he left on his holiday in Scotland. But for Jim, other events had intervened—the stairs, Jim's father's visit. Jim hadn't thought about paint for a while and Jonathan hadn't reopened the discussion. Jim had remembered it only this morning. Afterward, Jim will say, "Actually, I think as far as the communication goes, I presented them with the situation and I was waiting for their answer."

431

Actually, the way it looks to Jim, they don't have much to discuss. For once, the specs resolve the issue. He has his instructions in writing: "1 coat Cuprinol stain." If Jonathan wants two coats of paint, he'll have to pay for the second one.

That Monday morning, the day before Jonathan leaves for Scotland with Jules, Jonathan asks Jim to call him about the paint and to do so, please, before 10:00 P.M. The line is busy, though. By the time Jim gets through, Jonathan has gone to bed. Tuesday morning, Jonathan arrives early at the house. Everything about him speaks of haste to Jim. Jonathan seems cheerful, though. He worries about the latest bill from Apple Corps. Jonathan says he does not want to pay them for work not yet completed and he thinks their latest bill asks him to do so. But Jonathan won't insist on holding them to the letter of the payment schedule. He and Jim get that difficulty straightened out in no time.

"Okay," says Jim. "The stain on the outside. The specs say one coat stain."

"It says one coat paint, one coat primer," says Jonathan. "I could be wrong, but I don't think I am. All I can do is go back to my office. I'll bring you what I've got." Jonathan speaks rapidly. He's clearly a man in a race, a man with a list. "Judith is very anxious not to have to make a decision when I'm not here. I trust her, but if anything like that comes up and you can hold off, I'll be back here the thirtieth. If you can put something off, put it off, because she'll feel better if we both decide."

Jonathan goes on: "I'll tell ya. Strictly from a negotiating position it's a bad idea, but frankly I don't care. All these people from town say how beautiful the house looks. Others, who know more, think it's really nice. Two builders came here Sunday and they said it's just done beautifully. So I just thought I'd tell you now."

Jim smiles, faintly. "Okay," he says.

Jonathan vanishes.

"I don't know what I'm after," says Jim as he goes back to work. "It doesn't seem to be his praise."

The painters and the carpenters, all except for Ned, who is at home today, converge on the kitchen as soon as Jonathan's car clears the driveway. They might have just come in from a game of hide and seek. "I can't see negotiating something that's in the contract," Jim tells them.

"So what are you gonna do?" asks Richard.

Jim turns to Bert. "I want you to find that they don't have white, when you look at the chart." Jim means that he hopes Cuprinol does not advertise a white stain, which in fact they don't, at least not on Bert's chart. It's an odd way for Jim to say that, however. Jim might be holding a pretrial conference. He seems very calm.

"He wants us to feel guilty," Jim goes on.

"I don't feel guilty," says Richard. "Do you feel guilty?"

"No," says Jim, and to Bert, "You're not implicated in any way. He's going to want two coats. It'll look lousy otherwise. Actually, I'm not sure. If he's not going to pay for it, we're not."

"We'll pay for it," says Bert's partner, Tom, and everybody laughs.

"That's really nice," says Richard. "You're going to pay for it."

"It wouldn't be the first one," says Bert. "Last week we ate four-fifty in one day."

"We've done better than that," says Jim.

"But we're small, we're rinky-dink," says Bert.

"So are we."

"These flies," says Richard. "They're having an orgy in here."

"End-of-the job blues. Jonathan has them," says Jim. He lays a finger on his lips, which says that he is thinking.

"What you want is to put in new foundations," says Bert. "Everybody feels good then."

"Not always," Jim replies. "Sometimes people are still waiting for their loans." Jim seems then to speak to himself, in front of the others: "He's arguing without a leg to stand on." The others drift away. Jim shrugs and returns to laying tile, his post-staircase work, a job he thinks he should sub out but likes too much to give away. "There is far too much wild rose tile here."

Jim shakes his head over his ancient tile cutter. Its useful life has ended. He'll have to borrow Ned's. It's very hot. Heat like this is always disconcerting in September. Ninety-three degrees, the radio reported. "Both ends of jobs are hard," Jim says.

One by one that morning, the carpenters wander outside and up to the Wiffle Ball field, to watch Bert and Tom put color on the house. The first coat is nearly done. The carpenters bring back mostly favorable reports. "This house will look quite elegant all white," says Alex.

Back at his office, Jonathan can't find the specs right away. He has no time to search. Jim's probably right anyway, and anyway, the specs are not the issue to Jonathan. If you contract to build a house, you can't leave it only half-covered with one coat of paint, any more than you can in good conscience leave it with half a roof. If the specs say one coat, then the specs represent a mistake, for which Jim deserves at least some of the blame. Jim's own painter questioned that item; Jim has admitted that. Part of the unwritten agreement about this project obliged Jim to help guide his customers to a proper set of specs.

In fact, if this argument ended up in court— and to bring it there would cost more than the coat of paint in question—but if Jonathan took the matter to a judge and argued for the erasure of that item from the specs, he could muster a long list of cases in which contracts and pieces of contracts have been deemed invalid because of obvious errors in them. What's clearly a mistake is not a valid part of a contract. What's more,

there's that clause, "in a workmanlike manner."
Is it workmanlike to leave a house inadequately
painted? Jonathan wouldn't mind arguing his case
anywhere. What's most annoying is that he does
not have any time right now to do it.

He has a desk to clear and a plane to catch with
Jules and their golf clubs. He wishes he had not
accepted Jules's offer to treat him to this holiday.
Not that he hasn't looked forward to the trip or
that he doesn't think Judith could handle the
problem herself, but they have their own unwritten contract about this houseraising. She was going to deal with the house itself, and he was going
to handle the money. It would be wrong to leave
her alone with this problem, but he hasn't time to
work out the usual compromise himself.

This past weekend a lot of people had come by
and praised the house, just as Jonathan told Jim
this morning. Among them was a prominent citi-
zen of Amherst, a man who knows building and
architecture. He spoke with feeling about the
house, both the design and the workmanship.
This was, as Judith puts it, "a classy guy." He
had said, "I thought they didn't build them like
that anymore." Jonathan had never felt more
pleased about the place or about Bill and Jim. But
Jim is squeezing him now. If he didn't know
better, Jonathan would suspect Jim of playing a
particularly devious form of the lowball. The stakes
aren't large—some paint, a few hundred dollars—
but the situation is out of all proportion dire. Jim
is forcing him toward a concession he doesn't

believe he should have to make. By the time he gets through his list of crucial predeparture chores, rushing around in this oppressive heat, and returns to the house, Jonathan has an argument prepared and only a few minutes in which to deliver it.

Jim meets him near the front door. Jonathan begins by pointing out the ways in which he has already deviated from the letter of the contract for Apple Corps's convenience. He has bent the payment schedule to suit them. And what about the staircase? If the Wiener specs about the paint are to be enforced to the letter, then the Wiener stair, including the rounded bottom tread and banisters all at one height, are the proper model for the stairs inside this house. "The main thing is," says Jonathan to Jim, his preamble done, "is you're doing a good job and I don't want to tie you up for money. So here's the money." He hands Jim a check, for other work, not for that second coat of paint. He adds, "I didn't have time to find the documents."

Jonathan stands in the doorway between the mud room and the foyer, the front door open behind him. Jim leans against a bottom newel post, hands behind his back. This is one of Jim's attentive-looking poses. A schoolboy on his best behavior might affect it, but Jim looks comfortable. Jonathan, in sports clothes and sunglasses and shoes that go with finished floors, looks out of place, standing at the edge of the mud room's unfinished, dirty plywood floor. Jonathan stands at the door, no farther in than most unwanted visitors get, and Jim is within in a T-shirt, as if receiving him. Smells of paint and fresh wood and sweat lie within. Jonathan has paid for the house, but he doesn't look like the owner yet.

"So two coats?" asks Jim.

"I don't see how anybody can say they would only put one coat on," says Jonathan.

"Anyway, the question is moot, because it says so in the contract."

"Suppose it didn't say there was going to be a roof on the house?"

"That's different."

"It's not workmanlike, it's not acceptable," says Jonathan.

"Bert says you can put one coat of Cuprinol on."

"Nobody said anything to you about Cuprinol," says Jonathan.

"The contract says that." Jim still leans against the newel.

"You keep saying that."

"I don't see what the argument is," says Jim.

"I don't have any argument," says Jonathan.

"But you don't want to pay for it and we don't want to pay for it, and if you aren't going to, then we can't put two coats on."

Jonathan shifts slightly, an impatient movement. "I've told you my position, and if Bert and you decide one coat is not enough and you don't do something about it, I'll feel pretty bad about that."

"I don't blame ya for not wanting to pay for

it," says Jim. "So many things about the contract weren't clear. This is one where it's written down. It says, one coat."

"The contract also says good and workman-like."

Jim gazes at Jonathan. Jim looks polite, attentive, concerned. Then Jim brings his hands from behind his back and turns his palms up.

Jonathan's jaw stiffens. He looks, all of a sudden, larger than he is.

"I want it done!"

Jim offers his open palms again. "I'm not going to pay for it."

Up on the porch roof, Bert and Tom stop painting. Upstairs, Alex stops nailing baseboards. And in the kitchen, Richard, who has never in all the years Jim has known him spoken sharply to a customer, stops measuring for cabinet doors. The house is full of ears. In the mud room doorway, Jonathan pulls off his sunglasses. He whips them off. He has never raised his voice at Jim. He does so now.

"This is very unfair, to bring this back up the day before I leave. I'm very angry to deal with this on this basis. I've had a lot of stress the last two days."

"I told you about it two weeks ago," says Jim. Color has flooded over Jim's cheeks, but it stays only a moment. He leans back against the stair, arms folded. He looks, if anything, inquisitive. He keeps his eyes on Jonathan.

Jules has pulled up outside. It is past time for

Jonathan to go. Jonathan wheels, begins to leave, returns. ". . . And if the house *isn't* done with two coats I will not consider it done in a work-manlike fashion."

He turns again.

"I don't want to have them paint it, if we have to pay for it," says Jim to Jonathan's back.

Jonathan returns again. "I've dealt with you fairly on every economic issue. And I don't think it's fair to put me through this right now."

The car's horn honks.

Richard has appeared from the kitchen. He leans against a wall, one hand on his hip. "What we did," says Richard in his conversational bellow, to Jonathan, who stands poised to leave, one foot literally out the door, "we went through the specs and bid them and we looked at the specs and the contract, and it says, *one* coat of stain."

"Your painter said that was not adequate."

"We go with the contract sometimes and sometimes we don't go with it?" says Richard, head cocked to one side. "You stick with it when it's to your advantage."

"That's not true! I just paid you five thousand dollars you haven't earned."

Jonathan's departure proceeds as if it were a dance. He strides out of the house. Jim and Richard follow a little way. Jonathan turns and walks back toward them, a step or two. "I'm going to come back here on the thirtieth, I want the house painted with two coats, because your painter says it should be two coats, and I'm not saying I'm going to pay for it, but I will discuss it. You've had two weeks to get this resolved and you're asking me to resolve this now . . ."

Richard snorts and turns away. Jonathan descends from the porch. Jim follows him, to the front doorway and no farther. Jonathan turns back. "But you're not going to have me standing here now saying something . . ."

Jim watches Jonathan get in the car. Then Jim shrugs and returns inside.

It is utterly still in there, except for some banging that comes from the kitchen. Richard, his list of dimensions for cabinet doors complete at last, is packing up his tools, getting ready to go to Apple Valley and assemble the last of the kitchen cabinets. The clatter stops. "The hell I'll pay for his fucking paint job," says Richard's voice.

From the corners of the house, the workmen converge on the kitchen once again.

"What do *you* think, Jim? You're pretty quiet," Richard says. "Gettin' the last two thousand dollars out of this job is gonna be like pulling hen's teeth. I guarantee you that."

Jim looks at the ceiling. "Oh, the farmer is the man who feeds us all," he sings.

"Threaten us. Who's he think he is? Told him about this two weeks ago. *His* time is so valuable. Ours ain't worth anything," says Richard.

"Something's got him going," says Jim. "I don't know if it's entirely us."

Bert says he is worried. He has known his share of jobs in which owners refused to make the last payments to builders, who in turn could not or would not pay Bert. Jim says, "We're not gonna not pay ya."

"If I drop seven here I can just paint my name off the truck," Bert goes on. "When I lost two, it took eight grand before I was back where I should've been. If I drop seven here, I might as well go back to college and study psycho killers."

"It did not sound pleasant," says Tom.

"I didn't think he was like that," says Alex.

"Something else is bugging him," says Jim. "But that's not our fault."

Again, they disband, leaving Jim and Richard alone in the kitchen. Richard cleans the place. He makes an angry housekeeper. He takes it out on the trash. He mutters. He makes declarations. "I have lost complete respect for that guy. I want to have as little to do with him as possible. After the show he put on. All the pressure he's had on him the last few days. He's the one with the contract, architect and all that stuff. Big time. Contract doesn't work out for him now. So he's gonna be hurt. We're taking advantage of him. Take advantage of Jonathan Souweine? Guarantee you they can have the biggest party here and I won't come. *If* I'm invited."

Jim looks pensively out the windows. "Oh, well."

"They'll get a free stairway and deduct the money off for the paint job, that's what he'll do. And if we fight him, it'll cost us about the same. He's no dummy."

"If he wanted to be difficult about this, it could be really horrible," says Jim. "I don't have signed copies of all the change orders. They're all"—Jim loads his voice with irony—"*handshake deals.*" Jim does not look worried, however. He adds, "I think he'll be contrite when he gets back."

". . . And he *threatened* us," says Richard.

"How?" says Jim.

"Said, 'I expect it to be painted.' Painted or else. I hate that. I can put up with a lot of crazy bullshit . . . I'm glad Ned wasn't here."

"Yeah."

"I'm going home."

"I don't blame you."

Upstairs, Alex begins singing. Jim snickers to himself as he watches, through a window, Richard stomp his way to his truck. "Lindy's going to hear a lot about this tonight. I daresay." Jim smiles. "Jonathan *has* been reasonable. I think I'd be mad, if I didn't think I was completely right."

Out on the porch roof, Bert says to Tom, "I know we'll get paid, but I'm worried about how things are going to turn out. To please is part of it, too."

"Think he's pinched?" asks Tom.

"I don't know. I would be, if I was building this house."

"It's a hell of a house for the money, though. A hell of a house."

"Oh, well, it's not the first argument I ever heard," says Bert. "I hope it won't be the last. If it were, we'd be out of business. It just doesn't go smooth. The only way to get around it is to be a used car salesman. Then you know you're stuffin' and bluffin'."

Jim lingers in the kitchen, faintly smiling. He has affected coolness in arguments before, but he left signs of inflammation underneath. Now there's a serenity about him that seems completely his own. "I feel better in arguments now," he says. "More removed. I don't feel insulted . . . Oh, dear, general malaise. I'm glad I didn't lose my temper, though."

Outside the next afternoon, Judith looks up at her almost finished house, which is beginning to receive its second coat of paint, and she shakes her head, remembering her phone call to Jonathan in Scotland last night. Transoceanic heat. He told her to go ahead and agree to pay for the second coat, but he also said that if he were there, he'd throw the whole crew out of his house. "They think it's over," she says. "It's not over."

But as Judith well knows, Jonathan doesn't hold grudges, and the fight is in fact over by the time he comes home. Jim expects that Jonathan will apologize. Apology is far from Jonathan's mind. He does not intend to offer one, and he doesn't expect to receive one. Anger, Jonathan says, is usually useless at best, but he had no time and no other weapon to fight for what he's still sure was the right position. Jim played less than fair with him over the paint, he thinks, but there's no point raising the subject again or brooding on it.

Jonathan returns. Through the kitchen windows, Jim sees him coming toward the house. Jim waits inside. Jonathan smiles, talks a little business with Jim, describes Jules on holiday, and then departs. Jim looks out the window again, watching Jonathan leave, and then he says, "I guess we won't ever talk about it again."

Jim and Jonathan see each other only infrequently afterward. They talk pleasantly, almost exclusively about business. And Judith waits. She fears impending conflict. "Oh, there'll be lots more fights. Which I'm not looking forward to."

She has finished her carpentry work, for this season. She still has to get through her long list of details and choose coat hooks, towel bars, lighting fixtures, a microwave oven. "It seems like a lot of work just for a house." She feels tired of the process now and a little bored with it. She says so cheerfully. Mainly, what she wants now is to move in. She says she wishes for another sort of resolution, too.

While working inside one of her closets a couple of weeks ago, Judith overheard Jim and Norm, the plumber, reviling a certain brand of toilet. It wasn't the brand they were putting in her house, but it could have been. They spoke with such scorn about a thing that a homeowner could in all innocence be guilty of buying that it made her wonder. When she wasn't around, did they speak that way about choices she had made? "Is that what they say about us?"

A few days later, in the course of one of their many chats by phone, Bill asks her if the builders take some pride in the house now that it is nearly done.

She doesn't know, she says. "It really doesn't matter what they think. It's not worth a lot of energy waiting to find out."

She sits in her kitchen in Pelham on an October afternoon and adds what she didn't say to Bill: "But you care!" She smiles, apparently at herself.

Judith has worked among the carpenters. Now she knows on her own pulses what many people seem to have forgotten: that to admire a laborer's work but not the fruits of it makes the laborer feel glum, or even like a fool for having cared enough to apply all his skill. She knows why Jim has felt sad when his work has been praised and the design denigrated. Why wouldn't he? That isn't strange. But Jim does not seem to understand that she cares, too. Or if he does, he has the oddest way of showing it.

"I think Jim retains information and therefore you go looking to find out what he thinks," she muses. "It's kind of manipulative. For people like Bill and me, he's a very odd person to interact with. He's sort of a strong, silent Yankee type, which drives Bill nuts. I find it maybe not purposefully manipulative but a manipulative way to be. You have to ask him; he doesn't volunteer. He won't say, 'I like this pink tile.' You have to

446

say, 'Do you like this pink tile, Jim?' So you have to start looking for approval. Then I say, 'What do I care what he thinks. It's my house.' "

Judith has warmed to the subject, clearly. Everything about her shines: "If I were them I would be proud of being part of this nice house. Do they feel good about being part of this? I don't know. I think they like it. If I were a builder and someone picked something ugly, I would have such a hard time putting it in. You wonder, do they think this is yucky?

"The builder sort of becomes the judge, and for some reason, you care," she says. She laughs. "Jim studiously avoided questions of taste during the planning. He said"—she does a gruff voice— " 'That's not my job.' That sort of very moralistic view. We said, 'You can have an opinion, we can reject it.' Maybe that's why. He didn't want it rejected. It's safest on questions of taste not to offer an opinion. But it's totally alien to me. I always give opinions that no one ever asked me for."

8

Jim had recommended a certain make of front door. Bill had not liked it when it came. Until Jonathan settled the matter by liking the door himself, Jim had to worry about the cost of returning it. He nearly had to spend some of the good will Apple Corps enjoys with its suppliers, that bank account of favors owed, which any builder would prefer to draw upon for his own benefit and not his customer's. For Jim, there are tangible risks in offering opinions about items that haven't been chosen. Jim would court a different kind of risk if he spoke his mind about choices the Souweines and Bill have already made. To his partners, Jim has rarely expressed unmixed approval of the house or any of its important features. When he's alone and his eyes fall on something that he doesn't like, such as the hearth, he says, "It makes me mad." Then he looks as though it really does. More than any of the carpenters, Jim keeps close track of visitors, whose numbers have grown steadily. Often when a tour is in progress, Jim discovers an errand that takes him close enough to overhear what is being said about the house he has built. Most visitors praise it, especially the tax assessor, who likes everything he sees.

"White whaleish," Ned calls the building after the fight about the second coat of paint. Ned says he feels as though he must drag himself down out of the hills to work.

Richard stays at home for a couple of weeks now, to make cabinet doors. Jim keeps in touch with him by phone. Richard tells Jim that the house in Amherst now looks like "a big pimple."

"You have a bad attitude, Richard," says Jim.

Jim laughs to himself as he lays tiles in the mud room. Jim loves laying tile. "Feces play," he calls it. "You're supposed to get your hands dirty."

He's up to his wrists in mucky grout every day now, and now that the others have started denigrating the house so thoroughly, Jim has all but stopped criticizing it himself. He has no trouble getting out of bed and over to the job. In fact, he feels as though his truck chauffeurs him there. "I'm still wired about that job," he says as he makes his breakfast in the gray light before dawn.

He has a headache every day. He can't remember just when it became a daily fact. Sometimes it is sharp enough to make him grit his teeth, but more often it is merely dull, a little grayness that he carries with him. Jim gets these headaches every year, says Sandy. She thinks they're the residue of a carpenter's long building season. Jim seeks other explanations. He pauses every other day or so to wonder why his father disliked the design. Maybe that's the source, he says. Or maybe he gets headaches from his list of remaining chores. "Ephemeral but menacing," he calls that catalogue. He carries it in his mind, eschewing yellow pads now. The list seems elastic. It gets smaller. It grows. "Get and install sash locks, build door for closet on cellar stairs, purchase and install bath accessories, sand and urethane floors, build storm door, grout kitchen floor, install wood stove, put backsplash on vanity in powder room, build lattice for porch, lay granite steps, clean up and go to dump, buy light bulbs . . ."

While Alex installs baseboards, Ned and Jim attack the list.

"I'm looking for quick solutions. Contract solutions," says Jim.

Ned vows he'll do his best.

They contemplate an opening they've left, as the building code requires, a hole in an upstairs wall that opens into the crawl space above the master bedroom. Ned figures they should make a door, a real one with hinges. Jim says, "Nah." Ned should simply slap a piece of plywood over it.

Ned goes to work. "Contract solutions, right?" He'll just cob this together. He selects a piece of birch-faced plywood ($48 a sheet). No sense wasting time on this. He bevels the edges of the plywood, sands them smooth, faces the end grain, and attaches it to the wall with brass screws, carefully countersunk. "Good enough for South Amherst."

Ned does do one cobby piece of work that day. He builds a piece of something like a stair, between the folding stair and the attic floor above. He builds the thing neatly enough, but it doesn't do its job very well. Inspecting Ned's various accomplishments at the end of the day after Ned has left, Jim climbs the folding stair and gazes up at the half-baked piece of stair above. It seems that Ned couldn't bring himself to nail the thing in place. Jim laughs.

The carpenters' comments about the house soon soften, and then one evening in late September Ned stands in the kitchen and surveys the array of cabinet doors that Richard has brought down from the hills. Richard says he doesn't care at all about this house. Ned says, "He cares. Look at these cabinets."

Some of the treads in Jim's staircase squeak under the carpenters' feet. With shims and an armful of tools, Ned sets out to cure them. "I'm taking the squeaks out of the world."

Alex says that Ned must not remove them all. Some squeaks will serve as alarms for the parents of the house, says Alex, when their children become teenagers and try, as all teenagers must, to sneak silently up to their rooms after curfew.

The day when they begin to sand the floors, Richard's voice is merry. It's hard to do floor sanding well. You can easily make a floor ripple—enough, as Jim says, to make a person seasick. And with the floors, they return briefly to communal labor. "Glory work," says Richard.

"Pretty spiffy, guys," says Bert.

"We're building this house for Judith," says Richard.

"She's the only one we like anymore."

"Yeah, this house is going to come out okay. For Judith."

"This stair is real nice," says Bert.

"The Souweines don't like it," says Richard.

"Shoot," says Ned. "Then they don't *know*."

"Think it's done in workmanlike fashion?" says Richard. "That what it is? I hope we get paid for it. This is the glory job, though. We doing this in workmanlike fashion?"

The strips of red oak flooring have a mottled

grain, which has lain hidden in the grime. Now as they pad around in stockinged feet with brushes and buckets, applying coats of polyurethane, it is as if they were performing some trick for recovering disappearing ink. The grain emerges everywhere, its colors deep and radiant, the beauty underneath the bark of solemn oaks transported to a house. "Glory work," says Richard.

The air is bracing on the porch. Brewster romps outside. Long ago Judith won the argument on shutters, and on a gray October day Jim completes her victory. There will be shutters only on the temple end, and they won't be made of wood that she will have to scrape and paint. These shutters come in cardboard boxes. " 'Cellwood Shutters,' " Jim reads aloud. " 'An improvement to wood. Won't warp, chip, peel or rot. Hi-impact foam polystyrene.' Structural foam, they said. An oxymoron, thought I. But did I say it? I did not. I *did* snicker."

Jim has long boasted that he's never yet put up vinyl or aluminum siding, but he's begun to reconsider the value of his virginity. "I'm finally getting to where if someone likes something I don't, I don't feel they have a character deficiency. It's taken a long time," Jim said not long ago. Now out on the porch, he pulls the black vinyl shutters and enclosed hardware out of the boxes. He pauses and looks up. "Geese. Is that geese?"

The shutters seem to weigh only a few ounces apiece. They hang from aluminum hooks that hang in turn from fat aluminum nails, which Jim will have to drive through the clapboards. "God, this is fun. This is carpentry at its best." Jim nails up the first hanger. "This is going to change the looks of this place. Eh? In one swell foop. Eh, big moosey nails, eh? I'm very glad that they picked these instead of wood: They're cheaper. They'll probably want a credit, though. One thing wrong with these. If they were real old-timey shutters they'd hang the other side up. There."

Jim gives a boogieman's laugh, spits out a Bronx cheer, and sings a snatch of "The Tennessee Waltz." He says, "I haven't had so much fun around here since the hogs ate little sister. Sure are fun to install, too. Don't nobody go in there and tell those fellers about all the fun they're missing, or they'll all be out here clamoring for a chance. This is probably somewhat akin to putting on vinyl siding. In the judgment of the great carpenter in the sky, this is probably a severe demerit."

Jim cowers and looks skyward from around his shoulder: "But I was just doin' what I was told."

A stern, deep voice replies: "Cancel your subscription to *Fine Homebuilding.*"

Jim laughs. "They're really lousy. But this is what they ought to be, by God. For all the reasons they say on the box. I figure you ought to be able to put these on if you're really dumb. And if you cain't, it's a bad sign. You're a little high, there, Hortense." He lowers slightly the offending shutter.

At last, Jim climbs off the porch, walks to the driveway, does a soldier's abrupt about-face, and stops. He cocks his head. The temple end has black shutters. "Look at that, eh? That suds the sucker up or not?"

Richard joins him. "That looks nice, doesn't it?" says Richard. "I like shutters. Those guys inside don't like shutters. Shutters nowadays don't do nothin' anyways. Crisp, huh? These are good ones, you know that? Most people couldn't tell the difference probably."

Around the time when the first frost comes to Apple Valley, closing out Ned's and Richard's gardens, a man who lays carpet arrives at the house to cover the bedroom floors. The oak floor's last coat of urethane is still a little tacky, and the carpet man, pausing at the threshold of the foyer, says, "They don't have the heat on in here. That's why they're having problems with the floor."

Ned, in his socks, comes right out of the kitchen at these words. "Problems with the floor?" says Ned. His eyes are very wide, his chest quite high. "What problems? We don't have any problems with the floor."

"Okay, okay," says the carpet man, taking half a step backward from Ned. "You're the general."

Ned goes back to the kitchen, shaking his head all the way. He says to Jim, "Funny how reluctant I feel to share the house with anyone. So when a stranger comes in, mouthing off . . . I'm ready to give this house to the Souweines. I guess."

"I heard from a completely independent source that Jonathan is happy with this house," says Jim.

"Only that?" says Ned.

"What you want, boy?" says Jim. "You're gettin' paid."

"Well, jeez!" says Ned. "This house is the jewel of Amherst."

Ned needs to move an old bathtub, to get his own house ready for renters. Apple Corps needs to discuss their future and also the end of this job. So they gather one night at Ned's house. Two weeks, Jim says he figures. Richard and Ned can start the next job in a week. He and Alex can finish up. They can make their deadline easily. "Okay," says Jim. "The hell with the Souweine job."

"I think we're doin' okay," says Richard. "I think it held together real well."

Ned lies on the floor. "Yeah. A vote of appreciation from down here."

"I think you did *real* well, Jim," says Richard.

Alex nods assent.

"I feel better than I did," says Jim. Abruptly, he rises and turns to fetch another beer. His face has deeply reddened. Back turned for a moment, he asks, and his voice quavers slightly, "What's the state of the economy, Alex?"

Alex reads some figures. He asks Jim, "What do you figure? How are we doing?"

"I stopped keeping track in July," Jim says,

returning to the circle with his old face color back. "It made me sick."

"I think we're going to make some money," says Alex. "About ten thousand dollars. Maybe."

Jim asks them about the party. The Souweines have proposed one for the middle of a weekday. Jim says, "Thing I don't like is saying, 'Oh, everything's all right now,' because I don't feel that way. But I don't want to antagonize them."

"I've been on jobs where it felt real bad to leave," says Richard.

Richard and Alex have a short contest. Alex names bad jobs they've known. Richard names good ones. "Right," Richard concludes. "There's good and bad ones."

The next few days Jim canvasses everyone, his partners and all the subs. Finally, Jim has to tell Judith that she's chosen the wrong time of day for the party. In a busy season like this one, no one wants to take hours off from work. Perhaps another time, they say to each other, but Jim feels sure there won't be a party. There almost never is.

He feels pleased about the construction scheduling. They will beat the deadline. They can make a relaxed withdrawal. Clearly, he did some things right or that would not be about to happen.

At a bar in Northampton, after work, Jim goes over the last change orders, trying to tie up the last loose ends, for a last meeting with Jonathan. He wonders if he should exaggerate the costs of some of those changes, in order to gain position for bargaining. He shrugs. "I don't have a strategy. I'm just doing it for what it cost us." The endeavor takes Jim back through all of his old yellow pads. His attention wanders. "I've really been thinking about the issue of the art versus income," he says. "I guess I realized this summer that I'm not willing to trade it. The art."

Richard makes a mistake installing the kitchen stove, blames Bill and Judith for it, and the following Monday repairs the problem. Bill comes out to supervise the final grading of the land around the house, and Jim, a spectator for once, observes with amusement as Bill and Jonathan do a little sparring.

Bill wants more fill.

Jonathan does not want to pay for any more.

"The proverbial well is dry, buddy," says Judith.

"Hear me out, Jonathan," says Bill.

"All right," says Jonathan, softly. "One more time."

Jim points out that it may not take all that much fill to accomplish Bill's objectives, and the issue comes to rest.

A few days later, Jim and Richard drive a pickup to the barn. They load up the new appliances that have been stored inside. To Richard, Jim confesses, "I have trouble finishing anything."

"I like to finish things," says Richard.

"I don't," says Jim, lifting from one side of the refrigerator. "I think it's because when you finish something, then you're accountable for it. Then someone can say you did a good or bad job."

"Think that's it?" says Richard, on the other side of the icebox.

"Yeah," says Jim. They lift.

"I remember that one job, Jim," Richard says, as they go back to the barn for the dishwasher. "You left me a list of still-to-do. You said the job was three-quarters done, but what that meant was every piece of it was three-quarters done."

Richard cackles. Jim grins.

Back at the house, Jim says to Alex, "We were discussing the difficulty of finishing anything, for the children of critical parents."

"Yeah?"

"I guess that's what it is," says Jim.

A week or so before he's promised to surrender them, Jim throws away all the keys to the house. He hopes it was an accident. Alone in the kitchen, he consults his mental list of what remains and finds it short. "I don't want them living here yet," he says. "Because in some ways it's still ours."

Ned's way home is lit with autumn in the maples. "Usually one person is involved in the thing until Christmas," he says. "Somebody, I guess Jim, is going to space around on it one day a week, while the rest of us are at the next job. It never just stops. One person leaves, two people leave, most of the tools are gone, someone comes and picks up the planks, and then, you know, you're done. You don't go there anymore."

V

RETURNS

Coming ashore in New England, the Puritans faced what William Bradford described as "a hideous and desolate wilderness, fall of wild beasts and wild men." When the settlers cleared and fenced land and built houses, they thought of more than food and shelter. They had religion on their minds. To most seventeenth-century New Englanders, God's perfect creation had been drifting toward chaos and ruin ever since Adam ate the apple, but glimpses of God's original plan remained in debased Nature, especially in the human body, which had after all been made in God's image. Extending the conceits of English metaphysical poets, some of the New World's poets and diarists conceived of houses as human imitations of divine handiwork. A roof was like a head, rafters were like bones, posts were shoulders, clapboards were skin, windows were eyes, doors were mouths, a threshold was lips, and a chimney was the breast in which lay the heart, which resembled the hearth, which contained the flame, which stood for the soul. Employing terms such as "comely," "well and workmanlike," "of a rational bigness," "of a Suitable Proportion," building contracts of the period in effect asked that carpenters build houses to the standards God used in constructing the human body. "In a literal sense, houses represented the transfiguration of religious experience," writes the folklorist Robert St. George. Seventeenth-century New Englanders called God an architect, and to the passionate Puritan, raising a house to divine specifications in the desolate wilderness was a godly act that temporarily halted the effects of Adam's sin. "Housebuilding," says St. George, "was conceived as an heroic effort to stop time, suspend decay and interrupt the ordained flow to ruin that started with Adam's fall."

In ancient rituals and myths of construction and from architectural motifs, several investigators have glimpsed a similar desire to halt time and renew it. No one can say for sure what premodern builders had in mind when they buried under cornerstones and posts and thresholds and inside walls and chimney piles these among other items: food, gems, coins, pottery, plants, statues, arrowheads, bottles of wine, carcasses of cattle and sheep, horses' heads and hoofs, and, as many legends have it, living human beings. To the modern sensibility, real or figurative construction sacrifices seem weird and nightmarish. Mircea Eliade, perhaps the modern era's pre-eminent anthropologist of religions, argues persuasively that the rites weren't aimless. Sacrifices at foundations, Eliade believes, stemmed from a once widespread conviction that a building had to be animated. If it was going to stand and endure, a construction needed life. It needed inspiration. For Eliade, there is more. What he calls "traditional and archaic societies" did not view history as modern societies do—as a procession of irreversible events. Evading "the terror of history" the old religions held to a sense of renewable time. Human activities had reality only if they represented returns to primordial events. Building was one of those real activities. The creation of a building re-enacted the primordial Creation. Each building project was a repetition of the grandest construction project of all. In many old Creation myths, a divine being was sacrificed to make the cosmos. People began making sacrifices at foundations in order to re-enact that original sacrifice, Eliade believes.

Like the Puritans' metaphysical conception of the house, the foundation ceremony can be seen as a recognition that building is both an act of memory and also a fresh start. Rites of construction have lapsed and builders have forgotten the reasons for performing the ones that persist. What remains is only the activity on which the old rituals hung. "A construction is a new organization of the world and life," writes Eliade in *The Myth of the Eternal Return.* "All that is needed is a man with a sensibility less closed to the miracle of life; and the experience of renewal would revive for him when he built a house or entered it for the first time . . ."

It would revive for a man such as Jonathan. He goes about his life with so much enthusiasm for accomplishment that you might imagine he never finds time for reflection. In fact, two clocks seem to run in Jonathan, one spinning fast forward, the other turning slowly back. That is apparent on the first day of moving, which falls on a Thursday, the third week of October.

Jonathan wakes up around four in the morning, thinking about boxes and where they all go. He makes a trip to the dump and is so distracted he throws away a pair of garbage can lids. He wears corduroys, an orange turtleneck, and a yellow hat with a floppy brim. Mornings are becoming to Jonathan. On this one, he is all athlete. He's up on the balls of his feet, moving his shoulders around. He's grinning. "I'm in a lifting mode," he says. Jonathan climbs into Jules's pickup, to begin transplanting households. He has hired movers for the heavy stuff. He will handle the smaller items himself. He spends the day driving back and forth between his future and his past.

In the truck, Jonathan recalls a children's story in which one Mike Mulligan and his sensate steam shovel must dig a big cellar hole all in one day. "I feel like Mike Mulligan."

Jonathan wrestles the desk that he shares with Judith out the old doorways in Pelham and into the truck. He cleaned out the desk's drawers last night. It was a journey of sorts. "Another thing that happens when you move. You go through lots of old stuff, and you have the obligation, or maybe just the occasion, to throw away a lot of stuff. It's an externality. It's not the reason for moving, but something that happens because you are moving, and for me, there are a lot of memories. Some sad. I went through all the old D.A. stuff. I must have put it all in the basement and I hadn't looked at it in four years. When I lost, I guess I just . . . Well. And then there are the intentionally sentimental things that you keep, like these scrapbooks, which you never look at, except when you move. Then you look at them."

He sits at the wheel of the truck heading for Amherst, and in his mind Jonathan returns to the old house on the night when, against all the odds, he won the Democratic primary. He is by far the most radical candidate. "All these people are there, and we win! You know how the left has such a long and stunning history of losing. It's late that night and we're talking and these two guys show up, and they're pols. *Real* pols. Guys in three-piece suits, and everyone else is in jeans. I said, 'I *can't* believe it. The party regulars. I can't believe it.' All those things you read about and here it is happening." He remembered his Shakespeare then. He had the feeling he was in a play inside a play.

Behind the wheel, Jonathan smiles. "The feeling of doing something and the sense of watching yourself do something. I have that feeling now. I remember this process, from when I was a kid. I remember my parents doing this. It's one more indication of time moving along and roles changing. Seventy years, and it all happens in the twinkling of an eye. You can't hang on to it and you almost can't notice it passing, because it's so subtle. Moving. You're dying to get it over with, and yet you only do this so many times in your life. And only once with your in-laws helping." He adds, as if daydreaming, "Florence is particularly wonderful on these kinds of ceremonial occasions."

It's moving day and Jonathan, in the cab of the pickup and in the rooms of his old and new houses, is thinking about the meaning of things. It's as if nearly everything he sees today had a little nimbus around it. A quick trip to the dump to locate the garbage cans' lids reminds him of his childhood and of how as a boy he had no idea where water came from or sewage went. Bulldozers roam the littered ground. "I take the kids here to give them some notion of what happens to our solid waste. So much of what goes on in our lives is magic. TV! How can you show it to them? A kid asks why is the sky blue and you don't have any idea. I felt horrible. No idea! It's terrible to have kids ask good questions and not know the answer." Carrying a chair out through the living room that his family has shared for eight years with the family next door, he pauses near the fireplace, and he seems to see communal gatherings there. Children are born and growing up, their faces changing. In the empty common room around the hearth, a friendship blossoms between two families. "Of course, Bill and Jim are not aware of it, but for us moving into this new house is colored with a sense of loss," says Jonathan as he drives away toward Amherst. The unsentimental Jonathan adds, "I tell Judith you've got to keep this in perspective. A third of the world goes to bed hungry, and living a mile away from good friends is not the worst thing in the world."

Arms full of boxes, Jonathan edges down the old, familiar staircase and out through hallways whose contours he knows by heart. Arms full of boxes, he sidles gingerly through new doorways. He watches his feet with one eye as he ascends the new staircase. Heading out for Pelham, Jonathan says, "That's our new mailbox." He drives slowly by. "Those are the indices of a home. We called the paper boy, told him we want the paper Friday. And the kids' principal, so the bus will stop Monday. The phones are Friday. That means you got a house."

Into the truck goes Judith's doctoral dissertation. That was a happy, proud time, when her findings about school principals turned out to have statistical significance. Into the bed of the pickup he tosses a small, well-worn piece of rug. He and Judith bought it for their apartment, not long after they married. ("It cost twenty dollars from a remnant store. It was a big issue. Could we afford it?" He says once again, "Judith and I, we've always been married.")

There's a box full of liquor. ("This is good stuff.") A foot treadle for an old-fashioned sewing machine. ("God knows what to do with things like this.") A couple of old andirons for a fireplace that they no longer have. ("God knows what happens to them.") An aquarium. (Somehow, Judith and one of the children accidentally cooked the fish and it hasn't been used since. "That's in dead storage. A horrible experience.") A bunch of plastic signs designed to sit like caps on car roofs, and also bumper stickers. Both read, "SOUWEINE FOR D.A." ("We got such good bumper stickers no one could get them off. People are still driving around with my sticker on. People say to them, 'You must really like the guy.' They say, 'No, I hate the guy. I just can't get it off.' That is the truth, the absolute truth.")

Mounting the driveway to the new house, Jonathan spots a new lamppost out front. Jim must have just erected it—a large coach-style lamp of gleaming copper. "It's a bit much, don't you think?" murmurs Jonathan, gazing through the windshield. "I tell you, sometimes I feel that way about the whole house. I drive up here and I say, 'Nice house! Who lives here?'"

Back in Pelham, Jonathan's face lights up as he looks into the children's bedrooms. They will all sleep here in the old house tonight. He will bring the beds to Amherst tomorrow. He looks at the beds now, though. Two are a matched pair. They're old and battered and the hardware, notes Jonathan, approaches extinction. "These beds, my boys' double-decker bed, is my bed from when I grew up. And Judith's bed, listen to this, the bed Judith grew up in is going to be our daughter's bed. I don't know about you, but I like that stuff. One thing I like about things is the continuity they can provide. The other thing that matters to me is if somebody close to me made it. The stuff Judith's made is not as good as Jim or Richard could do, but I think it's pretty good, and I think that's really neat."

"Boy," says Jonathan, heading for the new house, "I definitely have the feeling of Mike Mulligan. But I think we're gonna make it." As he mounts the driveway this time, Jonathan says, "It's kind of neat to see some of the issues we discussed early on come together in this house. Now I can see how it all comes together, like a giant Erector Set." He goes on, softly, "Only now am I starting to feel it's my house."

He has planned to spend two days in moving. By late afternoon he has done all that he hoped to do on the first day. At the stop sign, about to turn onto Bay Road, Jonathan sees a panel truck up ahead. It's turning into the driveway, his driveway. "I wonder who's making a right turn there," he says. Perhaps it's the electrical inspector. "Obviously, he's going to my house."

Inside, Judith and Jonathan have begun to acquaint themselves with new light switches. Outside, the moon looks as if it might burst. Jim loads tools into his pickup. He has worked at the house all day. While Jonathan fetched boxes from Pelham and Judith unpacked them in Amherst and Jules wallpapered the new bathroom upstairs, Jim finished dozens of last little chores—hooked up the kitchen stove, planed a few edges of doors.

He worked hard to make the place inhabitable. He's finished his work now, but he isn't ready to leave.

Jim wanted to settle the final change orders today—for "symbolic" reasons, he'd said to Jonathan this morning. Jim imagined a ceremonial exchange—the Souweines would pay the bill; he'd turn over the house. But Jonathan hadn't studied the change orders yet, and Jim agreed to put off the issue of money until the following week. Jim waits, though, for some kind of summary. Jonathan and Judith and Jules all have work to do around the house this evening, and Jim has none. He feels awkward in the house now, but he goes back inside anyway.

"Cerveza!" cries Jules from upstairs. "Where's my beer?"

Judith and Jonathan are in the kitchen. "I hear you're selling beer," Jim says to Jonathan.

"Want one?" asks Jonathan.

"Have you got enough for yourselves?" asks Jim.

"Yeah, sure. No problem."

Jonathan opens a beer and hands it to Jim, but the chat Jim seems to have expected does not occur. Jim has caught Judith and Jonathan in midflight. They have a great deal to do before bed, and now Jonathan heads off upstairs, to begin arranging new rooms. Judith remains in the kitchen, unpacking boxes of plates and food.

Jim leans against a counter, as if it were coffee break. "I'm not sure if I want to let you have the

472

place or not," he says to her, the quaver of a small laugh in his voice. "I *like* it."

She looks up from a box, and she smiles at him. "You can come anytime. You don't even have to call."

Jim drinks down the beer. He walks toward the front door. He calls up the stairs, "Jonathan, if I don't catch you tomorrow, I'll catch you Monday. Good luck on your first night, if I don't catch you tomorrow."

Jonathan appears at the top of the stairs. "Thanks a lot. And thanks a lot for doing everything that had to be done for us to move in."

"You're welcome," says Jim.

Half an hour later, in his own kitchen, Jim says, "I wanted to hang around to see if anything would happen. It's funny. Every time Jonathan says you've been doing a good job, it's always in the context of some negotiation or some favor. It's not that I don't believe him, but it's always sort of tinged. I don't feel closure. I assume it will come. It doesn't always."

"Can you believe how sunny it is in here?" says Judith. "I came in here this morning and I couldn't believe how wonderful it is." Judith is brewing the kitchen's first pot of coffee. "Uh-oh, no spoons." On the drive to school this morning, she and her children passed their "favorite tree," a huge maple that they've passed each morning for a long time. The children said that they would miss their tree. "We'll have to get to work finding a new one," she says now. She digs into another box. "We have more mustard than any family in the world." She unpacks boxes and conveys the contents to the cabinets that Richard made. Little by little the cabinets fill up. "Jim left his lunchbox here last night," she says. Just a moment later, there's a knock at the front door.

"Come in!" calls Judith.

Jim appears in a wool jacket.

"Did you *knock?*" she asks.

Jim smiles. Suddenly, it's a functioning kitchen. He's never been here before. "Do I smell coffee?" he asks. He refuses a cup. He smiles some more. In a moment, without much further conversation, Jim heads down to the basement, to collect leftover wood and nails.

Yesterday Jonathan and Judith began to prepare their new house. Today, Friday, they'll begin to live in it. Judith's face is bright. She's like a tourist in some long-imagined country. Everywhere she looks she sees something that delights her. How thoroughly, for instance, sunlight penetrates the breakfast nook—she'd never fully realized that before. From the kitchen all morning come her cries of glee: "Oh, the rug is here!" and "It's the phone company!" (The young man who comes to hook up the phones says musingly that the house looks like an old farmhouse. "Oh, you said just the right thing!" says Judith. Later, she'll offer him lunch.) The morning wears on. Two orange moving vans—"THE CAREFUL MOVER," say the signs on them—pull up outside. Four men in coveralls come in and out, two by two, a man on either end of the heavy and bulky stuff that they lug down the ramps, out of the van, and in through the front door. Nearby, Jim is heaving staging planks into his pickup truck. The house is a hive when Jim returns to the kitchen. "Well, see you later," he says.

"You're going?" asks Judith.

"Yeah, you're not going to need me hanging around," he says. "I think everything works."

"Does the oven?" She tries it. It doesn't light.

"I lied," says Jim. He brings the oven to life in no time.

Jonathan joins Jim and Judith. "See you Monday."

Jim says, "Feel free to call if you have any questions."

Outside, Jim, in shirt-sleeves, climbs into his truck. The movers, all four of them now, grapple the black baby grand piano through the front door. Jonathan hovers, warning them to be careful, saying, "I've done three backs, for moving men." Jim's pickup moves down the drive.

The eldest-looking mover, clearly the boss, a smiling, burly man with gray hair, says to one of the children, who's just returned from school, "You want to stay away from school, become a dumb mover like us. A strong back and a weak mind." He laughs.

"You're supposed to be able to sit here and look out this window when you play this piano," says Jonathan to the movers. The four movers make a little ring around the piano, as Jonathan sits and plays the lively strains of "Jazz Holiday." The movers grin. They turn and laugh as Judith comes Charlestoning through the French doors and down into the living room. Jonathan starts into another song. "He has two songs," Judith explains to the movers. "That's his second."

The movers place the couch here, then there, as Judith ponders, directs, and redirects. Under a cushion she finds some children's things. "Look at all the goodies. Want some crayons?" she asks the men, who grin and laugh again. She sits. "This is great," she says to herself. "As my father says, who needs money?" She looks around her, at the chairs, at the Oriental rug, at the wood stove on the hearth, and she pats the cushions beside her. "This is a *great* room. I must call my friend, William Rawn, and tell him he done good."

The movers go back to work. Jules enters the living room. Jonathan sits and plays "Jazz Holiday" again.

"Do I have to listen to that?" asks Jules, with a crooked smile.

"My house, my songs," says Jonathan, winking to Judith.

Judith and Jonathan pause for lunch and a little eclectic rumination. It's that kind of day.

"Jim seemed a little down," says Jonathan. "Maybe he doesn't want to leave."

"Jim was upset, I think," says Judith. "He didn't know how to say good-bye. He's so shy. It is strange. He's sad and we're very happy."

They take their dishes to the sink by the kitchen window. "When I got here this morning, I had the I-can't-believe-I-live-here reaction. It's *so* beautiful," she says.

"All Amherst is wondering how long it will take the Souweines to wreck this house," he says.

"That's the sad part," she says. "Jim was so careful. It'll take us *no* time to make it a shabby house."

"Here's the dustpan, Jude."

"Dustpan. That's the story of my life. That's Jim's lunchbox. He's also got his jacket here."

"He doesn't want to leave," says Jonathan. "Le'ss go," he adds, and he heads out for Jules's pickup. It's time to resume moving.

"Here's the cable TV man. Hooray!" cries Judith's voice from back inside the house. Jonathan drives out. He stops at the mailbox on Bay Road. "Well, you think we got mail? We sure did. Let's see what it says. 'Boxholder.' Not so good."

He drives back to Pelham and the past once again. Years ago, Jonathan and Judith were moving into an apartment and their couch wouldn't fit up the stairs. Jonathan cut a leg off the couch and it still wouldn't fit. Then he cut off a piece of the landlady's banister and he has felt guilty ever since. He has kept that block of wood. "As a reminder," he says. He uses it in place of the old couch's missing leg. The movers have put the old couch in his new study, back in Amherst. The piece of banister is missing. He prowls through the old house. "Here it is. Gotta take this." It is a

477

thick block of wood, maybe maple, maybe oak, with some ornamental detailing and covered with a dark brown stain, the dingy color of hallways in old apartment houses.

On the way back to Amherst, Jonathan says, "Judith has an interesting look on her face. The look on her face reminds me of the look on her face when our first child was born. There was a six-month period where she was really different than before or since. A certain calmness, a certain feeling of order. That's not the word I want. Of having things in perspective. You run around and kill yourself and then you wonder, Why do this? For Judith it put things in perspective and clarified things. Six months and it never quite came back, but something about Judith's look reminds me of that."

Jonathan smiles out on the road ahead. "I realized that just now, sort of daydreaming. I feel filled with emotion, though not emotional. Contented. It may just be I'm hopeful that the last six months have come to an end, or that there's something focusing about having your house get in order. Unfortunately, I'm not that in touch with these kinds of things . . . I say, 'Judith, that was the time when you were happiest in all of your life, and I was happiest around you.'"

There is, in fact, high color in her face when he comes into the new house. She's dancing and appears not to know it. "We got cable!" She pirouettes. "I'm so excited! We're in the big time!"

Jonathan slips the piece of banister under the

old couch in his study. The phone rings. Jonathan answers it in the study, Judith in the kitchen. The phone man is just testing.

"Hello," says Judith.

"Hi, Jude," says Jonathan.

"Hi, Pook," she replies.

She sits down at the far end of the breakfast nook, her back to the east window, and looks through the kitchen and out through the living room. It's a vista through French doors from one end of the house to the other, and again, all at once, she thinks of Bill. She understands fully now why he was so fussy about lining up all those doors. "Nice? It's fabulous. This is the Bill part, the part that none of us mortals can do."

They have nearly run out of daylight. Enough remains for one last trip to their old house. Judith drives her car, Jonathan the truck. The old house looks ransacked, most of its furniture gone, discarded papers, toys, old coloring books on the floors, all the walls now exposed and crying out for paint. It is a small house, and looks smaller without its furniture. They have at least a weekend's work to do here, but this is, symbolically, their last visit. They will not sleep in this house again.

They work fast. The contents of the bathroom go into boxes. Into boxes go clothes, toys, shoes, tennis rackets, radios. "And, Jonathan, what do we do about the camera stuff?" Finally, both truck and car full, they stand in the bedroom.

"So, are you happy, Judith Souweine?"

"I'm very happy." Her nose has begun to redden.

Outside, Judith calls to the children, who are playing in the yard. "Come on, we're going home. To our *new* house." The children climb into the truck with Jonathan. In the car, Judith bows her head toward the steering wheel. Jonathan grins and climbs back out of the truck. He opens the door to her car and leans in.

"She's emotional. It's understandable. I don't feel it myself," says Jonathan, back in the cab of the truck. His voice is soft and slow. He grins broadly and he sings silly songs with his boys, all the way home.

Earlier in the day, Jonathan overheard Judith exclaim to her mother that this house would be just like the one in which she had been raised, that beloved home of Judith's childhood that her family had quit with reluctance years ago. Judith meant, Jonathan thought, that this house would be just like that one in spirit, and it seemed to him a fine way for a daughter to feel toward her parents.

"Oh, look at my mother!" Judith cries now, as she and Jonathan enter their new kitchen.

Her mother kisses her. "All good luck, dear."

On the round table in the breakfast nook, the one at which much of this house was planned, lie a new broom, a new box of sugar, another of breakfast cereal, the evening paper, and a carton of salt. In the living room, on the coffee table there are cold cuts, champagne, candles, and, as Florence says, "good Jewish bread."

The book of Deuteronomy establishes the custom for celebrating a new house: "Then the officials shall address the troops, as follows, 'Is there anyone who has built a new house but has not dedicated it? Let him go back to his home, lest he die in battle and another dedicate it.' " Of the ceremonial items, the most important in Jewish tradition are the salt, the bread, and the candles. The salt hearkens back to sacrifices at the Temple in Jerusalem. Sprinkled on bread, salt also recalls what God said to Adam when He expelled him from Paradise: "By the sweat of thy brow shall thou get bread to eat." The bread symbolizes the hope that there will always be enough to eat in the new household. Candles say that light and joy should prevail inside the house's walls.

Jules has rearranged the living room furniture. ("Two good chairs here articulating with the couch, and it's a perfect seating arrangement. I have spoken." He grins his crooked grin.) The family gathers around Jules and the couch. Jonathan has said that ceremony is the anchor for emotion in him. "I want to have a little Shabbes," Jonathan declares. It is past sundown, Friday evening, so both the Sabbath and the life of a new house have begun. The candles are lit, while Jules leads a prayer that they all say in Hebrew: *Baruch ato adonoy, eloheynu melech hoolom . . .* " "Blessed art Thou, O Lord our God, Ruler of the Universe, Who has sanctified us by Thy commandments and commanded us to kindle the Sabbath light." Jules leading again, they pray: *"Baruch ato adonoy . . ."* "Blessed art Thou, O Lord our God, Ruler of the Universe, Who has kept us alive, sustained us, and enabled us to reach this occasion." That simple prayer is said to come from Moses. It has, at any rate, great antiquity, and it can properly be tailored to suit as many occasions as life offers, including the opening of champagne. "Blessed art Thou, O Lord our God, Ruler of the Universe, who has created the fruit of the vine," Jules says in Hebrew. Judith's face is in rainbow condition, tearful and smiling. They raise their glasses high and toast the new house that resembles the old.

Among all the ordinary household goods arranged around the gleaming floors of the living room, Jim's gray lunchbox stands out, like boots on a carpet. It sits undisturbed and for now unnoticed, on the finished, painted TV cabinet beside the hearth.

Across the river in Northampton, Jim and Sandy have finished dinner, and Jim has decided that Jonathan won't call, when the phone rings. It's Jonathan thanking him. Jonathan says that everywhere he looks he sees things a person could not reasonably expect to have in his house until he had lived in it twenty years. Then Judith's voice is at Jim's ear, thanking him lavishly. He knows Judith far better and he likes her more than he does Jonathan now, but Jonathan's plain and unmixed thanks are what count for Jim. He has tears in his eyes when he hangs up.

"It was nice," says Jim the next day. "They still haven't paid," he adds.

2

For Judith, living in her new house is like a treasure hunt. She keeps finding little acts of genius in the design, and she calls Bill often to report her discoveries. She invites him to spend a night in his creation. Bill accepts with alacrity. "Not many architects get to do that."

When daylight-saving time ends, New England's afternoons turn into evenings. That is when a cozy house needs to feel coziest. Around dusk Bill drives up to the white house at the edge of the trees, and the windows are all lighted. He walks inside, and his friends really are living there. At a time that seems long ago, Judith and Jonathan told Bill that they did not want a formal living room from which everyone would shy away until company arrived. So Bill drew his vision of coziness, but a drawing stands only a small step away from an abstraction. The last time he saw this room the carpenters and painters had nearly finished it, but it was still unfurnished and untested, still an uninhabited room in his mind. Now Bill watches. When they come downstairs, bound for the kitchen, both children and adults often turn left, eschewing the hallway to the kitchen. Instead, they often go the long way around, just in order, it seems, to pass through the living room. And when Jonathan comes home that evening from a meeting, he and Judith head right for the living room for the day's summary. So does Bill, feeling, as he says later, "thankful."

In the morning, Bill rises early and watches the household awaken. The long sessions of planning and the decisions that came from them and the interpretations of those decisions that he made at his drawing board, all are collected in the way the house manages the bustle of a weekday morning. There are no traffic jams. Morning light really does stream in just as he dreamed it would. Bill sees the family off, first Jonathan and Judith and then the children, big old Uncle Bill with an ear cocked to youthful conversation, walking them down to Bay Road and the bus. Ambling back up the hill, he realizes that this is the first time he has ever approached the house with the intention of inhabiting it. He's walking in to stay awhile, he says to himself. How wonderful. He'll fix breakfast.

Bill wanders through rooms. He gazes out windows. He discovers a view of the woods that he had not foreseen, and he expresses at least as much pleasure about that as he does about the views that he planned. Those are pleasant, too, especially the ones that open along edges. Looking out along the woodline through the south windows of the master bedroom, Bill says, "Where meadow meets woods, that's where you want to put a house." He looks around the bedroom. "One always worried about dimensions. We were afraid this room would be too small, and it is by no means huge. I think they'll find it large enough." Upstairs, he pauses at the bathroom door. "The sinks are a little too close to the walls. That's something you learn. . . . This playroom has incredible views."

Bill tries out the house. He settles down at the round table in the breakfast nook. The cabinet-work looks just right to him, both the design and the execution. He must call Richard and thank him. He really must, Bill says, and, as it happens, he does, later on. (And Richard will say after that call, "Yeah, I'd like to work with him again. I learned a lot. I don't know about the fast track, though.") At this moment, Bill does not think of the south wall as an artistic composition, viewed from outside. Seen that way, it is just part of the house's clothing. The innards are what matter to him right now. "These windows, because they are mullioned, they make this wall very enclosing. Sitting here, the kitchen looks *much* bigger than I ever thought. Partly, it's the light. Because it does get in deeper than in most kitchens. They said they wanted sunshine. See how deep the sun comes in at this hour? The shadow line is at the halfway point of the room at ten o'clock in the morning, and it will get deeper for the next three months. I just haven't been in here when the sun comes out."

Bill remembers sitting in Pelham, with Judith

and Jonathan, worrying late into the night that the breakfast nook wouldn't be big enough for both table and people. Bill thought the nook had to be eleven feet wide, but if it were, he feared, the study adjacent would become virtually a closet. He moved the wall between the nook and study many times. Finally, he stole half a foot from the nook for the sake of the study, making the nook only ten and a half feet wide. He has worried ever since. "I thought it would be too tight, and if I weren't sitting here I would still believe that. The dimensions are tight and yet the room does not feel tight. It's something I had to learn. That's why architecture is such an experimental thing." Forty-year-old Bill adds, "And it's why so many architects flower in their fifties and sixties."

Bill expects that if his office prospers and grows, he will spend most of this last, best career of his designing buildings and not houses. As a rule, custom houses barely repay an architect's labors. But when Bill dreams of his firm grown large enough to sustain this sort of pleasure, he imagines that he will always have one new house on the drawing board. He will design other houses, and he says, "I'm sure that some of the Souweine drawings will become a standard for me on the next house." Bill gets a tape measure and, kneeling, stretches it across the breakfast nook. He measures the nook's width and length, just to make sure. Then it is clear what he has mainly been up to this morning. He's been storing up memories of decisions that seem right and ones that seem lucky, for the same reason that footings are laid—in order to build on. The tape snaps back into its case. "Now I understand what ten-feet-six by thirteen is," says Bill.

3

Bert Willey, the painter, heard this story at his father's knee: A mason builds a new fireplace for a wealthy man. When the mason finishes the job, he asks for his money, but the wealthy client says he can't pay just now. He doesn't have the right change. That's all right, the mason says. But if he has to wait, then the client does, too. The wealthy man agrees. He won't build a fire in his new chimney until he's paid the mason. The mason goes home. Just an hour or so later, his wealthy client appears at the door. "My house is full of smoke, goddammit!"

"I told you not to use that chimney until you paid me," says the mason. "When you pay me, I'll fix it."

So the client gets out his wallet, which is full of change after all, and the mason returns to the rich man's house. The mason brings a brick with him. He carries the brick up a ladder to the roof and drops it down the chimney, smashing out the pane of glass he had mortared across the flue.

Bert says his father told that story as if it had actually happened, but others tell the same story.

It must lie mainly among the wishful thoughts of the building trades, like the retort you think of only after the argument. In the course of a construction project, power often shifts among client, architect, and builder. Often it does so in unpredictable ways, until the end. In the end, power reverts to all but the most careless of clients. "And, remember, money is leverage. Always holdout twenty-five percent of the money until you are satisfied," said that radio show Jim and Bert listened to back in September, the one called "Getting Your Money's Worth from Home Contractors." All of the many books designed for would-be homeowners offer that advice. It's wise counsel. If you pay a builder in full before he's finished the job, it may be a long time before you see him again, and stories of such abandonments are legion. Every builder, meanwhile, knows stories of clients who make a practice of not paying the last bill, not because of real faults in the job, but just to save money. But whatever the merits of a given case, when clients withhold last payments, builders can't hope to get that money without spending some, often about as much as the last bill itself.

"I know all the tricks," says Jules privately, some days after the last change order meeting. "Jim couldn't win. Jonathan holds back fifteen thousand dollars. 'Sue me.' They get a lawyer. He calls Jonathan's lawyer, which would've been me. Their lawyer says let's settle this thing. If it went to court, the judge would order a settlement.

That's the way the world works. If I were an SOB, I'd have told Jonathan to give them nothing. But that was not the spirit of the job."

Maybe real virtue can't exist without an awareness of alternatives. Jonathan knows the stratagems. He owes Apple Corps money for work they have done and about which he has no questions or complaints. As for the cost of some other items, such as the extra $900 for the staircase, he doesn't believe that he owes Apple Corps anything. For still other items, such as the shingles, which were of a cheaper grade than specified—ones guaranteed for fifteen years instead of twenty-five—Jonathan believes that they owe him some money. There is a lot of sorting out still to do, and on the morning before the meeting, Jules tells Jonathan not to pay any of the last bill until he and Apple Corps have settled the whole. Jonathan does not take the advice. In his office, Jonathan writes out a check for the part of his debt that he doesn't question. It's for $6000. The costs of the other, questionable items amount to only a third of that.

Jonathan does not hand over the check at the beginning of the negotiations. He gives it to Jim midway through, when a compromise on the other issues is in the air. Jonathan does not withhold that uncontested payment. He does employ it, but gently, it seems.

As for Jim, he has done some tactical thinking. He does owe Jonathan a credit on the shingles. He comes to the meeting resolved not to mention the subject. If Jonathan has forgotten, Jim will forget. But when Jonathan mentions the shingles, Jim concedes the debt at once. The living room will see cozier scenes, but a rough symmetry governs these proceedings.

All of Apple Corps sits in the living room. Jonathan and Judith, who joins them midway, take the couch. Jules sits on one of Ned's little staircases, on the sidelines at first. Richard fiddles with the brim of a new hat. Sometimes he sighs. Ned arises to pace. Alex rests his forehead on the heel of a hand, studying puzzling figures. Jim wets his lips. He says to Jonathan, "I've got a general issue. What happens with this procedure each time . . . Let's see. When a situation comes up and we make a mistake, we eat it, but when it comes out less, in theory we make money, but . . ." Jim stops again, rewets his lips. "I don't know what I'm getting into. It just seems like it's a ratchet. It goes only one way." He tries again. "I'm not trying to collect. It's just a way I feel. It seems like . . . Maybe I can't say anything."

Jonathan leans forward toward Jim. "I want to say something that might make you feel better. I want you to listen carefully, because I don't want you to misunderstand me or get angry. There have been many, many times throughout the process when you looked at something as an extra and I didn't. But if your feeling is that it's all going one way, I think sometimes it went the other way. I'm not saying you did anything wrong by any means, but maybe that will make you feel better."

Apple Corps has a list. Jonathan has a list. They cannot agree about the stairs. Jonathan calls the staircase the one part of the house that does not please him. Mainly, he says, the railing is too low for safety. They can't decide who should pay for the extra costs incurred on what Ned nicknamed the brick day. Several other items stand between them. These make for a thicket of numbers. "And you won't listen to me, even though I have more gray hair than anybody," says Jules from the corner.

Everyone laughs. Eventually, they do listen. The whole argument boils down to $2000, Jules points out. Apple Corps thinks Jonathan owes them $1500, most of it on the staircase; Jonathan believes he owes nothing, but is on the contrary owed $500. "You're gonna end up with two thousand dollars in dispute on a hundred-and-fifty-thousand-dollar job and that's magnificent," says Jules. " 'Look, you guys, you'll spend at least five grand collecting the fifteen hundred, so I'll split it with you.' That's what my clients used to do."

"Of course, all your clients had broken noses," says Judith.

Jules proceeds. Jonathan should surrender his claim of $500. Apple Corps should give up $500 of theirs. That would leave $1000 in dispute, which they could split, Jonathan paying $500. Each side, in effect, gives up $1000.

"I'm willing to do that," says Jonathan. "Because if I don't, then we won't resolve the stairs and there will be bad feelings."

Apple Corps asks for time and privacy. Jules, Jonathan, and Judith leave the room. The carpenters stand in a circle by the hearth.

"It's hard, but I think we just oughta do it," says Ned.

"Okay with me," says Richard. "Come down here four or five more times and it'll cost us five hundred dollars." Richard turns to Jim. "I love the stairs. They're the prettiest stairs."

Jim cogitates with his lips. Then he says, "It makes me think of what happened in the beginning and of the two hundred dollars we gave them for Rawn."

"You can't go back over all that," says Richard.

"I guess you can't. If we do this, I just make some calls and it's all over."

"I'd say let's just do it," declares Richard.

"You agree, Alex?" asks Jim.

"Yup."

"Smile a little?"

"Nope. I don't have to do that."

When the champagne is opened and poured ("The ceiling's not guaranteed against corks," Jim says), Jonathan raises his glass to the carpenters. "I want to make a toast to you." It reads a little like a list. It's delivered with vigor and unmistakable feeling: "You're a very nice bunch of guys. You built a beautiful house. I'm very glad we got this resolved today. And, I hate to say it, but

Jules was probably helpful. And I am proud that I live in this house and that you built it, and I will tell everybody about that." He shakes hands with each of the carpenters, and when he reaches Alex, saying, "I love this house and I like you guys," Alex does smile after all.

"Thanks, Jonathan."

The familiar winnowing follows. Jonathan has a client whose interests need defending. He leaves at once. Alex, Richard, and Ned have suppers waiting. They move toward the door.

"This is not good-bye?" says Judith to them.

Ned grins. "Good-bye. Enjoy your house."

"We love our house," she says.

Jim remains behind awhile. To Judith, he says, "It was good to have a third party. Even this third party." He nods to Jules.

"I did not talk against you, Jim," says Jules.

"No. I know."

"So what have you guys got lined up?" asks Judith.

"Ned's going to South Carolina and Alex will be away this winter. Richard and I have a lot of inside jobs."

"So you and Richard are the winter crew, eh?" she asks.

"We have jobs for most of next summer, too."

"Aren't you selling yourselves short, working for time and materials?" asks Jules.

"Well, it's just so we don't have to do this," says Jim, beckoning at the scene of difficult and just completed negotiations.

"You won't make any money," says Jules.

Jim barks a laugh, rather like Ned's. "We didn't make any money on this!"

Jules grins. He winks. "Then you're stupid. If you couldn't rip *these* people off."

Jim grins at Judith. "Too bad he lives nearby. You can't tell him to just go home." The moment he says it, Jim feels he has overstepped his bounds, but Judith changes the subject gracefully, still smiling. Jim gets his leather case, also his lunchbox and jacket, and chatting pleasantly with Jules, thanking Jules for his help, Jim departs.

"So we only made three thousand dollars. But, pretty safe to say, we didn't make money on any other job this year."

This summer, from the Souweine job, the carpenters have earned better wages than ever before, but most of the profit they had hoped for has evaporated. They have dined together on pizza and wine. Now they sit with account books and calculators before them, at Alex's table. Outside, frost is gathering on windshields. Warmth swells from Alex's wood stove. Jim has taken off his wool shirt. He wears a white T-shirt. His eyes have red rims.

"Then where we really screwed up was our labor," Richard says. "How come we ended the job on time?"

"Because we put in so much at the beginning."

"Yeah, big weeks."

"Big ones."

"Aaaah," says Richard. "So how much did we blow the labor out? The partitions and frieze, we threw a lot out there."

"But not that much," says Ned. "Finish work. We deceived ourselves on the Colonial casing. It took a lot longer than we thought. And we spent an extra thousand for those silly stairs into the living room. We didn't charge for the windowsills."

"I thought about that," says Jim. "But I couldn't see doing it any other way."

"I'm glad we didn't," says Ned.

"How many days we put into it all?" asks Richard.

"We put in four hundred twenty-three days," says Ned.

Alex laughs.

"Oh," says Richard. "Now it's all making sense." He laughs. "What are we laughing for?"

"Well, it had to be in the labor," says Jim. "Especially in the finish work."

"So we should've estimated our labor at what?"

"A third more."

"I remember thinkin', 'Uh-oh, here comes the finish work,' when we finished the framing, because usually we're ahead by then," Richard says. "We built it, though, at fifty dollars a square foot. By God."

"Why didn't we lose our ass?" asks Alex.

"Because we were supposed to make fifteen

thousand, plus five percent on materials," says Jim. He makes a face.

"Yeah," says Alex. "We could've gone away with a lot of money in our pockets."

"If we knew what we were doing," says Jim. "This is depressing. Got any liquor?"

"We blew it out on the finish work," says Richard.

"Always do," says Ned.

They've gone back and forth through the numbers. Subcontractors and materials came out fine. The frieze and the bricks and the items they'd forgotten to estimate had been expensive, but some mistakes and underestimates are inevitable in a job and those had been roughly canceled out by the various overestimates they'd made. They had spent most of their hoped-for profit on their own labor. That is to say, they had spent most of the money building just so. In a real sense, they had spent their profit on themselves, and they know it. Ned finds a bottle of whiskey under Alex's desk and shoves it toward Jim. Alex has some more figures to report. On that job, they drove the following miles, he tells them: Richard drove 1700; Ned, 2687; Alex, 945; Jim, 1870. Alex has computed the ratio of miles driven to hours worked. "Jim is the most efficient of the crew."

"It's not gonna do me any good. We didn't make any money."

"Hey, you made your wages, man," says Ned.

"That's not enough." Jim stands, takes a shot of whiskey, sits down, and says, "Depressing. I wouldn't mind, but that you beat your brains out . . ."

"Oh-*Kay!* Let's leave fifty dollars in the account. Split up the rest. Susan's job is doin' real well." ("Susan's job" is the one they are working on now.)

Ned laughs.

"A little upbeat," Richard goes on. "Jim had the most hours by far."

"Yeah. For nothing," says Jim.

"Oh, come on!" says Ned. "We gotta give ourselves some credit."

"We put a lot into it and didn't get much out of it," says Jim.

Ned glares at Jim. "The things I got out of it through *you* are going to be significant, and there'll be a long-term payback," says Ned, and you might have thought he was threatening Jim— cheer up, Jim, or else.

"Look at it this way, too," says Richard. "We made three thousand dollars on that house. I don't know how much you *should* make on a house like that."

"I figured ten percent would take care of it," says Jim.

"And ten percent is not a lot, I agree," says Ned. "Not for custom builders of stature."

"Add the four of us up and you have quite a stature," says Jim. He laughs for the first time.

"Maybe we need someone to kick some more business into us," says Ned.

Jim looks around the table. He says, "I realized

this summer that I don't want to compromise the work for money."

"We don't want to do it cobby," says Richard.

"We *can't* do it cobby," says Jim. He looks glum again.

"So in that mode," says Ned, "we're gonna have to . . ."

"Charge more."

"Charge more."

Alex looks scholarly, in glasses, this evening. "But each of us made two hundred and forty dollars a month more than we did last year," he says, consulting the books.

"I'm just depressed," says Jim.

They divide the spoils. Richard plans to drive in convoy with Ned to South Carolina, a few weeks from now. He'll transport Ned's woodworking tools in his pickup. "Well, I got new tires. Truck's all tuned up. Wisht I'd gotten it painted. Oh, well," says Richard.

They talk about changes to come, about becoming employers themselves. They wonder who they might hire. Richard thinks they should hire inexperienced carpenters.

"Because we're sure to know more than they do," says Jim, and there's a ripple of laughter in his voice.

Richard makes a high, loud laugh. "That's what I was thinkin'!"

Jim says, "I remember guys, when I was first learning, guys who lorded it over you because they knew how to sweep a floor. 'You kids all think you know how to sweep floors.' " Jim turns to Ned and says he hopes Ned will return. Ned's place in the partnership will be waiting for him, if he does.

"Well," says Ned, "I fully intend to stay in touch with you guys, and I'd appreciate the same. As things go on."

"As money is lost," says Richard.

"As we screw up jobs," says Jim. "Help, we're in court."

"Please send money," says Alex.

Richard cackles. "Please send money."

"It's always the same," says Jim. "When you're done, the work's gone, and you focus on money. That's when you think, they have a house and you don't have very much to show for it." He thinks that he has probably served the hardest part of his apprenticeship in business. He also says he knows now that he loves this work that never ends and always changes. "It is a great job."

"Jules saved us in the end," Ned says. "Much as I disliked him at first, he came out smelling sweet to me. He allowed me to go away feeling all right. What I love most about this job, you leave one place and go on to the next, and it's all gone, really, the tension and anxiety. I love that cycle."

Susan's job, as Richard calls it, has progressed to stepladder height by the time Jim finishes the last details on the Souweines' house. Jim rejoins his partners full-time on Halloween, just soon enough to help them raise a huge hemlock beam, the main carrying beam for the second floor of the addition they are building.

Richard is the boss of Susan's job, which is the last on which they will all work together, for a long time to come. Ned is in high spirits this morning, nevertheless. Discussing the Souweine job over coffee earlier, he had said to Richard, "Good will at the end is worth some money. We *are* horrible businesspeople. But, by God, we can build a house!" They stand on stepladders now and on the top of the frame of the first-story walls—on thin, precarious perches.

"Jim's used to bein' in charge," says Richard to the others. "We gotta put him back in his place."

Jim smiles. "It's great to have a boss," he says.

"Thing is, we never listened to you anyways," says Richard.

All is ready. The beam is cut and mortised. The posts to support it are temporaried. They hoist the beam with collective grunts. The posts accept the load. The timber slides into place, and the client, Susan, asks them to wait. A snapshot is in order. She rushes inside and returns with a camera. They are wearing their gunslinger's belts again, big hammers hanging from their hips. Richard wears a new pair of suspenders, which Alex told Richard to buy for the sake of modesty, for proper elevation of the pants. The camera aims. The builders of houses turn and grin from their perches. Richard Gougeon raises his framing hammer high over his head. "This is my best pose right here," he explains. "When I'm swingin' my hammer."

EPILOGUE

The Boston Society of Architects annually confers awards for buildings that have been designed by local firms and erected outside the city and its suburbs. The awards carry prestige, and in the spring of 1985 two of them went to established, well-known companies and the third went to William Rawn Associates for the Souweines' house. Of course, the award really belonged to Bill alone, since he had no associates when he designed the house. Judith, Jim, and Sandy came to the ceremony. In his acceptance speech Bill praised his clients and builders.

Some things lose luster when they lose their newness, but for Judith and Jonathan the house kept improving, as it became a lived-in thing.

In the year and a half since they finished the Souweine job, Apple Corps had hired two experienced carpenters. They had built one new house, fixed up two old ones from top to bottom, and created a number of new bathrooms and kitchens. Ned was returning from South Carolina in the summer of '85, in time to help his partners on three new houses, which they had agreed to erect in that building season. All were contract jobs, and Jim wasn't nervous about any of them.

A NOTE ON TERMINOLOGY

Many of the terms in the housebuilder's technical vocabulary are serviceable heirlooms handed down through the centuries, and some are so well worn as to be universally understood. Other terms are relatively obscure, though. For the uninitiated, talk among professionals—the sort of talk you overhear at lumberyards—can be painfully mysterious. With apologies to those who wield a hammer, I offer a short glossary:

A *gable* is a triangular section of wall formed by the two sloping sides of a pitched roof. In the Souweine house, the *temple end* is the *gabled end* that contains the front door and that has *pilasters* (square, ornamental columns set into a wall) at the corners. A *pediment* is a wide, low-pitched gable. An *ell*, as every New Englander knows, is a wing of a building attached at right angles to the main structure. A *lintel* is the horizontal upper part of a door or window frame; it supports part of the structure above the door or window. Bill and Jim used *lintel* for the slab of granite laid horizontally across the top of the back of the hearth.

Lumber dealers usually sell moldings by the *lineal* or *running foot*—in that system of measurement only the length of the piece of wood is described. But in most cases, lumberyards deal in *board feet:* one board foot consists of a piece of wood that is nominally one inch thick, one foot wide, and one foot long. Baffling arrays of terms describe the quality of lumber. *Clear* or *select* lumber should be knotless, and lumber described as *number two* will contain some live knots. *Waney* lumber, like a waning moon, is missing pieces of its edges.

Housebuilders turn wood into these things, among many others: *sills* (the timbers that rest on the foundation walls, the first course of wood); *floor joists* (timbers laid horizontally to make the frames that support floors); *studs* (timbers standing upright to make the frames of walls); *collar ties* (timbers laid horizontally below the peak of a roof and fastened to rafters on either side of a roof, each collar tie tying one pair of rafters together); *gussets* (small pieces of wood or steel, usually triangular, applied to the corners of construction for strength). *Furring strips* are narrow boards applied to a surface—a wall or ceiling, say—to provide a base for some covering material such as plasterboard. *Clapboards* are beveled pieces of wood applied in horizontal, partially overlapping rows to the sides of buildings, and *casings* are the mostly decorative frames that surround doors and windows. *Bedmolding* is molding that is fitted in the joint between a vertical and overhanging horizontal surface. Staircases like the one Jim built have several sturdy *newelposts* and in between many thinner *balusters,* all of which hold up the *banisters* that children like to slide down. On such a stair, the *treads* that people walk upon have rounded *nosings* on their outward-facing edges, and for decoration, underneath each nosing, a strip of the delicately sculpted *scotia* pattern of molding. For the bottommost section of the banister, Jim used a curved section of handrail called an *easement.*

From the french *châssis* comes the term *sash,* the frame that holds the panes of a window. A *double-hung window* has two sashes, one over the other. The second half of this term, the "hung," is an artifact left from the days when the sashes of such windows were attached to balancing weights. *Sidelights* are windows, usually small and unopenable, placed beside a door. *Mullions* are vertical strips that divide the panes of a window; for some, the term *muntin* has the same meaning.

Sidewall brackets are items of temporary scaffolding—rigid arms of steel or wood anchored to the wall of a house and projecting outward to carry planks. *Bit,* an ancient term, refers to the part of a tool that does the biting, the cutting. A *dado bit* is used for cutting a groove into one board; another board is fitted into that groove and the result is a *dado joint.* Carpenters have, of course, invented myriad techniques for joining wood. Building kitchen cabinets, Richard made both dado joints and also *mortise and tenon* ones. (The *mortise* is a cavity cut in one piece of wood, and the *tenon* is a tonguelike projection that fits into the mortise.) Most woodworking shops con-

506

tain a *radial arm saw*, a bench-mounted, power-driven saw. The blade and motor are mounted on an arm that swings out over the work table. You can tilt the blade on both the vertical and horizontal planes, and so the tool is extremely versatile, but it is not especially convenient or precise for some cutting operations. Out of the enormous and still large variety of handsaws one can buy, Apple Corps regularly uses only the type called a *crosscut* saw, designed for cutting across the grain. A crosscut saw has small teeth shaped like knives, and the more teeth or "points" per inch the finer the cut such a saw will make. Jim uses a "ten-point" crosscut saw for making casings and a "twelve-point" for moldings, and when sawing by hand, he always keeps his working shoulder in a straight line with the cut. A *jig* is a tool for guiding another tool or for holding a piece of work in place. Apple Corps makes lots of jigs—sometimes, it seems, mostly for the fun of it.

ACKNOWLEDGMENTS AND SOURCES

My thanks to all of the people who appear in this book. I have not changed any names.

For their generous and painstaking help with the text, I am indebted, once again, to Richard Todd and Mark Kramer. Stuart Dybek and Mike Rosenthal helped me from start to finish. Jamie Kilbreth was, as usual, there when needed, as were Michael Janeway and Georges Borchardt. My thanks to Austin Olney for his support and to Upton Brady, Peter Davison, and William Whitworth for theirs. My thanks to the following for helping to keep me going: Jon Jackson, Martin Mahoney, John O'Brien, Bill McFeely, Bob Riddle, Tim Rivinus, Fred Wessel, Nat, Alice, and Jopa. For help on general research, my thanks to Dan Lombardo of the Jones Library in Amherst, to Elise Bernier Feeley at the Forbes Library in Northampton, and to the staff of the Neilson Library at Smith College, especially John Graiff, Mary McFeely, and Mary Courtney. Many people at Smith were kind and helpful, among others Don Robinson, Jane Bryden, and Anna Montgomery. Shirley Sagawa and Helen Gover helped with research. Eliza Childs got me organized, and

508

Deb Robson saw it through. Special thanks for special help to Barney Sneideman, Hugh Davis, and Sarah Flynn.

I relied on many people for the material that lies outside the narrative of this book. The foresters Perry Hagenstein and Lloyd Irland helped me on issues of the woods. Jeff Pidot, an assistant attorney general in Maine, mapped out the politics of Maine's Big Woods. Myron Fiering of Harvard put me onto studies about spraying and the spruce budworm. Michael Oppenheimer, a scientist with the Environmental Defense Fund, spoke to me at length about atmospheric pollution and forests, as did the atmospheric chemists Jim Anderson and Michael McElroy, both of Harvard. Kenneth Hodson and Randy Carron, executives of Pinkham Lumber, were good hosts to me in the Maine Woods. I am grateful to Russell Bisbee of Bisbee Lumber for a discussion we had about two-by-tens. I also relied on the following books and articles for information about forests and wood:

Carroll, Charles F. *The Timber Economy of Puritan New England.* Brown University Press, Providence, R.I., 1973.

Cronon, William. *Changes in the Land: Indians, Colonists and the Ecology of New England.* Farrar, Straus & Giroux, New York, 1983.

Harr, Jonathan. "The Golden Road." *New England Monthly*, Dec. 1984.

Hindle, Brooke, ed. *America's Wooden Age: Aspects of Its Early Technology.* Sleepy Hollow Restorations, Tarrytown, N.Y., 1975.

Hoadley, R. Bruce. *Understanding Wood: A Craftsman's Guide to Wood Technology.* The Taunton Press, Newtown, Conn., 1980.

Holling, C. S. "The Spruce-Budworm/Forest Management Problem."*Adaptive Environmental Assessment and Management.* John Wiley & Sons, New York, 1978.

Irland, Lloyd C. *Is Timber Scarce? The Economics of a Renewable Resource.* Yale University Press, New Haven, 1974.

———. *Wildlands and Woodlots: The Story of New England's Forests.* University Press of New England, Hanover, N.H., 1982.

United States Department of Agriculture. "America's Renewable Resources," a supplement to the 1979 *Assessment of the Forest and Rangeland Situation in the United States*, FS-22, Feb. 1984.

The economist John Pitkin tutored me on the economics of housing. Michael Stone of the University of Massachusetts in Boston, Kent Klitgaard of the University of New Hampshire, and Andrew Zimbalist of Smith College were generous and helpful. I relied on a number of publications from the Census Bureau and on many newspaper and magazine articles for my brief adventure into the economics of housing. The publications I found most useful were:

Goetze, Rolf. "The Housing Bubble." *Working Papers*, Jan.–Feb. 1981.

Hartman, Chester, ed. *America's Housing Crisis: What Is To Be Done?* Routledge & Kegan Paul, Boston, 1983.

For information about the setting of this book, particularly local history, I relied on the following:

Barnard, Ellsworth. *A Hill Farm Boyhood.* The Dinosaur Press, Amherst, Mass., 1983.

Carpenter and Morehouse (compilers and publishers). *The History of the Town of Amherst*, 2 vols., 1896.

Cronon, William. *Changes in the Land.*

[Various authors.] *Essays on Amherst's History.* The Vista Trust, Amherst, Mass., 1978.

The *Daily Hampshire Gazette*, Northampton, Mass. (From this newspaper, I got the statistics on how Amherst and Hadley voted in the presidential elections of 1824, 1828, and 1832.)

Howes, Frederick G. *History of the Town of Ashfield, From Its Settlement in 1742 to 1910.* Published by the Town, circa 1910.

Innes, Stephen. *Labor in a New Land: Economy and Society in Seventeenth-Century Springfield.* Princeton University Press, Princeton, N.J., 1983.

MacDonald, William L. *Northampton, Massachu-*

setts, Architecture and Buildings. Published by the author, Northampton, 1975.

Jochanan Wijnhoven, chairman of the Department of Religion at Smith College, directed me to many books about religion and building. He discussed the foundation sacrifice at length. He provided me with information about Jewish custom and about building rituals in Holland. John Stilgoe of Harvard related some of his findings about the roof tree ceremony, for which I am grateful. I went to the following books for information about ritual and custom in building:

Bradford, William. *Of Plymouth Plantation*, chapter 9.

Eliade, Mircea. *The Myth of the Eternal Return, or Cosmos and History*, trans. by Willard Trask. Princeton University Press, Princeton, N.J., 1954.

————. *Zalmoxis: The Vanishing God*, trans. by Willard Trask. University of Chicago Press, Chicago, 1972.

Evans, George Ewan. *The Pattern Under the Plow: Aspects of the Folk-Life of East Anglia.* Faber & Faber, London, 1966.

Frazer, James G. *The Golden Bough: A Study in Magic and Religion*, 3rd edition, 8 vols. Macmillan, London, 1911–1915.

Hastings, James, ed. *Encyclopedia of Religion and Ethics.* Scribners, New York, 1914.

Rykwert, Joseph. *On Adam's House in Paradise: The Idea of the Primitive Hut in Architectural History*. MIT Press, Cambridge, Mass., 1981.

Salzman, L. F. *Building in England down to 1540: A Documentary History*. Clarendon Press, Oxford, 1952.

Stilgoe, John, *Common Landscape of America, 1580 to 1845*. Yale University Press, New Haven, 1982. (Useful in other areas, too.)

Strassfeld, Michael, et al. *The Jewish Catalog: A Do-It-Yourself Kit*. The Jewish Publication Society of America, Philadelphia, 1973.

Robert St. George's forthcoming book, tentatively titled *The Disenchantment of Domestic Space: Material Life and Popular Culture in Early New England*, was the source for information about the metaphysics of building in seventeenth-century New England at the beginning of section V of this book.

The Biblical quotation in section V comes from *A New Translation of the Holy Scriptures According to the Masoretic Text*. The Jewish Publication Society of America, Philadelphia, 1962.

I am grateful to Dell Upton, of the University of California at Berkeley, for a chat we had about the professionalization of architecture in America, and to Kate Hutchins of the Winterthur Museum for getting me Upton's paper on that subject. I relied on that paper for part of the beginning of section

IV of this book. The following were my texts on architecture generally, on Greek Revival, and on relations between builders and architects:

American Institute of Architects. *The 1983 AIA Firm Survey.* New York and Washington, 1984.

[Anonymous.] "Important Trial: Compensation of Architects." *Architects' and Mechanics' Journal,* Vol. III, nos. 23, 24, and 25, Vol. IV, no. 1, March 9, 16, 23, and April 6, 1861. (These articles contain the trial transcripts that I mention in section IV.)

Baker, Paul R. *Richard Morris Hunt.* MIT Press, Cambridge, Mass., 1980.

Clark, Sam. "About the Business of Building." *Fine Homebuilding,* no. 22 (August/September 1984).

Le Corbusier. *Vers Une Architecture.* Editions Crés, Paris, 1923.

Downing, Andrew Jackson. *The Architecture of Country Houses.* D. Appleton & Co., New York, 1850.

Goldberger, Paul. *On The Rise: Architecture and Design in a Postmodern Age.* Times Books, New York, 1983.

Hamlin, Talbot. *Greek Revival Architecture in America.* Oxford University Press, London and New York, 1944.

Hofstadter, Richard. *The Americon Political Tradition.* Knopf, New York, 1949.

Kimball, Sidney Fiske. "Thomas Jefferson and the first Monument of the Classical Revival in

America," a doctoral dissertation at the University of Michigan.

Larkin, Oliver. *Art and Life in America*. Holt, Rinehart & Winston, New York, 1960.

Mumford, Lewis. *Sticks and Stones: A Study of American Architecture and Civilization*. Norton, New York, 1924.

Rawn, William L., III. "The Asymmetrical Spine: A Generator of Design." Thesis, MIT, 1979.

Saint, Andrew. *The Image of the Architect*. Yale University Press, New Haven, 1983.

Upton, Dell. "Pattern Books and Professionalism: Aspects of the Transformation of Domestic Architecture in America, 1800-1860." *Winterthur Portfolio* 19, nos. 2/3 (summer/autumn), 1984.

Wolfe, Tom. *From Bauhaus to Our House*. Farrar, Straus & Giroux, New York, 1981.

Wright, Frank Lloyd. *The Natural House*. Horizon Press, New York, 1954.

———————————

For information about the history and sociology of building, I went first of all and repeatedly to Bernie Herman of the University of Delaware. Herman's soon-to-be-published book about building and rebuilding cycles in rural Delaware from 1700 to 1900, tentatively called *Each Thing in Its Place: Building and Rebuilding Rural Architecture*, introduced me to the idea that houses can make for eloquent texts on social history. Hernan supplied me with dozens of articles and books. He spent a great deal of time explaining his views on

515

the Georgian house plan and on the "in workman-like manner" clause of old building contracts. He talked at length about the reasons for the rise of Greek Revival. Robert St. George, of Boston University, was extremely generous. He lectured me on the "Georgian moment," and on the early history of housing in America. He provided me with rough statistics on homeownership in Colonial times. He gave me many books and articles, including his own forthcoming work, already cited. Abbott Lowell Cummings of Yale and Richard Candee of Boston University were also generous and helpful. Ritchie Garrison, the director of education at Historic Deerfield, gave me a marvelous lecture on Greek Revival and introduced me to the daybooks of Calvin Stearns. He also arranged, through Rosa Johnston of the Northfield Historical Commission, for a tour of some Stearns houses. Mrs. Lawrence Hammond kindly loaned me some material about Stearns. Arthur Krim provided, among other things, the crucial paper on balloon framing. Jack Michel of the University of Pennsylvania explained old building contracts and the "in workmanlike manner" clause.

The Oxford English Dictionary was my text on the history of the names of tools and building techniques. I got my statistics on injuries and deaths in the construction trades from the Occupational Safety and Health Administration and from publications of the Bureau of Labor Statistics. To find my way into the history and sociology of building and housing, I used these books and articles:

Addy, Sidney Oldall. *The Evolution of the English House*. Macmillan, London and New York, 1898.

Butterworth, Benjamin. *The Growth of Industrial Art*. Knopf, New York, 1972 (originally published in 1892).

Cohn, Jan. *The Palace or the Poorhouse: The American House as a Cultural Symbol*. Michigan State University Press, East Lansing, 1979.

Cummings, Abbott Lowell. "Massachusetts Bay Building Documents, 1638-1726," appendix to *Architecture in Colonial Massachusetts*. The Colonial Society of Massachusetts, Boston, 1979.

———. *The Framed Houses of Massachusetts Bay, 1615-1725*. Harvard University Press, Cambridge, Mass., 1979.

Davison, Jane. *The Fall of a Doll's House: Three Generations of American Women and the Houses They Lived In*. Holt, Rinehart & Winston, New York, 1980.

Fitch, James Marston. *American Building: The Historical Forces That Shaped It*. Houghton Mifflin, Boston, 1947.

Glassie, Henry. *Patterns in the Material Folk Culture of the Eastern United States*. University of Pennsylvania Press, Philadelphia, 1968.

Hayden, Dolores. *Redesigning the American Dream: The Future of Housing, Work and Family Life*. Norton, New York, 1984.

Lynes, Russell. *The Domesticated Americans.* Harper & Row, New York, 1957.

Mercer, Henry Chapman. *Ancient Carpenters' Tools.* Bucks County Historical Society, Doylestown, Pa., 1960.

Nelson, Lee H. *Nail Chronology as an Aid to Dating Old Buildings.* American Association for State and Local History, Technical Leaflet 48, *History News*, Vol. 24, no. 11, Nov. 1968.

Perin, Constance. *Everything in Its Place: Social Order and Land Use In America.* Princeton University Press, Princeton, N.J., 1977.

Peterson, Charles E., ed. *Building Early America: Proceedings Held at Philadelphia to Celebrate the 250th Birthday of the Carpenters' Company of the City and County of Philadelphia.* Chilton Book Co., Radnor, Pa., 1976.

Reckman, Bob. "Carpentry: The Craft and the Trade," in *Case Studies on the Labor Process*, Andrew Zimbalist, ed. Monthly Review Press, New York, 1979.

Rose, Walter. *The Village Carpenter.* Macmillan, Cambridge, England, 1937.

Sprague, Paul. "The Origin of Balloon Framing." *Journal of the Society of Architectural Historians*, Vol. XL, Dec. 1981.

Stearns, Calvin. (His daybooks are on microfilm at Historic Deerfield and the originals are kept by the Northfield Historical Society.)

Upton, Dell. "Traditional Timber Framing," in *Material Culture of the Wooden Age*, Brooke

Hindle, ed. Sleepy Hollow Press, Tarrytown, N.Y., 1981.

Vara, John. "Nails." *Country Journal*, July 1984.

Wason, Betty. *It Takes "Jack" to Build a House: A Down-to-Earth Guide to Building (and Remodeling)*. St. Martin's Press, New York, 1968.

Winthrop, John. "A Modell of Christian Charity," in *The Puritans*, Vol. 1, Perry Miller and Thomas H. Johnson, eds. Harper & Row, New York, 1963.

Wright, Gwendolyn. *Building the Dream: A Social History of Housing in America*. MIT Press, Cambridge, Mass., 1981.

———. *Moralism and the Model Home*. University of Chicago Press, Chicago, 1980.

The publishers hope that this
Large Print Book has brought
you pleasurable reading.
Each title is designed to make
the text as easy to see as possible.
G.K. Hall Large Print Books
are available from your library and
your local bookstore. Or, you can
receive information by mail on
upcoming and current Large Print Books
and order directly from the publishers.
Just send your name and address to:

G.K. Hall & Co.
70 Lincoln Street
Boston, Mass. 02111

or call, toll-free:

1-800-343-2806

A note on the text
Large print edition designed by
Bernadette Montalvo.
Composed in 16 pt Plantin
on a Xyvision 300/Linotron 202N
by Henry Elliott
of G.K. Hall & Co.